Revitalizing the City

MAXINE GOODMAN LEVIN
COLLEGE OF URBAN AFFAIRS

Cleveland State University

Cities and Contemporary Society

Series Editors: Richard D. Bingham and Larry C. Ledebur,
Cleveland State University

Sponsored by the
Maxine Goodman Levin College of Urban Affairs
Cleveland State University

This new series focuses on key topics and emerging trends in urban policy. Each volume is specially prepared for academic use, as well as for specialists in the field.

SUBURBAN SPRAWL
Private Decisions and Public Policy
Wim Wiewel and Joseph J. Persky, Editors

THE INFRASTRUCTURE OF PLAY
Building the Tourist City
Dennis R. Judd, Editor

THE ADAPTED CITY
Institutional Dynamics and Structural Change
H. George Frederickson, Gary A. Johnson, and Curtis H. Wood

CREDIT TO THE COMMUNITY
Community Reinvestment and Fair Lending Policy
in the United States
Dan Immergluck

PARTNERSHIPS FOR SMART GROWTH
University-Community Collaboration for Better Public Places
Wim Wiewel and Gerrit-Jan Knaap, Editors

REVITALIZING THE CITY
Strategies to Contain Sprawl and Revive the Core
*Fritz W. Wagner, Timothy E. Joder, Anthony J. Mumphrey, Jr.,
Krishna M. Akundi, and Alan F.J. Artibise*

Revitalizing the City

Strategies to Contain Sprawl and Revive the Core

Fritz W. Wagner, Timothy E. Joder, Anthony J. Mumphrey Jr.,

Krishna M. Akundi and Alan F.J. Artibise

editors

CITIES AND
CONTEMPORARY
SOCIETY

M.E.Sharpe
Armonk, New York
London, England

Library of Congress Cataloging-in-Publication Data

Revitalizing the city : strategies to contain sprawl and revive the core / edited by Fritz W.
Wagner . . . [et al.].
    p.cm. — (Cities and contemporary society)
    Includes bibliographical references and index.
    ISBN 0-7656-1242-9 (cloth : alk. paper) ISBN 0-7656-1243-7 (pbk. : alk. paper)
    1. Cities and towns—United States—Growth. 2. Cities and town—Canada—Growth.
3. Metropolitan areas—United States. 4. Metropolitan areas—Canada. 5. Inner cities—
United States. 6. Inner Cities—Canada. 7. Urban renewal—United States. 8. Urban
Renewal—Canada. I. Wagner, Fritz W. II. Series.

HT384.U5R48 2005
307.76′0973—dc22

                                                                        2004017451

Printed in the United States of America

The paper used in this publication meets the minimum requirements of
American National Standard for Information Sciences
Permanence of Paper for Printed Library Materials,
ANSI Z 39.48-1984.

                                    ∞

BM (c) 10   9   8   7   6   5   4   3   2   1
BM (p) 10   9   8   7   6   5   4   3   2   1

Contents

Part 3. Central City Redevelopment

Part 4. Central City–Suburb Connection

Part 5. Conclusion

List of Tables, Figures, and Maps

Tables

Figures

Maps

Preface

This book is a collaborative effort by several researchers from Canada and the United States. The authors bring unique perspectives to the project. To date, few books have brought together studies of urban sprawl, metropolitan governance, central city revitalization strategies, and city-suburb cooperation under one umbrella. *Revitalizing the City: Strategies to Control Sprawl and Revive the Core* accomplishes that. It also presents the reader with a novel set of community-tested approaches for revitalizing the local economy. The book is divided into five parts:

Part 1. Urban Growth
Part 2. Metropolitan Administration
Part 3. Central City Redevelopment
Part 4. Central City–Suburb Connection
Part 5. Conclusion

Each of the first four parts of the book contains three chapters, each of which follows the same general format: an introduction of the question/problem, a review of related literature, a methodological description (i.e., qualitative or quantitative analytical approach), a report of findings, and recommendations. With respect to content, the authors

- Elaborate on key issues to consider.
- Describe specific local initiatives.
- Highlight effective policies or programs.
- Identify potential pitfalls to avoid.

Unfettered urban growth does impact the central city economy. The chapters in Part 1 describe this phenomenon. In Chapter 1, Akundi surveys the literature on metropolitan growth, suburban sprawl, and central city redevelopment. He then presents two perspectives on urban growth: the Edge City and

Interdependence hypotheses. These theoretical constructs set the framework for subsequent chapters. Finally, Akundi includes a profile of urban and rural growth trends. This description is followed by two chapters that debate the issue of whether to control or not to control urban growth. In Chapter 2, Bright considers whether having limits to regional growth is necessary to revitalize central cities. If so, then what containment strategies would be most effective? Calavita, Caves, and Ferrier, in Chapter 3, accept that containment or some form of growth control is needed. Sprawl has become all too commonplace in communities. Their chapter examines smart growth activities in the San Diego region of Southern California. Specifically, the authors attempt to evaluate the regional "smart growth" efforts being led by the San Diego Association of Governments (SANDAG) in one of the nation's largest urban areas.

The chapters in Part 2 suggest that a strong metropolitan economy—which is influenced by governance structures—could lead to a revitalized central city economy. Tranel, writing in Chapter 4, examines the evolving role of county governments in regional decisions regarding support of central city facilities and services. The author, focusing on the St. Louis region, asks, What is the impact of rapid geographic expansion on regional governance? Artibise and Meligrana, in Chapter 5, also examine the issue of governance and rapid geographic expansion, but from the Canadian perspective. They provide an assessment of regional planning efforts in the Greater Vancouver region of British Columbia. Whereas Tranel and Artibise/Meligrana analyze particular cases of regional governance, in Chapter 6, Nelson and Burby look at the impact of regionally instituted smart growth policies on population growth and residential and nonresidential new and rehabilitated construction.

The three chapters in Part 3 describe unique central city efforts at redevelopment. Burby makes the argument in Chapter 7 that enforcing municipal building codes may facilitate revitalization efforts. In Chapter 8, Deitrick and Farber contend that brownfields provide communities with an opportunity to reshape their built environment for the future. They examine five brownfield sites in Pittsburgh and evaluate the perceptions that community residents have of brownfields in general and the actual or potential redevelopment of these sites in particular. In Chapter 9, Leland introduces the reader to the novel technique known as PILOTs, Payments-in-Lieu-of-Taxes. She investigates the extent to which PILOTs, service fees, and voluntary contributions from local nonprofit organizations are a source of municipal revenue across the United States.

The chapters in Part 4 highlight some public policies that attempt to bridge the city-suburb divide, resulting in a strong metropolitan economy. The opening chapter in this part, however, contrasts the economic development priorities of central cities and suburbs. In so doing, Basolo and Huang demonstrate the enduring strength of the metropolitan economy. Chapter 11, by Schwartz and Tajbakhsh, considers those factors that make mixed-income housing developments financially viable and provide social benefits to low-income households of the central city and to upper- and middle-income households about to relocate to the suburbs and exurbs. In Chapter 12, Gross analyzes the impact of the Internet economy on Manhattan's built environment.

Artibise, in the book's final chapter, describes the lessons learned from previous chapters. He stresses those strategies that will assist elected officials and policymakers in revitalizing their local economies—specifically, those that rein in urban sprawl and in turn revive the urban core.

Acknowledgments

This book is the culmination of a large body of work on metropolitan growth and its effects on the urban core. Researchers at the National Center for the Revitalization of Central Cities (NCRCC) have also examined the successes and failures of well-established federal and state economic development grant programs and policies. A consortium of several academic institutions, the National Center analyzes critical problems facing America's central cities, evaluates strategies to address those problems, and recommends policy alternatives. It has addressed examples of human capital investment for revitalizing central cities and examples of managing capital resources—all in the context of federal retrenchment but increasing support from public-private partnerships. National Center Fellows have also investigated various tools of central-city redevelopment.

The idea for the National Center was born in 1991 as part of an urban development seminar series. Louisiana's former senator J. Bennett Johnston turned this academic discussion into a tool for research and policymaking and sponsored the National Center in Congress, which appropriated $500,000 to the project. Because of its initial success (1992–1994), the National Center received additional funding through the U.S. Department of Housing and Urban Development: about $280,000 per year between 1994 and 2002. The National Center has benefited from the support of many U.S. senators and representatives who are committed to urban policy research and to the nation's investment in central cities.

We recognize our National Center colleagues at Hunter College (Jill Gross), New School University (Alex Schwartz), San Diego State (Nico Calavita, Roger Caves, and Kathleen Ferrier), Virginia Tech (Arthur Nelson), Queen's University, Kingston (John Meligrana), and the universities of Missouri-St. Louis (Mark Tranel), North Carolina-Chapel Hill (Ray Burby), California Irvine (Victoria Basolo), Delaware (Pam Leland), Pittsburgh (Sabina Deitrick and Stephen Farber), and Texas at Arlington (Elise Bright). Their research and analyses have made a significant contribution to the urban planning/ urban development literature.

We also appreciate the work of many other people who were instrumental in this effort. Professor Richard Bingham, series editor of M.E. Sharpe's Cities and Contemporary Society collection, selected this manuscript for publication and recognized the important contribution our research could make to the urban affairs/urban studies discipline. Harry Briggs, executive editor, Management and Public Administration at M.E. Sharpe, and associate editor Elizabeth Granda guided us though the publication process. We are indebted to NCRCC Fellow Louis Crust, a Ph.D. student at the University of New Orleans, for his review and editing contributions. Finally, we wish to thank NCRCC graduate assistants Erin Elizabeth Stair and Sarah Beth Markway for formatting each of the research studies and consolidating them into a single manuscript, and for their patience with the editors.

March 2004
University of New Orleans
New Orleans, Louisiana

Fritz W. Wagner
Timothy E. Joder
Anthony J. Mumphrey Jr.
Krishna M. Akundi
Alan F.J. Artibise

Revitalizing the City

MAXINE GOODMAN LEVIN
COLLEGE OF URBAN AFFAIRS

Cleveland State University

Part 1

Urban Growth

KRISHNA M. AKUNDI

A Perspective on Suburban Expansion and Metropolitan Development

It does not matter exactly *where* it happened—central city or suburb—but that it *did* happen. A young man of twenty-four years walked out of his apartment toward the dumpster to throw out the trash. Having completed his task, he was about to return to his apartment when three teenagers surrounded him. They subsequently gave the twenty-four-year-old a beating. A young man had found himself at the wrong place at the wrong time, perhaps? But how could this have been the wrong place? It was where he lived; it was the place he called home.

No one wants to live with crime. No one wants to live in fear. So, if we can, we move. We move to a place where we feel safe. Joel Garreau in his groundbreaking 1991 book, *Edge City: Life on the New Frontier*, commented that people—by and large—prefer to live near others like themselves. And why is that? They do so because it gives them a sense of comfort and security. What does the phrase "others like themselves" suggest? It could mean people of the same race and ethnicity, age group, or income status. It could mean people with a similar religious affiliation, political persuasion, social interest, or intellectual curiosity.

Who lives where in the growing and ever-changing metropolis? Have the country's metropolitan areas and their component parts become culturally and racially diverse? On the other hand, have the component parts (the central cities and suburbs) become more homogeneous? In the Washington, D.C., metro region, for example, anecdotal observations—particularly of the public rail system—seem to support the idea of homogeneity. Most riders on Metro Rail's Orange Line who after work head west from the District of Columbia tend to be white and Asian, while most riders heading east tend to be African American. (See Table 1.1)

The data clearly indicate that all races in this region are moving to the suburbs. The outer suburbs (Frederick and Loudoun counties) are all but

3

Table 1.1

**2000 Racial Composition in the Washington, D.C., Metropolitan Region
by County** (by percent)

County	White	African American	Asian	Other
District of Columbia	30.8	60.0	2.7	6.5
Frederick	89.3	6.4	1.7	2.6
Montgomery	64.8	15.0	11.3	8.9
Prince Georges	27.0	62.7	3.9	6.4
Alexandria City	59.8	22.5	5.7	12.0
Arlington	68.9	9.3	8.6	13.2
Fairfax	69.9	8.6	13.0	8.5
Loudoun	82.8	6.9	5.3	5.0

Source: *American Fact Finder*, U.S. Census Bureau, http://factfinder.census.gov.

white, while the urban core and Prince Georges county, an inner suburb, have an African American majority. Montgomery and Fairfax counties, also inner suburbs of the metro region, have relatively large Asian populations. The Asian population in Fairfax County outnumbers its African American population. Is that a function of previous generations of Asian immigrants having established themselves in Fairfax and thus attracting new waves of immigrants to the same location? Or is it a recent phenomenon brought about by an industry's demand for a unique set of skills? This certainly is a question for future study.

Table 1.2 shows that suburban families—whether they are white, African American, or Asian—tend to be more affluent than their central city neighbors. Higher incomes afford families more choices. Thus, are people in the Washington, D.C., metropolitan region, or any metro region for that matter, moving to the edge because of fear? Are they moving because of overcrowding and build-out in the older suburbs?

Overcrowding may not be a valid reason. Few, if any, metropolitan regions in the United States are dense or compact. The urban landscape is marked by wide stretches of vacant land. Builders are leapfrogging. Government, business, homeowners, and commuters are all encouraging sprawl, and, sprawl has unanticipated consequences.

The National Center for the Revitalization of Central Cities is a consortium of universities where for the past ten years researchers have been studying the condition of the central city and evaluating strategies to redevelop and revitalize the urban core. The National Center has published several working papers and three books. One of its publications examined ways of managing capital resources in the urban core, and another considered the importance of supporting and developing human investments in the core.

Table 1.2

**2000 Median Household Income Distribution in the Washington, D.C.,
Metropolitan Region by County** (in U.S. dollars)

County	
District of Columbia	40,127
Frederick	60,726
Montgomery	71,551
Prince Georges	55,256
Alexandria City	56,054
Arlington	63,001
Fairfax	81,050
Loudoun	80,648

Source: American Fact Finder, U.S. Census Bureau, http://factfinder.census.gov.

Many of the strategies for revitalizing the central city, however, may be threatened by sprawl. Urban sprawl accelerates the decline of the central city. In this volume National Center researchers consider approaches for containing the frenetic pace of growth and thus revitalizing the city.

In this first chapter the author presents a perspective on suburban expansion and metropolitan development. Specifically, the author reviews recent literature on sprawl; a discussion of sprawl, however, covers any number of issues. In this brief survey the author summarizes the following: a history of sprawl best represented by central city decline and suburban growth, changes in metropolitan development patterns that not only cause but are caused by suburban sprawl, popular descriptions and definitions of sprawl, and the economic and social impacts of sprawl. Lastly, the author provides a bibliography of books and articles on the topic.

History of Sprawl

Throughout the mid-1990s the popular media focused on the costs of sprawl and the threat that unmitigated growth posed to the quality of life. How did we get to this point? We could lay the blame on the forces of suburbanization (suburban growth) and decentralization (central city decline), and on the neglect of our political leaders and their policies, but others would disagree.

Some researchers claim that the alarm over urban sprawl is misplaced. To them sprawl is the natural progression of metropolitan growth and development patterns. This natural progression started with a dense, active economic core that evolved into a ring of suburbs. People chose to "vote with their feet" and moved from the central city to the inner-ring suburbs; now, based once again on public choice, many are moving to the exurbs and beyond. The market met the initial demand and corrected for any externalities; the market will do the same in future expansions.

Central City Decline

Countless articles recount likely push factors behind the population exodus from the central city to the inner-ring suburbs (Tiebout 1956, Bradford and Kelejian 1973, Mills and Price 1984, Palumbo, Sacks, and Wasylenko 1990, Miezkowski and Mills 1993):

1. Declining levels of education expenditures.
2. Poor quality of infrastructure and amenities.
3. Increasing taxes.
4. High crime.
5. Racial tensions.
6. Greater population density.

Cumulative causation theories suggest that when middle- and upper-income households leave the central city, the city's tax base contracts. Because the local government now has fewer fiscal resources, it cannot meet all demands for the remaining central city residents (many of whom are poor and elderly) and central city businesses. To recover lost revenue, the local government increases taxes on landlords and other business owners but neglects needed infrastructure improvements. This leads to business closings and relocations and to financial disinvestments—these actions further erode the central city tax base. Cumulative causation theories assume that because suburbs depend on the central business district for jobs and services, a central city's eroding tax base will affect not only the central city but also surrounding suburbs and the entire metropolitan area (Akundi 1999).

Migration from the central city to the inner-ring suburbs did not happen overnight; it was a slow, gradual process that took nearly a century. It was only in the 1960s that the rate of central city out-migration increased and researchers began taking a much closer look at the reasons for that out-migration. After forty years of suburban development are we witnessing an exodus from the inner-ring suburbs to the exurbs and beyond? Has the cumulative effect of central city decline migrated to the inner-ring suburbs?

Mumphrey and Akundi (1998)—based on a review of a 1995 National Center for the Revitalization of Central Cities working paper—found that inner-ring suburbs do not follow the central city. That study examined changes in socioeconomic indicators (population, employment, and income) for forty-three metropolitan areas, including their central cities and inner suburbs.

National Center investigators found that between 1960 and 1990, the magnitude and rate of growth in metropolitan areas and suburbs exceeded growth in central cities. Trend data showed that population and employment declines in the inner suburbs did not follow central city population and employment declines. These investigators concluded that inner-ring suburbs could substitute for central cities as economic engines in metropolitan areas. So how did the suburbs achieve this independence?

Suburban Growth

The U.S. Census Bureau first used the term "suburb" in its analysis of Greater New York City in 1880. Twenty years later it became common practice to distinguish population characteristics of the central city from those of its adjacent cities or suburbs (Muller 1981). Fishman (1987), in his review of suburban development, describes suburbia as a place that included middle-class residences but excluded lower-income classes. It excluded industry and most commerce except for food stores and convenience shops. Thus, socio-economic homogeneity characterized suburbia. This definition was valid from the nineteenth century until into the 1950s. Muller (1981) finds that the idea of central city and bedroom suburbs ended for most metropolitan areas by 1969. During the 1970s the metropolitan structure had changed to include a central city, an inner ring of suburbs, an outer ring of suburbs, and edge cities.

The consumer's preference to reside in areas with low density, low land costs, low transportation costs, reduced travel time, less noise, less pollution, and virtually little crime marked the beginning of suburbanization and decentralization. Innovations in transportation technology and later in new construction techniques and financing mechanisms turned many residential preferences into a reality for American families.

Just as the electric streetcar contributed to the making of the nineteenth-century suburb, in the twentieth century, the automobile had the greater impact on suburban development; its influence began in the 1920s and increased considerably by the 1950s. Kenneth Jackson (1985) notes that among the pull factors that contributed to the rapid growth of suburban communities were the following:

1. Automobile.
2. Interstate highway network.
3. Mass production of single-family residential houses.
4. Government financing of home mortgages through the FHA and VA.
5. Low interest rates.

6. Higher wages.
7. Shopping opportunities.

Suburbs, exurbs, and the rural parts of metro areas also proved attractive to businesses because they offered lower factor costs (transportation, land, and labor) compared to central cities. Manufacturing plants and wholesale distributors began to locate in the suburbs and other outlying areas because of the large tracts of cheap land that allowed them to build horizontally.

Retailers followed consumers to the suburbs from the beginning. Since the 1960s, however, the suburban shopping experience changed. On average 48.5 percent of all 1963 metropolitan retail sales were concentrated in the suburbs; ten years later this average increased to 64.2 percent (Muller 1981, 121). The regional shopping mall was in part responsible for the transformation in consumer shopping patterns: Its enormous size (often more than 250,000 sq. ft. of selling space) essentially re-created the central business district shopping experience in a more controlled environment (Muller 1981). O'Sullivan (1993) reports that to benefit from one-stop shopping and comparison shopping, retailers with moderate-scale economies clustered in malls and plazas. Regional malls also offered recreational and entertainment activities for the consumer, and they offered close-in; free parking spaces—a perquisite not available in the central business district.

More than retail, manufacturing, or wholesale industry investment, it was suburban office investment that impacted the urban form and development patterns. According to Garreau (1991), the principal factors in suburban office investment were worker safety and commuting concerns. Cervero (1989) notes that 57 percent of all office space in 1980 was found in urban centers and 43 percent of all office space was in suburban centers. Six years later more office space was available in the suburbs than in the central cities: 60 percent in suburban centers and 40 percent in urban centers. This transformation may be attributed to the shorter commutation time for workers if offices were in suburbs rather than in the central business district: The suburb-to-suburb work trip was 50 percent shorter than the suburb-to-central city work trip (Cervero 1989).

Office developments are springing up not only in suburban communities adjacent to the central city but in clusters along freeway corridors. According to Pivo (1990), these clusters are characterized by high concentrations of workers amid low-density development. As office developments moved out of the central city to increase accessibility and reduce travel time for suburban residents, they also attracted other businesses and households to their new location—thus, creating a scattered development pattern as opposed to the contiguous pattern that once existed.

Metropolitan Development Patterns

A scattered development pattern is indicative of sprawl. The consequences of such a pattern will be discussed in a later section. Here the focus is on how the changing form of the metropolitan region affects the central city–suburb relationship.

Metropolitan development patterns are changing. The metropolitan region can no longer be described as a monocentric city surrounded by a ring of suburban residential communities. The monocentric city, for all intents and purposes, is dead. Metro regions are multinucleated or polycentric. In other words, the central city is just one among many employment centers (Bogart 1998, DiPasquale and Wheaton 1996, Helsley and Sullivan 1991, Giuliano and Small 1991, Richardson et al.1990). What does this mean for the location of jobs and households? How does this affect commuting patterns? Is there an urban core?

Relevance of the Central City

Mumphrey and Akundi (1998) evaluated six hypotheses that debate the relevance of the central city to the metropolitan region.

Should we dismiss as obsolete the suburban dependence hypothesis in which all other locations in the metropolitan region depend on the central city for jobs and income? Mumphrey and Akundi cite statistical evidence that this hypothesis is irrelevant.

Do we adopt the downtown dependence hypothesis, which claims that the central business district and the central city depend on the suburbs for workers and incomes? The reviewers contend that perhaps downtown dependence is the correct specification of the central city–suburb relationship. Yet, the downtown dependence hypothesis is consistent with the traditional monocentric model as opposed to the polycentric model of urban structure. Second, it assumes that suburban households make trips to the central business district for work. What about other employment agglomerations within the central city? Last, the downtown revitalization approach is not sufficient. If suburban households are to commute to the central city, whether for work or play, then central city neighborhoods and shopping districts need to be revitalized as well.

Is the tight labor market hypothesis the proper specification? It suggests that the metropolitan region's engine of growth swings between the central city and suburb based on the business cycle. This hypothesis is flawed. The investigators who proposed the theory in the first place discovered that central city labor does not substitute for suburban labor.

Are positive socioeconomic conditions in the urban core determined by the central city's ability to annex more land? The elasticity hypothesis is not a true evaluation of the city-suburb relationship, because it assumes that all communities have the authority to annex. They do not. Second, it accepts the traditional urban form: the monocentric model.

Does the central city—as put forth in the interdependence hypothesis—still wield influence over the metropolitan area's economic development priorities because it is the preferred location of dynamic industry? Mumphrey and Akundi believe that the interdependence hypothesis is the proper specification of the central city–suburb relationship: It takes into account the multinucleated urban form and makes a plea for public investment in the central city on the grounds of industry agglomeration to ensure regional growth and prosperity.

Have central business districts and central cities become irrelevant to metropolitan growth and development as proposed by Joel Garreau (1991)? The edge city hypothesis is a valid counterweight to the interdependence hypothesis. Mumphrey and Akundi (1998) contend that to disprove the edge city proposition, researchers ought to compare the net costs and benefits of central city revitalization against the net costs and benefits of edge development.

Thus, it would seem that the interdependence and edge city hypotheses play a pivotal role in defining the central city's place in a multinucleated metropolitan region. While supporters of the interdependence hypothesis find a unique and integral niche for the central city/the urban core, the edge city hypothesis—which finds the central city irrelevant—forces planners and policymakers to address the problem of urban sprawl and consider regional solutions such as urban growth boundaries, infill development, and revenue financing mechanisms.

Edge Cities

Robert Fishman (1987) foresaw a metropolitan region dotted with techno-burbs: low-density peripheral development, divorced from the central business district but invested with economic and technological dynamism. Examples of Fishman's techno-burbs include Silicon Valley near San Francisco, Route 128 outside Boston, Princeton, New Jersey's U.S. Highway 1, and the Research Triangle Park, in North Carolina.

Joel Garreau (1991) describes edge cities as any development activity that meets the following minimum criteria: five million square feet of leased office space and six hundred thousand square feet of leased retail space. In addition, it is an employment center—that is, it primarily has a day population. It is a single-end destination for jobs, shopping, or entertainment; and it has been in existence for only thirty years or less—before that time these edge cities were either rural locales or farmland. According to Garreau's count, in 1990 there were over two hundred edge cities in the United States. He lists several retail-oriented edge developments: King of Prussia outside Philadelphia, Las Colinas outside Dallas, the Buckhead section of Atlanta, the Westheimer corridor in Houston, Tyson's Corner in Virginia, and Beverly Hills in California, among others.

McKee and McKee (2001) bring some order to this list. They contend that edge cities can be grouped into six categories: entertainment, retail, office, corporate, research, and manufacturing. What has been missing from any discussion of edge cities is a theoretical framework. McKee and McKee place edge development in the context of growth-pole theory. They do not suggest that edge cities are necessarily growth poles but that edge developments may serve as either the supplier hinterland or consumer market for a growth pole.

The freeway system has facilitated the development of edge cities. The drive to pave the urban landscape with asphalt has made it easier to escape the central business district, the central city, and the inner suburbs. It is not, however, a causal factor. A reexamination of the bid-rent curve, on the other hand, may provide a better explanation for the rise of edge cities.

According to Burgess (1964) and other urban ecologists, the city grew outward because functions that lost out in central city competition relocated to peripheral areas—either to the inner-ring suburbs, the outer suburbs, or to the edge of older activity centers. This in turn led the remaining central city firms to seek competitive advantages within the city. The highest competitive land users (firms and residents able to pay high rents) located in the central business district, while less competitive land users (firms and residents able to pay moderate to low rents) located at the periphery. The farther from the center that residents and firms locate, the lower the rent. Alonso (1964) reiterated that the bid-rent set for land uses was determined by the returns accrued at various locations once the attendant transport costs were subtracted. The argument made by Burgess, Alonso and other urban ecologists may just as easily be applied to the metro region and its components— the urban core, the inner suburbs, outer suburbs, and exurbs.

Techno-burbs, edge cities, and subcenters all illustrate the same phenomenon: economic activity in a metro region that is locating outside traditional employment centers such as the central business district or older suburban downtowns.

Helsley and Sullivan (1991) contend that this multinucleic or polycentric form is simply the natural progression of urban development: the transformation from a region with a single employment center to a network of employment locations within a growing metro region. The authors hold that the transformation occurs in three phases: The first phase finds a single exclusive employment center (the central business district) that dominates the landscape. The second phase begins with the appearance of two or more peripheral employment activity centers. This shift of employment growth away from the central business district to other activity centers occurs because of external economies of scale in production and diseconomies of scale in transportation. Helsley and Sullivan suggest that this second phase is relatively short. The final phase shows both the employment center and employment subcenters developing simultaneously. Simultaneous development assumes that these centers provide unique products and services.

One of the characteristics of a multinucleated region, as described by Miezkowski and Smith (1991), is that it is peppered with vacant land. There is a center and, in some cases, contiguous older ring suburbs but then a sea of nothing before finding other subcenters. This is certainly the case in Houston and other Sunbelt cities. Giuliano and Small (1991) developed criteria for identifying subcenters. These measures include employment, land area, employment density (jobs per acre) and a jobs-to-population ratio. These same criteria may be used to identify sprawl. Miezkowski and Smith measured density in Houston by census tract. They found that the density gradient falls with distance from the central business district because of large tracts of vacant land between the central business district and other subcenters.

This review of edge cities allows for several conclusions including:

1. At some tipping point the central business district and the central city should be allowed to wither away. Economic activity in the metro region is better served by a dispersed pattern of employment subcenters.
2. Subcenters arise because firms that "win" in central city competition relocate to the edge of established settlements. And, in so doing, promote scattered development patterns that result in heavy economic and social costs to metro regions.
3. Perhaps employment subcenters provide unique products and services that actually support a metro region's economic engine, its growth pole. And perhaps that growth pole is located in the urban core. If this is the case, the edge city concept and interdependence concept may be reconciled.

Interdependence

Knowing how cities and suburbs relate to each other affects urban planning decisions, including the design of local and regional economic development strategies. Akundi (1999) contends that the relationship is explained by interdependence, an equal or nearly equal power relationship between cities and suburbs. Some industries (the suppliers or producers of goods and services) gain an advantage from concentrating in the core, while others gain an advantage from concentrating in the periphery. Each type of industry complements the other; that relationship reinforces metropolitan growth and development.

Akundi lays out three propositions for analysis:

1. The relationship between the urban core and periphery is determined by the types of economic activity that dominate in the metropolitan area.
2. Dynamic industries agglomerate in the core, from where they direct economic growth and development throughout the metropolitan area.
3. If dynamic industries are to develop or remain in the metro area, agglomeration economies in the core must be increased through public investment.

In a rather extensive literature review, he makes a case for interdependence. The statistical analysis does bear him out on some points; it is, however, quite narrow. Moreover, his geographic focus is the urban core and inner-ring suburbs of the metropolitan region not the exurbs or edge cities. Nonetheless, it is instructive and raises questions for future investigation.

Research on industry location indicates that suburbs rely on the central city because some types of economic activity agglomerate in the core (central city and central county); similarly, central cities rely on suburbs because other types of economic activity agglomerate in the periphery (suburbs). The literature further shows that agglomeration economies explain the spatial concentration of knowledge-based industries. Thus, the issue becomes how to maintain the central city's agglomeration economies. Drennan (1992, 2002) contends that if agglomeration economies in the core deteriorate, core area firms may leave not only the core but the metropolitan area, the region, and even the country. Thus, to sustain the profitability of the urban core, attract new firms and retain existing firms, municipalities need to enhance the economies of agglomeration.

Studies by several investigators including Akundi (1999) find that knowledge-based industries concentrate in the urban core of metropolitan areas. Information-processing industries such as banking, insurance carriers, and securities and commodity brokers prefer an urban core location. Intellectual-oriented industries such as business services, legal services, and engineering/management services also prefer a core location.

Coffey (1996) and Schwartz (1993) agree that, within the metropolitan area, the central city is an important location for business, professional, and financial services. Coffey (1996) examined information industry trade flows (i.e., sales and purchase data) in the Montreal census metropolitan area for a sample of 324 establishments. The study shows the positive role information industries play in linking cities and suburbs. Schwartz examined the distribution of 5,000 financial firms within the nation's consolidated metropolitan statistical areas. The results of his analysis indicate that 48 percent of all corporate offices locate in the central city, 45 percent in the suburbs, and 7 percent in rural areas. He also finds that most corporate offices—wherever headquartered—purchase their services from central city vendors.

The view that a knowledge-based economy would make dense developments unimportant has been discounted by empirical evidence; they are more likely to concentrate in a particular location. Kutay (1989) has suggested that innovation-based industries are pulled to sites with social and physical amenities, modern transportation, and communications infrastructure, and with many business services firms nearby. Thus, Kutay's study implies that infrastructure investment in the core or periphery affects industry location.

Akundi's (1999) literature review shows that investments in the physical infrastructure and human capital of regions (i.e., states, metro areas, and counties) affect economic development and particularly agglomeration economies. Agglomeration economies are strengthened by investments in physical infrastructure and human capital. Akundi conducted several least squares regression tests which indicate that public investment in the urban core— over the long term—does influence economic growth and development in the metropolitan area. The results also seem to indicate that population growth leads to job growth and that the urban core's services industry has a greater impact on metro jobs than the core's manufacturing industries.

The urban core or central city has an advantage over other locations when it comes to physical infrastructure. Central cities contain the wealth of the country's physical infrastructure. Yet, as the nation matures, demands on infrastructure services outrace the central city's capacity to provide them. This circumstance has led—in Tiebout-like fashion—to households and large firms voting with their feet and moving to locations that meet their needs. Large firms usually have the internal scale economies that allow them to move from the central city to the suburbs or exurbs. They also have the resources to construct a new infrastructure system or to support municipalities in constructing the infrastructure—whether they actually do so or not is a different matter. Small-sized firms are more reliant on external economies. Thus, unless the public infrastructure is maintained, small firms may be forced to move to other metropolitan areas or fail.

The need to build new infrastructure in peripheral settlements is a consequence of sprawl. Future research ought to measure costs associated with such construction. These costs may be mitigated by economic interdependence between the core and periphery. Preserving this link requires dense development and strong agglomeration economies.

Describing Sprawl

Sprawl, as it is called in the popular lexicon, can trace its beginnings to the forces of decentralization and suburbanization. These forces also explain changes in the urban form of the metropolitan region. Although a polycentric region is the inevitable progression of urban development, the growth of edge settlements only aggravates sprawl. The term has been so overused that it would appear no formal definition is needed—you will know it when you see it.

The Sierra Club in a 1998 report listed the 30 Most Sprawl-Threatened Cities. The number one city on the list was Atlanta, followed by St. Louis and Washington, D.C.

The Sierra Club defines urban sprawl to mean "Low-density development beyond the edge of service and employment, which separates where people live from where they shop, work, recreate, and educate—thus requiring cars to move between zones."

Bolioli (2001) uses a similar definition in his examination of the population dynamics behind suburban sprawl in Rhode Island: low-density, large-lot residential and commercial development that is scattered across a large land area. This land area is separated into distinct zones requiring regular interzone travel. Sprawl changes the rural landscape of farmlands, parks, and other natural areas into man-made environments.

Squires (2002) offers this definition of sprawl: "Sprawl can be defined as a pattern of urban and metropolitan growth that reflects low-density, automobile dependent, exclusionary new development on the fringe of settled areas that often surround a deteriorating city."

Galster and colleagues (2001) reviewed several definitions of sprawl. They found that the term has too often been described in terms of its consequences or resulting physical pattern:

- Sprawl is continuous low-density residential development on the metropolitan fringe.
- Sprawl is low-density ribbon development along suburban highways.
- Sprawl is development that leapfrogs past undeveloped land and leaves a patchwork of developed and undeveloped tracts.

Galster et al. contend that sprawl is a process of development and should be treated as such. "Sprawl is a pattern of land use in an urbanized area that exhibits low levels of density, continuity, concentration, clustering, centrality, nuclearity, mixed uses, and proximity."

Common to all five definitions is low density. Density appears to be the key to resolving the sprawl issue. However, Burchell et al. (1998) caution that American cities and suburbs are generally less dense than their counterparts in other countries. Thus, density is a relative matter. What is the ideal density? Ewing (1995) suggests seven houses per acre. This desire for higher density, however, appears to conflict with consumer choice. Consumers find benefits to our current pattern of sprawl development (Burchell et al. 1998):

1. Unlimited use of the automobile.
2. Homes and shopping far from the social and fiscal problems of central cities and older inner suburbs.
3. Diverse economic base not just retail.
4. Larger lots as well as rising home values.
5. Better and safer schools.
6. Relatively low property taxes.

The Council of State Governments in its 1998 fall newsletter, *State Trends*, reported on the efforts of fifteen state governors to implement smart growth policies and programs. Smart growth is a means to inoculate a metropolitan area from sprawl. Some of the more common characteristics of suburban sprawl that local governments battle include:

1. Unlimited outward expansion.
2. Strip development.
3. Leapfrog development.
4. Traffic congestion.
5. Income and racial segregation.
6. Fiscal disparities.
7. Environmental contamination.
8. Loss of open space.
9. High-priced housing.
10. Inadequate housing for low-income households.
11. Fragmentation of powers among municipalities.
12. Stress on the physical infrastructure of rural areas because of new, large-scale projects and rapid development.

Myers and Kitsuse (2001) also reviewed descriptions of sprawl. They juxtapose competing arguments in the sprawl debate: Reid Ewing's support of compact development against Gordon and Richardson's implicit support of decentralized development, and the views of the Bank of America against those of Wells Fargo.

The Bank of America is California's largest financial institution and also a major lender to real estate developers. In 1995 Bank of America and three other government and nonprofit agencies drafted *Beyond Sprawl: New Patterns of Growth to Fit the New California*. Myers and Kitsuse applaud the authors for undertaking the report and for making the argument that traditional land-use decision making has failed the state. However, the report does not provide any prescriptions. It is a largely static review of development patterns in California and the consequences they pose for economic growth and quality of life. Bank of America defines sprawl as "low-density, single use development removed from the core of the central city and older inner suburbs, and indexed by long hours spent driving." The Wells Fargo Bank prepared *Preserving the American Dream*, a response to the Bank of America and all those who spout the conventional wisdom behind sprawl. On the basis of statistical evidence and academic research, the Wells Fargo team argues against compact development, finds mass transit inefficient, and claims that leapfrog development will eventually lead to higher infill densities. Wells Fargo does not consider the social and environmental costs posed by sprawl. Yet, it is these costs that perhaps make the best case for controlling development.

Parris Glendening, the former governor of Maryland, said, "Inner city disinvestments and suburban sprawl are two sides of the same coin." The Council of State Governments agrees that fiscal and social costs of sprawl impact every corner of society.

The Economic and Social Costs of Sprawl

Robert Freilich is a well-respected land-use lawyer with over thirty years experience. In his 1999 text, *From Sprawl to Smart Growth*, he discusses the losing battle that local governments are waging against urban sprawl. Freilich cites the case of *Golden versus Planning Board of Town of Ramapo* as presenting local and state governments with the best set of tools for controlling the frenetic pace of growth.

In Chapter 2 of his text, Freilich describes the costs of sprawl in terms of its impacts on the community, housing, jobs, transportation, government finances, farmland and open space, and the political debate. He lists six main crises that sprawl causes in metropolitan regions:

1. Deterioration of central cities and inner-ring suburbs.

2. Environmental degradation—specifically, the loss of wetlands and sensitive lands; poor air and water quality.
3. Overconsumption of petroleum.
4. Fiscal insolvency, infrastructure deficiencies, and taxpayer revolts.
5. Transportation congestion.
6. Unaffordable housing.

Market Failure

Reid Ewing (1995) views sprawl as a market failure. This idea is echoed by economists at the St. Louis Federal Reserve Bank who find that the market has failed when it allows sprawl or uncontrolled development to continue despite the costs to local governments because of the public infrastructure generated by new development, the time costs associated with commuting, and the intangible benefits of open spaces that may be lost (Hernandez-Murillo 2001). Brueckner (2000) contends that a market correction would require developers and residents to pay the full costs imposed on others.

With respect to public infrastructure demands brought on by housing subdivisions and apartment complexes—the first wave of sprawl—the best strategies to control such growth are taxes and fees. In Montgomery County, Maryland, the planning commission imposes impact fees on residential developments to pay for transportation and education infrastructure.

Traffic Congestion

The most visible of these crises is traffic congestion. It affects commuters every day. Nationally, according to the Census Bureau's Journey to Work data, the mean commutation time to work increased from 22.4 minutes to 25.5 minutes between 1990 and 2000. In the Washington, D.C., metro area, mean travel time increased from 28.2 minutes to 31.7 minutes. The Federal Highway Administration (2003) reports that nearly 13 percent of the Washington, D.C., labor force spends over 60 minutes commuting to work. In 1980 only 9.3 percent were spending that much time, and by 1990 nearly 10 percent were spending an hour. The number of people who spend less than 15 minutes commuting to work has consistently declined—in 2000 it was only 17.7 percent of the Washington, D.C., labor force. Time spent commuting does impact worker productivity—by how much has not been estimated, but it is an interesting avenue of research. Time spent sitting in traffic also affects air quality.

The Federal Highway Administration finds that, despite ten years of sprawl debate and over thirty years of discussion on environmental quality and energy

Table 1.3

2000 Journey-to-Work and Travel Times in the Washington, D.C., Metropolitan Region by County

County	Travel Time (in minutes)	Percent Working Outside the County (in percent)	Percent Choosing Public Transportation (in percent)
District of Columbia	30.0	27.0	33.2
Frederick	32.0	41.0	1.4
Montgomery	33.0	41.0	12.6
Prince Georges	36.0	60.0	11.9
Alexandria City	30.0	75.0	16.4
Arlington	27.0	70.0	23.3
Fairfax	31.0	47.0	7.3
Loudoun	31.0	59.0	1.5

Source: American Fact Finder, U.S. Census Bureau, http://factfinder.census.gov.

conservation, more people are driving alone. In 1990, 66.1 percent of Washington, D.C., area commuters drove to work alone, but by 2000 that figure increased to 70.4 percent. In the New York metropolitan area the figure went from 55.4 percent to 56.3 percent; in Los Angeles it went from 72.3 percent to 72.4 percent. American society prefers its automobiles. It must be said that the increased percentages may also have to do with metropolitan expansion. People living farther out have no other means of transportation but the automobile.

Other modes of transportation such as rail and bus are having a minor impact in most metro regions. In the Washington, D.C., metro region, workers riding the bus fell from 6 percent to 4 percent but rail ridership increased from 4.5 percent to 5.0 percent. The New York metropolitan region also witnessed a decrease in bus ridership from 7.2 percent to 6.8 percent. Rail ridership has a strong following in that region: 17.1 percent of New Yorkers take the train to work, up from 16.7 percent in 1990.

The Sierra Club's award to the Washington, D.C., metropolitan area as the third most sprawled city may be well deserved. The amount of time people spend commuting—regardless of their mode of transport—is also impacted by where they live.

Washington, D.C., commuters spend anywhere from a half hour to over an hour on their journey to work. Consider the Washington, D.C., metropolitan public transportation system—which includes Metro, MARC (the Maryland Rail Commuter), VRE (the Virginia Railway Express), and a number of bus services. These transit systems are not simply transporting residents from nearby suburban communities to jobs in the central city or

Table 1.4

2000 Suburb-Suburb Commuting in Washington, D.C., Region Suburban Counties to/from Montgomery County

County	To Montgomery County (in percent)	From Montgomery County (in percent)
District of Columbia	5.2	23.1
Frederick	6.1	1.0
Montgomery	71.4	61.9
Prince Georges	10.8	6.2
Arlington	1.2	2.3
Fairfax	4.5	5.1
Loudoun	0.7	0.4

Source: Maryland National Capital Park and Planning Commission.

from central city neighborhoods to jobs in downtown. The rail lines are also carrying people from suburb to suburb—for example from residences in northern Virginia to jobs in suburban Maryland and vice versa.

Census data indicate that the number of residents commuting from the D.C. metro region's inner suburbs to the urban core declined 6 percent in the last ten years. The number of residents commuting from the region's outer suburbs to its urban core has increased by 46 percent. One can infer from the suburb-to-core declines that suburb-to-suburb commuting has increased. Table 1.4 shows commuting patterns to and from Montgomery County.

Other Costs

The National Resources Defense Council (Benfield et al. 1999) reports that sprawling land development is gobbling up the American countryside at 365 acres per hour. The American Farmland Trust reports that between 1982 and 1992 the United States lost 400,000 acres of prime farmland—land with the best soils and climate for growing crops—to urban and suburban development. They cite that California's Central Valley, the Northern Illinois Drift Plain, and the Northern Piedmont region near Washington, D.C., are the most threatened farming regions.

Sprawl or, more specifically, overdevelopment also threatens aquifers, underground water tables, and drinking water supplies. Paved areas prevent billions of gallons of rainwater from seeping through the soil to replenish groundwater. The other main problem is that in sprawling developments storm-water runoff—which is contaminated by oils and other pollutants—must be prevented from entering sensitive areas (Doggett 2002). According to a Reuters news article, the three top metro areas most affected by water loss are Atlanta, Boston, and Washington, D.C. It reports that between 1982 and 1997 Atlanta lost 38 billion gallons of water per year on average, Boston lost 29 billion gallons of water per year on average, and Washington, D.C., lost an average of 16 billion gallons of water per year.

Conclusion

The metropolitan region is expanding and will continue to expand, but the issue is what form that expansion will take. If we contend that decentralized, low-density development (sprawl) is unacceptable, then we must encourage approaches that will create higher density development. Higher density development is the key to continued economic growth and development in the metropolitan area. Myers and Kitsuse (2001) hold that the main issue in revitalizing the city and controlling the pace of development, especially in a polynucleated metropolitan region, is increasing density. Dense development may be achieved through growth management, housing affordability, sustainability, new urbanism, and compact cities. Amy Liu of the Brookings Institution concurs. In a presentation before the Urban Land Institute in October 2003 Liu discusses the benefits and realities of high density development.

The interdependence hypothesis suggests that central city influence stems from its advantage as the preferred location of dynamic industries in the metropolitan area. Thus, unless agglomeration economies are maintained in the central city through investments in physical and human infrastructure, dynamic industries may not develop to begin with or may exit the region if already present. It would appear that containing frenetic growth and reviving the core is necessary for the economic viability of the metropolitan region.

In the chapters that follow, my colleagues consider avenues—though not explicitly—for higher density development in older central cities. Higher density may be achieved through the redevelopment of abandoned properties and brownfields, through the enforcement of regulatory controls, and through the creation of mixed-income housing in the center.

References

History of Sprawl: Central-City Decline and Suburban Growth

Bradford, D., and H. Kelejian. 1973. "An Econometric Model of the Flight to the Suburbs." *Journal of Political Economy* 81, no. 3 (July): 566–89.
Cervero, R. 1989. *America's Suburban Centers.* Boston, MA: Unwin-Hyman.
Chudacoff, H., and J. Smith. 1994. *The Evolution of American Urban Society.* Englewood Cliffs, NJ: Prentice Hall.

Downs, A. 1993. *New Visions for Metropolitan America.* Washington, DC: Brookings Institution.

Fishman, R. 1987. *Bourgeois Utopias: The Rise and Fall of Suburbia.* New York: Basic Books.

Garreau, J. 1991. *Edge City: Life on the New Frontier.* New York: Doubleday.

Jackson, Kenneth T. 1985. *Crabgrass Frontier: The Suburbanization of the United States.* New York: Oxford University Press.

Kunstler, J. 1993. *The Geography of Nowhere: The Rise and Decline of America's Man-Made Landscape.* New York: Simon and Schuster.

Margo, R. 1992. "Explaining the Postwar Suburbanizations of Population in the United States: The Role of Income." *Journal of Urban Economics* 31, no. 3: 301–10.

Miezkowski, P., and E. Mills. 1993. "The Causes of Metropolitan Suburbanization." *Journal of Economic Perspectives* 7, no. 3: 135–47.

Mills, E., and E. Price. 1984. "Metropolitan Suburbanization and Central City Problems." *Journal of Urban Economics* 15: 1–17.

Muller, P. 1981. *Contemporary Suburban America.* Englewood Cliffs, NJ: Prentice Hall.

O'Sullivan, A. 1993. *Urban Economics.* Boston, MA: Richard D. Irwin.

Palumbo, G., S. Sacks, and M. Wasylenko. 1990. "Population Decentralization Within Metropolitan Areas: 1970–1980." *Journal of Urban Economics* 27, no. 2: 151–67.

Pivo, G. 1990. "The Net of Mixed Beads: Suburban Office Development in Six Metropolitan Regions." *Journal of the American Planning Association* 56, no. 4: 457–69.

Schneider, W. 1992. "The Suburban Century Begins." *Atlantic Monthly* (July): 33–44

Tiebout, C. 1956. "A Pure Theory of Local Expenditures." *Journal of Political Economy* 64, no. 5: 416–24.

Metropolitan Development Patterns

Akundi, K. 1999. "Is There a Case for Public Investment in the Urban Core of Metropolitan Areas?" Ph.D. diss., College of Urban and Public Affairs, University of New Orleans.

Alonso, W. 1964. *Location and Land Use: Toward a General Theory of Land Rent.* Cambridge, MA: Harvard University.

Bingham, R. 2000. "Beyond Edge Cities: Job Decentralization and Urban Sprawl." *Urban Affairs Review* 35 no. 6: 837–55.

Bogart, W. 1998. *The Economics of Cities and Suburbs.* Upper Saddle River, NJ: Prentice Hall.

Burgess, E. 1964. *Contributions to Urban Sociology.* Chicago: University of Chicago Press.

Coffey, W. 1996. "Forward and Backward Linkages of Producer-Services Establishments: Evidence from the Montreal Metropolitan Area." *Urban Geography* 17, no. 7: 604–32.

DiPasquale, D., and W. Wheaton. 1996. *Urban Economics and Real Estate Markets.* Englewood Cliffs, NJ: Prentice Hall.

Drennan, M. 1992. "Gateway Cities: The Metropolitan Sources of U.S. Producer Service Exports". *Urban Studies* 29, no. 2: 217–35.

———. 2002. *The Information Economy and American Cities*. Baltimore, MD: John Hopkins University Press.

Giuliano, G., and K. Small. 1991. "Subcenters in the Los Angeles Region." *Regional Science and Urban Economics* 2, no. 2: 163–82.

Gordon, P., H. Richardson, and H. Wong. 1986. "Distribution of Population and Employment in a Polycentric City: The Case of Los Angeles." *Environment and Planning A* 18, no. 2: 161–73.

Helsley, R., and A. Sullivan. 1991. "Urban Subcenter Formation." *Regional Science and Urban Economics* 21: 255–75.

Kutay, A. 1989. "Prospects for High-Technology Based Economic Development in Mature Industrial Regions: Pittsburgh as a Case Study." *Journal of Urban Affairs* 11, no. 4: 361–77.

McKee, D., and Y. McKee. 2001. "Edge Cities and the Viability of Metropolitan Economies: Contributions to Flexibility and External Linkages by New Urban Service Environments." *American Journal of Economics and Sociology* http://www.findarticles.com/cf_dls/m0254/1_60/74643765/p1/article.jhtml (accessed February 21, 2004).

McMillen, D. 2001. "Polycentric Urban Structure: The Case of Milwaukee." *Economic Perspectives*. Chicago: Federal Reserve Bank of Chicago, http://www.chicagofed.org/publications/economicperspectives/2001/2qepart2.pdf (accessed February 21, 2004)

McMillen, D., and J. McDonald. 1998. "Suburban Subcenters and Employment Density in Metropolitan Chicago." *Journal of Urban Economics* 43: 157–80.

Miezkowski, P., and B. Smith (1991) "Analyzing Urban Decentralization: The Case of Houston." *Regional Science and Urban Economics* 21, no. 2: 183–99.

Mumphrey, A., and K. Akundi. 1998. "The Suburban Dependency Hypothesis, Reconsidered." *Journal of Planning Literature* 13, no. 2: 147–57.

Richardson, H., P. Gordon, M. Jun, E. Hekkila, R. Peiser, and D. Dale Johnson. 1990. "Residential Property Values, the CBD, and Multiple Nodes: Further Analysis." *Environment and Planning A* 22, no. 6: 829–33.

Schwartz, A. 1993. "Subservient Suburbia: The Reliance of Large Suburban Companies on Central City Firms for Financial and Professional Services." *Journal of the American Planning Association* 59, no. 3: 288–305.

Describing Sprawl

Bolioli, T. (2001) "Population Dynamics Behind Suburban Sprawl." Master's thesis, Center for Environmental Studies, Brown University, Providence, Rhode Island, http://envstudies.brown.edu/Thesis/2001/tbolioli (accessed February 21, 2004).

Burchell, R. et al. 1998. "The Costs of Sprawl, Revisited." *Transportation Research Board*. Washington, DC: National Research Council, http://www.landuse.msu.edu/related/trans_sprawl.pdf (accessed February 21, 2004).

Council of State Governments. 1998. "States Battle Suburban Sprawl." *State Trends* 4, no. 4: 1–3, http://stars.csg.org/trends/1998/fall/fa98trends1.pdf (accessed February 21, 2004).

Ewing, R. 1995. "Characteristics, Causes, and Effects of Sprawl: A literature Review." *Environmental and Urban Issues* (Winter): 1–5.
Galster, G., R. Hanson, M. Ratcliffe, H. Wolman, S. Coleman, and J. Freilage. 2001. "Wrestling Sprawl to the Ground: Defining and Measuring the Elusive Concept." *Housing Policy Debate* 12, no. 4: 681–71.
Sierra Club. 1998. "Sprawl: The Dark Side of the American Dream," http://www.sierraclub.org/sprawl/report98/report.asp (accessed January 18, 2002).
Squires, G. 2002. "Uneven Development of Metropolitan America." *Urban Sprawl: Causes, Consequences, and Policy Responses.* Washington, DC: Urban Institute.

Economic and Social Costs of Sprawl

Benfield, K., M. Raimi, and D. Chen. 1999. "Once There Were Greenfields." New York: National Resources Defense Council, http://www.nrdc.org/cities/smartGrowth/greenfiled.asp (accessed February 21, 2004).
Brueckner, J. 2000. "Urban Sprawl: Diagnosis and Remedies." *International Regional Science Review* 23: 160–71.
Ciscel, D. 2001. "The Economics of Urban Sprawl: Inefficiency as a Core Feature of Metropolitan Growth." *Journal of Economic Issues* 35, no. 2: 405–14.
Doggett, T. 2002. "Suburban Sprawl Blocks Water, Worsens U.S. Draught," August 29, Reuters Newswire, http://enn.com/news/wire_stories/2002/08/08292002/reu_48291.asp (accessed February 21, 2004).
Federal Highway Administration. 2003. "Journey-to-Work Trends in the U.S. and Its Major Metro Areas, 1960–2000." Washington, DC: U.S. Department of Transportation, http://www.fhwa.dot.gov/ctpp/jtw/contents.htm (accessed February 21, 2004).
Freilich, R. 1999. *From Sprawl to Smart Growth: Successful Legal, Planning and Environmental Systems.* Chicago: American Bar Association.
Gale, W., J. Pack, and S. Potter. 2001. "The New Urban Economy: Opportunities and Challenges." Washington, DC: Brookings Institution, http://www.brookings.edu/dybdocroot/comm/conferencereport/cr07.pdf (accessed February 21, 2004).
Hernandez-Murillo, R. 2001. "Suburban Expansion," Regional Economist, St. Louis: Federal Reserve Bank of St. Louis, http://www.stls.frb.org/publications/re/2001/d/pages/economic-briefing.html (accessed October 11, 2001).
Myers, D., and A. Kitsuse. 2001. "The Debate Over Future Density of Development: An Interpretive Review." Boston, MA: Lincoln Land Policy Institute, http://www-rcf.usc.edu/~dowell/qualife.htm (accessed February 21, 2004).
Staley, S. 2001. *Market-Oriented Approaches to Growth: Outsmarting Sprawl's Impacts.* Los Angeles: Reason Public Policy Institute.

2

Elise Bright

Is There a Need to Contain Growth?

In a speech several years ago at an Urban Affairs Association (UAA) conference in New Orleans, Michael Stegman (a former Assistant Secretary for
Research at HUD under the Clinton administration) stated that there were
37,000 vacant, abandoned, dilapidated housing units in New Orleans alone.
He then asked, "What federal policies contributed to this?" and called for
ideas on how to redirect HUD funds to help "do something" with these
homes and their counterparts in other American cities.

Since then National Center researchers at the University of Texas, Arlington, have been studying the causes, effects, and keys to the reuse/redevelop-
ment of abandoned properties (often called TOADS—temporarily obsolete,
abandoned, derelict sites) in cities throughout America. We have documented
the extent of these properties and found them to be far more ubiquitous than
we ever anticipated. We discovered that, more than any other single factor,
bringing these sites into productive use is critical for successful central city
revitalization, and we have identified barriers and developed recommendations for achieving successful reuse (Bright 1999).

We can now answer Mr. Stegman's question. Although many federal policies have adversely affected central cities, perhaps none have done more
damage than those that favored new construction over rehab and greenfields
development over infill—sapping the central city's economic base (Frieden
and Sagalyn 1992), placing it at a competitive disadvantage, undermining
regional cooperation (Rusk 1995), and causing the existence of tens of thousands of abandoned properties (Wagner, Joder, and Mumphrey 1995). Now
federal policy seems to be swinging toward promotion of "smart growth"—
including infill central city development that features mixed use, mixed income, transit-centered development on TOADS.[1] Yet, in an ironic application
of devolution, despite the prominent role of federal policies in creating the
abandonment problem that many cities have today, the barriers to their redevelopment are still being left to local governments to overcome. If these

barriers are not removed, the renewal of central cities through smart growth and regional cooperation will be stillborn—it will become a suburban phenomenon or at best a phenomenon only for wealthy new urban residents.

Sadly, local response to abandonment over the past thirty years gives ample evidence that local governments cannot, or will not, overcome these barriers alone. If smart growth is to benefit central cities—and particularly their poorer residents—we also need federal involvement to reduce these barriers. Thus, the time appears to be ripe to address Mr. Stegman's call for ideas on redirecting federal funds to facilitate property reuse in central cities throughout the nation.[2]

In particular, work is needed to identify effective policies that slow or even reverse the federally subsidized sprawl that has taken over our urban hinterlands. What is the role of growth containment strategies and other regional approaches in producing healthier central cities? In regions with regional growth containment strategies, demand for central city property seems to be relatively high—suggesting that perhaps the growth controls limit the supply of developable land, creating a market for long-abandoned property. On the other hand, some of the most successful TOADS reuse programs for low-income people have occurred in cities without regional growth management (for example, Cleveland and Boston). Could it be that, contrary to popular wisdom and logic, regional growth containment strategies are not necessary for successful central city revitalization of even the poorest neighborhoods? Is the common belief that "sprawl is bad and growth management is good" an oversimplification—perhaps even a myth?

The research question that evolved from this line of explorative thought is simply this: Is regional containment of sprawl an important factor in determining central city health?

Research Design

Four hypotheses were derived from the research question. This chapter focuses on Hypothesis B; the approach and disposition of all four hypotheses is described below.

> *Hypothesis A.* Retention and attraction of jobs is more important for central city health than is population retention and attraction. Specifically, the more central city jobs per resident, the lower the vacancy and abandonment rates will be.
> Methodology: TOADS measures were correlated with 2000 census data on employment and population for the 27 central cities, 24 freestanding cities, and 36 suburbs with a population of at least

100,000 in 1990 or 2000 that responded to our previous survey. Poverty rates for several decades and vacancy rates for 1970, 1980, 1990, and 2000 were correlated with census employment and population data for all 46 central cities, 102 freestanding cities, and 96 suburbs with a population of at least 100,000 in 1990 or 2000. Results are summarized briefly in this chapter; details will be contained in a separate publication.

Hypothesis B. Regional sprawl containment strategies are important facilitators of central city health. Specifically, greater containment means lower vacancy, poverty, and abandonment rates.

Methodology: For all 148 freestanding cities and central cities with over 100,000 population, the extent of containment was indicated via Lopez's index of sprawl, double-checked with our own index. These data were then correlated with census vacancy and poverty data. The same analysis was done using data from the 87 cities that responded to a previous survey of vacant abandoned property (the TOADS survey), with groupings of central cities alone, central and freestanding cities, and all cities. Results of this investigation were extensive; describing them will take up much of the remainder of this chapter.

There is a great need for further research on the two remaining hypotheses, which were not pursued at this time because of the reasons given below.

Hypothesis C. The better the fit between a neighborhood's salaries and the local population's income, the lower the vacancy, poverty, and abandonment rates.

Methodology: This should be testable when all the census 2000 data are made available. Unfortunately, the necessary data were not all released in time for this publication.

Hypothesis D. Targeted strategies work better than either comprehensive or no strategies, especially when coupled with other strategies such as neighborhood control.

Methodology: This hypothesis was dropped for an unexpected reason: When cities with reported containment strategies were more closely examined, it became clear that in reality the level of containment was too weak to have a significant effect. Even in Portland, Oregon, a city widely considered to have more effective regional containment than any other in America, local experts reported

extensive leapfrog development in the surrounding countryside outside the growth boundary—and their views are reinforced by data
on sprawl reported in several recent publications (Carruthers 2002,
Carson 2002, El Nasser and Overberg 2002). There are simply too
few cases of effective containment strategies to allow investigation
of this hypothesis, at least using data from the United States.

Defining Central Cities, Suburbs, and Freestanding Cities

Before data could be collected and analyzed, working definitions of the
various city types had to be compiled. This proved to be more troublesome
than expected. Nearly every other urban researcher whose work we examined utilized the census definitions of central cities. However, upon perusal
of these definitions, we found them far too broad for our purposes. The
census definition causes far more cities to be labeled as central than is the
case in reality, and an examination of the census list of central cities revealed
anomalies that made us question the validity of their categorization. For
example, Irving, Texas, is listed as a central city, but it is quite clear to any
resident of the Dallas–Fort Worth area that Irving is, and always has been, a
suburb of Dallas—it grew because of its proximity to Dallas and is often
cited as a prime example of a suburb's ability to "steal" office development
from a central city.

Instead, using census data, maps, knowledge of the area, and occa-
sional phone calls for verification, we pared the census list down by
counting only the largest city in an urbanized area as the central one.
This was easy to do in most cases, but a few cities proved troublesome.
Thus, if a second city exists in the same urbanized area with a population
that is over 100,000, is more than half the central city's population, and
is either adjacent to (thus really forming a single central city) or at least
thirty miles from the primary one, it was also considered central (for
example, Fort Worth, Texas), and the urbanized area would be considered as "dual-hubbed." Some areas were still difficult to deal with
though—Brownsville-Harlingen-McAllen, Texas, is an area with a
plethora of rather small cities, none of which is clearly central; and
Clearwater-Tampa-St. Petersburg is a three-hubbed city with a bay in the
middle, as is San Francisco-Oakland-San Jose.[3] The remaining cities in
the urbanized areas were considered suburbs.

Also, the decision as to whether to consider a city to be without suburbs—
that is, freestanding—or a central city proved to be a tricky call, since almost
every city has some surrounding towns, but they are often quite small. We
decided to consider cities with one suburb of 100,000 people or more, two

suburbs of 50,000 people or more, or numerous small suburbs to be central; the others were considered as freestanding. This categorization is important, because regional containment affects mainly freestanding cities and urbanized areas—although a few cities (Phoenix, Fort Worth, etc.) are considered central but elastic (unconstrained), since they can still expand in one or two directions. In a sense, freestanding cities share characteristics with central cities in that they both contain the historic urban hub of the region. Fortunately, the categorization regarding containment proved to be far more important for our purposes (see below).

Finally, the issue of whether to include the suburbs in the analysis had to be resolved. The research question necessitated correlation of containment levels with central city data on vacancy rates, poverty rates, and numbers of abandoned properties. Also, a large number of inelastic, contained suburbs were found in the Los Angeles urbanized area—enough to heavily bias any suburban analysis. On the other hand, comparing central city and freestanding city data with the suburbs might be interesting. Thus, on the advice of UAA conference session attendees, the suburban data were left in for the correlation analyses done while investigating Hypothesis A, but were removed from the containment analysis.

Defining and Measuring Central City Health

For purposes of this research, central city health was defined as having low rates of abandonment, vacancy, and poverty. The author's previous research has shown that levels of vacancy and abandonment correlate very well with city health, and has also provided a database of the existence and characteristics of vacant abandoned properties in 87 cities with populations of 100,000 or more located throughout the United States. The data were collected via a survey done for a previous grant and constitute the only known nationwide database of abandoned properties. In order to include all 243 cities with 100,000 people and to allow for analysis over time, we added 1970, 1980, 1990, and 2000 residential vacancy rates (single and multifamily combined) as a second measure of health.[4]

Finally, at a presentation of this work at the UAA annual conference in Boston in 2001, members of the audience suggested having three categories of analysis: central cities alone, central plus freestanding cities (since freestanding cities by definition contain a central core), and all cities. This would allow the effect of the suburbs to be separated, which was important because the numerous contained suburbs in the Los Angeles area were skewing the results. They also suggested using income, employment, and poverty data as measures of central city health. Unfortunately, 2000 census data were not available at the levels of analysis that we needed for any of these; however, we did add poverty rates for three decades to the database.

Defining and Measuring Containment

Before attempting to develop an index of regional containment, we began with a search of existing indices of sprawl. Most were not useful for our purposes. Some sprawl indices are based on annexation, so they suffer from the same flaws as Rusk's work. Others are based on population density and are more useful, but they ignore other important determinants of sprawl such as concentration of development in an urban core. After an extensive search we found an index developed by Russ Lopez of Boston University (Lopez 2003) that looked theoretically sound and well suited to our purposes. Lopez's index includes measures of urban concentration as well as density and is adjusted to remove rural parts of each Metropolitan Statistical Area (MSA) from the analysis. We verified his rankings with our own independently developed classification of cities and urban areas as contained, somewhat contained, or uncontained. Our classification was based on interviews with local experts, material in the academic literature, and extensive study of urbanized area maps (see below). The fit with Lopez's scale was good, so we decided to use his index in our work.

Results

> *Hypothesis A.* Retention and attraction of jobs is more important for central city health than is population retention and attraction. Specifically, the more central city jobs per resident, the lower the vacancy and abandonment rates will be.

TOADS Data

Results of extensive correlation analysis reveal that the greater the jobs/person the fewer the total TOADS. However, the total number of TOADS varies directly with population; thus, the next step was computing a TOADS/person figure and a jobs/person figure.

In all cities, when we control numbers of TOADS for population as well (that is, compare jobs/person to TOADS/person ratios), we get a negative correlation (–.289) significant at the .01 level—so the more jobs/person the fewer TOADS per person.[5] When we look at data for central cities only, the relationship gets much stronger, with a significance level of just .011 and correlation of –.484. This seems to be strong evidence that as jobs/person ratios increase, TOADS/person decrease, particularly in central cities.

These statistics are strong evidence that attracting and retaining jobs is important for central city health—but what about attracting and retaining people? The relationship between central city TOADS/person and total 2000 population is not at all significant ($p<.816$, correlation strength .047)—apparently, in central cities the TOADS per capita rate does not increase with population but is fairly stable across all city sizes. Similar results, although less dramatic, were obtained when freestanding cities were added to the analysis, when all cities were analyzed, when 1990 population data was used (although here a .236 correlation with $p<.05$ was found when all cities were analyzed), and when total jobs was substituted for total population. These results reveal a lack of relationship between per capita TOADS rates and city size.[6] Clearly, the common notion that abandonment is a big city problem is false.

We can safely conclude that these statistics strongly support Hypothesis A: They show that attracting and retaining jobs is important for central city health, but attracting people is not.

Comparing the two per capita rates, Macon, Georgia, Detroit, and Baltimore were the only cities in which the TOADS/person ratio was more than 10 percent of the jobs/person ratio in 2000; these were followed by Buffalo and Pittsburgh. All five of these cities lost population from 1990 to 2000, however, St. Louis and Cleveland also lost population but did not have such a severe TOADS problem: Why? Both of these cities have a unique and effective governmental mechanism for recycling abandoned property: the Land Reutilization Authority—St. Louis and Cleveland may have controlled the number of TOADS better than most shrinking cities because of their use of this unique tool. Baton Rouge, Louisiana, lost more than 150,000 people but had a TOADS/person rate that was one-third of Baltimore's and Detroit's. Soon, however, Baton Rouge may approach the rates found in these two cities: Between 1990 and 2000 only Baton Rouge's TOADS/person ranking changed significantly, rising from number thirettn to number seven in the nation. Savannah and Columbus, Georgia; Lansing, Michigan; Green Bay, Wisconsin; Cheektowaga, New York; New Haven, Connecticut; Peoria, Illinois; and Norfolk, Virginia, all had high TOADS/person rates but little population loss. Perhaps, unlike St. Louis and Cleveland, these cities suffer from state and local laws or regulations that make reuse of TOADS difficult. All other cities' rankings did not vary much.

What about the effect of changes over time? We compared changes in jobs/person over the past decade with per capita rates of abandonment (TOADS/person), and got consistently significant results. A correlation of −.505 with $p<.01$ level was found between per capita abandonment and changes in jobs from 1990–2000 in central cities, and a −.356 correlation was found with $p<.05$ for central/freestanding. The relationships were even stronger when per capita abandonment rates were correlated with population change from 1990–2000: .01 level of significance was found for all cities—central and freestanding, and central alone—with the strongest relationship (–.624) occurring in central cities and the weakest (–.382) when suburbs were included. If TOADS numbers remain constant but the population increases, the abandonment ratio will fall—and changes in job growth mirror changes in population. Thus, the conclusion seems to be that growth in jobs helps greatly to curb the growth of abandonment, but does not substantially reduce the existing inventory of abandoned properties.

Vacancy Data

Vacancy data were available from the census; thus they were available for many more years than was the TOADS data and for many more cities (244, of which 46 were classified as central, 102 as freestanding, and 96 as suburbs).

Comparing vacancy/person data with jobs/person data, in 1980 significant negative correlation was found for all 46 central cities (–.417) at the .01 level and for all 244 cities (–.155) at the .05 level. Finally, negative correlation significant at the .05 level was found in 1990 (–.137) and 2000 (–.144) for all cities. One can conclude that, especially in central cities and suburbs, the more jobs, the lower the vacancies. This again provides evidence of support for the hypothesis.

Correlation of vacancy rates with change in jobs revealed a mix of significant and insignificant results. In 2000 central city vacancy rates and vacancy/person were significantly negatively correlated (–.336 and –.326) with 1990–2000 job change at the .05 level; central plus freestanding were negatively correlated at the .01 level for changes in jobs 1970–2000, for both vacancy rates (–.226) and vacancy/person (.278). However, this effect disappears when jobs are adjusted for city size.

Controlling the jobs data to account for city size reduced the number of significant relationships. As with the data on change in total jobs, for 1980 this analysis found significant relationships at the .01 level for central cities (–.480) and for all cities (–.250); however, there was no relationship for the central plus freestanding category (–.032). This held true for both vacancy rates and vacancy/person (correlations –.454, –.056, and –.318, respectively). The only other significant relationship for vacancy rates was between the 2000 rate and changes in jobs/person for all cities from 1970–2000, which was negative (–.163) and significant at the .05 level—and which was not significant when change in total jobs was used.

Finally, change in population for 1970–80, 1980–90, and 1990–2000 was compared with vacancy rates and vacancy/person for the final year of each decade. The only correlation of significance with regard to both vacancy measures (−.206 for rates, −.142 for vacancy/person, $p < .01$) was for central cities in 2000, using 1990–2000 population data. This makes logical sense: The greater the population change, the lower the vacancy rate. For vacancy/ person, weak negative correlations significant at the .05 level were found for central plus freestanding cities (−.206) and for all cities (−.142), using 1990– 2000 population change data.

Poverty Rate Data

Eight out of nine correlations between jobs/person and poverty rates were negative and significant at the .01 level over three decades; only the relationship for all cities in 1969–70 was insignificant. Correlations ran as high as −.718 (for central cities, using 1989 and 1990 data); by 1990 even the "all cities" category—which had the weakest correlations in 1970 and 1980— received a −.652 correlation with $p = .000$. In 1970 and every decade thereafter, for central cities alone and with freestanding cities, correlation strength was over .3—and in three cases (two in 1990 and one in 1980) they exceeded .6. Thus, one can conclude that from 1969–90 the more jobs/person, the lower the poverty rate was in all types of cities, but especially in central and freestanding ones.

This conclusion is reinforced by comparing poverty rates to changes in jobs for 1970–80 and 1980–90. In every case a negative relationship with a .01 confidence level was found. Relationships were very strong: For central cities results were −.60 using 1980 data and −.65 using 1990 data, and −.33 was the weakest correlation in the data set. Clearly, the faster the job growth in the previous decade, the lower the poverty rate will be.

Looking further at changes over time, five out of six correlations run between the poverty rate and change in jobs/person for the decades 1970–80 and 1980–90 were negatively significant at the .01 level; only the central city figure for the 1979 poverty rate was not significant. Like nearly all previous correlations with poverty level, these were stronger overall than those involving vacancy measures; the central city figure for 1989 (−.592) was the highest of all, and five out of six correlations were over −.3. Clearly, an increase in jobs means a reduction in poverty for all types of large cities.

Finally, the poverty rates were strongly correlated with change in population for the previous decade. In all six runs, for all types of cities and all decades from 1970–1990, negative correlations significant at the .01 level were found. Somewhat surprisingly, it seems that an increase in population means a reduction in a city's poverty level as well, although the relationship is weakest in freestanding cities; reasons for this remain a mystery.

Although the relationship between poverty rates and population change is strong, it cannot match that between poverty rates and jobs discussed above. Thus, these results provide very good evidence that retention and attraction of jobs is even more important for central city health than is retention and attraction of residents. Clearly, Hypothesis A is correct.

> *Hypothesis B.* Regional sprawl containment strategies are important facilitators of central city health. Specifically, greater containment means lower vacancy, poverty, and abandonment rates.

Results paint an interesting picture of the effects of containment on urban health as measured by vacancy, abandonment, and poverty. For all 148 central and freestanding cities analyzed, significant positive correlations were obtained at the .01 level for 1970 (.003) and 2000 (.001) vacancy rates, but there was no significant relationship using 1980 or 1990 data, and in 1980 the sign even reversed. Controlling directly for city size by using vacancy per person produced very similar results, the only difference being that the significance level for 1970 dropped to .05.

Analyzing data for the 46 central cities alone reveals a much stronger relationship between the two variables. Significant positive correlations were found between containment level and vacancy rates at the .01 level for 1970 and 1980 vacancy data and at the .05 level using 1990 and 2000 census data, with strength of the relationship falling between .3 and .4; the highest values were found for central cities. When vacancy/person ratios were used, a .01 significance level was still obtained for 1970 data and a .05 level for 1980 and 2000 data; strength was .275–.39, and only the 1990 figure for central/freestanding cities was not significant. Central city strengths were usually over .3 and were consistently higher than those for the central/freestanding category. This appears to be evidence that supports Hypothesis B: Places that seem to have regional containment—that is, high values for population density and concentration—are associated with lower central city residential vacancy.

When TOADS data were analyzed, however, opposite results were obtained. For the 27 central cities a 0.05 significant negative relationship was found (.047, strength .385) between containment level and total number of TOADS—that is, the more uncontained the central city, the fewer TOADS. The correlation is weaker here than with central and freestanding cities combined, where analysis revealed a correlation significant at the .01 level ($p<.002$, strength .424). This result is logically consistent with the idea that elasticity is good for central city health: By absorbing their suburbs, it appears that freestanding cities have lower numbers of TOADS. However, this may not be a causal relationship; instead, both may be caused by differences in city size—the most contained central cities tend to be in our larger urban areas (Lopez 2003), and big cities also have more TOADS. Sure enough, when we controlled for population size, the significance disappeared entirely—using both 1990 and 2000 population data to compute TOADS/person (the weakest was .002, $p <.988$).

Correlation of containment and poverty rates produced similar results. For central and freestanding cities using 1969, 1979, and 1989 data, results were only significant (.05 level—$p <.014$, strength .204) for 1969. When the data were analyzed for the central cities alone, no significant relationships were found.

What can we conclude from all this? The vacancy data appear to give evidence that supports Hypothesis B: Regional containment is associated with lower central city residential vacancy consistently since 1970. Can these results be attributed to containment strategies? We know of no city that had regional containment strategies in place well before 1969; thus, we must conclude that the positive correlation we find for these data—as well as the 1970 and probably the 1980 vacancy data—is not evidence of the effectiveness of any intentional containment strategy but probably results from containment by happenstance (geography, political boundaries, etc.). The positive correlations for the 1990 and 2000 vacancy data might be evidence of the effect of containment strategies, but since they are generally weaker than those for the earlier years, they could simply be due to the same non-strategy factors at work in the 1960s–1980s. Further research is needed here to identify the strategies used by cities with high containment scores, dates they were put in place, geographic and other constraints compared to urban growth patterns, and so forth.

The results of this part of the study show that regional containment seems to have some positive effect on central city health as measured by residential vacancy rates, but none on overall abandonment or poverty. Perhaps this stems from the fact that regional containment has its greatest effect on residential development patterns: The TOADS data include commercial and industrial property, and poverty rates are strongly related to employment data, so analysis using these variables would be less likely to produce significant results if containment mainly affects residential property. Further research is needed to resolve this question.

Geography: The "Hiding Hand" Behind the Data?

Some of our strongest relationships were found between the TOADS data and the geographic region of the country in which the city is located. The

Northeast and Midwest had by far the highest mean number of TOADS/ central city (28,966.14 and 21,159.17, respectively). For all six geographic regions, however, the standard deviation nearly equaled or exceeded the mean, with the Northeast and Midwest having large differences between the means and standard deviations, but the other four regions not sharing this trait. Also, the Midwest had a much higher mean number of TOADS for central cities (21,159.17) than it did for central and freestanding (9,581.36), indicating that TOADS are a central city problem in the Midwest; the same pattern held in almost all other regions but with less difference between the two. For example, in the South-central region the mean number of TOADS in central cities was 12,850.0, but it dropped to 5780.3 when freestanding cities were added. The exception was the southeastern region, which had a mean of just 287.5 TOADS for its central cities but 951.7 when freestanding cities were added. The remaining two regions had means for central cities of 242.67 (West) and 100.67 (California) for central cities and 169.6 (West) and 75.5 (California) with freestanding cities added. This unusual pattern was reflected in the TOADS/person data as well. We think this may be due to the fact that Macon, Georgia—a freestanding city—has one of the highest numbers of TOADS in the country and ranks first in TOADS/person. However, there could be any number of explanations for this: Perhaps there are more freestanding cities in the South or there are more large cities in the Midwest and Northeast, thus making the findings a mere reflection of city size.

To test this, we controlled for population by computing the mean TOADS/ person ratio for the cities in each region. This made the Northeast the clear winner both for central city data alone and for central and freestanding cities. For central cities, the Northeast had a mean TOADS/person value of .02353 using 1990 data and .02440 using 2000 population data (Note: The decline is meaningless, because the same TOADS figure was used in both cases; thus the decline simply reflects declining population). When freestanding cities were added, the means were still high: .021396 for 1990 and .022149 for 2000. The next closest regions were the Midwest, with .001029 mean TOADS/person using 1990 central city population data and .001597 using 2000 data (.0096458 and .0096709 with the addition of freestanding); and the South-central, with .01223 mean TOADS/person using 1990 central city population data and .01131 using 2000 data (.007170 and .007460 with the addition of freestanding). In all cases the results for the other regions were considerably lower than these figures, with the West and California having the lowest rates by far.

Finally, the six regions were numbered from east to west and correlations run. Although it is not statistically valid to correlate ordinal data with nominal, since the numbers were not assigned randomly but as a function of distance from the Northeast, hopefully there is some validity to the results. For total TOADS there was a .05 significant negative correlation, as would be expected (the Northeast was assigned number 1, and California was assigned number 6), with strength of the relationship being −.282 for the 51 central/freestanding city group and −.268 for all 87 cities. When TOADS/person data were used, the p value was .000 for all cities and <.002 for the central/freestanding group, with strengths of −.402 to −.411 for all cities and −.42 to −.431 for the central/freestanding group (the range is for 1990 and 2000 population data). Thus, it is clear that geographic location may be an important determinant of central city health; the regional differences remain even after controlling for population. Future studies should probably conduct analyses within regions, so this effect will be controlled.

Why would geography affect abandonment rates? Probably because there has been a massive resettlement of people and jobs from the Northeast and upper Midwest to the South and West over the past thirty to forty years. Further research is needed to compute these job and population losses for 1960–1990 for all cities studied, then correlate those figures with data on TOADS, jobs, and vacancy. If these correlations prove to be strong, then the classification of the nation into regions and analysis by region could be dropped, since regions serve merely as surrogates for population and employment shifts.

Conclusions

The data show that regional containment may help to keep residential vacancy at bay, but it seems to have little effect on measures of central city health that include a nonresidential component. The evidence also indicates that although both employment and population growth are somewhat important to central city health, job growth is the most important of the two. One can conclude that containment strategies hold promise as tools to foster and support central city health, but they would be more effective if they focused on capturing jobs for central cities rather than residents. This is an important conclusion, given the current focus on using subsidies for infill residential development for middle- and upper-class residents as central city revitalization tools and the claims being made for comprehensive growth management strategies as the cure for urban ills.

There are many good reasons for governments to adopt regional containment strategies. But if we want to retain public support for containment-related initiatives like smart growth and infill development, we must be careful not oversell them—they are not panaceas. Comprehensive regional containment alone will not revitalize our cities or even make much positive change in their current state; the damage done by the massive exodus of people and jobs from the North and East (as reflected in the strong relationship of our measures of health and geographic region) cannot be undone so easily. This leads to a few final thoughts and radical suggestions.

- Regional containment is helpful, but not necessary, in keeping vacancy, poverty, and abandonment away from central cities.
- Regional containment may be less necessary in the future because of changes in urban growth patterns due to the Internet, a rapidly aging population, and immigration—all of which are more likely to generate pressure for infill and/or rural development, not suburban sprawl.
- Regional containment strategies that work are rare. Most effective regional containment in the United States is due to accidents of geography and land ownership.
- Regional containment—and especially regional governance (the most extreme containment strategy)—is often politically unfeasible. Therefore,
- Increasing central city employment densities—by targeting jobs instead of people, even by deannexing urban residential areas and further fragmenting the region if need be—may be better for successful revitalization than is regional containment of population.

Notes

1. Of course, reuse of abandoned property is not synonymous with policies of smart growth, regionalism, or sprawl control, but it is an important part of these efforts, because most available sites in central cities are by definition TOADS. There are reasons why these sites have been passed over, and these reasons need to be addressed or they will continue to stymie reuse even with federal smart growth policies in place. If good developable sites are not available in central cities, then smart growth, regional containment, and sprawl control will have little effect.

2. Some needed reforms are now clear—including the need for assistance with site assembly, title clearance, replatting, recovery or waiver of development fees and back taxes, conversion of abandoned properties to appealing open space, removing liability and providing funds for brownfields cleanup, federal incentives for reforming state laws and local policies to allow donation of TOADS, use of eminent domain, waiver of taxes and fees, land banking, streamlined foreclosure, and so forth. But other directions for reform are less clear.

3. Experts from the areas in question agreed that Tampa and St. Petersburg are central cities but Clearwater is a suburb; that Ventura/Oxnard are suburbs of Los Angeles but Lancaster/Palmdale are not; and that San Francisco and San Jose are central cities but Oakland is a suburb.

4. Vacancy rates are very different measures from TOADS/person for many reasons: Vacancy rates apply to structures, but TOADS include many vacant lots;

vacancy rates are for residential property only, whereas TOADS include commercial and industrial; and vacancy rates are computed by dividing vacancies by total housing units, whereas TOADS are divided by population.

5. Jobs/person ratios for all 146 cities are concentrated between >.3 and <.7: Could this be the ratio of jobs needed to keep a city viable? Obviously, a city would be hard-pressed to exist with no jobs, but at the other extreme not every resident can hold a job either; the ratio must be greater than zero and less than 1. Only Honolulu had a jobs/person ratio greater than 1.

6. The presence of many TOADS does not correlate well with an ailing economy: Houston ranked third in the nation in TOADS, Dallas was fifth, and Boston was seventh, despite their healthy economies (other cities with good economies and high TOADS rankings include Grand Prairie, sixteenth; Corpus Christi, twentieth; and Amarillo, twenty-fourth). Perhaps this is due to the poor laws and policies regarding getting TOADS back into use that prevail in Texas, Massachusetts, and many other states.

References

Bright, Elise. 1999. "TOADS: Instruments of Urban Revitalization," in *Managing Capital Resources for Central City Revitalization*, ed. F. Wagner, T. Joder, and T. Mumphrey, pp. 545–80. New York: Garland.
———. 2000. *Reviving America's Forgotten Neighborhoods*. New York: Taylor and Francis.
Carruthers, John. 2002. "Evaluating the Effectiveness of Regulatory Growth Management Programs: An Analytic Framework." *Journal of Planning Education and Research* 21: 391–405.
Carson, Richard. 2002. "A Tale of Two Cities." *Planetizen*, July 8.
Cox, Wendell. 2002. "Trouble in Smart Growth's Nirvana." *Planetizen*, July 1.
El Nasser, H, and P. Overberg. 2002. "A Comprehensive Look at Sprawl in America." *USA Today*, April 1.
Frieden, B., and L. Sagalyn. 1992. *Downtown Inc.: How America Rebuilds Cities*. MIT Press, Cambridge, MA.
Gober, P., and E. Burns. 2002. "The Size and Shape of Phoenix's Urban Fringe." *Journal of Planning Education and Research* 21: 379–90.
Greenberg, M., and F. Popper. 1994. "Finding Treasure in TOADS." *Planning* magazine 60 no. 4 (April): 24–28.
Lopez, Russ. 2003. "Sprawl in the 1990s: Measurement, Distribution and Trends." *Urban Affairs Review* 38 no. 3 (January): 325.
Real Estate Center. 1990–present. *City and Town Civilian Employment and Unemployment Data*, http://recenter.tamu.edu/data/empct. Total Employment and Unemployment Rates by City.
Rusk, David. 1995. *Cities Without Suburbs*, 2d ed. Baltimore, MD: Johns Hopkins University Press.
U.S. Census Bureau. 1990. Census of Population and Housing. *Population and Housing Counts*, CPH-2–1, United States. Washington, DC, 1993. www.census.gov/prod/cen1990/cph2/cph-2-1-1.pdf. 1970–1990 city population, housing units, total and land areas, population and housing densities (Table 45). 1940–1990 city (100,000+) population and housing units; 1790–1990 population (Table 46).

———. 1998. *Housing Vacancies and Homeownership Annual Statistics*. Washington, DC. www.census.gov/hhes/www/housing/hvs/annual98/ann98t6.html.

Homeowner Vacancy Rates for the 75 Largest Metropolitan Areas: 1986 to 1998 (Table 6).

———. 2000. Census of Population and Housing. *Summary Social, Economic and Housing Characteristics*, PHC-2–1, United States Summary. Washington, DC, 2003.

www.census.gov/prod/cen2000/phc-2–1–pt1.pdf

www.census.gov/prod/cen2000/phc-2–1–pt2.pdf

Work Status and Income, 1999 (Table 53). Contains 2000 total housing units for cities 100,000+ population (Table 58)

———. 2000. *Housing Vacancies and Homeownership Annual Statistics*. Washington, DC. www.census.gov/hhes/www/housing/hvs/annual00/ann005.html.

Rental Vacancy Rates for the 75 Largest Metropolitan Areas: 1986 to 2000 (Table 5).

www.census.gov/hhes/www/housing/hvs/annual00/ann00t6.html.

Homeowner Vacancy Rates for the 75 Largest Metropolitan Areas: 1986 to 2000 (Table 6).

U.S. Department of Labor, Bureau of Labor Statistics. 1970–present <<?>>. *Local Area Unemployment Statistics (LAUS) Database Series*, "Cities and towns above 25,000 population." Accessed July 1, 2001. www.bls.gov/lau/

1970–present (variable with location) annual employment counts; not seasonally adjusted.

Wagner, F., T. Joder, and T. Mumphrey, eds. 1995. *Urban Revitalization: Policies and Programs*. New York: Garland.

3

Nico Calavita, Roger Caves, and
Kathleen Ferrier

The Challenges of Smart Growth: The San Diego Case

During the 1990s "smart growth" supplanted growth management as the principal mechanism to deal with problems of growth. While growth management sought to regulate "the amount, timing, location, and character of development" (Levy 1988, 218), smart growth calls for the *accommodation* of growth because, it is maintained, growth is inevitable but the problems associated with it are not. Smart growth proponents argue that by creating more compact development patterns, promoting urban reinvestment, and designing communities that are mixed-use, higher density, transit-oriented and pedestrian-friendly, we can eat the growth cake and have it too.

This vision of a strategy of development that promises growth accommodation while at the same time rejuvenating our decaying communities and saving our endangered ecosystems is a powerful one—but extremely difficult to realize. First, for smart growth to succeed, state intervention is essential. Several states have undertaken initiatives to limit sprawl and encourage development within existing communities and neighborhoods, but it is unclear whether these efforts can counter the impetus to decentralize. For example, states such as Oregon, Washington, Vermont, Maryland, and Delaware are dealing with sprawl in a variety of ways. Through the leadership of Governor Parris Glendening, Maryland embraced smart growth and emerged as a leader in this movement.

The state of Delaware is also concerned with the effects of sprawl and how infrastructure and sprawl might affect the area's quality of life. In response to these and other concerns, Delaware enacted its Livable Delaware program, which is designed to be proactive in directing growth to areas with sufficient infrastructure that are ready to accommodate growth. State activity in the area of smart growth continues to increase. In a recent report

Johnson, Jordan, and Salkin (2002, 14) indicated that "17 Governors issued 19 executive orders on planning, smart growth and related topics during the past two years compared to 12 orders issued during the previous eight years combined."

Second, in addition to the need for state intervention, smart growth cannot succeed without a regional approach that integrates physical planning with environmental, equity, and economic goals (Calthorpe and Fulton 2001, Wheeler 2002). Implementation of regionalism, however, runs up against powerful political barriers, especially the unwillingness of local governments to release the stronghold they have on land-use power and suburban constituents' opposition to the socioeconomic integration of the region. Further, claims that it is cheaper to build in existing communities are generally unproven, and NIMBYism (Not in My Backyard) is a powerful deterrent to densification and infill.

It is important, then, that the enthusiastic claims of smart growth proponents be checked against the results of actual attempts to implement that strategy. Also, specific approaches to smart growth might not fit all regions. Planners and practitioners need to analyze what works, or fails, and under what circumstances.

This chapter presents a case study of the attempt to plan according to smart growth principles in San Diego, California, a region experiencing high levels of growth and with a long tradition of growth-related conflicts. The chapter starts with a brief description of smart growth principles and its politics and challenges. This is followed by an analysis of efforts to implement smart growth in San Diego, first at the regional, and then at the local level, with an emphasis on the City of Villages plan of the city of San Diego. The chapter concludes with a discussion of the implications of the San Diego case for the future of smart growth.

Principles of Smart Growth

Smart growth represents the antithesis and, one might hope, the nemesis of sprawl. It attempts to rein in the tendencies of sprawl by limiting expansion at the metropolitan edges and redirecting development to the already urbanized communities. By so doing, existing infrastructure and public facilities are reused and existing cities and suburbs revitalized. Growth is directed to higher density, mixed-use community centers, to what Calthorpe (1993) has called Transit Oriented Developments (TODs), increasing opportunities for mass transit. Smart growth can be summarized by the following six processes (Burchell et al. 2000, Dreier et al. 2001, Downs 2001, Orfield 2002, Calthorpe and Fulton 2001, Katz 2002):

1. Creation of a more compact urban form by limiting sprawl at the metropolitan fringe through Urban Growth Boundaries (UGBs) and open space conservation.
2. Revitalization of existing communities through infill/densification and good community design while optimizing existing public facilities.
3. Enhancement of the tax base of inner city and first-ring suburbs through regional tax-base sharing. Also, creation of affordable housing in suburban areas through regional fair-share housing.
4. Redesign of old and new developments on the basis of "new-urbanism" principles that call for mixed-use centers, job-housing balance, pedestrian-friendly communities, grid-street patterns, alleys, porches, and other design elements that make neighborhoods vital and diverse.
5. Reorientation of the transportation system to reduce dependency on the automobile through land-use measures as in (4), reallocation of funds to transit, and monetary disincentives, such as higher gasoline taxes.
6. Preservation of wildlife habitats, prime agricultural lands, and open space, especially at the urban fringe.

The implementation of most of these actions requires a regional approach that addresses the physical design of the region "to help overcome sprawl" and "the region's social and economic opportunities, which can help overcome inequity" (Calthorpe and Fulton 2001, 63). While other authors have stressed smart growth's equity aspects (Dreier et al. 2001, Downs 2001, Orfield 2002), and physical design aspects (Duany et al. 2000, Katz 1994, Kreiger and Lennertz 1991), Calthorpe and Fulton (2001, 63) have made the strongest call for a holistic approach that addresses "these two policy imperatives responsibly, comprehensively, and in an interconnected way. . . . Physical design must be married to social and economic incentives in ways that are mutually reinforcing." Given these twin policy imperatives, what are the chances for smart growth to succeed? The challenges that smart growth faces are threefold: cultural, political, and economic.

Cultural Impediments

While it is true that the mass expansion of the suburbs after War World II was made possible by federal policies such as the interstate highway program and the Federal Housing Administration's mortgage financing and subdivision regulations, it is also true that the phenomenon coincided with the cultural aspirations of white middle-class Americans for the single-family detached home and the automobile. Similar trends are being observed in other countries, now that the expansion of highways and the greater wealth of a large sector of the population make it possible to own a home in the suburbs. Gordon and Richardson (1998, 23), frequent critics of smart growth, maintain that "it is hard to avoid concluding that 'sprawl' is most people's preferred lifestyle." Similarly, another author (Easterbrook 1999, 545) declares that "the axial truth of this issue is that most Americans want a detached home with a lawn." A recent California survey confirms the preference. Asked if they would choose to live in a low-density neighborhood where driving is a necessity, 66 percent said yes. Eighty-six percent said that ideally they would like to live in a single-family detached home (Baldassare 2002). It is not surprising, then, that higher densities are routinely opposed by neighborhood groups. Densification, an essential element of smart growth, entails types of buildings—such as apartments—that are different from the single-family home and usually associated with poor, racial minority, or transient populations, the same groups that white middle-class Americans fled from when they left the cities en mass during the 1960s, 1970s, and 1980s.

Political Impediments

Smart growth, with its proposal for a complete overhaul of the way we grow, runs counter to the basic human inclination to resist change, a trait that is especially strong in those who are comfortable in their present positions. We actively fight to resist change (Schon 1971). Baldassare's survey, mentioned earlier, confirms this point. A majority acknowledges that growth does lead to traffic congestion and housing affordability problems, yet, they would resist changing their suburban way of life to reduce these impacts of growth. That is especially true of densification, particularly if accompanied by affordable housing. Not surprisingly, proposals for change at the neighborhood level usually lead to NIMBY community organizing in the city as well as in the suburbs. Such attitudes are not lost on local politicians, who will not go out of their way to accommodate more population growth, especially in the form of higher-density housing. This is typically the case in suburban communities, where regulatory barriers are erected to both multi-family and lower cost, single-family housing (Downs 2001, 23).

The equity component of smart growth—regional fair-share housing and tax-base sharing—faces the longest odds in planning and implementing smart growth. Tax-base sharing proposals face strong opposition from suburban communities enjoying the fruits of a privileged position in the metropolitan context (Dreier et al. 2001). In fact, the only region in the country to successfully establish tax-base sharing is the Minneapolis–St. Paul region, a feat made possible by the leadership and indefatigable organizing work of the former Minnesota state senator Myron Orfield (Orfield 2002). An attempt to create a similar tax-base sharing system in the Sacramento region of California in 2002 failed because of strong opposition from localities.

Herein lies the dilemma of smart growth. Politically, smart growth seems to have succeeded in bringing together an unlikely coalition of urban planners, businesses, environmentalists, developers, labor unions, urban minorities, fiscal conservatives, farmers, historic preservationists, and government officials. As Downs (2001) has pointed out, though, they all come to the table with varied and conflicting agendas. While there seems to be consensus on the need for the revitalization of existing communities and the preservation of large open-space areas, there is less agreement on the limitation of outward extension of development at the metropolitan fringe and even less on the regional redistribution of affordable housing and tax revenues. Katz (2002, 27–28) goes even further, calling for smart growth to "recognize the central role of race . . . smart growth advocates will need to move beyond the relatively 'safe ground' of open space acquisition, environmental protection and infrastructure investment. If they are serious about curbing sprawl, they will need to embrace and push fundamental changes . . . to development patterns that have isolated the racial poor and undermined the economic and fiscal vitality of cities and inner suburbs."

Economic Impediments

Smart growth proponents, especially environmentalists and urban planners, want to rechannel growth to existing communities, contending that it is cheaper than sprawl because of existing public infrastructure and public facilities. However, infill and densification face economic-viability obstacles, in addition to the political problems outlined above. In a study of infill in Baltimore and Washington, Bowman and Piesen (2002, 3) found that in "older cities, aging and poorly maintained infrastructure may be more of an obstacle than an advantage to development." In newer areas huge deficits in public infrastructure in urban communities may doom infill and densification efforts (Calavita 2002). Farris (2001), in his analysis of barriers to infill development, identifies several obstacles, including land assembly and infrastructure costs, excessive risks, and the complexity of public/private partnerships. These and other political/administrative constraints "suggest that very little of this forecast new development will occur in presently built-up areas . . . and economic obsolescence will continue to plague many older neighborhoods, and outlying development

Map 3.1   **San Diego Region**

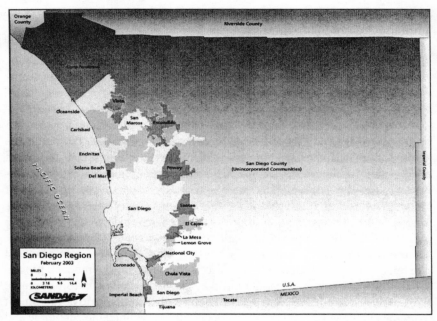

Source: Sandag, 2003.

will continue. . . . While supporting infill, smart growth advocates should focus primarily on encouraging higher-density, quality suburban and outlying growth" (Farris, 2001, 1).

Regional Planning in San Diego

Let us now examine how San Diego is responding to the challenges of smart growth, beginning with the regional planning attempts of the San Diego Association of Governments (SANDAG).

The San Diego region is coterminous with San Diego County and covers 4,261 square miles, approximately the size of Connecticut, with a 2002 population total of 2.8 million. Administratively, the San Diego region encompasses eighteen cities and the unincorporated areas of the county. The region, then, contains a single county, a rarity among metropolitan regions in the United States. It might be assumed, therefore, that regional planning in San Diego would encounter fewer difficulties than planning for multicounty regions. Before analyzing recent efforts at applying smart growth at the regional level, we will trace the evolution of regional planning in San Diego.

Table 3.1

Total Population for the San Diego Region

	Estimated Growth, 2000 to 2030			
	2000	2030	Numbers	Percentage
Carlsbad	78,247	124,922	46,675	60
Chula Vista	173,556	282,664	109,108	63
Coronado	24,100	25,536	1,436	6
Del Mar	4,389	5,103	714	16
El Cajon	94,869	109,044	14,175	15
Encinitas	58,014	78,762	20,748	36
Escondido	133,559	166,119	32,560	24
Imperial Beach	26,992	31,866	4,874	18
La Mesa	54,749	60,932	6,183	11
Lemon Grove	24,918	30,008	5,090	20
National City	54,260	67,430	13,170	24
Oceanside	161,029	214,696	53,667	33
Poway	48,044	55,932	7,888	16
San Diego	1,223,400	1,613,355	389,955	32
San Marcos	54,977	106,772	51,795	94
Santee	52,975	69,221	16,246	31
Solana Beach	12,979	14,411	1,432	11
Vista	89,857	113,969	24,112	27
Unincorporated	442,919	718,862	275,943	62
Region	2,813,833	3,889,604	1,075,771	38

Source: SANDAG, Preliminary Cities/County Forecast, October 2002.

The Evolution of San Diego's Regional Planning

In response to 1966 federal legislation the county administration, along with the existing thirteen cities in the San Diego region, signed a Joint Powers Agreement (JPA) to create a Comprehensive Planning Organization (CPO), to be managed under the county administration. In 1970 the state of California designated San Diego's CPO as the Metropolitan Planning Organization (MPO), enabling the organization to receive state highway dollars for the San Diego region. In 1975 the MPO produced its first Regional Transportation Plan (RTP)—as required by federal legislation—in order to win federal dollars and began reviewing all applications for state and federal aid to ensure they were consistent with regional plans and were coordinated with other federal aid projects.

In 1980 the board of directors approved a name change for the MPO to reflect its identity as San Diego's regional government agency. It would now be called the San Diego Association of Governments. By the late 1980s SANDAG was managing transportation, airport-land use, criminal justice issues, and housing for the San Diego region. Twenty years after state authorization, the agency had expanded its authority to encompass almost all the major public concerns that confronted the region.

In 1987 the region's voters approved a half-cent sales tax increase to create the San Diego Transportation Improvement Program—a program dedicated to the funding of regional transit, highway, and local road projects over the following twenty years. The program, commonly known as TransNet, generated nearly $2 billion for the region between 1988 and 2001 and is expected to collect an additional $1.3 billion for transportation improvements through 2008.

The county ballot in November 1988 was largely dedicated to growth control measures—two in the city and two in the county and a regional advisory initiative (Proposition C) to create a Regional Planning and Growth Management Review Board (Caves 1992). Prop C passed, and SANDAG, through an amendment to its Joint Powers Agreement, assumed the role of Regional Planning and Growth Management Review Board.

With its new role as regional growth policymaker, SANDAG had a significant opportunity to strengthen its policymaking powers. In June of 1991 SANDAG presented a draft version of the Regional Growth Management Strategy through its board of directors. The strategy was officially adopted in 1993 and is important for several reasons: It launched a new policymaking standard for SANDAG in setting quantitative goals and measures; it laid the foundation to add new elements for SANDAG's constantly expanding scope of work; and it officially made the connection between land-use and transportation policy.

In the fall of 1988 SANDAG compared current land-use plans with three variations of a land-use scenario that located highest densities near transit stations and along major bus corridors, encouraged mixed land uses and mixed housing types, and included residential uses within or near major employment centers (see Figures 3.1a and 3.1b, which compare the likely distribution of housing units using current plans and a smart growth scenario that accommodates the projected 2020 population).

The results of the comparison were, according to a SANDAG report, "decisive, if not surprising." The most striking finding was the difference in land consumption. Under the smart growth scenarios, about 200,000 acres of land would be consumed between 1995 and 2020, mostly for residential use. However, if we are to continue with our current general and community plans, there is the potential to consume more than 600,000 acres of now vacant land. Under the smart growth alternatives, much of that land could be preserved for habitat, recreational or agricultural uses" (SANDAG 1999, 6). In addition to open space preservation, the smart growth alternatives would

Figure 3.1a **Likely Distribution of New Housing Units Using a Smart Growth Scenario**

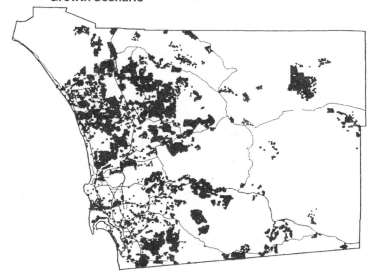

Source: Sandag 1999.

Figure 3.1b **Likely Distribution of New Housing Units Using Current Plans**

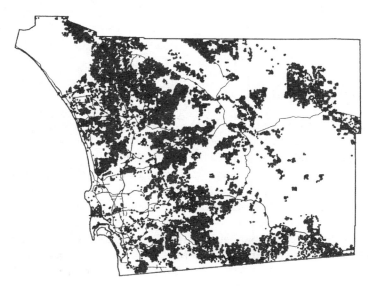

Source: Sandag 1979.

lead to "less traffic congestion, shorter trips, lower travel costs, less air pollution and more transit use." In reality, while traffic was considerably reduced under the smart growth scenario in the eastern portion of the region, it was increased in the mostly developed western portion to reflect the shift of population from the east to the already urbanized western areas.

The 2020 Regionwide Forecast, released in 1999, indicated a need for about 408,000 new homes between 1995 and 2020 to accommodate the projected population growth of 1 million people. Existing general plans could accommodate only 312,000 homes, about 100,000 units short of demand over the forecast period. It also found that 59 percent of future housing would be single-family homes at an average density of 2.4 homes per acre, while existing single-family development densities average 5.5 units per acre. While the density planned for multifamily homes was about 19 homes per acre, the amount of land dedicated to multifamily housing was abysmally low. How could future growth be accommodated? The solution was to apply smart growth principles, as envisioned under the land-use scenarios discussed above, to the REGION 2020 Growth Management Strategy also released in 1999.

The gap between housing needs and actual construction potential is not a theoretical or future threat. Observers have already pointed out that we may be undersupplying housing at the national level (Lang 2002) and that in California we demonstrably built fewer housing units than needed (Myers and Park 2002). This was especially true in San Diego during the 1990s, when the market was unable to keep up with demand. San Diego County, with a median-priced home costing $323,000, is one of the least affordable housing markets in the country.

Issues of Governance

Another noteworthy outgrowth of the regional governance issue came in early 2000 with California state senator Steve Peace's sponsorship of Senate Bill 329 that would have established a Regional Infrastructure and Transportation Agency (RITA). According to Peace, RITA was a constructive response to the fact that the fragmented local and state agencies in San Diego had failed to cooperate on the problems, challenges, and opportunities facing the region. RITA would have consolidated SANDAG, the San Diego Unified Port District, the San Diego Air Pollution Control District, the Metropolitan Transit Development Board (MTDB—in charge of transit for southern San Diego County), and the North County Transit District (NCTD).

RITA eventually led to a new bill that consolidated transportation planning in the San Diego region under one agency that would control planning and the allocation of funding for transportation projects. The consolidation of the planning functions of the three agencies—SANDAG, MTDB, and NCTD—has already taken place.

The debate over attempts to create a regional planning agency deserves more space than is allotted here. It must be said, however, that while a major step has been taken to coordinate transportation planning, control and power over local land use was left untouched. However, progress is slowly being made. The most recent steps in this incremental and piecemeal process are the preparation of a Regional Comprehensive Plan and the apparent willingness of SANDAG to employ a system of incentives and disincentives tied to its authority to disburse transportation funds.

The Regional Comprehensive Plan

The idea of a Regional Comprehensive Plan (RCP) stems from the need to integrate local plans and policies with those of neighboring jurisdictions, neighboring regions, and the international border. The problems that the RCP attempts to address are common to many jurisdictions: "consumption of large amounts of undeveloped land, low planned densities on currently vacant lands, job housing imbalance, and regional infrastructure financing" (SANDAG 2000). In typical SANDAG consensus-building fashion, a number of committees were established to undertake this effort, and a series of workshops were held throughout the region during 2003.

In December 2003 SANDAG released a draft of the RCP for comment. The elements that the RCP addresses are urban form, enhanced mobility, housing, healthy ecosystems, regional infrastructure needs and financing, and environmental justice/social equity. Each element will be structured and monitored by analyzing its impact on environment, equity, and economy, the three *E's* usually associated with sustainable development. From a smart growth perspective the "key tenet of the RCP is to identify smart growth opportunities areas and to reward communities that create compact, higher density, mixed-use, pedestrian-oriented neighborhoods with supportive transportation and infrastructure improvements. When it comes to transportation funding and smart growth, the RCP directs SANDAG to put its money where its mouth is . . . (SANDAG 2003, xx). A decision on the RCP is expected by the end of 2004.

Regional Open Space Preservation

An essential element of smart growth is the preservation of regionally significant open space, the definition of which will vary depending on the history and ecology of place. In San Diego, a region blessed with the highest level of biological diversity in the continental United States, the regionally significant open space consists of the remaining habitats that house a great variety of animals and plants. For the long-term preservation of these species, their habitats have to be interconnected, thus creating the potential for a regional open space network that could work as a greenbelt—in effect an urban growth boundary—separating developable from nondevelopable land at the regional level. In the San Diego region an intensive planning process has been taking place for the past ten years and has produced multiple habitat conservation programs that are currently being implemented. The first was the Multiple Species Conservation Program (MSCP) for the southwestern portion of the county. Approved in 1997, it represents a good case study of the feasibility, opportunities, and pitfalls of such an approach.

Multiple Species Conservation Program

In 1991 San Diego became a pilot project for the statewide Natural Community Conservation Planning (NCCP) program, which gives local governments control over streamlined endangered species permitting. This is in exchange for developing a long-term habitat preserve system meant to define and preserve large areas of habitat, rather than individual species. The program established three subregional habitat conservation planning programs in the region. The first in the county—and in the nation—was the MSCP, covering 582,000 acres of southwestern San Diego County, and including the cities of San Diego, Chula Vista, Imperial Beach, National City, Santee, El Cajon, Lemon Grove, La Mesa, and a portion of San Diego County's unincorporated area.

The protection of sensitive plant and animal species by the MSCP eliminates the need to list the species as endangered under federal and state endangered species acts and reduces the costly and time-consuming permitting process for private landowners and public agencies. In the past, mitigation of development impacts had created small protected areas that were disconnected from other habitat areas. As local and federal agencies scrambled to protect species listed as endangered, uncertainties and delays in the development process were created.

The goal of the MSCP was to maintain and enhance biological diversity in the region through the maintenance of viable populations of endangered, threatened, and key sensitive species and their habitats. Planning for the 172,000–acre MSCP preserve (98,379 acres of which are in the unincorporated area) also promoted regional economic viability through streamlining the land-use permit process—a significant benefit to landowners.

Interior Secretary Bruce Babbitt heralded the MSCP as a national model for the protection of all rare animals and plants. Some problems, however, have begun to surface in its implementation:

1. Funding. In politically conservative San Diego the protection of property rights was of utmost concern to the politicians overseeing the planning process. The County Board of Supervisors even recommended at one point that private land be excluded from the MSCP area. This attitude eliminated from consideration mechanisms like Transfer of Development Rights (TDRs) that could have limited the need of funding for the acquisition of the private portions of the proposed reserve.
2. Loss of open space in developable areas. In exchange for providing land in the reserve, developers outside the reserve can build on areas that in the past would have remained undeveloped. The result is less open space in developing areas.
3. Vague and discretionary policies resulting from the need to achieve consensus.

This has led to the destruction of rare habitats, such as vernal pools (Rolfe 2001).

In spite of these and other problems, habitat conservation planning is probably the best approach to the protection of species and long-term conservation planning, and the San Diego experience can provide guidance for similar efforts in the country.

The analysis of the evolution of SANDAG has shown that progress has been made on many fronts. These include tying together land-use and transportation planning, regional open space planning, creating a regional transportation superagency, and initiating a regional comprehensive planning process. SANDAG, however, still remains an association of governments with—until now—no land-use powers. Will localities change their plans to implement smart growth by increasing densities? Recent experiences of the city of San Diego, the county of San Diego and the city of Carlsbad seem to indicate that, left on their own, localities will not.

Smart Growth at the Local Level

City of San Diego

Before describing the recent city of San Diego's City of Villages effort and failure it is necessary to go back about twenty-five years, for the roots of this recent failure are found in failed growth management policies of the past. San Diego began its growth management program in the early 1970s, fueled by the national environmental movement and antigrowth sentiment. In 1975 Mayor Wilson hired Robert Freilich to prepare a growth management plan for San Diego. Freilich was the land-use attorney who had developed and successfully defended in the courts the Ramapo, New York, growth management plan. The result was a tier approach to growth management. This strategy encouraged infill and denser development in the already urbanized communities by not assessing fees for development, while major new growth was to be accommodated in the "planned urbanizing" tier, where all capital facilities (the parks, libraries, schools, streets, etc.) would be financed through fees paid by the developers. To phase growth, a "future urbanizing" tier was established, with outlying areas to be kept off-limits to development for at least twenty-five years.

During the early 1980s San Diego's growth management strategy seemed to be working well. Infill development proceeded at a brisk pace in the urbanized communities, and, following a spate of legal wrangling, "facilities benefit assessment" fees were collected from developers to pay for public infrastructure in the planned urbanizing tier. For a while the city was considered a model for effective management of growth, with planners and elected officials from other U.S. cities coming to San Diego to learn about how to implement growth management.

Nevertheless, this model begun to unravel in the 1980s, a decade of rapid growth. In 1982 the city authorized the construction of 4,000 new units; in 1986 more than 19,000 were approved, and a similar number of units were authorized for the rest of the decade. The urbanized communities took the brunt of this growth, with developers paying no development impact fees. The assumption was that there were already enough parks, libraries, and schools to accommodate new growth. Not surprisingly, developers took advantage of this ability to construct new housing without paying for new facilities. One after another, single-family neighborhoods were invaded by multifamily buildings (many of them insensitively designed), and community facilities were overwhelmed by the onslaught of newcomers. Some observers have commented that the adopted plan had worked too well, by bringing too much growth to the urbanized communities (Fulton 1999).

The plan, however, was flawed from the start. It was generally understood, when the infill strategy was being debated, that there were already serious deficiencies in some of the urban neighborhoods. It was also understood that those deficiencies could be eliminated with general fund dollars. In 1978, however, Proposition 13 was passed, capping property taxes at 1 percent of assessed value and yearly increases at 2 percent, seriously

Figure 3.2   **City of San Diego Growth Management Tiers**

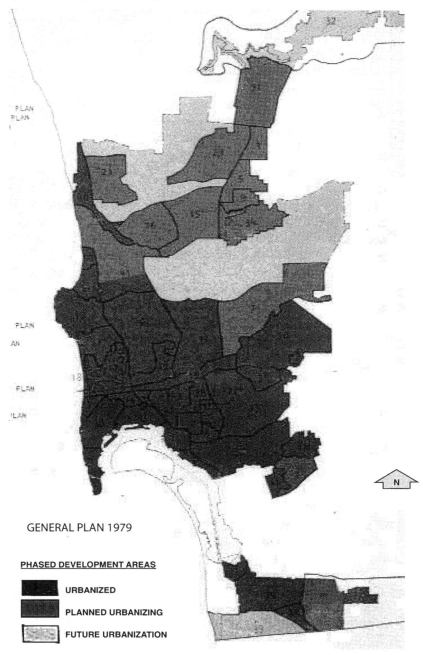

GENERAL PLAN 1979

PHASED DEVELOPMENT AREAS

URBANIZED

PLANNED URBANIZING

FUTURE URBANIZATION

undermining the ability of the city to raise revenue. This came at the end of almost a decade of conflicts over growth management and the tier system in particular. To avoid opening another Pandora's box, the plan was not changed, and it was approved the following year. It was probably difficult at the time to predict the serious effect of that decision, but the deficit originated then and increased every year after that as the urbanized communities grew rapidly, without new public facilities to accompany that growth. Not until 1987 did the city council begin imposing fees on new development in the urbanized communities, too little and too late to avert a huge shortfall in public facilities (Calavita 1992, Caves 1992). How huge? The city's most recent estimate for funding the backlog of parks and recreation, transportation, fire, and library needs is $2.5 billion. Such a staggering figure needs to be contrasted with San Diego's unwillingness to tax itself. Until recently San Diego prided itself on being a fiscally conservative city. Compared to other California cities, general fund revenues are low. In San Diego they amount to $425 per capita, about half that in Los Angeles or San Francisco. Business tax and hotel taxes are among the lowest in the state. San Diego is the only city in the region that does not charge a separate fee for refuse collection.

It is especially damning that San Diego's inaction intensifies an ominous drift toward a socially, economically, and racially fractured city. If the most important function of local government is the equitable distribution and provision of public facilities and services to its citizens, then San Diego has failed miserably. Public facilities deficits plague its older, urbanized neighborhoods south of Route 52, where most of the minority, lower-income population of the city is concentrated. Newer communities, on the other hand, enjoy public facilities that actually exceed city standards. Although built with developers' fees, they exact a disproportionate share of the city budget intended for ongoing maintenance and operation (Calavita 1997). It is within this context that San Diego decided to update the 1979 tier-based general plan. The new strategy was evocatively called a City of Villages.

The City of Villages Strategy

A new strategy was necessary because the old tier strategy had become irrelevant. The city of San Diego was running out of vacant land. The "planned urbanizing" tier, where developers were made to pay development impact fees, had worked well, but not much land was left for development. Could the city accommodate a significant share of regional growth under this new scenario?

In 1999, as the general plan update efforts were beginning, SANDAG released its population forecast for the year 2020. It was projected that the region would grow by approximately 1 million people, and the share of the city of San Diego would be approximately 400,000 people. As discussed above, the new projections called for the local jurisdictions to increase the capacity of their general plans. This did not generate an enthusiastic response in many jurisdictions. The county of San Diego, for example, was able to bargain with SANDAG to bring its share of future population down considerably. In the city of San Diego, instead, the planners made the accommodation of 50,000 more units above what the existing plans could accommodate—approximately 100,000 units—the main objective of the general plan update.

To guide the process, a number of committees were impaneled, core values established, and alternative strategies evaluated. The approach that was chosen was the City of Villages. Planning department documents describe a village "as a community-oriented center where residential, commercial, employment and civic/education uses are integrated . . . and served by a world-class transit system" (City of San Diego 2002a, 27). The village strategy would reinforce "the existing pattern of development by utilizing community nodes or centers for further intensification and enhancement" (City of San Diego 2002a, 27).

During the first two or three years of citizen involvement, with endless meetings in various parts of the city, the response seemed to be positive. Beautiful examples of housing at various densities were shown to the public, and a brochure, *What Does Density Look Like?* also gave many examples of how housing at densities varying from 11 du/ac (dwelling units/per acre) all the way to 151 du/ac could indeed be attractive. The concept of villages became enticing to many people. Whatever goodwill the planners' images of villages had evoked, it was quickly dispelled by the harsh reality of a first-draft map indicating the location of the villages. The map indicated areas where densities could be increased and by how much. Additional growth was to be concentrated in the urbanized communities, the same areas with the $2.5 billion deficit in public facilities and with the highest concentration of low-income and minority people. The rationale provided by the planners for this approach to the distribution of future population in the city was that those areas had the highest redevelopment potential.

Opposition to the City of Villages strategy found an institutional outlet in the Community Planners Committee (CPC). The CPC is comprised of all the chairs of the planning groups and makes recommendations on citywide policies and programs. In June 2002 CPC had given qualified support to the concept of villages if certain conditions were met. When those conditions were not met, CPC worked against staff recommendations.

Environmental and community groups opposed the plan because of their concerns with the program-level Environmental Impact Statement (EIR) for the plan update. They felt that the EIR was inadequate in assessing the true costs of growth. The most glaring fault was that the EIR failed to measure the impact of development possible under existing community plans *plus* the proposed additional units, but measured only the impact of the additional units.

The second major obstacle was the difficulty in finding land for parks—and schools—to eliminate existing deficiencies and accommodate the future population. San Diego is unlike other cities, such as Cleveland, that have experienced sharp declines in population. There is practically no developable land of any significant size in San Diego's urbanized communities; its Unified School District was forced to tear down hundreds of housing units to build schools in the community of City Heights. The lack of land in the urbanized areas led to the EIR statement that "The current guideline of 20 acres per thousand people is difficult to attain for the higher density, attached homes envisioned by the proposed growth strategy . . . these guidelines need to be revised or alternatively applied for the mixed-use, higher density attached homes" (City of San Diego 2002c, iv–105). Common sense would tell us that parkland is essential precisely where densities are high, where housing does not have backyards, and where the only open space is public open space. Densification and infill would need to be accompanied by open space and recreational opportunities, especially in neighborhoods with many low-income children.

Flexibility, revision or alternative application of park standards, and more intensive use of existing parks were mentioned as solutions to this conundrum. People in the urbanized communities saw these alternatives as euphemisms for lower standards. In spite of assurances to the contrary, and contrary to what the City of Villages was supposed to achieve, the future seemed to promise a lower quality of life. If higher densities would lead to lower standards and lower quality of life, community activists felt they needed to know before the approval of the strategy. For them, public parks were the sine qua non of higher densities.

Perhaps the most persistent and damning criticism of the plan was the existing deficit in public facilities in the urbanized communities, where the bulk of growth was supposed to occur. As part of the updating process, the city hired economic consultants to analyze alternative revenue sources available for "financing infrastructure in those existing urbanized areas, so as to bring them up to current standards prior to their absorbing additional population growth" (City of San Diego 2002b, 1). The consultant proposed several major revenue categories and outlined constitutional and other constraints, the most significant being that most possible revenues would need to be approved by two-thirds of the voters. At a city council public hearing, the consultants suggested that to begin the process, surveys should be conducted to establish which of the measures the voters were more likely to support. No action was taken, though, and neither council members nor the mayor showed any intention of initiating a process that could lead to more taxes.

These were the main criticisms of the plan that were out in the open. A more dangerous and creeping obstacle was fear of density. City planners valiantly tried to dispel notions that density would worsen the quality of life of communities. On the contrary, they maintained, it would create vibrant village centers, add needed affordable housing, generate opportunities for walking and public encounters, and make transit viable. The great majority of residents were not easily swayed.

The first city council hearing drew heavy opposition from community planning groups, residents, the CPC, environmentalists, and limited-growth activists. The council had given earlier support to the plan, but now the opposition had solidified and grown stronger, and the council was reluctant to impose higher densities on communities. They were in a bind. SANDAG unwittingly provided a way out. A few days after the first council hearing, SANDAG declared the 2020 population projections too high and released new, lower preliminary estimates for 2030.

The 2000 census had shown that SANDAG underestimated the number of people who had left the county during the recession of the early to middle 1990s and overestimated fertility rates, especially for Latinas. In December SANDAG had communicated to the city that instead of the additional projected 50,000 units, a smaller number was likely. A new range of 17,000 to 37,000 units was given as a preliminary number. When the draft projections came out for 2030, it was discovered that the city did not to have to accommodate additional population beyond the capacity of the community plans—108,000 units.

The city council could have easily extended the time frame for the City of Villages to 2030, in line with SANDAG's time frame for their RCP and Regional Transportation Plan. In so doing, the additional densities so essential for the integrity of the City of Villages and the viability of transit would have been protected. Various communities were opposed to the higher densities, and the council was unwilling to impose them without the public facilities. A memorandum authored by the mayor and two council members recommended "delete all density increases" in the plan, because "We agree that no community should be asked to accept increased density, unless it is accompanied with adequate public facilities to support these densities. However, given the legal and fiscal constraints that the City faces, it will be challenging to provide full funding of pre-existing infrastructure deficits on a citywide basis at the time" (Murphy et al. 2002, 2). In this way, the council declared its inability or unwillingness to do anything about the public facilities deficit.

The City of Villages was adopted without the 2020 housing goals by community planning areas and with the strategy changed from accommodating more growth to the shifting of the 108,000 planned units into a "smarter" pattern. The process continues with Pilot Villages. Four communities were chosen in February 1994 "to demonstrate how a village will evolve and function depending on the neighborhood and community in which it is sited. This program will require finding funds to support the pilot's village infrastructure needs" (City of San Diego 2002a, 59). Funding of public facilities, however, is not likely to be part of the help that the city will provide to the Pilot Village sites.

Other Localities

How are other localities in the region addressing Smart Growth? Space limitations allow for only a short presentation of two jurisdictions' approaches and for some general comments about the others.

County of San Diego

The county is in the process of updating its general plan. The thrust of the proposed plan is to move away from a sprawl pattern of development to concentrating growth in existing communities. This entails a massive downzoning of vast areas of the unincorporated area of the county, and that has generated a great deal of controversy. Transfer of development rights or purchase of development rights are being discussed; both are fraught with different implementation problems. Nevertheless, the county has chosen the right (and difficult) path toward establishing a smart growth pattern of development—and that is good. Unfortunately, the county has reduced its capacity to accommodate development from 880,000 to 660,000 people, and is willing to accommodate only 17 percent of future growth. Given the difficulties in implementing infill and densification in the city of San Diego, the county's decision, quietly agreed to by SANDAG, raises questions about a worsening mismatch between housing demand and availability of land for residential development.

Carlsbad

In 1986 the city of Carlsbad approved a growth management plan that established the ultimate number of units to be built in the city. The plan cut the maximum number of units from 108,000 to 54,600, with the great majority of the residential land dedicated to single-family homes. At the end of 2002 about 38,000 units had been built, with approximately 16,000 remaining under the plan. In several cases developers have built at densities lower than those allowed by the plan, with the excess units going into an "excess dwelling units bank." The excess dwelling units were to be used when developers wanted to build at higher densities in areas favored by the city, such as redevelopment areas. The Carlsbad city council became alarmed when the number of units in the bank reached almost 6,000, and it slashed the number by half in 2002. Pleadings from SANDAG, affordable housing developers, and many others were to no avail. Apparently, even the potential for higher densities (within the parameters of the built-out growth management plan) was too threatening for Carlsbad. SANDAG's efforts seem to have fallen on deaf ears in this wealthy coastal city.

Other Approaches

Other cities, such as Chula Vista, located near the U.S.-Mexican border, are planning for more growth. Otay Ranch, a new town being built in accordance with new-urbanist principles, was welcomed in Chula Vista. Several cities have built or are planning to build mixed-use centers. San Marcos, in collaboration with Cal State San Marcos, is planning to accommodate considerable growth consistent with smart growth principles. Carlsbad is developing a mixed-use core and is locating a new transit center near the original town center, within walking distance of many shops. Lemon Grove and Santee are developing transit-oriented town centers. Responses to growth, then, are varied. Most cities use new-urbanist principles in conjunction with redevelopment projects or transit station development. A few cities, usually situated in the southern part of the county, welcome growth. The opposite is true in northern San Diego County. The question is whether a coherent and unified regional approach to smart growth can be shaped from such a vast array of attitudes and approaches to coping with growth.

Discussion and Conclusion

Smart growth has been touted as the planning savior, capable of accommodating population growth while revitalizing declining communities—protecting wildlife habitats and agricultural lands, encouraging transportation alternatives to the automobile, fostering social integration, and engendering a sense of community—truly a comprehensive and ambitious agenda. The question is whether it can deliver on its promises.

We have examined the San Diego case to ascertain the viability of smart growth in a particular context at a particular time. The San Diego region has experienced and continues to experience high rates of growth, although projections for 2030 indicate that it will grow more slowly than in the past. Absolute growth figures remain staggering, with forecasts of an additional one million people by 2030, bringing the regional population to 3.8 million. In attempting to deal with growth problems, San Diego has developed a long tradition of growth-management programs and attempts at growth limitations. Recent efforts to implement smart growth must be considered within this context.

Regional growth is guided by an association of governments, not by an elected body with broad mandates. While SANDAG is similar to the great majority of regional bodies that exist in the country, it is singular in that it involves only one county, which is bounded along its entire southern edge by an international border with Mexico. Is smart growth possible in San Diego? Put another way, can San Diego accommodate growth without losing its much touted quality of life? Success will depend on three interrelated factors: effective regional governance, smart growth at the local level, and equity. Threading through all these factors are the thorny issues of adequate infrastructure and public facilities.

Effective Regional Governance

To be successful, smart growth must extend beyond local strategies, which are inevitably piecemeal, and focus on regional interconnections between older neighborhoods and newer suburbs, land use and transportation, tax-base inequities, and the social and economic health of communities. The region—no longer the city, state, or nation—is emerging as the dominant economic unit of the twenty-first century. Related industries form clusters at the regional level, establishing networks that tie the region together. Their viability demands regional planning for transportation, public facilities, open space, land use, and social and cultural networks. To plan efficiently and equitably, an elected body, such as Metro in Portland, sustained by state legislation, would be the most effective and democratic mechanism to implement smart growth. Nevertheless, "Regional planning agencies with broad mandates are not likely to be created in most places" (Wheeler 2002, 275). Absent that, our best hope lies with local government ad hoc working groups, including joint powers authorities such as SANDAG, to work to their highest potential (Savitch and Vogel 1996). SANDAG is in a good position to do so.

Because of SANDAG's organizational nature, progress in fostering smart growth will continue to be slow and incremental. Looking back at SANDAG's achievements over the past decade, we can identify the creation of a regional open space system through habitat conservation planning; the institution of the land-use/transportation connection as the foundation of their planning function and as a criterion that informs funding decisions, and the establishment, through state intervention, of a regional transportation superagency. Finally, a regional comprehensive planning process has been initiated, creating a forum for debate and problem solving at the regional level.

An equally important challenge is the task of funding the regional public facilities and infrastructure necessary to maintain the quality of life in the region in the face of concentrated growth. Huge financial investments are required not only for highways and arterials but also for a first-class transit system, acquisition of habitat lands, and water quality protection. At a time of federal retrenchment and state budget crisis, San Diegans will need to look to themselves to find the bulk of the necessary resources. Securing voter reapproval of TransNet—the program created with the county's half-cent sales tax, which will expire in 2008—is essential. Since a two-third voter approval is now required for passage of this extension, the future of TransNet may hinge on a proposed state ballot measure that would reduce the standards for voter approval. Even if passed, the TransNet tax would fund only a portion of the necessary transportation infrastructure and not other needs.

Smart Growth at the Local Level

SANDAG's success will depend to a large extent on the willingness and ability of local jurisdictions to apply smart growth principles within their own borders. However, the San Diego County and Carlsbad stories show that, left to their own devices, local jurisdictions will tend to act parochially, with little consideration for the surrounding region. Not mentioned in this chapter is the confounding issue of local initiatives that subject general plan changes to voter approval (Fulton 1999). In San Diego County two cities, Escondido and Solana Beach, have passed such initiatives; San Marcos might do so in the near future.

Even in cases where a locality is willing to accept additional density, as in the city of San Diego, past planning mistakes often resurface to block efforts to increase density. At least for the foreseeable future it is very unlikely that funding for infrastructure will be forthcoming, and it is not clear at this point where funds can be tapped for even three or four pilot projects.

Equity

Smart growth is a powerful concept but fraught with pitfalls. In order for it to succeed, a full range of elements must be implemented, most importantly the equity component. If implemented piecemeal, smart growth can actually lower a community's or a region's quality of life. It could become the Trojan horse that, with false promises of unlimited growth and improved quality of life, would create havoc, especially in low-income and minority communities. For example, choosing to protect open space at the fringe unaccompanied by ample opportunities for infill and densification will lead to more limited housing opportunities and higher housing costs. According to Pyatok (2002, 5) "physical intervention is not the end, but rather the means, for building jobs, community self-sufficiency and political empowerment . . ." otherwise "'sticks and bricks' interventions will merely raise property values and displace the very people we should be trying to help."

Other major equity issues are regional in nature, specifically tax-base sharing and overcoming racial and income segregation. The San Diego region is roughly divided into a northern and a southern section—with Interstate 8 representing the dividing line. The northern section is where the majority of jobs have been created during the past twenty years, where wealth is concentrated, and where practically no affordable housing has been built. The southern section is where most racial minorities and low-income people live. A job-housing imbalance of huge proportions has led to significant problems of traffic congestion. People who live in the urbanized communities of the city of San Diego cannot afford to move where the jobs are and are forced to live in areas with inadequate public services and to commute long distances on congested freeways.

SANDAG has emphasized equity as a necessary element to ensure the sustainability of the San Diego region and has included equity as a criterion to evaluate the various elements of the RCP, which is a step in the right direction. It is highly unlikely, however, that localities that are unwilling to accommodate additional population would be willing to make a large part of their new housing affordable to low-income families. In the RCP, SANDAG has not made the provision of affordable housing a condition for transportation funds. Tax-base sharing necessary to avoid fiscal zoning and ameliorate the tax-base disparities in the region (Orfield and Luce 2002) has never been seriously discussed.

Future Uncertainties

San Diego has made some progress in the long process toward the implementation of smart growth principles, but the nature and intensity of the problems require a long-term, comprehensive, cooperative response by local jurisdictions. It remains to be seen whether SANDAG can succeed with its present structure. If the RCP process fails, the debate on regional governance will, of necessity, be renewed. Densification in the city of San Diego may be an ultimately desirable outcome but is problematic under conditions of public infrastructure deficits, scarcity of land, high land costs, and community opposition. Moreover, without an increased supply of affordable housing and replacement programs, gentrification and displacement will occur, exacerbating social ills along with traffic congestion and employment disparities. Smart growth would be easier to achieve in San Diego if California had a strong mandate for regional planning with enforceable guidelines for smart growth. While states like Oregon, New Jersey, Washington, and others have responsibly stepped forward, California has retreated from its former leadership role. Given the state's financial crisis, it is unlikely that financial incentives will be available to encourage smart growth in the foreseeable future. Without greater state involvement that can provide both financial incentives and regulatory direction, it is likely that San Diego will pick and choose rather than fully incorporate all the ingredients necessary for successful smart growth.

* * *

The authors would like to thank Parke Troutman, Ph.D. student, University of California, San Diego, for his assistance in researching and drafting parts of this chapter.

References

Baldassare, Mark. 2002. *A California State of Mind: The Conflicted Voter in a Changing World.* San Francisco Public Policy Institute of California and the University of California Press.

Bowman, Michelle, and Ann Piesen. 2002. "Challenges of Infill Development," Paper presented at the annual conference of the Association of Collegiate Schools of Planning, Baltimore, November 23.

Burchell, Robert W., David Listokin, and Catherine C. Galley. 2000. "Smart Growth: More than a Ghost of Urban Policy Past, Less than a Bold New Horizon." *Housing Policy Debate* 11 no. 4: 821–80.

Calavita, Nico. 1992. "Growth Machines and Ballot-Box Planning: The San Diego Case." *Journal of Urban Affairs* 14, no. 1: 1–24.

———. 1997. "Vale of Tiers." *Planning* (March): 18–21.

———. 2002. "Smart Growth as Trojan Horse: The Case of San Diego." *Planners Network* 150, (Winter): 26–28.

Calthorpe, Peter. 1993. *The Next American Metropolis.* Brooklyn, NY: Princeton Architectural Press.

Calthorpe, Peter, and William Fulton. 2001. *The Regional City.* New York: Island Press.

Caves, Roger W. 1992. *Land Use Planning: The Ballot Box Revolution.* Thousand Oaks, CA: Sage.

City of San Diego. 2002a. *Draft Strategic Framework Element.* Planning Department, July 10.

————. 2002b. *Facilities Financing Study.* Planning Department.

————. 2002c. *Environmental Impact Report: The City of Villages Growth Strategy.*

Downs, Anthony. 2001. "What Does 'Smart Growth' Really Mean?" *Planning* (April): 20–25.

Dreier, Peter, John Mollenkopf, and Todd Swanstrom. 2001. *Place Matters: Metropolitics for the Twenty-First Century.* Lawrence: University Press of Kansas.

Duany, Andres, Elizabeth Plater-Zyberk, and Jeff Speck. 2000. *Suburban Nation.* New York: North Point.

Easterbrook, Gregg. 1999. "Comment on Karen A. Danielsen, Robert E. Lang, and William Fulton's 'Retracting Suburbia: Smart Growth and the Future of Housing.'" *Housing Policy Debate* 10, no. 3: 541–48.

Farris, Terrence. 2001. "The Barriers to Using Urban Infill Development to Achieve Smart Growth." *Housing Policy Debate* 12, no. 1: 1–30.

Fulton, William. 1999. *Guide to California Planning*, 2nd ed. Point Arena, CA: Solano.

Gordon, P., and H. Richardson. 1998. "Prove It: The Costs and Benefits of Sprawl." *Brookings Review* (Fall): 13–29.

Johnson, Denny, Jason Jordan, and Patricia Salkin. 2002. "Introduction," *Planning for Smart Growth: 2002 State of the States*, pp. 13–29. Chicago: American Planning Association.

Katz, Bruce. 2002. "Smart Growth: The Future of the American Metropolis?" Centre for Analysis of Social Exclusion, London School of Economics, CASE Paper 58, July.

Katz, Peter. 1994. *The New Urbanism: Toward an Architecture of Community.* New York: McGraw-Hill.

Kreiger, Alex, and William Lennertz, eds. 1991. *Andres Duany and Elizabeth Plater Zyberk: Towns and Town-Making Principles.* New York: Rizzoli.

Lang, Robert. 2002. "Is the United States Undersupplying Housing?" *Housing Facts & Findings* 4, no. 2: 1, 5–7, Washington, DC: Fannie Mae Foundation.

Levy, John M. 1988. *Contemporary Urban Planning.* Englewood Cliffs, NJ: Prentice Hall.

Murphy, Dick, Council Members Tony Atkins, Scott Peters. 2002. "Memorandum: Strategic Framework Element Modifications," October 16, City of San Diego: Office of the Mayor.

Myers, D., and J. Park. 2002. "The Great Housing Collapse in California." *Housing Facts and Figures* 4, no. 2 (May). Washington, DC: Fannie Mae Foundation.

Orfield, Myron. 2002. *American Metropolitics: The New Suburban Reality.* Washington, DC: The Brookings Institution.

Orfield, Myron, and Thomas Luce. 2002. *California Metropatterns.* Minneapolis-St. Paul: Metropolitan Research Corporation.

Pyatok, Mike. 2002. "The Narrow Base of the New Urbanists." *Planners Network* 151 (Spring): 3–5.

Rolfe, Allison. 2001. "Understanding the Political Realities of Conservation Planning." *Fremontia* 29, nos. 3–4 (July–October): 13–18.

SANDAG. 1995. "Land Use Distribution Element of the Regional Growth Management Strategy," February. San Diego, CA.
———. 1999. "SANDAG INFO: 2020 Cities/County Forecast for the San Diego Region," September–October, No. 5. San Diego, CA: SourcePoint.
———. 2000. "Indicators of Sustainable Competiveness." San Diego, CA.
———. 2002. "Project Evaluation Criteria," October. San Diego, CA.
———. 2003. "Planning for the Region's Future Starts with You." Brochure announcing future workshops on the Regional Comprehensive Plan. San Diego, CA.
Savitch, Hank, and Ron Vogel, eds. 1996. *Regional Politics: America in a Post-City Age.* Thousand Oaks, CA: Sage.
Schon, Donald. 1971. *Beyond the Stable State.* New York: Random House.
Wheeler, Stephen. 2002. "The New Regionalism: Characteristics of an Emerging Movement." *Journal of the American Planning Association* 68, no. 3: 267–78.

Part 2

Metropolitan Administration

4

MARK TRANEL

The Role of County Governments in Metropolitan Administration: A Study of the St. Louis MSA

In the sixth century King Arthur needed the support of a group of knights to both protect and project his kingdom. When the knights gathered at Camelot in late spring for an annual meeting, King Arthur had a problem seating them. The knights were each so great in dignity and power (at least in their own minds) that one could not occupy a higher-ranking seat than another. The king's solution was to seat them at a round table that all might occupy chairs of equal importance.

Central city officials in the twentieth century need support, not as was the case with Arthur to respond to military threats, but to protect their territory from economic, social, and technological challenges, and to project their territory in the global economic arena. The central city sits at the table, not with knights, but with officials of county governments in the metropolitan area. The shape of the table does not, however, resolve the structure of political governance in contemporary American metropolitan areas. Not the least of the issues is who needs to be at the table. King Arthur set his own limit on the number of knights at his table. The geographic growth of the metropolis in the last several decades, however, has expanded the governmental landscape at an unprecedented rate to include an ever-growing number of jurisdictions. And these local officials are becoming more and more temperamental as they feel themselves equal to, and frequently superior to, the central city.

Neil Pierce and Curtis Johnson advanced the contemporary concept of the round table in their 1997 book, *Boundary Crossers*, in which Lesson 1 describes how the table of regional governance gets "larger and rounder." In recent decades the table has grown considerably, and the new faces at it are county officials or their designates. The significance of county governments in metropolitan governance has been a rapidly evolving phenomenon over the past three to four decades. Urban sprawl has quite literally reached out and embraced many formerly rural counties. Between 1980 and 1990 the U.S. Census Bureau redefined over 50 counties from outside a Metropolitan Statistical Area (MSA) to part of a MSA. The pace accelerated over the next decade. From 1990 to 2000 the Census Bureau reclassified 167 counties as metropolitan. The increasing participation of these new metropolitan counties has not been matched by county-level research, in particular regarding their relationship to the central city.

The American federal system is typically examined in terms of local governments (with the emphasis on municipalities and special districts), states, and the national government (Morlan, 1966). While counties are an important link between the states and local governments, they have not been included in examinations of critical decision makers in metropolitan regions (Duncombe 1977). Indeed, it has been stated that academic researchers have a bias against examining county government in the metropolitan context because of the "unflattering image of counties as backward suppliers of rural services and the still enigmatic nature of county governmental forms" (Streib and Waugh 1991, 140).

St. Louis is a useful example of a metropolitan area where the number of counties at the table of regional decision making keeps getting larger. Metropolitan St. Louis consisted of four counties and the central city in 1950. Seven counties had been added by the year 2000. This chapter examines how the city of St. Louis and its surrounding metropolitan counties have evolved geographically, demographically, and structurally; what county leaders think about regional relations (and how that compares to the perceptions of the general population); and how issues are handled in the expanded geography with dissimilar demography.

Evolving Urban Counties

The literature on counties is for the most part concerned with descriptive assessments of their legal and organizational structure and the extent of service delivery. Most county studies are also quite normative. They advocate that counties should have greater authority to raise revenue and provide services.

When county governments have been considered in academic studies, the topic normally falls into one of several categories:

- *Rural to urban evolution* (Streib and Waugh 1991)—county service delivery responsibilities are changing with an expansion from traditional functions of road maintenance and modest law enforcement to include land use and zoning, water supply and sewage, and environmental issues such as toxic waste management and ground water contamination.

- *Fiscal crisis* (Boroughs, Black, and Collins 1991)—particularly in the early 1990s when all governments' resources were stressed by an economic recession, county governments were examined along with the local, state, and national governments.
- *County service delivery* (U.S. Advisory Commission on Intergovernmental Relations 1993)—a debate continues regarding the efficiency of centralizing service delivery in fewer government structures, which would push a broader range of services up to the county level, or the responsiveness of many small municipalities delivering a customized package of locally preferred services.
- *Impact of reform structure* (DeSantis and Renner 1994, Marando and Reeves 1993)—as was the case with the impact of reform structures on municipal governments in the first half of the twentieth century, studies of changing to a professional administrative staff in county governments have examined whether or not there has been increased efficiency and effectiveness in service delivery.

Park (1997) reported on one of the few studies to include counties in an analysis of intergovernmental relations at the metropolitan level. Table 4.1 outlines his application of the "competition" verses the "cooperation" theories of fiscal response. Park conducted a test of the competition and cooperation hypotheses by examining fiscal data for 186 metropolitan areas. He calculated increases and decreases in spending over time as the multitude of governments in metropolitan areas responded to changes in expenditures by other governments. One of the dimensions Park sought to measure was interaction between cities and counties. Previous work had focused on horizontal interaction, that is, city-to-city or county-to-county. Park's question was do "cities compete with counties as well as with other cities." If they do, he said, "future researchers may have to extend their scope to include the concept of vertical competition in order to provide a more holistic view of service delivery practices in metropolitan areas." Park states the choice of expenditures was based on the lack of nationwide data on "activities" of cities and counties. His expenditure data showed that "traditional conceptions of county governments as administrative arms of the state should be reevaluated. Instead of passing through or allocating state resources objectively to their nominally subordinate local governments, county governments appear to be self-seeking entities competing with their own local governments in a few policy areas such as development."

Table 4.1

Multijurisdictional Competition vs. Cooperation

	Competition	Cooperation
Horizontal (interjurisdictional)	Two cities match policy	City provides services other cities lack or cut services other cities provide
Vertical (intergovernmental)	City matches county policy	City provides services not provided by county or cuts services provided by county

Source: Park, "Friends and Competitors," 1997.

Park examined expenditure patterns under conditions of fiscal stress. The present case study of metropolitan St. Louis examines the longer-term process of evolving governance structures under conditions of geographic expansion. A case study provides the opportunity to examine "activities," particularly the evolving role of county governments in metropolitan affairs.

One City, Multiplying Counties

Issues of county growth and central city decline are very real in the metropolitan St. Louis area. The metropolitan area has expanded exponentially while the population of the central city has dropped precipitously. The structure of government has evolved, and the level of intergovernmental activity has increased, stimulating both competition and cooperation between the central city and the metropolitan counties.

Expansion

The U.S. Census Bureau uses counties as a fundamental unit in defining an MSA.[1] Using this definition, the geographic expansion of the metropolitan St. Louis area over the last fifty years is shown in Maps 4.1 and 4.2. In 1950 the U.S. Census Bureau defined the St. Louis MSA to include the city of St. Louis (shown in solid gray on the maps), two Missouri, and two Illinois counties. In both 1960 and 1970 the Census Bureau added one additional Missouri county to the St. Louis MSA. Two Illinois counties were added in 1980 and another Illinois county in 1990. In 1992 the Census Bureau added three Missouri counties.

Metropolitan St. Louis expanded so rapidly and so extensively that it outgrew several definitions of "district." The 1947 city of St. Louis comprehensive plan based its analysis on "the St. Louis Metropolitan District." At

Map 4.1 **St. Louis Metropolitan Area: 1950**

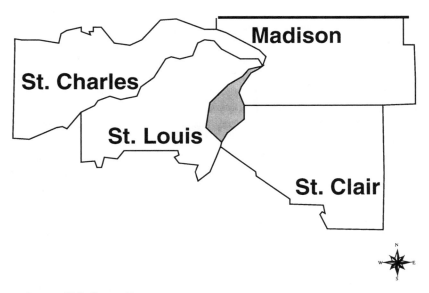

Source: U.S. Census Bureau.

Map 4.2 **St. Louis Metropolitan Area: 2000**

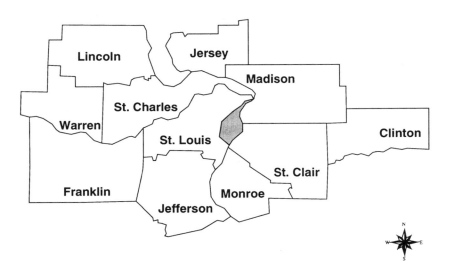

Source: U.S. Census Bureau.

that time the Census Bureau designated portions of Madison, Monroe, and St. Clair counties in Illinois and portions of St. Charles and St. Louis counties and the city of St. Louis as the Metropolitan District. The 1947 plan projected that in 1970 the population of the city of St. Louis would be 900,000, accounting for 54 percent of the population of the five-county Metropolitan District. As it turned out, the city of St. Louis was no longer sitting at the head of the table in 1970. Its population in 1970 was 622,000. The Metropolitan District had grown by two counties. Only 26 percent of the metropolitan population lived in the City of St. Louis in 1970.

In the mid-1960s the East-West Gateway Coordinating Council was established as the metropolitan planning organization (MPO) for St. Louis. As the MPO, the council was mandated not only to plan the region's transportation system but also "to help create a better sense of region among our unique local government constituency by acting as a catalyst to achieve consensus on regional issues, plan alternative actions, and aggressively pursue positive change in the physical, economic, and social environment."[2] At the time of its founding, East-West Gateway's boundaries were set to include the developed metropolitan area: the city of St. Louis and seven surrounding counties in Missouri and Illinois. With the addition of four more counties in the 1980s and 1990s, metropolitan St. Louis outgrew the coverage area of the MPO. Today the St. Louis region is divided among three regional planning organizations. In addition to the jurisdictions represented by East-West Gateway, Lincoln and Warren counties in Missouri are parts of the Boonslick Regional Planning Commission, and Clinton and Jersey counties belong to the Southwest Illinois Regional Planning Commission. In this instance, the table has not gotten bigger; there are more tables.

Demographic and Structural Anomalies

There are two contextual issues—one demographic, the other structural— that influence the relationship between the central city and the metropolitan counties in St. Louis.

A compelling element of the geographic evolution that impacts the relationship among the growing number of counties in metropolitan St. Louis is the almost stable total population compared to the explosive geographical expansion. The metropolitan counties pride themselves on growth although, in fact, for the past thirty years these jurisdictions have been in competition for essentially the same people, jobs, and capital. From 1970 to 2000 metropolitan St. Louis had a net increase of 147,000 people, less than a 6 percent growth in population. During the 1970s the metropolitan area actually experienced a population loss of over 42,000. The 6 percent net increase in the last thirty years is in stark contrast to the population gain of over 600,000 in the 1950s and 1960s. It is almost as if the geographic expansion is in inverse relationship to the population growth.

In the conclusion of Park's article on intergovernmental policy action in metropolitan areas, he discusses the governmental structure in St. Louis. Because the statistical analysis calculated less vertical than horizontal competition, he states that competitive pressures would automatically ease if the city of St. Louis became a municipality within St. Louis County. As the following discussion explains, that is much easier measured than managed. The lack of population growth in metropolitan St. Louis creates competitive attitudes and actions that compound structural issues.

In the nineteenth century St. Louis succeeded in taking two steps toward political independence that at the time were considered vital for economic growth. In 1822 it revised its charter to become the first city in America to directly elect its mayor. Previously mayors were gubernatorial appointments (Frisby 1999, 39). Then, in 1876, voters in the city of St. Louis approved a proposal to secede from St. Louis County, essentially saying they didn't want to have to sit at the table with anyone. Ironically, the perception at the time was that St. Louis would not grow beyond the approximately sixty square miles of the boundaries then set. Because the city of St. Louis is independent of any county, the judicial and revenue collection functions usually performed by a county government are part of the city of St. Louis. The eight "county offices" are each separately elected offices with separate staffs and are independent of the mayor. They are each elected to four-year terms. St. Louis is unique in that it is a home rule city, but it is not a home rule county. Its county functions and offices are subject to state restrictions on county governments and are not governed by the charter of the city of St. Louis.

In the twentieth century political independence turned out to be economic isolation. There were several proposals to bring the city of St. Louis and St. Louis County back together, and all were unsuccessful (Judd 2000, 14). Table 4.2 records the ballot initiatives. The history has been for city voters to approve the change and for county voters to reject it, although in 1962 there was a reorganization proposal that was rejected not only by city and county voters, but also by voters throughout Missouri.

While the city of St. Louis has been repeatedly unsuccessful in looking to its primary county as the means for structural reform, voters in metropolitan counties have consistently supported initiatives to modernize their governmental organizations. St. Louis County voters approved a charter in 1950 that modernized its government. The charter replaced the three-judge county court with an elected full-time executive and a seven-member county

Table 4.2

Structural Reform Proposals

1926   Consolidate city of St. Louis and St. Louis County: Passed in the city,
          failed in the county

1930   "Greater St. Louis" a metropolitan government: Passed in the city, failed in
          the county

1959   Metropolitan Service District: Failed in the city, failed in the county

1962   · Municipal County (constitutional amendment): Failed statewide, failed in
          the city, failed in the county

Source: Jones, *Fragmented by Design*, 2000.

council. County services were organized into eleven departments. The first charter left sixteen administrative leadership positions as partisan elected offices. Amendments approved by voters in 1968 and 1979 converted all the administrative positions to appointment by the county executive with approval of the council. St. Charles County went through a similar transformation after approval of a charter in 1992.

The opportunity for the city of St. Louis to reorganize its county offices requires that it first be granted authority as a home-rule county. In November 2002 voters in Missouri approved a constitutional amendment that would give the city of St. Louis county home-rule status. City voters will decide on a charter amendment in November 2004.

Changing Character of Demographics and Capital

Considerable attention has been given to the fact that older central cities have become the repositories of low-income persons. It is necessary, however, to examine the relative change in income between the central city and the metropolitan counties to appreciate the position of the city in regional affairs. Table 4.3 records how the proportion of median family income in seven of the metropolitan St. Louis counties has changed compared to the median family income in the city of St. Louis over the last fifty years.

In 1950 median family income in five of the seven counties was relatively close to that of the city of St. Louis. St. Clair County was almost at parity, just 1.5 percent less than the city. Jefferson, St. Charles, and Monroe counties ranged from just over 5 percent to just over 7.5 percent below city median income. Franklin County and St. Louis County were significantly different at over 28 percent below and more than 23 percent above,

Table 4.3

Metropolitan County Change in Median Family Income Relative to the City of St. Louis

County	Metropolitan County Median Family Income/City of St. Louis Median Family Income (in %)						
	St. Louis	St. Charles	Jefferson	Franklin	St. Clair	Monroe	Madison
1950	23.3	−6.9	−5.1	−28.2	−1.5	−7.6	8.8
1960	40.5	10.4	7.6	−9.1	9.0	0.5	18.5
1970	51.4	32.6	19.0	7.0	16.6	14.2	25.2
1980	65.5	58.3	37.8	23.0	26.0	49.3	40.3
1990	86.2	83.8	46.5	34.6	31.5	62.6	47.0
2000	89.2	97.6	58.9	53.8	45.4	91.4	56.0

Source: U.S. Census Bureau.

respectively. By 2000 only St. Clair County had a median family income less than 50 percent above the median family income in the city of St. Louis. St. Charles County increased to a median family income almost double that of the city.

Another indicator of the difference in constituencies between the city and the metropolitan counties is the number of one-person households. One-person households comprise the largest part of nonfamily households. For incorporated places of 100,000 or more across the nation, St. Louis City's proportion of one-person households, at 40.3 percent of total households, is tied for seventh largest. If the one-person household category were subdivided into one-person households over age sixty-five, the city's 32 percent would be second only to Pittsburgh's 34.9 percent.

All metropolitan St. Louis counties had more "traditional" (married couple with children under age eighteen) than one-person households in 1990. St. Louis City was the exception at 42,879 more one-person than traditional households (39.2 compared to 13.3 percent of all households). In 2000 the city's one-person households exceeded traditional households by 43,322 (while the city lost 17,855 total households). Although the number of one-person households increased in all parts of the metropolitan area during the decade of the 1990s, they continue to represent a far higher percentage of households in the city of St. Louis than in any of the metropolitan counties.

These changing demographics in household income and household composition isolate the city of St. Louis. When the metropolitan counties sit down with the city at the table of regional discussion, they find less and less in common.

The changing character of the city of St. Louis compared to the surrounding metropolitan counties is also seen in the structural environment. There is a concentration of population movement about forty miles west of the city. This area of intense development is in St. Charles County. St. Charles County was not in the first phase of post–World War II suburban expansion. It did not begin to experience significant population increases until the 1970s and later. The data in Table 4.4 show the total assessed value of property in the central city of St. Louis compared to far suburban St. Charles County over the decades of the 1990s. Expressed as a ratio, total property value in the city of St. Louis was 1.24 percent of the value of property in St. Charles in 1990. By 1997, the ratio for the city was only 91 percent of the St. Charles value and it dropped to less than 75 percent in 2001. Assessed value is important for several reasons. First, one of the criteria in Missouri state law for the classification of a county is assessed value; St. Charles becomes technically equal to the central city based on assessed value. Second, many local services, such as education, are funded primarily through property taxes based

Table 4.4

Comparison of Assessed Value (in U.S. dollars)

Calendar Year	City of St. Louis	St. Charles County	Ratio of St. Louis to St. Charles
1990	2,438,918,024	1,966,402,939	1.24
1991	2,477,277,432	2,053,600,867	1.21
1992	2,487,760,181	2,102,917,352	1.18
1993	2,669,680,540	2,150,370,910	1.24
1994	2,789,339,672	2,219,655,709	1.26
1995	2,785,220,679	2,435,033,835	1.14
1996	2,707,668,977	2,684,959,069	1.01
1997	2,759,999,398	3,045,308,530	0.91
1998	2,871,401,678	3,177,730,357	0.90
1999	3,005,394,940	3,544,870,980	0.85
2000	2,995,438,069	3,767,094,533	0.79
2001	3,196,243,121	4,308,569,584	0.74

Source: Missouri State Tax Commission.

on assessed value. St. Charles County moves into a superior position to fund these services compared to the central city. While Park explained changes in expenditure patterns as policy responses, an alternative explanation may be response to the changing metropolitan development pattern. St. Charles County can spend more than the city of St. Louis because it has more. Finally, there is the perceptual impact of a county, which was largely rural until thirty years ago, developing a built environment that is not only newer than the central city but literally worth more.

The transfer of value is not limited to St. Charles County. The assessed value of the combined counties of Franklin and Jefferson began the 1990s at 70 percent of the value of the City of St. Louis. They achieved parity with the city in 2001.

One Region, Many Tables

There has been a persistent reluctance to change the structure of metropolitan government as St. Louis has evolved; at the same time, however, there has been a very active process of changing governance. Table 4.5 profiles ten organizations that have been created within the existing structure of government to provide regional services. The authority for appointing who sits at the table of these regional organizations generally has gone to the counties.

These regional governance structures predominately operate in the city of St. Louis and St. Louis County. Until 1980 a regional service area composed of the city of St. Louis and St. Louis County made numeric, if

Table 4.5

St. Louis Regional Authorities

Regional Agency	Jurisdictions	Appointing Authority
East-West Gateway Coordinating Council	City of St. Louis; Missouri counties: Franklin, Jefferson, St. Charles, St. Louis; Illinois counties: Madison, Monroe, St. Clair	Illinois, Missouri governors
Bi-State Development Agency	City of St. Louis, Missouri counties: Jefferson, St. Charles, St. Louis; Illinois counties: Madison, Monroe, St. Clair	Illinois, Missouri governors
Metropolitan Sewer District	City of St. Louis, St. Louis County	St. Louis mayor, St. Louis County executive
Zoo-Museum District	City of St. Louis, St. Louis County	St. Louis mayor, St. Louis County executive
Community College District	City of St. Louis, St. Louis County	Publicly elected trustees
Convention/Visitors Bureau	City of St. Louis, St. Louis County	St. Louis city and county governing bodies
Cultural/Performing Arts District	City of St. Louis, St. Louis County	St. Louis city and county governing bodies
Convention Center/Sports Authority	City of St. Louis, St. Louis County	St. Louis mayor, St. Louis County executive, Missouri governor
Metropolitan Parks and Recreation District	City of St. Louis; Missouri counties: St. Louis County, St. Charles County, Illinois counties: St. Clair, Madison	St. Louis mayor, County executives in St. Louis, St. Charles, St. Clair counties, Board chairman, Madison County

Source: City of St. Louis, Planning Department.

not geographic, sense, because the majority of the population lived in those two areas. As shown in Figure 4.1 the population of the metropolitan counties outside the city of St. Louis and St. Louis County had grown to be almost equivalent to those two jurisdictions by the year 2000. This has stimulated considerable discussion, and some action, about enlarging the table to include more counties in regional service production.

Data from the U.S. Census Bureau and other secondary sources provides an objective assessment of the changing shape of and participation at the table of regional affairs. County officials in metropolitan St. Louis find themselves more and more sitting at the table of regional governance or appointing their constituents as their representative at regional tables. How do these changes manifest themselves in the perceptions of local government officials? Responses to a survey of county elected officials indicate deep differences of opinion with city officials about regional issues. Their perceptions often are in stark contrast to the opinions of their constituents. The following data were collected in a survey of metropolitan St. Louis elected officials conducted in the spring of 2002.[3] The survey asked questions about the connection between the central city and the metropolitan counties and about specific regional issues; the same questions had been asked in an earlier general population survey.

- County question: What is the connection between the quality of life in the city of St. Louis and the quality of life in your local community?
- City question: What is the connection between the quality of life in suburban counties and quality of life in your local community?

| | Counties | | City | |
| | | General | | General |
Question	Officials	Population	Officials	Population
Quality of Life Connection (in %)				
Not a close connection	39	56	36	31
Somewhat close connection	24	33	7	46
Close connection	28	7	50	11
Don't know	9	4	7	12

City of St. Louis officials see the closest connection between their quality of life and the quality of life in the metropolitan counties. An equal percentage of their constituents feel there is a close connection, but the majority of them feel it is only "somewhat close." A majority of county officials feel there is a close connection between their quality of life and that of the city of St. Louis (although they are almost evenly divided as to whether that connection is "close" or "somewhat close"). Most of their constituents, however, feel there is not a close connection. County residents were the most decisive

Figure 4.1 **Relative Service Populations, Core and Outer Areas, 1950–2000**

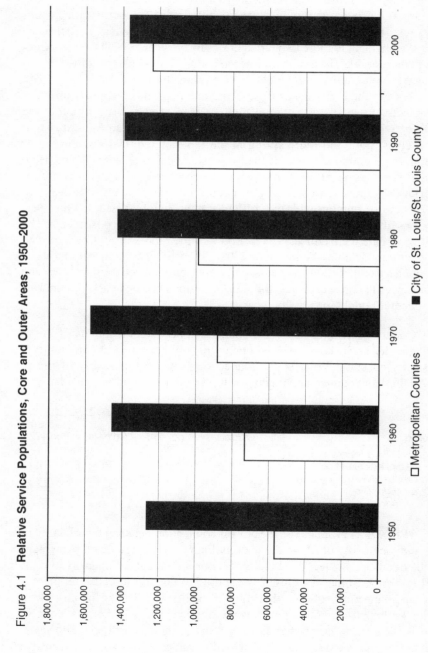

Source: U.S. Census Bureau.

of the four groups, with only 4 percent unable to answer how close the connection is.

- Both county and city officials and the general population were asked, "Which of the following statements comes closer to your point of view?"

	Counties	City	General Population
Shared problems (in %)			
Everyone should help to solve the problems in the city of St. Louis	48.9	92.9	58
The city of St. Louis should solve its own problems	51.1	7.1	32

Clearly the city of St. Louis feels the problems it faces are a regionally shared responsibility. A majority of the general population agrees. County officials are about evenly split between helping the city and leaving it to solve its own problems.

- Both county and city respondents were asked, "Would you favor or oppose a proposal which would have the better-off parts of the St. Louis metro area share some of their tax revenues to help meet the needs of some of the worse-off parts of the area?"

	Counties	City	General Population
Tax sharing (in %)			
Oppose	61.6	14.3	23
Favor	25.1	57.2	62
Don't know	13.3	28.5	15

While almost every city official felt there should be regional help for city problems, not everyone agreed that meant financial help. A majority of city officials, nearly 60 percent, felt tax sharing is a good idea. But while they were very decisive about regional help for city problems, almost 30 percent of city official respondents didn't know whether they favored or opposed tax sharing. The general population was somewhat more decisive. They favored the idea of tax sharing just a little more than did city officials. As much as city officials and the general public favored tax sharing, that's just how much metropolitan county officials opposed the idea.

- Both county and city respondents were asked, "Would you favor or oppose having the Zoo-Museum District include other counties in the

St. Louis metro area so that property tax dollars from residents of these counties would also help support these institutions?"

	Counties	City	General Population
Broader Zoo–Museum District Support (in %)			
Oppose	55.6		17
Favor	40.0	92.9	79
Don't know	4.4	7.1	4

A question was asked about a specific instance of tax sharing. There is a special tax district to support the St. Louis Zoo, Art Museum, and Science Center that includes St. Louis City and St. Louis County. All of the facilities are located in the city of St. Louis. When asked if additional counties should contribute property taxes to support these cultural institutions, city officials overwhelming favored the idea, as did a strong majority, almost 80 percent, of the general population. While 4 in 10 favored this tax proposition, most county officials opposed the idea.

- Both county and city respondents were asked, "As a regional infrastructure project, how important is the Lambert Airport expansion project to your jurisdiction?"

	Counties	City
Lambert Airport Expansion Importance (in %)		
Not Important	49.0	
Important	44.6	100
Don't know	6.4	

There was a question regarding regional infrastructure asked of city and county officials that was not included in the general population survey. As explained below, Lambert St. Louis International Airport is constructing an expansion project to increase the airport's capacity. When asked whether or not the project is important to their jurisdiction, every city official agreed, but less than a majority of county officials felt it was important to their jurisdiction.

Regional Control and the Role of the Counties

These perceptual issues form a backdrop for continuing evolution of who sits at what table to make regional decisions in metropolitan St. Louis. The following examples of both cooperation and contention indicate how the structure of governance continues to grow and the nature of the relationship between the central city and the metropolitan counties continues to change.

Airport

While a large percentage of county officials may feel the expansion of Lambert St. Louis International Airport is not important to their jurisdiction, operation and ownership of the airport has become a contentious issue, with repeated proposals to reshape the table of regional control. One of the complicating factors is that, while the city of St. Louis both owns and operates the airport, it is not in the city. The city purchased what then was known as Lambert Airfield in February 1928; it was located outside the city's boundaries in unincorporated St. Louis County, about eight miles from the city limits.

In the years following World War II, Lambert grew to be one of the nation's busiest airports. Operational growth ultimately meant physical growth. This required more land in St. Louis County and some of its incorporated municipalities. To promote further growth and to streamline operations, the City of St. Louis Board of Alderman passed an ordinance in 1968 that created the Airport Authority and the Airport Commission. The Airport Commission was given responsibility for oversight of airport operations. The ordinance allowed the airport to exercise increased control over its own planning and operation, distancing itself from direct city management. One result was the passage of a $200 million bond issue utilized for airport improvements in the years that followed.

Today Lambert is the fourteenth busiest airport in the United States with just under 6 million passengers for the first quarter of 2002. Although Lambert continues to be owned by the city of St. Louis, the structure of the Airport Commission and the Airport Authority has evolved over the past thirty years. The Airport Commission has seventeen members: ten appointed by the city of St. Louis, five by the St. Louis county executive, one by the St. Charles county executive, and one appointed by the St. Clair county executive.

In the early 1990s the Airport Authority proposed a major expansion: construction of a second parallel runway. This would require doubling the airport's physical size and the relocation of over 1,800 households and 400 businesses. The new runway would shift landing and takeoff patterns further to the west. This would lower aircraft operations and noise impact over eastern St. Charles County. There was a growing sense among the metropolitan counties that not only was the central city demographically different but also that it was becoming a political bully and that something had to be done to rein it in.

In 1997 Missouri state senator Steve Ehlmann sponsored a bill (SB 278) that would have effectively turned over control of Lambert to a regional governing body. The governing body would have included appointees from St. Louis, St. Charles, Jefferson, and Franklin counties and the city of St. Louis. The distribution of representation on the committee would have been based on the populations of each of these jurisdictions. The city of St. Louis would, however, have retained ownership of Lambert under the bill.

The proposal drew immediate fire from those opposing a change in the existing operational structure of Lambert. Francis Slay, at the time the president of the St. Louis Board of Aldermen, said Ehlmann's effort to reorganize control of Lambert "caught St. Louis City officials completely by surprise. Ironically, although the bill purportedly is aimed at regional cooperation, it was introduced without prior notice or warning to the city. As a result, city officials were backed against a wall and, from the outset, the city was placed in an adversarial position relative to its neighboring counties. The bill, therefore, sets the wrong tone for meaningful and productive discussions toward regional cooperation" (*St. Louis Business Journal*, February 24, 1997).

Ehlmann's 1997 initiative failed to pass out of committee, but he again sponsored similar pieces of legislation in 1998 (SB 623), 1999 (SB 123), and 2000 (SB 624). During the four-year period that Ehlmann was sponsoring bills in the state senate addressing Lambert governance, a fellow legislator in the House of Representatives was sponsoring similar proposals. Chuck Gross, who at the time was a state representative, sponsored House bills with wording similar to Ehlmann's bills in 1997 (HB 385) and 2000 (HB 1286). All of the bills failed to garner widespread support in their respective legislative bodies.

The proposed transfer of control of Lambert from the city of St. Louis to a board dominated by metropolitan counties resulted in acrimonious debate among partisans on both sides. State representative Quincy Troupe of St. Louis City labeled Ehlmann a racist for proposing the legislation. In a widely publicized radio interview Troupe complained that Ehlmann's legislation implied, "that black people are incompetent and incapable of running things." Troupe added that St. Charles County and its politicians "think that black people can't run anything." He went on to say, "They are overt racists and Senator Ehlmann, he leads the charge . . . he just needs to put on his hood and declare himself the grand dragon or the imperial wizard." Ehlmann responded to Troupe's outcry, characterizing his words as "racial McCarthyism" (*Jefferson City News Times*, April 6, 2000).

Ehlmann left the legislature to become a judge in St. Charles County after the 2000 legislative session. His successor, Representative Gross, sponsored unsuccessful bills addressing Lambert governance in 2001 (SB 469) and 2002 (SB 1046). When SB 1046 again fell short of the needed support,

Gross sponsored Senate Resolution 1719. SR 1719 was approved in the 2002 session of the Senate. It established the Senate select committee on the regional control of Lambert. While the bills sponsored by Gross and Ehlmann were specifically aimed at changing the operational control of Lambert, SR 1719 is broader in its exploration of the impact of the airport on the region. Testimony at the hearings held by the select committee documented that revenues generated by the airport were both regulated by the FAA and in an amount sufficient to cover only the cost of airport operations. Further efforts in 2003 to introduce changes in Lambert governance were not approved by the Missouri General Assembly SB564, which had been approved out of committee, was never brought to the floor for final vote before the end of the 2003 session.

In this case, competition between the metropolitan communities is not manifest in a program or service expenditure. There is an initiative to exercise control by affecting who sits at a table to direct management of a major regional transportation facility.

Parks

Table 4.5 showed that most of the "regional service areas" included only the city of St. Louis and St. Louis County. As metropolitan St. Louis has sprawled, so has interest in a broader base of regional services. A case in point is the Metropolitan Parks and Recreation District. The district had its start as an initiative of St. Louis 2004, a regional nongovernmental planning effort sponsored by the Danforth Foundation. It began under the rubric of "Clean Water, Safe Parks, and Community Trails," as one of the action plans that emerged from a strategic planning process to invigorate St. Louis on the centennial of the 1904 World's Fair. As a policy initiative it required legislation in Illinois and Missouri authorizing the establishment of an umbrella district upon approval by voters in participating counties. Financially it required a one-tenth of one-cent sales tax. Politically it required spreading the new money around. After a general population survey and extensive meetings with county officials and parks and recreation professionals, a proposal emerged to allocate one-half of the money to municipalities and counties for projects they would determine and one-half to regional projects approved by a district board. The district board would include representatives from the participating counties, with board members appointed by the county chief elected official. In November 2000 a proposition to create the district was on the ballot in the city of St. Louis and six metropolitan counties. The proposition was approved in the city of St. Louis and four of the metropolitan counties.

Although district board members sit around one table to make decisions, the structure is actually designed to evolve. The legislation authorizing the structure of the governing body of the Metropolitan Parks and Recreation District institutionalized a process of adapting to intrametropolitan population migration and economic distribution. Section 67.791 of the Revised Statutes of the State of Missouri was changed to state:

"The distribution of board members shall reflect such factors as the intent and purpose of the district, *each county's population, each county's financial contribution to the district*, the amount and quality of land dedicated to metropolitan district use in each county, the existing and planned locations of district improvements and organizational efficiency. *During the period between September 1, 2011, and January 1, 2012, and during any identical period every ten years after such initial period, the executives of each member county shall meet to determine the appropriate allocation of board members among counties.* . . . [emphasis added]

Authority to alter representation on the board of the regional district was placed solely in the hands of county executives. Every ten years, when new census information is available, there is a mandatory review of population and economic shifts within the region. This codified intrametropolitan migration and the need to be flexible over time in adjusting who sits at regional decision-making tables.

Downtown Revitalization

At about the same time the Metropolitan Park and Recreation District formed, a proposal for regional support of downtown revitalization was quashed. The Downtown St. Louis Development Action Plan was prepared by Downtown Now!, a public-private partnership. A collaboration of city and regional organizations led a two-year process of visioning and technical work by a team of consultants. Stakeholder and task force meetings produced a master plan for residential and commercial development and public improvements. The ambitious, detailed plan was estimated to cost $1.129 billion over a projected 1999–2004 implementation schedule. A breakdown of the development costs estimated the private investment at $751 million and the public investment at $378 million. The implementation schedule was severely limited by the city's lack of $50 million to $80 million a year.

To close the funding gap, a Downtown Revitalization District was proposed. The Downtown Revitalization Act (HB 1915/SB 827) was filed in the 2000 session of the Missouri legislature. The act would have established a Downtown Revitalization District including the city of St. Louis and St. Louis County. The district would have been authorized to impose (upon voter approval) a four-tenths of one-cent retail sales tax. The sales tax would have been deposited in a Downtown Revitalization Trust Fund. Expenditures from the fund would have been made only in "the area comprising the primary business district of the city with the largest population wholly within the downtown revitalization district, which shall not contain more than five percent of the total geographic area of such city." Management of the district was to be vested in a nine-member board of trustees. Determining who sat at the trustees' table was a complex structure of fiscal and political equity.[4] What the act proposed was that sales tax collected throughout the city of St. Louis and St. Louis County could support only the proposed projects in the Downtown St. Louis Development Action Plan.

An army of downtown civic, and political leaders supported the act. Speaking for both the county and its member municipalities, the St. Louis County Municipal League strongly opposed the Act. The league had three objections. First of all, St. Louis County officials did not accept the assumed linkage between public improvements and private investments as detailed in the downtown plan. The only guaranteed expenditures were from the trust fund. The private investment in the plan was based on the desired projects that came out of the planning process. There were no private developers committed to any of the residential and commercial projects. "If you build it (civic improvements), they will come," was too speculative for St. Louis County officials to support. Second, the inner areas of St. Louis County were experiencing depopulation and the attendant decline in their older commercial districts. The league would have supported an act that would have allowed expenditures from the trust fund to support revitalization throughout the district, or some broader definition of downtown than just the traditional central city downtown. The downtown St. Louis interests would not, however, negotiate access to the trust fund. Their master plan required all the funds that would potentially be raised by the sales tax. Third, the league objected that the burden for financing downtown St. Louis revitalization would fall primarily on St. Louis County. As shown in Figure 4.1, by the year 2000 the population of metropolitan St. Louis had decentralized to the point that the metropolitan counties were equal in population (and shoppers) to the city of St. Louis and St. Louis County. The league would have had fewer objections to the act if the district had included some or all of the metropolitan counties.

In the case of the Metropolitan Parks and Recreation District, there was interest in sitting at the regional table because participants in the counties had been consulted on the development of the financial plan and had a stake in the distribution of the finances. The downtown St. Louis interests wanted to invite others to the table to pay, but to have no access to the use of their money. The argument that what's good for downtown is good for the region just did not sell.

Setting the Table

The indication from this case study of metropolitan St. Louis is that counties are now, and are likely to become even more, present at the table of regional decision making. Metropolitan areas continue to grow geographically, converting additional counties from rural to urban. Not only do their governments frequently transform to modern, full-service organizations, but they also inevitably engage in regional intergovernmental relations. Metropolitan counties are separated from central cities by distance and by demography. When counties sit at regional decision-making tables with the central city, they can feel at odds with the city's interests because they serve such different constituencies. These differences can be manifest through attitudes and through actions; the actions can be competition or cooperation.

Park chose to examine the fiscal response of metropolitan counties in part because of a lack of information on the activities of counties. While there is not a database from which to easily draw comparative records, state legislatures are a fertile source of "activity" information regarding regional table setting. It would appear that the state often is the playing field for promoting metropolitan county and central city interests. Legislative bills that become law, and those many that do not, can tell much about the relations between metropolitan counties and their central cities. But while the state enables, county voters are typically the arbiters authorizing seats at regional decision tables. Election outcomes, therefore, are another data source for regional activity. Ultimately the decision about who sits at the regional table is left to the discretion of the county government leadership.

The governance structure of metropolitan areas is complex and evolving. Metropolitan counties are assuming a greater role in regional decision making, including decisions that impact the central city. While it is challenging to investigate, it is possible. And as metropolitan areas continue to grow, it is increasingly necessary.

* * *

The author would like to thank Jeff Roorda, Public Policy Research Center research assistant, who prepared a draft version of the Lambert Airport expansion issue, and Tim Fischesser, Executive Director, St. Louis County Municipal League, for his 2002 interview regarding the legislative history of the Downtown Revitalization Act.

Notes

1. The U.S. Census Bureau's 2000 Census glossary states that an MSA is "A geographic entity defined by the federal Office of Management and Budget for use by federal statistical agencies, based on the concept of a core area with a large population nucleus, plus adjacent communities having a high degree of economic and social integration with that core. Qualification of an MSA requires the presence of a city with 50,000 or more inhabitants, or the presence of an Urbanized Area (UA) and a total population of at least 100,000. The county or counties containing the largest city and surrounding densely settled territory are central counties of the MSA. Additional outlying counties qualify to be included in the MSA by meeting certain other criteria of metropolitan character, such as a specified minimum population density (at least 1,000 people per square mile of land area) or percentage of the population that is urban." Definitions can complicate an analysis of central city relationship to surrounding counties. Metropolitan St. Louis actually has six central cities:

Alton, Illinois
Belleville, Illinois
East St. Louis, Illinois
Granite City, Illinois
St. Charles, Missouri
St. Louis, Missouri

For purposes of this analysis, the central city will be defined as the traditional and largest central city area, the city of St. Louis.

2. East-West Gateway mission statement. http://www.ewgateway.org/aboutus/Staff/ MissionStatement/ missionstatement.htm.

3. The University of Missouri-St. Louis Public Policy Research Center conducted the public officials' survey in March 2002. A survey instrument was mailed to the chief elected official and all members of the legislative body in the city of St. Louis and the metropolitan counties, a total of 145 potential respondents. Responses were received from 61 officials, 47 from the metropolitan counties, and 14 from the city of St. Louis, a 42 percent response rate. Data for the general population was taken from "How We See It," a report on a survey conducted in 1999 by the East-West Gateway Coordinating Council.

4. There was a complicated formula for appointing St. Louis County board members: Four of the six were to come from municipalities in St. Louis County, the other two from unincorporated St. Louis County; no more than three of the six could come from the same political party; and no two board members could reside in the same county council district "at the time of appointment." Trustees would not be penalized for moving to another council district once they were appointed. For the three trustees appointed in the city of St. Louis, one would be appointed by the mayor, one by the president of the board of aldermen, and one by the comptroller.

References

Bass, Bernard M. 1983. *Organizational Decision Making.* Homewood, IL: Richard D. Irwin.

Bollens, John C. 1969. *American County Government.* Beverly Hills, CA: Sage.

Connery, Robert H., and Richard H. Leach. 1960. *The Federal Government and Metropolitan Areas.* Cambridge, MA: Harvard University Press.

DeSantis, Victor S., and Tari Renner. 1994. "The Impact of Political Structures on Public Policies in American Counties." *Public Administration Review* 54, no. 3 (May–June): 291–298.

Downing, R.G. 1991. "Urban County Fiscal Stress: A Survey of Public Officials' Perceptions and Government Experiences." *Urban Affairs Quarterly* 27, no. 2 (December): 314–325.

Duncombe, Herbert S. 1977. *Modern County Government.* Washington, DC: National Association of Counties.

Frisby, Michele. 1999. "Separating the Powers." *American City & County* (November): 39.

Hays, Samuel P. 1964. "The Politics of Reform in Municipal Government in the Progressive Era." *Pacific Northwest Quarterly* (October): 157–169.

Jones, E. Terrence. 2000. *Fragmented by Design: Why St. Louis Has So Many Governments.* St. Louis: Palmerston & Reed.

Judd, Dennis. 2000. "City, County Cooperation Not New." *St. Louis Journalism Review* (February): 14.

Kettl, Donald. 2000. "The Transformation of Governance: Globalization, Devolution, and the Role of Government." *Public Administration Review* (November/December): 488–96.

Marando, Vincent L., and M. Reeves. 1993. "County Government Structural Reform: Influence of State, Region, and Urbanization." *Publius* (Winter): 1993.

Marando, Vincent L., and Robert D. Thomas. 1977. *The Forgotten Governments: County Commissioners as Policy Makers.* Gainesville: University Presses of Florida.

Martin, Roscoe C. 1961. *Decisions in Syracuse.* Garden City, NY: Anchor Books.

Meyer, C. Kenneth, and Charles H. Brown. 1989. *Practicing Public Management: A Casebook.* New York: St. Martin's.

Morgan, David R., and Kenneth Kickham. 1999. "The Changing Form of County Government: Effects on Revenue and Expenditure Policy." *Public Administration Review* (July): 315–27.

Morlan, Robert L. 1966. *Capitol Courthouse and City Hall.* Boston, MA: Houghton Mifflin.

Murin, William J., ed. 1982. *Classics of Urban Politics and Administration.* Oak Park, IL: Moore.

Murphy, Thomas P. 1970. *Metropolitics and the Urban County.* Washington, DC: Washington National Press.

Nalbandian, John, and James Oliver. 1999. "City and County Management as Community Building." *Public Management* (May): 20–22.

National Association of Regional Councils. 1995. *Working Together on Transportation Planning: An Approach to Collaborative Decision-Making,* May.

Orfield, Myron. 1999. *Metropolitics.* Washington, DC: The Brookings Institution.

Park, Keeok. 1997. "Friends and Competitors: Policy Interactions Between Local Governments in Metropolitan Areas." *Political Science Quarterly* (December): 723–50.

Pierce, Neil, and Curtis Johnson. 1997. *Boundary Crossers: Community Leadership for a Global Age.* College Park, MD: Academy of Leadership Press.

Rusk, David. 1993. *Cities Without Suburbs.* Baltimore, MD: John Hopkins University Press.

Savitch, H.V., and David Collins. 1992. "The Paradox of Diversity: Social Difference Amid Common Regions." *National Civic Review* (Summer–Fall): 326–34.

Schnore, Leo F. 1957. "Metropolitan Growth and Decentralization." *American Journal of Sociology* (September): 171–80.

Streib, Gregory, and W.L. Waugh Jr. 1991. "The Changing Responsibilities of County Governments: Data from a National Survey of County Leaders," *American Review of Public Administration* (June): 139–57.

Teaford, Jon C. 1979. *City and Suburb: The Political Fragmentation of Metropolitan America, 1850–1970.* Baltimore, MD: Johns Hopkins University Press.

U.S. Advisory Commission on Intergovernmental Relations Metropolitan Organization. 1993. *Comparisons of the Allegheny and St. Louis Case Studies.*

Wallis, Allan D. 1993. "Governance and the Civic Infrastructure of Metropolitan Regions." *National Civic Review* (Spring): 125–139.

Ward, Janet. 1997. "Can Two Live as Cheaply as One? (Consolidation of City and County Governments)." *American City & County*, Feb 1992 v107. *St. Louis Business Journal* (February 24).

5

ALAN F. J. ARTIBISE AND JOHN MELIGRANA

Regional Governance and Sustainability: The Case of Vancouver

This chapter describes, assesses, and critiques the governance of urban/regional planning in the Greater Vancouver Region of British Columbia, Canada. This region is an important component of the Canadian space-economy as it is the destination of choice for a significant percentage of migrants, immigrants, and economic investment. The study of urban policy formation and implementation provides insights into how, within this Canadian context, local-regional-provincial structures are coping with rapid demographic and economic change.

The chapter's objectives are fourfold. First, it places the Greater Vancouver Region within the broader North American context. City-regions, although unique in terms of their geographic reality, cannot be studied in isolation from the broader forces of global economic change. Thus, any urban policy for development or redevelopment is a local attempt to control forces that are often outside the region's direct control. Second, the chapter explores the historical evolution of local and regional governmental institutions and their mandates over urban and regional policies in the Greater Vancouver Region. It is important to take stock of the behavior and relationships of various local and regional authorities within the city region as shaped by a unique historical trajectory that presents both opportunities and constraints on future institutional reform and reorganization.

Third, the chapter describes the organization, functions, and characteristics of the key regional institution, the Greater Vancouver Regional District (GVRD). This focuses on one institution that has recently received considerable attention from other jurisdictions. Last, the chapter provides a critique of the GVRD's and other institutions' abilities and inabilities to formulate and implement urban policies to develop and redevelop the urban environment in the effort to prepare the region for future economic, environmental, and social challenges.

Figure 5.1   **Prospective Urbanization in the Georgia Basin/Puget Sound Region**

Source: Based on the Georgia Basin Initiative, BC Round Table on the Economy and Environment.

Growth and Change in the Greater Vancouver Region

The Greater Vancouver Region forms part of a larger bioregion, the Georgia Basin, that includes the areas surrounding Puget Sound in Washington State. The Georgia Basin–Puget Sound Region (often also referred to as Cascadia) is ringed by the crest of the Olympic Mountains, the Vancouver Island Ranges, the Coast Ranges, and the Cascades. The inland sea stretches from Olympia, Washington, in the south to Campbell River and Powell River in the north (Figure 5.1). The region is one of the most ecologically diverse areas in North America, containing a wide range of vegetation and fish and wildlife habitats of significance.[1]

In 1960, 2.6 million people lived in the Georgia Basin–Puget Sound Region. By 1990 that number had doubled. Expectations are that it will double again by 2020 (Greater Vancouver Regional District 1996). Notably, the city of Vancouver and the surrounding metropolitan area are affected by the pressures and trends of a highly popular, rapidly growing region. What has developed is a "Lotusland myth," where the forces of urbanization may be placing in jeopardy the reasons that draw people to this area. Growth on this scale and speed challenges conventional notions of how to manage and plan natural and man-made environments (Murchie 1995, 9–10).

Well over 50 percent of the province's population is within the British Columbia portion of the Georgia Basin. This region is the economic core of the province. It is also very significant in national terms as Canada's gateway to the Asia-Pacific region and as the country's third largest metropolitan area after Toronto and Montreal. The metropolitan Vancouver area is the overwhelming choice of residence for migrants to this area from other parts of the province, the country, and other nations. These facts, coupled with the Greater Vancouver Region's environmentally sensitive setting, pose tremendous planning challenges.

The population of the Vancouver metropolitan region increased from 890,000 in 1961 to 1.75 million in 1991 and is projected to grow to 2.97 million by 2021 (Figure 5.2). This will involve the largest absolute increase in population in the region's history. Over the past decade one-third of the population growth in this region has been the result of natural increase, one-third from net migration to the area from the rest of British Columbia and the rest of Canada, and one-third from net migration to the region from other countries (Baxter 1993).

Recent government reports suggest that a critical choice will confront the residents and the governance of the Georgia Basin in the coming decades: unplanned growth or managed growth (B.C. Round Table 1993). The outcome of the choice is illustrated in Figure 5.1. The former is a "do nothing" approach that will see rapid, unplanned growth wastefully using the land and placing a strain on the region's ability to provide a healthy and vibrant place to live and work. The second approach contains and manages growth to accommodate new development with the least amount of threat or damage to the natural environment. Thus, there are serious concerns, planning issues, and important policy choices to be made that require a comprehensive understanding of regional governance and regional government.

Downtown Vancouver, the metropolitan core, is at the western edge of the Fraser Valley on the shore of the Strait of Georgia and the Pacific Ocean (Figure 5.3).[2] It is the historic core of an evolving network of regional centers and an ever-expanding urban landscape making its way eastward

Figure 5.2   **Population Growth of Metropolitan Vancouver Region, 1921 to 2021**

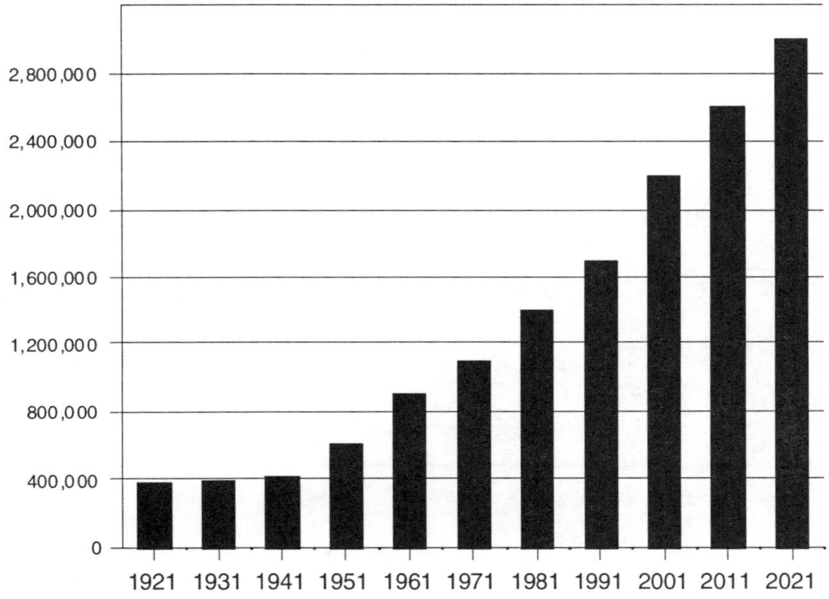

Source: Planning Department, Greater Vancouver Regional District.

along the Fraser River. The geographic context has shaped, to a significant degree, the pattern of development that is constrained to the west by the ocean, to the south by the international border, and to the north by the coast mountains, leaving the only option to be eastward expansion up the Fraser Valley.

The natural setting means that communities outside the Lower Mainland have limited direct access to other centers in the national and international economy. Thus, one of the primary economic strengths of the metropolitan Vancouver region is its gateway function for the rest of the province and for Canada.

Strength of the Central City

The revitalization of Canadian central cities poses unique problems and challenges from their American counterparts. The postwar metropolitan areas of Canada and the United States are both alike and different in terms of their internal spatial structure and the economic and demographic forces shaping metropolitan form. Canadian central cities are generally more compact and

Figure 5.3 **Greater Vancouver Area and Fraser Valley**

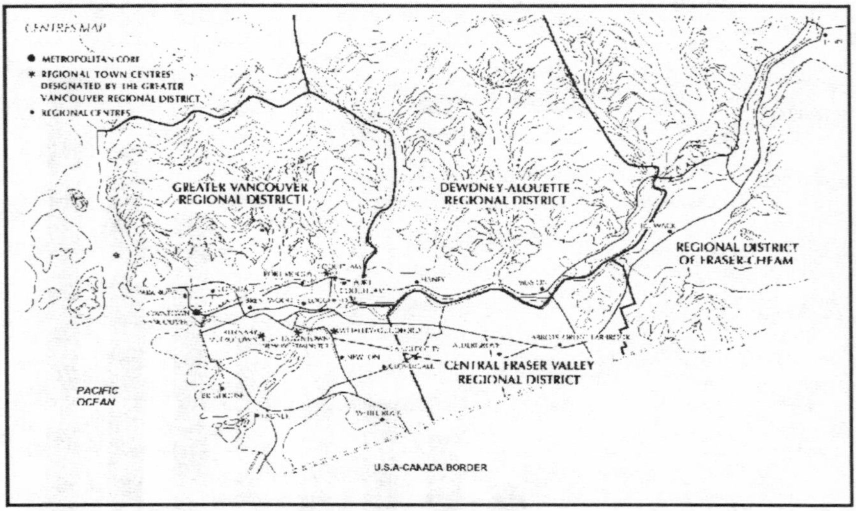

Source: Greater Vancouver Regional District.

of higher densities than U.S. central areas, translating into higher usage of public transit. The U.S. postwar investment in expressways has led to lowering density gradients at a faster rate than has occurred in Canada. Canadian central areas have maintained their hold on the middle and upper-middle classes, with the central city retaining an image of an acceptable place to live and raise a family. The phenomenon of "white-flight" to the suburban fringe that has shaped the social geography of American cities was not as powerful a force for Canadian cities. Also, the Canadian downtown core has proved a powerful draw for a variety of economic activities, while the American central city has shown trends toward uniformity or only key sectors congregating downtown (Mercer 1979, 119–39; 1991).

Figure 5.4 shows that Vancouver ranks eighth in terms of total office floor space and fourth in terms of total office floor space in the central business district (CBD) when compared with other North American metropolitan areas with over one million population. Thus, the Greater Vancouver area has been very successful in attracting office investment; it appears that the downtown core continues to enjoy being the preference of investors in office buildings (Figure 5.5).

Visible on Vancouver's skyline are numerous construction cranes busily erecting new office towers. This is evidence of the rapid economic transformation of Vancouver from employment in manufacturing, the hallmark of the industrial era, to the postindustrial service economy built on trades and

Figure 5.4 **Comparison of Office Floor Space in North American Cities**

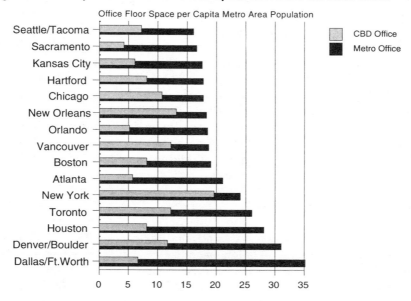

Figure 5.5 **Downtown Vancouver as the Dominant Office Location**

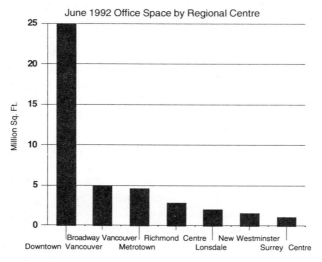

Sources: Major Centres in Greater Vancouver: Current Status and Policy (Vancouver GVRD, 1993), p. 15; City of Vancouver: *City Plan Tool Kit: Office Development* (Vancouver 1993).

services. The skyline of Vancouver is rather young, with most office towers built in the last twenty-five years to accommodate the growing number of office workers. Since the late 1960s office space within the downtown area has more than tripled to almost twenty-five million square feet. By the early 1980s business and personal services and trade had grown enough to overtake manufacturing as the region's largest employers (City of Vancouver 1993).

The focus of attention of building for the new postindustrial era favors the downtown metropolitan core of Vancouver (Figure 5.5). This has posed planning challenges in terms of the pressure on downtown Vancouver. Regional planning strategies are focusing on development of alternative or "second" downtowns in suburban areas. Meanwhile, continued office growth is placing pressure on transit, housing, and other services.

The Suburban Challenge

Vancouver's downtown core has, since the 1960s, been almost completely built up and occupied (with a few important exceptions noted below). The urban land-use pattern comprises a skyline with many office towers and a high-rise apartment zone in the "west-end," ringed by commercial and industrial land uses. The metropolitan core was and still is clearly dominant. Before the 1960s the land beyond the urban core, within the Fraser Valley, was primarily agricultural. A mixture of private and public decisions and investments, however, has lead to the development of a peripheral, polycentric land-use pattern (Hardwick 1971).

The concept of "edge cities" that exemplify the outward migration of office parks and office complexes within major U.S. metropolitan areas has not yet found its expression in the urban spatial structure of the Greater Vancouver Region (see, for example, Garreau 1991). This is not to suggest, however, that the suburbs, the areas to the east of the metropolitan core along the Fraser River (Figure 5.6), are not developing and capturing impressive commercial and industrial facilities.

High population growth rates in the regional districts next to the GVRD are the result of spillover. Population growth along the mainland coast to the north, that is, the Sunshine Coast, and the rapid urbanization of the southeastern portions of Vancouver Island, that is, Cowichan Valley, Nanaimo Regional District, and the Capital Regional District (centered on the provincial capital of Victoria), have resulted in an expansion and emergence of an interconnected regional economic zone centered on the metropolitan Vancouver area (Figure 5.7). In short, there is an expanding suburban peripheral zone, known as the Lower Coast of British Columbia.

The housing starts from both the Vancouver and Victoria Census

Figure 5.6   **British Columbia's Lower Coast**

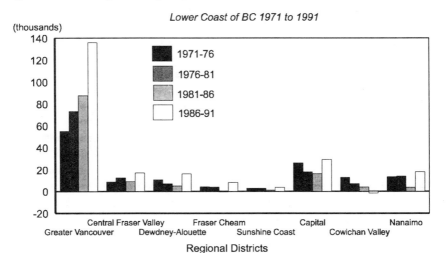

Source: Province of British Columbia.

Figure 5.7   **Net Migration by Regional District**

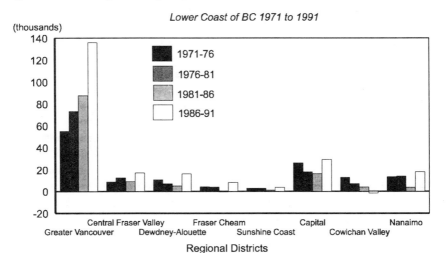

Source: Statistics Canada.

Metropolitan areas reveal the cyclical economic trends of the economy, with stronger trends evident during the late 1980s and early 1990s. The economic spinoffs from housing construction have been concentrated in the metropolitan areas of the province; however, recent trends (1991 and 1992) show that housing starts in areas outside the metropolitan areas have also increased (Figure 5.8).

Within this regional space economy, suburban municipalities immediately surrounding the city of Vancouver (Figure 5.6) are absorbing much of the "spillover" growth. Although the city of Vancouver is the largest municipality, with a population of more than 477,000 in 1991, its share of the metropolitan population has declined from 65 percent in 1921 to less than 27 percent in 1991.

Institutional Evolution

The evolution of metropolitan organization in the Greater Vancouver Region reflects the western and strongly populist sentiments of this geographical area. Following the populism of British Columbia's political traditions, the municipal level of government in B.C. has maintained significant autonomy and power compared with both the provincial government and regional institutions; and individual municipalities have tended to maintain a fierce independence from one another.[3] In this context the evolution of intermunicipal governance and regional government over the past eight decades has been based upon "ad hoc incrementalism, an approach that creates intermunicipal institutions only where continued delivery of a service by municipalities alone is unfeasible" (Cameron and Karlsen 1992, 2). In a positive sense this approach—"an upward delegation of municipal authority"—is adaptive and flexible, having evolved over a period of decades during which the province maintained an arm's-length, yet responsive, approach to local self-determination (Cameron and Karlsen 1992; Artibise, Cameron, and Seelig 2004). There is, however, a negative aspect to this evolutionary, ad hoc approach. For all its successes—and they are considerable—the evolution of intermunicipal governance has left many critical regional issues unresolved and the future of the region in jeopardy.[4] On balance, the Greater Vancouver Regional District is a notable North American example of the ability of local government to find innovative ways to meet the needs of its citizens. Nevertheless, several key challenges remain either unresolved or ignored, suggesting that for all its innovation, the GVRD may not be well equipped to successfully guide the region into the next century. At a 1992 policy workshop on regional governance in Greater Vancouver, for example, "the basic critique of the present system of intermunicipal confederation was that it had worked for "choosing

Figure 5.8 **Housing Starts, 1983 to 1992**

Housing Starts, 1983 to 1992
Vancouver, CMA; Victoria CMA and British Columbia

Source: Statistics Canada.

our future" (i.e., the consultative process of goal, value, and vision definition), but is not working for "conveying our future" (i.e., the implementation
of the identified goals, values, and vision of a livable region) (Hill 1992, 94).
In short the GVRD is an institution in evolution.

History of Municipal Organization in Greater Vancouver

In recent years there has been a lively debate about governing city-regions in
North America, and the literature on the subject is growing dramatically
(see, for example, Sancton 1994, Pierce 1993, Rothblatt and Sancton 1993).
Much of the analysis involves rather cursory examinations of existing systems and crude attempts to rate systems on ideal scales of effectiveness. In
this context several observers have suggested that while the "GVRD is far
from perfect," it nonetheless seems to "best represent" a middle ground and,
implicitly at least, one that might be copied elsewhere (Sancton 1994, 99).

This view, however, does not start from an understanding of the history
of the evolution of regional governance in the Greater Vancouver Region.
This context is critical since it explains in large measure the distinctive B.C.
approach of regional governance; an approach that is a result of a particular
political culture and tradition. It is also an approach that is not easily ex-
ported elsewhere (see Paget 1995).

The Early Years, 1911–1966: Single-Purpose Special Authorities

In 1911, less than thirty years after the city of Vancouver's incorporation in 1886, Vancouver and three adjacent municipalities formed a Joint Sewerage Committee. Provincial legislation followed this initiative in 1914 to form a Joint Sewerage and Drainage District. Similar special districts were created to meet other special and common needs of neighboring municipalities. In 1925 the Greater Vancouver Water District was created, and from 1936–1948 four health and hospital boards were formed (see Artibise et al. 2004).

The history of these districts and boards is an example of the gradual amalgamation of single-purpose bodies due to the circumstances, convenience, and personalities of both local politicians and civil servants. Notably, municipal participation in these and other single-purpose bodies was completely voluntary. This fact is significant since it has become a distinguishing characteristic of all metropolitan organization in the Greater Vancouver Region. In fact, the term "regional government" is rarely used, since it would imply a compulsory structure. In encouraging expansion of the original sewerage authority to include adjacent municipalities, a draft bill in the early 1950s ran into objections until it was redrafted to make certain that membership remained completely voluntary. In 1956 the new act was passed and the district's name was changed to Greater Vancouver Sewerage and Drainage District.

Weighted voting, a characteristic that remains in today's regional district boards, was also introduced in the early single-purpose boards. For example, Vancouver, which purchased the largest amount of water from the water district, was given more than half the votes on the board. Each of Vancouver' board members had several votes, while other municipal representatives had one each.

The focus on this early history of metropolitan organization in Greater Vancouver has been on the sewerage and water functions because they demonstrate an important pattern in metropolitan organization in this geographic area. They began as local consortia of municipalities and were later augmented by provincial legislation. They contributed two major characteristics in working and voting styles which persist to this day in the organizations that succeeded them: weighted voting and voluntary participation.

It is important to note, however, that other regional organizations existed in these early years. In 1938 medical health officers of Vancouver and adjacent municipalities established a Metropolitan Health Committee. In 1944 provincial legislation (the health act) provided officially for the committee. In 1959 a Metropolitan Hospital Planning Board was created to coordinate planning of hospital construction. In 1942 an intermunicipal committee was created to deal with park issues. It was called the Lower Mainland Regional Park Advisory Committee.

One of the most high-profile and controversial of the single purpose boards was one that dealt with land-use planning. In 1938 Vancouver and five other municipalities formed an informal planning body called the Lower Mainland Regional Association. In 1948 the Town Planning Act was revised to provide for regional planning authorities. In 1949 the entire Lower Mainland, containing twenty-eight municipalities, was designated as a planning region by the minister of municipal affairs. Municipal council members were nominated to serve on the Lower Mainland Regional Planning Board (LMRPB), which was to develop a regional plan.

The LMRPB did in fact create an official regional plan, based on the concept of "a series of cities in a sea of green" (LMRPB 1963, 6). The official regional plan was formally adopted in 1966. Municipal planning was required to be in accordance with the official regional plan, and an official amendment procedure was introduced. The plan continued to exist even after the demise of the Lower Mainland Regional Planning Board. It was officially updated in 1980 in a cooperative effort of the four regional districts which succeeded the Lower Mainland Regional Planning Board.

It is clear from this early component of metropolitan Vancouver history's that municipal independence has always been a cornerstone of any regional organization. The various regional authorities were accepted as an offshoot of local government and not in any way superior to them. The regional authorities all depended on voluntary participation by individual municipal governments and on a consensus-building approach.

The Middle Years, 1967–1983: The Province's Role in Establishing a Regional Organization

The introduction of regional districts marks a distinct shift in the provincial nonintervention policy in the general history of metropolitan organization in Greater Vancouver. The critical date was 1965, when the province enacted regional district legislation. The legislation was enabling in nature, empowering the lieutenant-governor-in-council, on recommendation of the minister of municipal affairs, to incorporate a regional district, to set its boundaries, to name it, and to assign functions. The minister went on to set up thirteen (out of a total of twenty-eight) other regional districts before creating the one covering the Greater Vancouver area. The Greater Vancouver Regional District was created in 1967.

The creation of regional districts is significant because it represents a provincewide approach rather than an effort to create regional government for the two large urban areas of the province centered on Vancouver and Victoria. The entire province was divided into twenty-eight regional districts, with the one in Vancouver being the most urbanized and the one that eventually provided the greatest range of services to its member municipalities.

As a concession to the traditional of municipal autonomy, the province included an "opting out" provision in the 1965 legislation. Under the regional district legislation, all municipalities would have to be part of regional districts, but they could choose to opt out of particular functions assigned to that district. "Undoubtedly this provision, which was very well publicized, served to reduce any lingering local fears about provincial motives and to allay fears of smaller municipalities and unincorporated areas about domination by neighboring large municipalities. Clearly the opting out provision would mean that the regional districts would be significantly different from other metropolitan governments" (Tennant 1980, 3–5; see also Tennant and Zirnhelt 1972).

The term used for the process of creating regional districts is "gentle imposition." This term is particularly appropriate for the imposition of regional district boundaries in Greater Vancouver. The former Lower Mainland Regional Planning Board was officially abolished, and four regional districts subsequently covered its territory. The original name for the district in the Vancouver area did not even include the word Vancouver. It was called Regional District of Fraser-Burrard—a tactic used to obscure the event of creating a Vancouver-centered regional district. In 1968 the name was changed to Greater Vancouver Regional District.

The district was created by being tacked onto an already existing single-purpose authority, the hospital district. The board of directors of the new regional district was identical to the hospital district board of directors. "The creation of the regional district was thus a most innocuous event" (Tennant 1980). In his speeches the minister of municipal affairs took great pains to deny that a regional government was being created.

The regional district structure allowed for the gradual addition of new functions at the initiative, and with the consent, of member municipalities. The only functions required by legislation were hospitals and regional planning, which the GVRD took on; it took on the function of borrowing for municipalities in 1968; and it took on the air pollution control function in 1972. Also in 1972 the Parks District was absorbed into the GVRD by mutual consent. The solid waste disposal function was transferred from four municipalities to the GVRD in 1973. The GVRD received the public housing function in 1972 and the collective labor relations function in 1974. The one function that it requested and was denied, in 1971, was public transit.

The Contemporary Years, 1984–1996: The "Wings Are Clipped and Regrown"

In a recent article on Greater Vancouver by two local experts, it was noted that the GVRD "is not a full-fledged regional government. It does, however, play an important—even a central—role in the governance of the metropolitan Vancouver region" (Oberlander and Smith 1993). This distinction between "government" and "governance" characterizes today's regional district pattern in British Columbia and is a logical outcome of the earlier history of single purpose boards and of minimal provincial involvement. It stands in contrast to metropolitan governments in Toronto and Winnipeg, for example, which involve integration of regional functions in a more powerful "unicity" approach. In recent years, however, the contrast between government and governance did cause controversy in the region, suggesting that not everyone was comfortable with the slow growth of the profile of the GVRD. Earlier, in the mid-1960s, the predecessor to the GVRD and other regional districts, the LMRPB, posed a threat to provincial power by engaging in open criticism of provincial land-use policies (Oberlander and Smith 1993). Again in the early 1980s, the GVRD planning committee was at loggerheads with the province—this time over a particular piece of land in the suburban municipality of Delta. The provincial cabinet supported the land's exclusion from the Agricultural Land Reserve (ALR).[5] The owner of the property was a longtime supporter of the Provincial Social Credit Party, which was then in power. The province responded by stripping all regional districts of their planning powers. All official regional plans prepared before this date were canceled. The province justified its action by saying that regional planning was redundant, in view of the advanced level of local planning then in place.

Thus, in 1983 the province revoked all regional planning authority in the Municipal Amendment Act and the legal status of regional plans was eliminated and replaced by local plans. At the GVRD the planning department even changed its name to development services department to reflect its new, diminished role. Nonetheless, the GVRD continued to work closely with member municipalities, providing coordination, research, and analytical services related to the region's growth and development.

It was from this rump of regional planning that the GVRD board began to develop a response to the very rapid growth of the 1980s. By 1990 the rapid growth of the Greater Vancouver Region led to an even more ambitious goal—the production of a new, updated regional plan, even though such a document would have no legal status. Given the history of municipal relationships in the region, the process was from the outset a "consensus, partnership-based regional strategic planning process." This process, called Creating Our Future, actively sought community participation and involvement and by 1994 resulted in the approval in principle by all member municipalities of a *Livable Region Strategic Plan (LRSP)*. Concurrently the Provincial New Democratic Party defeated the Social Credit government and came to power promising a return to "regional planning." In 1995 the province passed the Growth Strategies Act, which returned some of the regional planning authority to regional districts, including the GVRD. Finally, in 1996, both the GVRD and the province formally approved the *LRSP* as the GVRD's official plan (GVRD 1996).

It must be stressed, however, that the *LRSP* is a confederal document rather than a hierarchical one; its success depends upon the voluntary consent of all member municipalities. There is no doubt that the agreement of the members to the plan is a significant achievement. What remains in doubt is whether the implementation of the plan will be as effective as was the planning process (Artibise 1995a).

Current Organization of the GVRD

The GVRD in 1998 is the result of more than eighty years of developing and practicing the principle of voluntary membership, upward delegation of power, and local solutions validated by provincial legislation (except for the 1983 removal of regional planning authority). The GVRD is a partnership of twenty-one municipalities (twelve cities, six districts, and three villages) and two electoral areas. It occupies more than 3,300 square kilometers at the southwest corner of British Columbia's mainland. The GVRD board of directors first met on July 12, 1967.

According to official GVRD publications, "the role of the GVRD is to deliver to the area's 1.8 million people—half the population of B.C.— essential services that are regional rather than local . . . Working through the GVRD, the municipalities provide these services on a regional basis for reasons of economy, effectiveness and fairness. Yet the system is structured so that each partner maintains its local autonomy" (GVRD 1996).

While it makes little difference in day-to-day practice, the GVRD is in fact five legal entities that operate under a common umbrella: the GVRD itself, the Greater Vancouver Water District, the Greater Vancouver Sewerage and Drainage District, the Greater Vancouver Hospital District, and the Greater Vancouver Housing Corporation. They are all in the same offices, have a common administrative staff, and virtually the same board.

Organization Characteristics

Membership

All municipalities and electoral areas (areas that are not incorporated under the Municipal Act) are represented on the GVRD board of directors; that is, the board is made up of municipally elected officials who are then appointed by the respective municipal governments to serve on the board. There is no automatic representation by mayors or by councillors receiving the highest number of votes in local elections.[6] The two electoral area directors are elected directly from their areas during municipal elections.

Each area has one vote for every 20,000 population to a maximum of five votes. Thus, in 1997 the city of Vancouver—with a population of 521,000 in 1995—had a maximum of five votes. The village of Belcarrra—with a 1995 population of 647—had one vote. The 1997 board had thirty-one directors with a total of ninety-six votes. Notably, using the weighted-vote system is rare for the GVRD board; the vast majority of "votes" are by consensus.

Finances

GVRD funds are obtained from member municipalities by billing them for services rendered. This gives municipalities a measure of control over the level of services. The cost of most services is apportioned on a property assessment basis. On municipal homeowner's tax notices, a separate item is listed for most GVRD activities. Other regional costs are contained within municipal charges for water, sewer, and solid waste. Generally, GVRD services total about 12 percent of a property owner's total tax bill. More than 90 percent is for capital costs for hospitals, water, sewerage and solid waste disposal programs.

Administration

The regional manager is the chief administrative officer of the GVRD board and is appointed by the board of directors. He or she serves as commissioner under the Water District Act and the Sewerage and Drainage Act. Reporting to the regional manager are nine divisional managers and two administrators (Figure 5.9). The GVRD board has eleven standing committees, which represent the board's main functions, for example, Air Quality; Communications and Education; Sewerage and Drainage; Parks; Solid Waste Management; Water; and Transportation and Strategic Planning 1.

The GVRD board also elects, on an annual basis, a chair and vice-chair. In turn, the chair appoints, again on an annual basis, the chairs of the eleven standing committees. The chair receives an annual stipend of $28,788; the vice-chair receives $14,400. Board members receive $125 for meetings lasting four hours or less, and $250 for meetings of more than four hours. Remuneration varies according to the level of activity, with some committees being far more active than others. Average remuneration for board members in 1995 was $6,500.

Figure 5.9 **Administrative Structure of the GVRD**

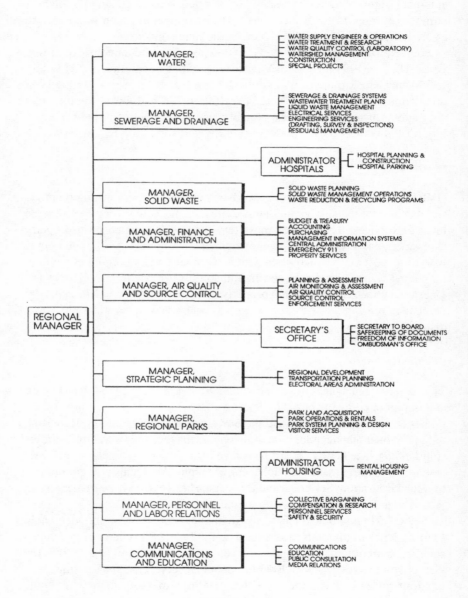

Source: GVRD.

GVRD Functions

In general terms the GVRD provides some twelve distinct functions including regional utilities for water, sewer, and solid waste; regional services such as parks, housing, and an emergency 911 exchange; and planning for growth management, transportation, health care, air quality, and solid and liquid waste. It employs about 1,000 staff and has an annual budget of over $350 million.

The Strengths and Achievements of the GVRD

As is evident from the history and current operations of the GVRD, the institution has evolved over time in a pattern of ongoing, gradual acquisition of functions (with at least one major setback in 1983). One analysis called this "do-it-yourself" regional government (Artibise et al. 2004). The original provincial legislation provided for only the basic structure of the organization and gave it the two mandatory functions of hospitals and planning; this grew to encompass some twelve distinct functions in 1998.

Does this gradualism and deference to municipal autonomy constitute success? The answer is a complex yes and no. On the yes side, the haphazard development of the GVRD has been quite successful in a limited number of areas, particularly when viewed in the context of the independent nature of municipal government in British Columbia and the generally passive attention of the province to municipal and urban affairs.[7] Compared with some other North American jurisdictions, the successes of the GVRD may not be highly notable, but in the B.C. context they are worthy of considerable attention. In particular, it is possible to single out the successes of the GVRD in several areas.

There is virtually unanimous agreement between both participants and observers that the most important and obvious successes of the GVRD are in the provision of certain key, basic services: water, sewerage, and drainage. The GVRD and its predecessors have provided good quality utilities on a regional basis for many decades and, with few exceptions, without major disputes over politics or finances. There are major current challenges, particularly in the expensive move to secondary treatment (a long overdue improvement), but the GVRD is well on its way to becoming a solid environmentally conscious region. Certainly, no matter what new structure a reformed or revamped GVRD might take, there would be few major changes to these fundamental utility functions. A few critics have noted that the district should be exploring private-public partnerships more than it has, and that it should be carrying out environmental goals more quickly, but overall there are few complaints in these fundamental areas (Artibise 1996).

114 METROPOLITAN ADMINISTRATION

Similar praise is focused on the GVRD parks function. While the original intention of this department was to complement local and provincial park policies and programs, the GVRD regional park function has come to dominate. While local authorities continued to spend on parks and recreational budgets, it was increasingly assumed that the acquisition of large parks was the role of the regional district. Parks acquisition is therefore an area where the GVRD has taken a leadership role. It is also a role that has given the district a good deal of favorable publicity (Oberlander and Smith 1993).

While the GVRD handled utility management and parks acquisition and management skillfully, these were relatively straightforward areas. In contrast, planning for land use and air quality directly infringed on traditional municipal areas, provincial jurisdiction, and the rights of individual property owners and citizens. Nonetheless, the GVRD has managed, particularly over the past several years, to record significant achievements in both areas. The *Livable Region Strategic Plan* and the *Air Quality Management Plan* are both recognized as high-profile, consensus-based documents that rival the best produced anywhere on the continent. Notably, the GVRD produced both plans without hierarchical planning authority, attesting to the fact that planning for certain areas on a regional level has been established as a staple of governance in the metropolitan Vancouver Region (Oberlander and Smith 1993, see also Tomalty 1997).

The GVRD is not a particularly high-profile organization. During municipal elections, politicians do not tend to make statements about the GVRD, since they are not running for election to its board. Since GVRD board members are mayors or councillors whom their own municipal councils subsequently appoint, politicians must first be elected at the local level. These local elections are the politicians' paramount concern. The lack of direct political accountability seems to free GVRD board members to take more controversial stands at the regional level than they might do at the local level, because such a stand is less likely to jeopardize their reelection chances.[8] When local politicians wear their regional hats, they seem freer to judge each issue on its merits.

By the mid-1970s most mayors were willing to accept a regional office which "entailed some commitment (and in the performance of which their fellow mayors would judge them) . . ." (Artibise et al. 2004). During the 1970s the GVRD leadership became an important status factor among municipal politicians. Also during the 1970s the GVRD undertook to develop support not only among politicians, but also among the public. The Livable Region Program was developed as a wide-reaching public participation process. Citizens' advisory committees on topics such as airport development and the future of oil spills in the region were examples of citizen involvement in policymaking.

In the 1980s and 1990s land-use planning (the Creating Our Future process) and air quality management processes again developed a broad consensus on regional goals. Both exercises developed an agenda for a wide range of initiatives in land-use and environmental planning. The fact is that lacking either local or provincial leadership, the region has become the (low key) focus for citizen concern about the future of the region. Given the confederal model of the GVRD, the decisions made have generally widespread support and are only rarely directly challenged by any municipality or provincially elected official. This evolution toward a leadership position is based upon three principles that the GVRD follows consistently in almost everything that it does.

The GVRD has the most comprehensive knowledge base about the past, present, and future of the region. The knowledge resource, sustained and nurtured through various jurisdictional and budgetary disruptions, brings to the regional table the powerful decision-making mandates: the municipalities for land use and local services, and the provincial government for transportation, environmental, and social policy.

Once at the regional table, the power of good and sensible ideas can seduce the decision-making mandates, provided these are advocated consistently and convincingly. An example is the concept of the regional town centers, which was developed in the mid-1970s and appeared to be a naive dream in the early 1980s. By the 1990s, through consistent and vigorous pursuit by regional and municipal planners and councils who kept the faith, Greater Vancouver's regional town centers were a reality attracting worldwide attention.

There are few examples where a thorough and honest decision-making process, often agonizingly slow, has not produced a strongly supported concept of the regional interest. To those who believe that such processes are too slow to make the decisions required for sustainable growth and the protection of livability, one can only observe that fast-track processes seem, at least in Greater Vancouver, almost always to derail. The most important lesson from Greater Vancouver is that the absence of a theoretically appropriate regional government is no excuse for inaction. Communities can forge the regional institutions they need by doing it themselves. In that respect, the Greater Vancouver Regional District is a notable example of the ability of local government to find innovative ways to meet the needs of their citizens.

In addition to demonstrable successes in the utility area, regional parks, planning, and regional leadership, the GVRD has claimed and can claim more modest achievements in such areas as the 911 service and a fairly high-profile public communications and education service. In a more general vein, it has played a key role in maintaining the integrity of the region in the areas where it has jurisdiction, no municipalities have opted out of the services provided by the GVRD, and it has also been able with modest success to expand its boundaries in an effort that deals with the effective urban region.

In short, within its very limited areas of jurisdiction the GVRD has an enviable track record. At the same time this enviable track record must be examined in a broader context that raises the questions of not how well the GVRD does in its areas of responsibility, but, rather, what is not being done within the region as it faces the challenges of the next century.

The Weaknesses and Failures of the GVRD

In the past three decades the major high-profile failures of regional governance in the Greater Vancouver region followed on the heels of the greatest successes. For example, the most successful of the earlier regional authorities, the Lower Mainland Regional Planning Board, produced a concise and inspiring document, *Chance and Challenge* (1963), which outlined the major factors that would influence land development in the Greater Vancouver Region. It also produced a formal land-use plan for the region, a plan that all municipalities in the area formally adopted. The very success of the LMRPB bred its demise. The provincial government felt the sting of LMRPB criticism of certain of its land-use decisions and ultimately abolished the LMRPB, replacing it with regional districts in 1967. The planning efforts of the LMRPB remained in the form of the official regional plan, but the organization itself failed.

Some fifteen years after the abolition of the LMRPB, planning was again the subject of controversy, once more following on the heels of a highly successful program. After development and publication of the widely supported Livable Region Program, the GVRD's planning department had a fairly high profile. As described earlier, controversial land-use decisions relating to the Agricultural Land Reserve angered provincial authorities. Eventually, in 1983, the planning function was eliminated from all regional districts, although the action was aimed primarily at the GVRD.

In both cases, these failures were political. In any power struggle between the regional and provincial levels of government, the province has prevailed. Indeed, in virtually every area of weakness and/or failure, the problem of the GVRD is a result of the province either acting against the region's interest or, more commonly, failing to act at all. Certainly that is the case in the most obvious and critical areas of weaknesses for the GVRD.

Issues related to transportation have a high profile in the GVRD. Both the *Livable Region Strategic Plan* and the *Air Quality Management Plan* devote a good deal of attention to transit and transportation issues, and the GVRD's education department gives considerable attention to traffic issues. In 1997 the GVRD renamed its strategic planning committee; it became the transportation and strategic planning committee. Yet, despite this high and growing profile, the GVRD has no direct control over critical transit and transportation issues. BC Transit is controlled directly by the province, while interregional roads are controlled by the province and local services by municipalities. The middle ground, interregional roads, is an area of confusion about who should make decisions and who should pay, particularly with respect to the supply of road and transit services. Meanwhile, the GVRD's approach is to combine its knowledge base with its limited mandates in air quality and growth management to forge a partnership with the province to advance regional objectives.[9]

The critical nature of these issues, combined with plans for a $1 billion new light rail transit system, have led both the province and the GVRD to begin to negotiate a new policy and funding arrangement for the region. During these discussions the GVRD's goal is to gain the legal and financial power to play the central role in regional transportation. It is too early to tell what the outcome will be, although both sides recognize that changes are long overdue. It is safe to predict, however, given the province's actions and statements to date, that the results will be incremental change and a further worsening of Vancouver's already poor transportation situation. Without radical change, however, the region's success in implementing the air quality and land-use plans will be in jeopardy.

Currently the strategic planning department collects economic data for the region. Beyond these basic functions, economic development is left to the province and to local governments. Notably, during the "Creating Our Future" process, a seminar on the regional economy was added almost as an afterthought, and no serious discussion of this critical function has ever occurred at the regional level. This is despite the fact that nearly all local experts noted that this was an essential regional function.

Indeed, in a recent article on the region's future, two noted experts commented on the region's unwillingness to promote itself.[10] What is more important, perhaps, in terms of the GVRD's weakness, is that this issue has no profile at the GVRD board or within the bureaucracy. Board members, fearful of competition from other municipalities, prefer the status quo; bureaucrats, fearful of disturbing the enforced calm of the status quo, stay silent. In the meantime, Vancouver has little chance of becoming what it sees as its destined future, a world economic center. But as one observer noted, to become a world center you need more than luck—you need leadership, a common plan, and a joint effort by governments, businesses, and other institutions (McCullough 1997, see also Kelly 1995, Artibise 1996).

That has yet to occur, and, furthermore, there is not even talk of trying to make it come about.

The *Livable Region Strategic Plan* is a valuable and sophisticated document. Its adoption by the GVRD board in 1996 was an important milestone for the region. But, in relative terms, the plan making was the easy part. The real challenge has now begun—implementing the plan in the municipalities. Under current regional and provincial legislation, there is no clear-cut implementation process or, more importantly, penalty for municipalities that do not implement the goals of the regional plan. There are, it is true, complicated procedures when there are disagreements, but in the end, the consensus approach prevails. When consensus is thwarted, little can, or will, be done.

The *LRSP* is a well-meaning attempt to sell regionalism through a partnership based on clear regional goals, which it is assumed will prevail over local goals. Nevertheless, the fact is that both provincial power and local autonomy can stymie the GVRD in its efforts. The province controls transportation decisions, and the province is not formally committed to the plan. Municipalities, on the other hand, control zoning and development permits. The GVRD's role is strategic, but when disputes arise, it is the province that must step in to resolve problems—and the record suggests that they are likely to favor municipalities over the region. In short, only the very optimistic suggest that the future for a consistent and comprehensive realization of the *LRSP* is possible.

Beyond a role in managing existing social housing units and a very modest role in health services, there is no profile and no discussion of social issues at the regional table. The advantaged, the young, and the high-profile ethnic groups clearly have trouble discerning or accessing the present arrangements or regional governance, let alone the disadvantaged, the aged, and minority groups. At a 1992 workshop on regional governance, many commented on the need for a process of devising and implementing a system of regional governance that relates to people in their daily lives (Hill 1992, 95). While the GVRD occasionally profiles social issues in the *LRSP*, the action on these areas of "community" are left in the hands of local government and the province. Given that such issues as housing and racism must be tackled at a scale larger than local government in an economically and geographically integrated region, this is a serious failure.

Except for the 911 service, policing, firefighting, and other issues of public safety do not fall within either the legal or even the political purview of the GVRD. As with economic planning, municipalities jealously and parochially guard their own services, seemingly fearful of losing out in any realignment based upon models of efficiency and effectiveness. The room here for major change is almost as acute as with transportation planning and transit delivery.

The current situation in terms of hospitals is one area where the GVRD is clearly and openly ready for change. Under the current situation the GVRD simply pays for 40 percent of the capital cost of new facilities, but it has a very minor role in siting decisions and no role in operations. One hope is that the province will pick up these costs in exchange for the GVRD's assuming a significant role in transit and transportation planning. This approach will be put forward in the negotiations with the province on transit and transportation.

In the provision of utilities the GVRD has developed a fair system based on the level of service provided. In other areas, however, the same model is not at work. Cultural, recreational, and municipally funded social services in the core area of Vancouver are largely or wholly supported by city of Vancouver taxpayers, even while they are enjoyed by residents throughout the region. Similarly, profitable inner-city bus routes subsidize money-losing services in the suburbs. To date, neither the province nor (not surprisingly) the municipally dominated GVRD board has ever discussed these issues of fairness and equity.

It has already been noted that the GVRD, as a body, has assumed a level of leadership in the region, particularly in terms of discussions of issues within its mandate. Nevertheless, while the present system of intermunicipal confederation is capable of tracking and identifying the regional implications of local decisions and those made by the province and federal government, it is incapable of ensuring that the regional interest prevails. The power of the mandate is sufficient to identify impacts but insufficient to take a proactive stance.

There are several important reasons for this critical weakness. First, the GVRD has a very limited mandate granted to it by the province. Indeed, it is not an exaggeration to say that the mandate is, in fact, the limited and conditional authority delegated to the district by member municipalities. And delegation can, and sometimes is, undelegated. It changes with the fortunes of the regional interest at the local ballot box. A second reason is that no one speaks—clearly, consistently, and loudly—for the region. The GVRD chair (together with all the other board members) is a part-time regional politician. He or she also serves as a mayor (the usual situation) or councillor of a municipality. The board tightly constrains the chair. Open election by the GVRD board fills the position annually. The third reason is that GVRD committees, where the real work of the body is done, are similarly constrained by the part-time chairs and members and annual appointments. A further constraint is that none of the GVRD board members receive any budget for staff accountable to them, and they are quickly overburdened by two jobs that can both be full-time. In this situation the GVRD staff takes on an inordinate importance, unshaken and unmotivated by close political attention. At best, the GVRD politicians give very broad political direction and the GVRD staff "really run the place."[11]

Related to these issues of politics are the themes of accountability and representative democracy. Observers and experts agree that, at best, one citizen in ten in the region would understand how the GVRD works, how members come on the board, or how decisions affecting their taxes are taken. Certainly few would understand or support the voting system where in one area (Lions Bay Village) 647 citizens have one GVRD vote, whereas in another (the city of Vancouver) a similar vote is shared by 104,210 citizens. The principles of representative democracy are strongly violated by the structure of the GVRD.

In this context it is no surprise that the regional voice is a muted one in Greater Vancouver. It is true that the GVRD chair does speak on the region's behalf to provincial and federal governments, and—occasionally—to other private and public bodies. But in the day-to-day events of the region it is rare for the regional voice to be heard from within the GVRD itself. Some people outside the GVRD attempt to speak on behalf of the region. But the GVRD chair, regional manager, and committee chairs are not heard often enough. If, in fact, good regional ideas are to triumph over bad local ideas, this situation must be rectified.

Conclusions

Regional Governance Without Regional Government

The GVRD is the result of almost eight decades of developing and practicing the principles of voluntary membership, upward delegation of power, and local solutions validated by provincial legislation. The challenges faced by this regional governance system, like those of most city-regions, are daunting. Operating in a globalized economic situation, severely constrained by the region's geography (mountains, the Pacific Ocean, and the Canada-U.S. border), and with minimal financial support from the national and provincial government, the region needs to take strong actions on a variety of fronts to preserve livability in the social, economic, and environmental spheres. As a regional entity that conventional analysts would regard as relatively "weak," the GVRD can be considered less prepared than it should be to meet these challenges. An alternative view, based on the heavy weather being encountered by "strong" regional governments elsewhere, would be that the GVRD is better prepared than most.[12]

A balanced assessment of the GVRD experience, however, must conclude that while it has done well under the circumstances, the Greater Vancouver city-region faces severe current challenges and is not, in fact, reaching its considerable potential. In short, the current GVRD needs to be rethought and restructured if it is to meet the goal it set for itself in 1990:

"Greater Vancouver can become the first urban region in the world to combine in one place the things to which humanity aspires on a global basis: a place where human activities enhance rather than degrade the natural environment, where the quality of the built environment approaches that of the natural setting, where the diversity of origins and religions is a source of social strength rather than strife, where people control the destiny of the community, and where the basics of food, clothing, shelter, security and useful activity are accessible to all" (GVRD 1996). Within this self-proclaimed context the GVRD faces the important question of regional reform and policy implementation.

The Need for Reform

The GVRD works well within a political tradition where local autonomy is very strong and provincial involvement in municipal and urban affairs is very weak. Nonetheless, even the strongest proponents and designers of the current system admit that "the challenges of growth will require increased provincial direction for local government and devolution of the powers that regional governments need to manage growth and change.[13]

Whenever regional governance in the GVRD is discussed formally, as at a policy workshop attended by over two hundred persons in 1992, there is lively debate and recognition about the shortcoming of the current system. "A livable region was thought to require a system of regional governance that is effective, accessible, responsive, affordable, accountable and equitable. To the participants in the seven working groups, the present system did not appear to embody these principles to any great degree. The basic critique of the present system of intermunicipal confederation was that it had worked for choosing our future (i.e., the consultative process of goal, value and vision definition) but it is not working for conveying our future (i.e., the implementation of the identified goals, values and visions of a livable region)" (Hill 1992, 94).

Notwithstanding these views, policy workshop attendees had a contradictory view about changing the current system. They displayed a "marked attachment to the current system." Generally, the attendees concluded that the present system was not doing a bad job and that it needed "minor realignments" rather than a "major overhaul." Most participants "seemed to prefer familiar problems to unfamiliar solutions" (Hill 1992, 94).

This view of general support for the status quo was shared by virtually all the persons interviewed for this study. Most agreed there were serious problems and shortcomings, but there was little appetite for radical change. It was also widely agreed that there was very little chance of the GVRD reforming itself; change would have to be forced on it by the province.

Two main concerns have been identified in the analysis of the GVRD system. The first relates to the present system of delegated upward authority as opposed to the alternative of legislated and integrated regional authority (i.e., regional government). The merits of the system of delegated authority rest on the importance of local autonomy, diversity, and the preservation of the distinct identity of member municipalities. The demerits relate to the system's ineffectiveness in ensuring that regional concerns are taken into account in local decisions. The second concern relates to accountability and the relationship between regional and municipal powers. The issue is whether indirect accountability (through elected representatives of member municipalities) serves the region well or whether a directly elected regional board would better serve the region.

Many, indeed most, of the weaknesses and failures of the GVRD can be attributed to its lack of a clear mandate; generally it can do only what it is delegated to do by its members (a fact that is mentioned at virtually every board meeting). This is a failure of member municipalities to recognize both the need to enlarge the mandate under changed circumstances and the need to give the GVRD the power to enforce the consensus once it has been achieved.

The failures and weaknesses of the GVRD are also the result of the inability of successive provincial governments to recognize that in the changed circumstances of the 1990s, British Columbia's most important metropolitan region—indeed, the province's economic engine and face to the country and the world—requires a revamped, comprehensive, and directly accountable regional government if it is to thrive in the coming decades. As it stands, it is no exaggeration to say that Greater Vancouver is living on borrowed time and—sooner or later—must reorganize itself into an effective city-region to face the challenges of global competitiveness. The sustainability challenge—thinking globally and acting locally—must be revised to allow—in fact to encourage—regional actions. Only at this level can many of the social, economic, and environmental challenges be turned into opportunities.

Notes

1. For a detailed discussion of Cascadia see Artibise 1994, Artibise et al. 1996, Artibise 1995b, and B.C. Round Table 1993.
2. In 1997 the regional districts of Dewdney-Alouette, Fraser-Cheam, and

Central Fraser Valley were amalgamated to form the new Fraser Valley Regional District. For the purposes of this chapter, we have utilized the organization in place until 1997.

3. During the preparation of this chapter there were two notable examples of this fierce independence. One is the ongoing debate about possible amalgamation between the city of North Vancouver and the district of North Vancouver. While the city is in favor of amalgamation, neither the district nor the province is prepared to actively pursue the matter (see *Vancouver Sun* 1997a, B3. Similarly, in a later story in the *Vancouver Sun* (1997b), the city of White Rock, which separated from the city of Surrey in 1957, reiterated its "fierce independence" from its larger and surrounding neighbor. The point is that there is very little appetite for municipal amalgamation or rationalization in the region.

4. For three such views see Seelig and Artibise 1991, Jones 1996, and Artibise 1996. All three studies rely on wide-ranging interviews and thus represent more than the views of the authors. In the same vein a 1992 policy workshop on regional governance concluded that "all the working groups were effusive in their critiques of the present system" (Hill 1992, 94).

5. The ALR was established in 1972 to protect agricultural land. Development of land in the reserve was impossible unless the land was excluded by the decision of an independent, provincially appointed Agricultural Land Commission (ALC). The cabinet overturned the decision of both the GVRD and the ALC.

6. In January 1997, for example, the recently reelected mayor of the city of Richmond and immediate past-chair (1994–1996) of the board of directors of the GVRD was not selected by his council to serve on the GVRD.

7. B.C., unlike many other Canadian provinces, has no Ministry of Urban Affairs. The Ministry of Municipal Affairs deals with all municipal issues, and Greater Vancouver and other urban regions receive no special attention.

8. The exceptions are the electoral area directors, who are directly elected.

9. The GVRD has devoted a good deal of time and resources on transportation planning. Some of the results can be found in the Transport 2021 reports.

10. The two experts are John Hansen of the Vancouver Board of Trade and John Wiebe of the Vancouver Economic Development Commission. They are quoted in McCullough (1997, 151–53).

11. A sentiment that was expressed by many persons interviewed for this study.

12. Interview with Ken Cameron, Manager, Strategic Planning, GVRD, 1996.

13. Paget 1995. This view was also confirmed in an interview.

References

Artibise, Alan F. J. 1994. *Opportunities for Achieving Sustainability in Cascadia*, Publication 1. Vancouver: International Centre for Sustainable Cities.

———. 1995a. "Our New Regional Plan Needs a Plan—To Police Planners and Politicians," Op-Ed article. *Vancouver Sun*, November 9.

———. 1995b. "Achieving Sustainability in Cascadia: An Emerging Model of Urban Growth Management in the Vancouver-Seattle-Portland Corridor," in *North American Cities and the Global Economy*, ed. P. Kersl and G. Gappert, pp. 221–250. Beverly Hills, CA: Sage.

————. 1996. "Regional Governance: Without Regional Government: The Strengths and Weaknesses of the GVRD." Report Prepared for the Regional Municipality of Ottawa-Carleton, Vancouver.

Artibise, Alan F. J., E. Seltzer, and A. Verney Moudon. 1996. "Cascadia," in *Cities in Our Future*, ed. Robert Geddes, Washington, DC: Island.

Artibise, Alan F. J., Ken Cameron, and Julie Seelig. 2004. "Metropolitan Organization in Greater Vancouver," in *Metropolitan Governance Without Metropolitan Government*, ed. D. Phares, pp. 147–76. Aldershot: Ashgate.

Baxter, David. 1993. *Natural Increase, Migration and Immigration as Components of the Population Growth in the Metropolitan Vancouver Region*. Burnaby, BC: Strategic Planning Department, Greater Vancouver Regional District.

B.C. Round Table on the Environment and the Economy. 1993. *Georgia Basin Initiative: Creating a Sustainable Future*, Victoria.

Cameron, Ken, and Erik Karlsen. 1992. "Regional Governance and Improved Regional Coordination: The Contest," in *Conveying Our Future: Proceedings of the Policy Workshop on Regional Governance in the Pacific Fraser Region*, ed. J. Hill, pp. 2–12. Vancouver: School of Community and Regional Planning, University of British Columbia.

City of Vancouver. 1993. *CityPlan Tool Kit: Office Development*. Vancouver.

Garreau, Joel. 1991. *Edge City: Life on the New Frontier.* New York: Doubleday.

Greater Vancouver Regional District. 1996. *Livable Region Strategic Plan*. Burnaby, BC.

Hardwick, Walter. 1971. "Vancouver: The Emergence of a 'Core-Ring' Urban Pattern." *Geographical Approaches to Canadian Problems*, ed. R.L. Gentilcone, pp. 112–19. Scarborough, BC: Prentice Hall.

Hill, J., ed. 1992. *Conveying Our Future: Proceedings of the Policy Workshop on Regional Governance in the Pacific Fraser Region*. Vancouver: School of Community and Regional Planning, University of British Columbia.

Jones, D. 1996. "The World's Next Great City?" *Report on Business Magazine*, November.

Kelly, M.J. 1995. *The Role of Canadian Municipalities in Economic Development*. Toronto: ICURR.

Lower Mainland Regional Planning Board. 1963. *Chance and Challenge*. Vancouver.

McCullough, M. 1997. "Are We There Yet?" *BC Business* (April 1997): 151–53.

Mercer, John. 1979. "On Continentalism, Distinctiveness and Comparative Urban Geography: Canadian and American Cities." *Canadian Geographer* 23, no. 2: 119–39

————. 1991. "The Canadian City in Continental Context: Global and Continental Perspectives on Canadian Urban Development," in *Canadian Cities in Transition*, ed. T. Bunting and P. Filion, pp. 55–75. Toronto: Oxford University Press.

Murchie, Graham. 1995. "Looking Beyond Vancouver's Picture Postcard Beauty." *Plan Canada* 35, no. 3 (May): 9–10.

Oberlander, P.H., and Patrick J. Smith. 1993. "Governing Metropolitan Vancouver: Regional Intergovernmental Relations in British Columbia," in *Metropolitan Governance: American/Canadian Intergovernmental Perspective*, ed. D.N. Rothblatt and A. Sancton, 329–373. Berkeley: Institute of Governmental Studies Press.

Paget, Gary. 1995. "Managing Growth in Metropolitan Areas: Governance and Planning with and Without Hierarchy." Paper presented to Annual American Association of Planners and Canadian Institute of Planners Conference, Toronto (April).

Pierce, Neil. 1993. *Citistates*. Washington, DC: Seven Locks.

Rothblatt, D.N., and A. Sancton. 1993. *Metropolitan Governance: American/ Canadian Intergovernmental Perspectives*. Berkeley: Institute of Governmental Studies Press.

Sancton, Andrew. 1994. *Governing Canada's City-Regions: Adapting Form to Function*. Montreal: Institute for Research on Public Policy.

Seelig, Michael, and Alan F.J. Artibise. 1991. *From Desolation to Hope: The Pacific Fraser Region in 2010*. Vancouver: School of Community and Regional Planning, University of British Columbia.

Tennant, Paul. 1980. "The Evolution of Regional Government in Greater Vancouver, 1914–1979." Unpublished manuscript, pp. 3–5.

Tennant, Paul, and David Zirnhelt. 1972. "The Emergence of Metropolitan Government in Greater Vancouver." *BC Studies* 15 (Autumn).

Tomalty, Ray. 1997. *The Compact Metropolis: Growth Management and Intensification in Vancouver, Toronto and Montreal*. Toronto: Intergovernmental Committee on Urban and Regional Research.

Vancouver Sun. 1997a. March 14, p. B3.

———. 1997b. April 14.

6

Arthur C. Nelson and Raymond J. Burby

The Effect of Regional Smart Growth on Metropolitan Growth and Construction: A Preliminary Assessment

Since the end of World War II the United States has seen a transformation of its built landscape. Downtown and central city dominance has given way to urban sprawl, leading to what some now call the "edgeless city" (Lang 2003). Many bemoan this transformation (e.g., Kunstler 1994) while others consider it to be the natural course of events (e.g., Mills and Hamilton 1989). In recent decades some local, regional, and even state governments have embarked on various "smart growth" initiatives to rein in urban sprawl such as statewide growth management and urban containment (see Nelson and Duncan 1995).

In this chapter we engage in a preliminary assessment of the extent to which regional smart growth efforts affect growth and construction measured at the metropolitan scale over the period 1985 through 1995. We begin with a review of urban sprawl and the role of smart growth in managing it. We continue with preliminary assessments of the differences between regional smart growth and business as usual on metropolitan growth and construction activity. We conclude with general observations but caution that this is merely a preliminary assessment.

Urban Sprawl and Regional Smart Growth

Urban sprawl is fueled by pull and push factors. Among the pull factors are a variety of economic, technological, cultural, and public policy influences. Certainly, exurbia exists because of the shift of jobs from central cities and first-tier suburbs to the suburban employment ring of metropolitan areas. The problem in many central cities and close-in suburbs is a dearth of available land at competitive prices; this is not a problem in exurbia. New development is thus lured to or pulled into exurbia. The result is that formerly rural areas have become accessible to workers looking for new places in which to live.

Population and employment deconcentration is made possible largely through significant improvements in technology. While neither a push nor pull factor per se, new technologies such as the personal computer, cellular telephones, satellite linkages, and the Internet allow millions of people to live and work practically anywhere.

Economic and technological changes merely make living farther out possible but do not explain households' underlying desire to do so. What may drive households farther out is cultural antiurbanism, characterized by the Jeffersonian "gentleman farmer" ideal—a potent pull factor. While households may be pulled to the rural landscape for cultural reasons, many others are pushed in their search for locations allowing them to escape from the noise, congestion, pollution, micro-climatic conditions, ethnic and racial diversity, and crime associated with urban areas.

Facilitating urban sprawl are a variety of public policies supporting a vast highway system, home mortgage programs and tax subsidies, underpriced fossil fuels, and disaster insurance or relief that enable development of hazardous and sensitive landscapes. Bourne (1980) argues that is it the implicit urban policy of the United States to favor development of outlying areas over reuse, redevelopment, or rehabilitation of central areas.

Another important push factor is uncoordinated development within metropolitan regions. Most regions do not engage in coordinated land-use planning, with the result that local governments—usually cities and counties—go it alone in fashioning their development patterns. The consequence is that while some attempt to accommodate their proportionate share of a region's growth, many others cater to only the kind and amount of the region's development they wish to have. The rest is pushed outward. How much of exurbanization is attributed to pull or push factors is not known.

The effect of urban sprawl has become of concern to a growing number of public policy-makers. Urban sprawl requires that resources be plowed into public services, facilities, and transportation systems that are very costly to provide over large areas and at low density. For example, in terms of roads, urban sprawl may exacerbate existing or imminent problems. One outcome is more and longer trips. Moreover, because urban sprawl is highly diffuse, connecting outermost areas to employment centers via bus or rail lines is not cost-effective. Alternatives such as pricing schemes to discourage urban sprawl or change travel behavior may be difficult to implement. At the same time the presence of households in sprawling areas may encourage even more deconcentration of employment. This appears to be happening in the manufacturing industries.

There is also the concern that urban sprawl will eventually demand, or require, urban level services spread over vast territory and at high cost. Households locating at the suburban fringe may enjoy low taxes that pay for low-quality services, or no services, but in time they may demand higher-quality services. More insidious would be the proliferation of private on-site or small-scale water and wastewater systems that, over time, fail and need to be replaced with public systems. At low development densities, these systems would cost considerable amounts of money. Suburban fringe residents may pay for some of the cost, but much of the cost could be borne by small-town residents who have the systems, state agencies under health hazard provisions, and the federal government.

Ultimately there is the concern that urban sprawl weakens efficiencies associated with urban agglomeration. That is the concern of this analysis.

In response to urbanization patterns leading to what may be termed urban sprawl, dozens of local, regional, and state governments have embarked on smart growth. Although perceived popularly in such forms as the "new urbanism" and "transit-oriented developments," for our purposes we consider regional smart growth initiatives that aim to contain urban sprawl or at least reduce its extent. At its heart regional smart growth aims to synchronize key public facilities with urban development pressures, preserve open spaces, and facilitate development in ways that preserves public goods, minimizes public costs, and accounts for development impacts by those who cause them (Nelson and Duncan 1995, Nelson and Dawkins 2002).

Does regional smart growth improve the metropolitan economy? This preliminary assessment has two elements. The first evaluates the difference in growth rates among the thirty-five largest metropolitan statistical areas (MSAs) or largest primary metropolitan statistical areas (PMSAs) in consolidated metropolitan statistical areas (CMSAs) during the 1990s with respect to "business-as-usual" (non-smart growth) and regional smart growth metropolitan areas. Regional smart growth metropolitan areas are those with metropolitan-wide growth management or growth management in large sub-metropolitan areas such as counties. The second element uses a sample of data collected for a study sponsored by the National Science Foundation to compare new construction activities between a group of business-as-usual and regional smart growth metropolitan areas. This is followed by a discussion suggesting results are consistent with expectations that regional smart growth generates measurable benefits for the metropolitan economy. Policy implications and qualifications combined with a call for more rigorous research conclude this preliminary assessment.

Does Regional Smart Growth Dampen Development?

We apply this question to the thirty-five largest MSAs as ranked by the U.S. Census Bureau (http://www.census.gov/population/cen2000/phc-t3/tab03.pdf). While the rankings include consolidated MSAs, we believe it was more appropriate for this analysis to focus on contiguous metropolitan/urban fields, so the largest MSAs or primary MSAs within CMSAs as defined in 1990 were used to analyze population and urbanized area changes from 1990 to 2000. Future research may be more inclusive and include all MSAs/PMSAs of more than 1 million population in 2000. Table 6.1 shows the MSAs/PMSAs, ranked by their population growth rate in the 1990s. This table also shows the degree to which urban containment is employed, whether none, natural, weak, or strong based on work recently reported by Nelson and Dawkins (2002).

Only about a third of metropolitan areas analyzed utilize some type of regional smart growth. Los Angeles, Las Vegas, and Phoenix are naturally contained. We say "naturally" because in the case of Los Angeles, oceans and mountains rising to more than 10,000 feet hem development into a basin.[1] Las Vegas and Phoenix are naturally contained because of public ownership of vast amounts of land around them, and water that is expensive to acquire, treat, and distribute. Eight metropolitan areas have what we call regional smart growth: Orlando, San Francisco, Twin Cities, Miami, Portland, Sacramento, San Diego, and Seattle. We included MSAs/PMSAs that employed containment policies since 1990, which means we classify Denver, Milwaukee, and Philadelphia as having no regional smart growth even though each implemented some form of metropolitan-wide smart growth effort later in the 1990s. It is interesting to note that among the top ten fastest-growing metropolitan areas, half have some sort of regional smart growth and half do not. Among the bottom ten in growth rates, only one has some form of regional smart growth and all the rest do not. It seems sensible that regional smart growth is more likely to be used where growth occurs and not where growth does not.

In any analysis of the sort we are conducting, namely comparing changes in outcomes over time between different regimes of metropolitan growth management, one must be cognizant of "logical fallacy"—assuming an effect when it comes before the cause or the issue of interaction between causes and effects. There is little absolute certainty of avoiding this, but we can start with estimating the statistical relationship between growth rate and containment regimes. In the model:

$$\% \text{ population change } (1990–2000) =$$
$$f \text{ (smart growth, natural containment)}$$

Table 6.1

Total Metropolitan Population Growth Rate by Rank

MSA/PMSA	Regional policy	1990 Population	2000 Population	Change	Percent
Las Vegas	Natural	693,486	1,332,116	638,630	92.1
Atlanta	None	2,450,009	3,588,326	1,138,317	46.5
Phoenix	Natural	2,016,557	2,940,555	923,998	45.8
Charlotte	None	858,386	1,194,106	335,720	39.1
Orlando	Smart	973,728	1,329,992	356,264	36.6
Dallas	None	2,341,044	3,127,857	786,813	33.6
Denver	None	1,543,161	2,018,398	475,237	30.8
Portland, OR	Smart	1,305,506	1,689,578	384,072	29.4
Houston	None	3,046,597	3,868,908	822,311	27.0
Salt Lake City	None	1,019,106	1,279,993	260,887	25.6
Sacramento	Smart	1,322,801	1,631,443	308,642	23.3
Indianapolis	None	1,060,336	1,284,812	224,476	21.2
Seattle	Smart	1,837,763	2,202,300	364,537	19.8
Tampa	None	1,867,420	2,211,981	344,561	18.5
San Antonio	None	1,179,558	1,394,810	215,252	18.2
Miami	Smart	1,894,156	2,227,073	332,917	17.6
Twin Cities	Smart	2,173,122	2,543,126	370,004	17.0
Columbus	None	1,140,773	1,326,787	186,014	16.3
Washington, DC	None	3,729,991	4,262,228	532,237	14.3
San Diego	Smart	2,335,227	2,639,250	304,023	13.0
Kansas City	None	1,368,375	1,532,529	164,154	12.0
New York	None	8,548,640	9,314,235	765,595	9.0
Norfolk	None	1,272,522	1,384,597	112,075	8.8
Chicago	None	6,005,800	6,483,652	477,852	8.0
Los Angeles	Natural	8,739,001	9,416,396	677,395	7.8
Cincinnati	None	1,293,911	1,392,266	98,355	7.6
San Francisco	Smart	1,546,765	1,660,953	114,188	7.4
Boston	None	3,622,560	3,853,480	230,920	6.4
Detroit	None	4,039,377	4,276,490	237,113	5.9
Milwaukee	None	1,323,325	1,392,283	68,958	5.2
Philadelphia	None	4,602,147	4,809,778	207,631	4.5
New Orleans	None	1,139,953	1,175,419	35,466	3.1
St. Louis	None	2,173,853	2,235,106	61,253	2.8
Cleveland	None	1,704,437	1,740,300	35,863	2.1
Pittsburgh	None	1,774,754	1,718,259	(56,495)	-3.2

Source: Prepared by Raymond J. Burby.

where the independent variables (binary) are regional smart growth or natural containment, the null hypothesis is no statistically significant association between metropolitan population growth and regional smart growth or natural containment type. If the null hypothesis is rejected, we might be concerned that regional smart growth is influenced by growth or vice versa, and that more complex interactions between growth and policies need to be explored. In the ordinary least squares regression of the model, we find:

% population change (1990–2000) =
0.151 + 0.054 × smart growth (0.064)
+ 0.334 × natural containment (0.097)*

where standard errors are in parentheses. The coefficient of determination is modest at 0.27, meaning that 73 percent of the variation in percent population change is attributable to factors other than those represented in the model. Among the independent variables, only natural containment is statistically significant at conventional levels ($* = p<0.05$). This simple test suggests that there is no association between growth and regional smart growth. Although we do find an association with respect to natural containment, we surmise that it is nonetheless not influenced by explicit containment policy.

In general we do not find support for the proposition that regional smart growth per se dampens growth measured in terms of population change. If regions grow with or without smart growth, is there a difference in *how* they grow from the perspective of construction activity related to growth? That question is addressed next.

Regional Smart Growth and Construction Activity

To compare construction activity between business-as-usual and regional smart growth metropolitan areas, we use data compiled by Raymond J. Burby and others for research sponsored by the National Center for the Revitalization of Central Cities. The data include the value of residential and nonresidential construction for a sample of 155 metropolitan areas covering the period 1985 through 1995, a total of eleven years. The data are organized by the U.S. Census Bureau's 1993 definition of metropolitan status. This period covers a complete business cycle that takes into account periods of peak construction, downturns and upturns, and periods of recession. Per capita values per new resident are used to control for variations in population across central cities and metropolitan areas.

Because developers base construction decisions on different location factors when considering residential and various types of nonresidential construction, we include seven types of construction activity: new single-family detached and multifamily housing; industrial, office, and retail/warehouse buildings; and residential and commercial rehabilitation projects. Separate analysis of each category of construction helps to avoid potential counteracting forces that are not revealed when all categories of construction are combined into a single measure of construction activity (see Bartik 1991). Construction data come from building permit information provided annually by cities and counties to the U.S. Census Bureau. For this preliminary assessment, however, we report aggregate residential and nonresidential construction. As a footnote, "construction" does not include land, exactions, costs associated with permit processing, or other activities (see Census Bureau definitions for construction costs).

The status of regional smart growth in each metropolitan area in the sample was determined through a telephone survey in 1999 and 2000 of planning directors in each metropolitan area. Regional smart growth is determined to exist by the presence of a formally adopted containment policy (growth boundary, service extension limits, or greenbelt) in each metropolitan area prior to the start of the study period in 1985. In addition, we determined the year in which regional smart growth programs were established to test the proposition that effects would be more pronounced the longer programs were in existence (no consistent effects of length of program were found, however). More complete survey work on regional smart growth has recently been completed by Nelson and Dawkins (2004).

Nearly all regional smart growth metropolitan areas comprising this sample can be characterized as "growth accommodating." That is, nearly all (there are only five exceptions) have plans designed to explicitly accommodate projected metropolitan growth and long-range infrastructure plans in place to facilitate this. The usual suspects include some of the nation's fastest-growing metropolitan areas including Miami, Orlando, Portland, Oregon, San Diego, and Seattle and some that are growing at or below the national average such as Baltimore, Lincoln, Milwaukee, and Rochester, Minnesota. Such "growth restrictive" metropolitan areas as Boulder/Longmont, Ventura County, California, and Loudon County, Virginia, are not included in the sample.

Descriptive comparisons are presented in Table 6.2. Of the 155 metropolitan areas sampled, 32, or about 20 percent, have some form of regional smart growth present while the remaining 123, or about 80 percent, do not. Growth rates of the two groups are surprisingly similar, being 5.5 percent and 7.1 percent for business-as-usual and regional smart growth metropolitan areas, respectively. Both groups also saw reasonably robust construction activity: $647 billion for business-as-usual metros compared to $272 billion for regional smart growth metros. For the most part, however, the similarities appear to stop there.

On the basis of new construction per new resident, regional smart growth metros saw more activity than business-as-usual metros in terms of both residential and nonresidential construction. For residential construction, regional smart growth activity averaged about $296,000 per new resident compared to about $212,000 per new resident in business-as-usual metros, about 39 percent more. Because land and other costs are not included, the results

Table 6.2

Construction in Smart Growth and Business-as-Usual Metropolitan Areas, 1985–1995

Indicator	Business as usual	Smart growth
Population growth		
Population 1980	37,509,474	9,392,202
Population 1990	39,575,862	10,058,309
Population growth	2,066,388	666,107
Growth rate (in %)	5.5	7.1
Number of metros sampled	123	32
Residential construction		
Res. const. 1985–95 ($000)	439,069,192	196,889,455
Res. const./new res. ($)	212,481	295,582
Smart growth difference ($)		83,101
Difference (in %)		39.1
Nonresidential construction		
Nonres. const. 1985–95 ($000)	208,341,079	74,782,990
Nonres. const./new res. ($)	100,824	112,269
Smart growth difference ($)		11,445
Difference (in %)		11.4
Total construction		
Total construction ($000)	647,410,271	271,672,445
Total const./new res. ($)	313,305	407,851
Smart growth difference ($)		101,979
Difference (in %)		30.2

Source: Prepared by Arthur C. Nelson and Raymond J. Burby.

indicate that residential units of higher value were being constructed in regional smart growth metros relative to business-as-usual metros. We suspect that the difference is attributable to the higher costs associated with infill and redevelopment, and the usually higher unit cost of renovating older buildings than constructing new. Also, we suspect that existing residential properties are more likely to be renovated in regional growth management areas than not. This is only speculation, however. More rigorous assessment should be undertaken.

The situation is similar but less dramatic for nonresidential construction, where regional smart growth metros saw an average of about $112,000 per new resident compared to about $101,000 per new resident, or about 11 percent more. The difference may be attributable to higher costs associated with more intensive development, such as more multilevel buildings requiring elevators than may be seen in sprawling suburban areas. Infill and redevelopment and renovation costs may also be a factor.

One of the explanations for the difference between construction figures in smart growth and business-as-usual metropolitan areas is the extent to which rehabilitation construction occurs. Modern building codes may make it more expensive to rehabilitate older buildings, thus making it relatively less expensive to build on greenfield sites rather than rehabilitate older buildings in central areas. If development is constrained from sprawling outward, closer-in sites become more attractive, but because building codes drive up the cost of rehabilitation, the amount of construction money spent per new resident also goes up. Table 6.3 compares rehabilitation investments between smart growth and business-as-usual regions. Here we find that rehabilitation investments are in the range of $100,000, or 167 percent, more per new resident in smart growth regions than in business-as-usual regions. This is essentially the entire difference noted in Table 6.2.

Other comparisons can be made. Table 6.4 compares construction in three broad areas in business-as-usual and regional smart growth metropolitan areas. Industrial construction was somewhat higher in business-as-usual metropolitan areas, but retail/warehouse construction was somewhat higher in regional smart growth metropolitan areas. A substantial difference exists in office/bank/professional building construction, decidedly favoring regional smart growth metropolitan areas. We surmise that regional smart growth is usually associated with higher-quality construction of these kinds of buildings. In addition, more intensive development associated with regional smart growth brings with it higher building costs such as elevators and steel-reinforced concrete construction of multilevel buildings. This implies that while the actual cost of new construction is not necessarily different between smart growth and business-as-usual regions, more rehabilitation investment is stimulated.

Summary, Interpretation, Limitations, Recommendations, and Implications

On the whole we find that per new resident, new construction in regional smart growth metropolitan areas averaged about $102,000, or 30 percent, more than in business-as-usual metropolitan areas. The entire difference appears to be attributable to rehabilitation investments. Our initial speculation is that while regional smart growth does not per se inhibit growth, it may stimulate more rehabilitation than business as usual. This may be consistent with a growing literature suggesting that one element of regional smart growth, densification, leads to more economic activity and, by implication, more construction activity than lower densities (see Cervero 2000 for discussion). Our preliminary interpretation of the descriptive analysis is that regional smart growth appears to generate more total construction activity per new resident than business as usual, albeit not any more *new* construction per

Table 6.3

Rehabilitation in Smart Growth and Business-as-Usual Metropolitan Areas, 1985–1995

Indicator	Business as usual	Smart growth
Rehabilitation ($000)	124,384,084	60,708,076
Rehabilitation/new resident ($)	60,194	160,828
Smart growth difference ($)		100,634
Difference (in %)		167.2

Source: Adapted from Nelson, Burby et al. 2004.

Table 6.4

Selected Nonresidential Construction, Smart Growth and Business-as-Usual Metropolitan Areas, 1985–1995

Indicator	Business as usual	Smart growth
Industrial construction		
Industrial ($000)	38,808,919	11,226,951
Value per new resident ($)	18,781	16,855
Smart growth difference ($)		(1,926)
Difference (in %)		−10.3
Office/bank/professional building construction		
Office/bank/prof. bldg ($000)	53,763,192	21,944,997
Value per new resident ($)	26,018	32,945
Smart growth difference ($)		6,927
Difference (in %)		26.6
Retail/Warehouse construction		
Stores/warehouse ($000)	58,935,149	19,935,753
Value per new resident ($)	28,521	29,929
Total value per new res. ($)	73,320	79,728
Smart growth difference ($)		6,409
Difference (in %)		8.7

Source: Adapted from Nelson, Burby et al. 2004.

new resident. Until more research is conducted, however, we are unsure about the reasons.

This analysis has important limitations that need to be addressed in future, more rigorous research. For one thing, some of the data upon which it is based are almost twenty years old. For another, many more metropolitan areas today have some form of regional smart growth than did during our study period. Third, we did not control for a variety of factors that may help explain differences in construction activity such as central city–suburban interactions, land area, central city "elasticity" (Rusk 1993), market conditions, development constraints, and so forth. Nor did we control for the possibility that regional smart growth per se may make such regions more attractive and therefore more prone to seeing higher construction activity than business-as-usual metropolitan areas. Finally, this analysis was of less than half the metropolitan areas; it would be better to have analysis that includes them all. Given these and certainly many other limitations, we recommend rigorous multivariate statistical analysis with more recent data that is applied to all metropolitan areas.

An overarching implication may be derived from this preliminary assessment. If there is very little difference in growth rates based on business-as-usual or regional smart growth (see Table 6.1 and regression analysis), does regional smart growth really make a difference in other ways? The answer would appear to be affirmative. On the whole, with minor exceptions, building activity per new resident is decidedly higher in regional smart growth than in business-as-usual metropolitan areas.

There are other benefits to smart growth, as the literature is beginning to show. They relate to higher incomes (Nelson and Peterman 2000, Nelson and Foster 1999), improved public health (our interpretation of Frank, Engelke, and Schmid 2003), reduced sprawl and improved land preservation (Nelson 1999), reduced racial segregation (Nelson, Sanchez, and Dawkins, 2004a, 2004b), improved regional economic welfare (Nelson and Moody 2000), and apparently improved quality of life (Nelson 2000). Perhaps it is because of the accumulation of perceived and measurable benefits relative to business as usual that more communities and entire metropolitan areas are embarking on regional smart growth efforts. Not all such efforts improve or even facilitate development, however, as one of us (Nelson 2002) has speculated. A final call for research is therefore to understand the institutional composition of different varieties of regional smart growth to determine those that do the best job to sustain growth while also maximizing benefits and minimizing costs.

Note

1. It is not sprawl that makes Los Angeles what it is; it is actually the nation's most densely settled metropolitan area.

References

Bartik, T.J. 1991. *Who Benefits from State and Local Economic Development Policies?* Kalamazoo, MI: W.E. Upjohn Institute for Employment Research.
Bogart, W. 1998. *The Economies of Cities and Suburbs.* Upper Saddle River, NJ: Prentice Hall.

Bourne, L.S. 1980. "Alternative Perspectives on Urban Decline and Population Deconcentration. *Urban Geography* 1, no. 1: 39–52.

Burchell, Robert, et al. 1998. *The Costs of Sprawl Revisited: Literature Review.* Washington, DC: Transportation Research Board.

———. 2002. *Costs of Sprawl—2000.* Washington, DC: Transportation Research Board.

Cervero, R. 2000. *Efficient Urbanization.* Cambridge, MA: Lincoln Institute of Land Policy.

Ciccone, A., and R. Hall. 1996. "Productivity and the Density of Economic Activity." *American Economic Review* 86: 54–70.

Frank, Lawrence D., Peter O. Engelke, and Thomas L. Schmid. 2003. *Health and Community Design.* Washington, DC: Island.

Kunstler, James Howard. 1994. *The Geography of Nowhere:* The Rise and *Decline of America's Man-Made Landscape.* New York: Touchstone.

Lang, Robert E. 2003. *Edgeless City.* Washington, DC: The Brookings Institution.

Marshall, A. 1952. *Principles of Economics.* New York: Macmillan.

Mills, Edwin S. 1972. *Studies in the Structure of the Urban Economy.* Baltimore, MD: Johns Hopkins University Press.

Mills, Edwin S., and Bruce Hamilton. 1989. *Urban Economics,* 4th ed. Glenview IL: Scott, Foresman.

Muth, Richard. 1969. *Cities and Housing.* Chicago: Chicago University Press.

Nelson, Arthur C. 1992. "Characterizing Exurbia." *Journal of Planning Literature* 6, no. 4: 350–68.

———. 1999. "Comparing States With and Without Growth Management: Analysis Based on Indicators with Policy Implications." *Land Use Policy* 16: 121–27.

———. 2000. "Smart Growth or Business as Usual? Which is Better at Improving Quality of Life and Central City Vitality?" in *Bridging the Divide: Making Regions Work for Everyone,* ed. Susan M. Wachter, R. Leo Penne and Arthur C. Nelson, chap. 3, pp. 83–106. Washington, DC: HUD.

———. 2002. "How Do You Know Smart Growth When You See It?" in *Smart Growth: Form and Consequences,* ed. Terry Szold, Armando Carbonelle, Cambridge, MA: MIT Press and Lincoln Institute of Land Policy.

Nelson, Arthur C., and James B. Duncan. 1995. *Growth Management Principles and Practices.* Chicago: American Planning Association.

Nelson, A., and K. Foster. 1999. "Metropolitan Governance Structure and Economic Performance." *Journal of Urban Affairs* 21: 309–24.

Nelson, A., and M. Moody. 2000. "Effect of Beltways on Metropolitan Economic Activity," *Journal of Urban Planning and Development* 126, no. 4: 189–96.

Nelson, A., and D. Peterman. 2000. "Does Growth Management Matter?" *Journal of Planning Education and Research* 19: 277–85.

Nelson, Arthur C., and Casey J. Dawkins. 2002. *Urban Containment–American Style(s).* Washington, DC: The Brookings Institution.

Nelson, Arthur C., and C.J. Dawkins. 2004. *Urban Containment in the United States.* Chicago: American Planning Association.

Nelson, Arthur C., Thomas W. Sanchez, and Casey J. Dawkins. 2004a. "Urban Containment and Racial Segregation." *Urban Studies* (forthcoming).

————. 2004b. *Urban Containment and Society*. Draft monograph. Alexandria: Virginia Tech.

Nelson, Arthur C., R.J. Burby, E. Feser, C.J. Dawkins, E.E. Malizia, and R. Quercia. 2004. "Urban Containment and Central-City Revitalization." *Journal of the American Planning Association* 70, no. 4: (in press).

Office of Technology Assessment. 1995. *The Technological Reshaping of Metropolitan America*. Congress of the United States, Washington, DC.

Rusk, D. 1993. *Cities Without Suburbs*. Woodrow Wilson Center Press: Washington D.C.

Part 3

Central City Redevelopment

7

RAYMOND J. BURBY

Impacts of Building Code Enforcement on the Housing Industry

Building codes regulate residential construction in virtually every central city in the United States. These codes consist of standards and specifications designed to provide minimum safeguards in the construction of buildings to protect the people who live and work in them from the dangers of building collapse. While they obviously are important for public safety, building codes have been blamed by a series of national commissions and academic experts for the crisis in affordable housing in the United States and for the inability of central cities to compete successfully for economic growth (e.g., Downs 1991, Dowall and Landis 1982, Dowall 1984, Field and Rivkin 1975, Fischel 1990).

Here are what three national commissions had to say. The National Commission on Urban Problems (Douglas Commission) first brought the problem to light in 1969. According to the commission's final report, *Building the American City,* "their influence extends beyond the physical relationships that are their primary concern, affecting such diverse matters as employment opportunity, housing opportunity, and local tax rates. . . . Critics charge that regulations act to reinforce racial and economic segregation, raise the costs of housing and stifle interesting and innovative design" (p. 199). President Reagan's Commission on Housing concluded in 1982 that the supply of housing could be increased if cities substantially deregulated the development process (President's Commission on Housing 1982). In 1991 the Advisory Commission on Regulatory Barriers to Affordable Housing came to a similar conclusion. In the commission's report, *Not in My Backyard: Removing Barriers to Affordable Housing* (1991), it cited building codes and other development regulations as a serious obstacle to affordability. The commission found that "Local building codes often are not geared to supporting cost-effective construction of affordable housing," and that "Virtually all of the construction work in (central) cities consists of infill and rehabilitation rather than large tracts of new homes built on open land, necessitating that city officials rethink their regulations" (p. 3–1).

The primary targets of regulatory reform and the primary subject of most previous research on this subject has been building code standards and, more broadly, restrictive land-use regulations. Building code standards are formulated by three large-model code groups and then adopted (and modified in the process of adoption) by states and local governments. (The principal model code group in the East and Midwest is the Building Officials Conference of America—Basic Building Code; in the West, the International Conference of Building Officials—Uniform Building Code; and in the South, the Southern Building Code Congress International—Southern Standard Building Code.) Land-use regulations are embodied in thousands of local zoning, subdivision, and other development regulations. Changing building code standards is a highly technical, tedious, time-consuming, and politically contentious process that often takes years to accomplish. Local development regulations are easier to alter, but substantial change still requires considerable effort (staff and political) to accomplish. As a result of the difficulties of making significant changes in codes once they have been adopted, little progress has been made in dealing with the problem of unreasonable code standards, as is indicated by the reports of the three national commissions over a twenty-two-year period.

The impacts of code standards, however, depend not only on the standards themselves but also on the manner in which they are administered. All model codes permit local officials to accept alternate materials or methods that will improve the efficiency and reduce the costs of urban development and rehabilitation. Local officials also have the discretion to enforce codes in a flexible fashion that relaxes standards and other rules that make little sense in given applications but increase costs substantially. This local discretion may provide an important means to alleviate the building code burden on central cities and allow them to compete more successfully for housing construction (and the population that comes with it) within their metropolitan areas.

The conventional wisdom has been that few local governments use the discretion they have available (see, for example, Advisory Commission on Regulatory Barriers to Affordable Housing 1991, 3–7). However, we believe the conventional wisdom may be incorrect. In this chapter we describe the code enforcement strategies being pursued by central cities in the United States and examine their effects on the success of central cities in capturing new housing construction within their metropolitan areas. We show that enforcement strategies vary widely and that a number of local governments do use the discretion they have available to facilitate new construction. Our analyses indicate that strict enforcement does, in fact, hinder the ability of central cities to capture a larger share of the market for new single-family-detached and multifamily housing within metropolitan areas. Furthermore, we show that minor changes in strategy, such as increasing the flexibility with which codes are enforced, will not alter this effect. Instead, central cities that have embraced a strict approach to enforcement will need to completely rethink their enforcement strategies if they want to be more successful in competing with suburban areas for new housing construction.

In the next section we describe the data collection procedures we used to gather information on code enforcement and to explore the effects of enforcement on housing construction in central cities relative to their metropolitan areas. We then present our conceptualization of code enforcement systems, look at the code enforcement strategies actually being employed by central cities, and report the results of analyses of the association of code enforcement strategy with housing construction. The paper concludes with a discussion of the implications of the findings for central city code enforcement policy.

The Data

In order to characterize the enforcement actions of central cities and their effects on housing construction, we extracted data for 155 central cities from a national database assembled in 1995 through a mail survey of city and county building code enforcement agencies (see Burby, May, and Paterson 1998). The response rate for the mail survey was 82 percent after a postcard follow-up and two additional follow-ups with replacement questionnaires. To provide a representative profile of central city code enforcement and its effect on housing construction, the sample data are weighted on the basis of each state's proportion of the total number of central city governments in the United States. Comparison of the sample of 155 central cities with the universe of 362 central cities in the United States in 1990 indicates that the sample overrepresents larger central cities. However, the sample of central cities does not differ from the remainder of central cities in terms of per capita income in 1990, or the percentage of population growth, percentage of income growth, and percentage of employment growth between 1980 and 1990. Thus, we believe the sample data are reasonably representative of all central cities.

Central city success in attracting single-family and multifamily housing construction, our dependent variables, is measured with respect to the number of housing units constructed in each central city relative to its surrounding metropolitan area. For each type of housing, we calculated the per capita ratio of building permits issued by central cities over the eleven-year period 1985–1995 in relation to the corresponding permits issued for the metropolitan area in which the central city is located. Data from individual jurisdictions in metropolitan areas were spatially aggregated for each year of the study period, based on the 1993 census definition of each metropolitan area. The data were aggregated over an eleven-year period in order to include a complete business cycle that takes into account periods of peak construction, downturns and upturns, and periods of recession. Per capita values are used to control for variation across central cities and metropolitan areas in population.

The measurement of enforcement practices, strategies, and effort is discussed below. To isolate enforcement effects on housing construction, we used OLS regression analysis in which we controlled statistically for other factors, in addition to enforcement, that can affect the success of central cities in capturing single-family-detached and multifamily housing construction within their metropolitan areas. The selection of control variables is based on literature and theorizing about key decision-making considerations for homebuilders and multifamily developers. In this regard a key premise is that construction decisions hinge on considerations of financial feasibility. That is, housing projects will not be undertaken unless the cost of a potential project is less than expected project value. Cost depends on the cost of inputs—land, labor, and materials—used for capital outlays and for operating expenses and indirectly on the cost of local public facilities and services. Value depends on expected sales price and rental income. This, in turn, is a function of market conditions—local demand and supply, local quality of life and climate for development, credit availability, and national economic conditions. Based on this conceptualization, we formulated indicators to capture the effects that cost and value can have on construction activity in central cities relative to their metropolitan areas. In addition, we take into account the potential effects of the size of each metropolitan market area and its economic attractiveness relative to other metropolitan areas. Measurement of the dependent, policy, and control variables is described further in the appendix.

Code Enforcement Practices and Strategies

Our conceptualization of building code enforcement draws on previous theorizing about regulatory enforcement (e.g., see Kagan 1994) and builds on our earlier work on code enforcement systems and their effects on compliance with code standards and on economic development (e.g., see Burby, May, and Paterson 1998, May and Burby 1998, and Burby et al. 2000). Here we focus on three related enforcement concepts: practice, strategy, and effort. An agency *practice* is the most fundamental of these concepts and can be easily observed in the field. Practices consist of such things as supervising field staff, carrying out inspections, issuing notices of violation and field citations, and providing technical assistance. Agency *strategy* consists of combinations of the practices that agencies pursue, either explicitly or implicitly, to enhance their effectiveness in bringing about compliance. For example, an agency can pursue a strict enforcement strategy that involves the use of a number of coercive practices, or it can emphasize other practices, such as the use of incentives. Finally, *effort* refers to the vigor with which agencies pursue enforcement. In this regard some agencies are proactive in employing enforcement practices and strategies, while others are more dormant.

To measure enforcement practices, we created a set of indexes that correspond to different actions identified in the enforcement literature: standardization and supervision, deterrent enforcement, technical assistance, discretionary enforcement, and use of incentives. The items within each category of practice are shown in Table 7.1. For each category, we created a summated index from the individual items, based on central city enforcement agency reports of the use of the different tools. Summary statistics for each index and measures of reliability (Chronbach's alpha) are provided in the appendix.

Several points about the enforcement practices that we measured are important to note. First, these are measures of the use of different practices and not whether they simply exist on paper or not. As such, they reflect actions of code enforcement agencies. Second, the amount of effort put into different practices is not included in these measures. Third, by constructing indexes of different practices, our analysis is at a more aggregate level than considering individual practices one by one. This has an advantage of increasing the reliability of measures and enables us to talk about categories of practices that are consistent with those discussed in the regulatory literature.

Our measures of effort that agencies put into different activities are based on ratings provided by code enforcement agencies. These provide relative ratings among seven different categories of activities (public information, surveillance, plan checking, inspection, legal prosecution, technical assistance, and public relations).

The enforcement strategy of a given agency can be characterized in terms of the mix of different practices that the agency chooses to pursue. We think of strategy as a bundle of discrete choices concerning such things as inspection, technical assistance, and use of deterrence. In order to identify enforcement strategies in practice, we employed iterative cluster analysis to identify

Table 7.1

Enforcement Practices of Central City Code Enforcement Agencies

1. **Standardization and supervision**
   - Inspection checklists and forms
   - Agency policy or procedure manual
   - Periodic review of inspectors' work
   - Inspectors required to consult supervisor/building official on hard calls
   - Rotate field inspectors' territories
   - Intensive training of inspectors in agency policy and procedures
   - Annual performance evaluation of inspectors
   - Follow-up field inspections of inspectors' work
   - Productivity measures used to evaluate inspectors' work
2. **Deterrent**
   - Notice of violation
   - Notice of corrective action
   - Stop-work order
   - Revocation of building permit
   - Revocation of certificate of occupancy
   - Temporary restraining order
   - Preliminary injunction
   - Permanent injunction
   - Infraction field citation/fine
   - Misdemeanor prosecution/fine
   - Fine levied for working without permit in past 12 months
   - Fine levied for not following approved plan in past 12 months
   - Fine levied for not following code provisions in past 12 months
3. **Technical assistance**
   - One-on-one technical assistance during plan review
   - One-on-one technical assistance at construction site
   - Booklets describing code enforcement procedures and policies
   - Workshops to explain code provisions
   - Newsletter, bulletin
   - Self-contained slide, audio, or videocassette modules
4. **Discretionary**
   - Inspectors authorized to bluff in order to attain compliance
   - Inspectors allowed to be lenient when life safety not threatened
   - Inspectors can spend extra time on site to develop good relations with regulated entities
   - Inspectors can badger contractors who are chronic violators
   - Inspectors can relax standards based on extenuating circumstances
5. **Incentives**
   - Prior record of violator taken into account in decision to prosecute
   - Attitude of violator taken into account in decision to prosecute
   - Less frequent inspections
   - Bend over backward to be cordial
   - Other incentives
   - Modify standards for firms with good records with approval of higher authority

Table 7.2

Comparison of Cities with Different Enforcement Strategies

| Characteristic | Mean values for clusters comprising different strategies[a] | | |
	Strict enforcement strategy	Creative enforcement strategy	Accommodative enforcement strategy
Enforcement practices that comprise the strategy			
Standardization and supervision	85	65	53
Deterrent enforcement	58	59	46
Technical assistance	75	56	36
Discretionary enforcement	40	72	47
Incentives	29	46	10
Enforcement effort associated with the strategy			
Overall enforcement effort	74	74	67
City characteristics associated with use of each strategy			
Population, 1990	623,780	195,030	210,806
Population growth, 1980–89 (in %)	15	8	5
Median per capita income, 1989 ($)	14,084	13,070	12,319
Unemployment rate, 1990 (in %)	6.8	7.1	8.3
Median home value, 1990 ($)	96,847	74,960	70,620
Housing built prior to 1940 (in %)	18	26	26
Political demand for enforcement	51	53	39
Political opposition to enforcement	19	25	16
Politicization of enforcement	2	16	15
Cluster sample information			
Number of cases (weighted)	43	47	65
Percent of sample	28	30	42

Note: [a]Except for the cluster sample information, cell entries are the mean values of designated items for central cities that comprise the designated strategy (cluster) for the weighted sample of central city enforcement agencies. The difference of means F-test is statistically significant at $p < .05$ for all items except housing built prior to 1940, political opposition, and politicization, which are significant at $p < .10$.

three groupings of code enforcement agencies with similarities in use of different practices.[1] By examining the practices employed by the central cities in each group, we could deduce the strategy each employed to bring about compliance with code standards. We labeled these strategies as strict, creative, and accommodative.

An accommodative strategy was being used by the largest percentage of cities (43 percent), followed by cities using a creative strategy (29 percent), and those using a strict strategy (28 percent). The attributes of each cluster are shown in Table 7.2. The first set of entries lists the mean scores for the practices used to label each strategy. Each set of practices is an index measured on a scale of 0 to 100. Central cities that used a strict enforcement strategy are noteworthy for their emphasis on standardization of fieldwork and provision of technical assistance. Those that employed a creative enforcement strategy stand out for their use of flexible enforcement practices and use of incentives. Both strict and creative strategies feature relatively large doses of deterrence. The cities that employed an accommodative strategy used more flexible enforcement practices than the strict enforcement group, but used fewer of each of the other types of practices than cities that used strict or creative strategies. This is also reflected in enforcement effort, which tended to be lowest among the cities that pursued an accommodative strategy.

Our characterization of enforcement strategies is consistent with other studies in showing that agencies employ a mix of practices. What we found, however, differs in important details from the stylized versions of enforcement strategy found in the literature. In particular, deterrence tends to be employed in equal measure by agencies that employed strict and creative enforcement strategies, and both groups of agencies made a strong effort to enforce code requirements. What separates the strategies of these agencies is the use of flexibility and incentives. These are added to the enforcement strategy of agencies that have to cope with a more highly politicized environment and have more opposition to strong enforcement from constituencies such as builders, developers, and contractors (shown in the bottom rows of Table 7.2).

Our finding that a large proportion of code enforcement agencies follow an accommodative strategy is not as easily characterized and not found as a separate strategy in the literature. It might be considered as similar to what Kagan (1994) labels as a retreatist approach, in which regulatory officials, with more limited support for strong enforcement, merely create an appearance of enforcement. As shown in the bottom rows of Table 7.2, an accommodative strategy is likely to also be a response to economic circumstances. Cities that used an accommodative strategy, as a group, tended to be poorer, growing at a slower rate, and experiencing weaker economies than cities that used strict or creative enforcement strategies.

Impacts of Enforcement Choices on Housing Construction

At issue is the question of whether a strict enforcement strategy has constrained housing construction in the central cities that have used it. Equally important is the question of whether creative and accommodative strategies, each of which employs more flexibility in dealing with builders and contractors, has mitigated this adverse effect in the cities where these strategies have been employed. To investigate these questions, we ran multiple regression models that control for other factors that can affect central city success in capturing housing construction activity within their metropolitan areas.

The results of these analyses are summarized in Table 7.3. The columns labeled Model A use strict and accommodative dummy variables to estimate the effects of central city approaches to enforcement. The columns labeled Model B look at the effects of strict and creative enforcement strategies. Our discussion of the model findings looks first at the effects of enforcement strategy on single-family-detached housing and then at effects on multifamily housing.

Model A indicates that relative to a strategy of creative enforcement (the omitted dummy variable), strict enforcement had little effect on central city success in attracting single-family-detached housing over the period 1985–1995, while an accommodative strategy had a fairly strong, statistically significant positive effect. The positive effects of the accommodative strategy are also shown by the results of Model B, which indicates that relative to accommodative enforcement, both strict and creative enforcement have statistically significant negative effects on the proportion of single-family-detached housing that central cities were able to capture. In contrast to enforcement strategy, we find that enforcement effort has only a modest (and statistically insignificant) negative effect on the construction of single-family-detached housing in central cities relative to their metropolitan areas. We turn to this finding in more detail below.

The single-family-detached housing model summarized in Model B indicates that the negative effect of a systematic approach to enforcement is not ameliorated by the greater employment of flexibility and incentives associated with a creative enforcement strategy. Both strict and creative enforcement strategies have an equivalent negative effect on the ratio of single-family-detached housing captured by central cities. This occurs because both strategies rely heavily on the use of deterrent enforcement practices. In a separate analysis employing the index of deterrent practices (see Table 7.1) in place of enforcement strategy, we found that deterrence is negatively associated with construction of single-family-detached houses (beta $= -.15, p < .01$). In contrast, an accommodative strategy (as shown in Model A) that is characterized by little attention to deterrence has a positive effect on the construction of new homes.

In the case of multifamily housing, we find that enforcement strategy has little effect on the ability of central cities to capture new multifamily housing units. However, enforcement effort does. Central cities that were more proactive in enforcement were less able to capture multifamily housing than were those that exerted less effort. Enforcement effort summarizes activities such as public information about code requirements, frequency

Table 7.3

Multiple Regression Models of Success of Central Cities in Capturing Housing Construction Activity in Metropolitan Areas, 1985–1995

| | Standardized regression coefficients[a] | | | |
| | Single-family housing units | | Multifamily housing units | |
Variables	Model A	Model B	Model A	Model B
Enforcement choices				
Strict enforcement strategy	−0.01	−0.14**	0.06	0.10
Accommodative enforcement strategy	0.15**	—	−0.04	—
Creative enforcement strategy	—	−0.14***	—	0.04
Enforcement effort	−0.04	−0.04	−0.18**	−0.18**
Other explanatory variables				
Demand for housing				
Population—proportion of metropolitan population living in city, 1990	0.42***	0.42***	0.22**	0.22**
Income—ratio of city to metropolitan area median per capita income, 1990	0.28***	0.28***	0.13	0.13
Spending power—ratio of city to metropolitan area per capita retail sales, 1982	0.20**	0.20**	0.44***	0.44***
Population growth (metro area), 1980–1989	−0.002	−0.002	−0.03	−0.03
Income growth per capita (metro area), 1980–1989	−0.04	−0.04	0.09	0.09
Development opportunities				
Land area—increase in city land area, 1980–1989 (in %)	0.10*	0.10*	−0.004	−0.004
Obsolescence—1990 ratio of city to metropolitan area percentage of housing built prior to 1940	−0.28***	−0.28***	−0.17*	−0.17*
Housing shortage (metro area), 1990	0.09*	0.09*	0.06	0.06
Development costs				
Cost of land—ratio of city to metropolitan area population density, 1990	0.03	0.03	0.09	0.09
Construction cost (metro area), 1993	0.16**	0.16**	0.06	0.06
Property tax rates (metro area), 1990	0.15**	0.15**	0.08	0.08
Quality of life				
Crime—ratio of city to metropolitan area number of crimes per capita, 1990	0.01	0.01	−0.002	−0.002

Poverty—ratio of city to metropolitan area increase in persons in poverty, 1980–1989 (in %)	−0.12**	−0.12**	−0.09	−0.09
Schools—students in private schools (in %)	−0.11*	−0.11*	0.02	0.02
Metropolitan area controls				
Population (metro area), 1990	−0.09	−0.09	0.02	0.02
Unemployment rate (metro area), 1990	−0.02	−0.02	0.02	0.02
Development constraints— miles of shoreline per capita (metro area)	0.03	0.03	0.01	0.01
Model statistics				
Adjusted R2	0.62	0.62	0.26	0.26
F–value	12.49	12.49	3.51	3.51
Significance	0.001	0.001	0.001	0.001
Number of cases	141	141	141	141

Notes: ªDependent variables are ratios of central city construction activity per capita to metropolitan area construction activity per capita, 1985–1995.

$*p<.10$

$**\ p<.05$

$***\ p<.01$ (one–tailed test)

of plan checking and building inspections, and vigor with which legal prosecution is pursued. Apparently these activities tend to discourage multifamily housing, while the practices that comprise the measures of enforcement strategy do not have such an effect. Decomposition of the effort index into its constituent parts indicates that the effort enforcement agencies put into public information about code standards, plan checking, inspections, and legal prosecution accounts for the negative effect. Effort expended on surveillance to detect building without a permit, on technical assistance, and on public relations does not have a negative effect on the construction of multifamily housing.

There are two possible reasons for differences in the effects of enforcement strategy and effort on the construction of single-family-detached and multifamily housing. First, homebuilders active in central cities may be smaller firms that are more sensitive to the hassles and costly delays implied by the use of deterrent enforcement practices such as stop-work orders. Firms building multifamily housing may be larger and more adequately financed, so that they can take these costs in stride. In addition, they may be more professional in orientation, so that they are less likely to violate code standards and less subject to the costs of deterrent enforcement actions. Second, enforcement effort also implies that firms are less likely to be able to evade the costs of complying with code standards. For example, in our previous research we found that enforcement effort is a strong predictor of the degree of compliance with code requirements that enforcement agencies have been able to achieve (Burby, May, and Paterson 1998, Burby et al. 2000). If they are unable to evade the extra costs of complying with code standards, developers of multifamily housing may shift their construction projects to suburban jurisdictions where these costs are less burdensome or where less effort is expended on securing compliance. These explanations are mutually consistent and seem plausible given the likely characteristics of the firms constructing single-family-detached and multifamily housing in central cities.

Policy Implications

This chapter has examined the effects of building code enforcement strategy and effort on the ability of central cities to capture single-family-detached and multifamily housing construction within their metropolitan areas. We have seen that in response to pressures in their operating environment, agencies pursue different strategies in their attempts to attain compliance with building code standards. Larger cities and those with strong political support for enforcement tend to pursue a strategy of strict enforcement, which emphasizes standardization of enforcement tasks, provision of technical assistance, and the use of deterrence (e.g., stop-work orders, fines, etc.) to bring about compliance. Smaller cities that want to exert a strong effort on enforcement, but have to cope with more politicization of enforcement and greater opposition from various constituencies, tend to employ a creative strategy of enforcement. This strategy also emphasizes the use of deterrence, but it tolerates more flexibility in the way inspectors and plan checkers actually apply it. Smaller cities that are less intent on making a strong enforcement effort, typically in response to economic stagnation and political pressures to avoid antagonizing economic interests, tend to use an accommodative enforcement strategy. This strategy involves the use of fewer enforcement practices and less effort in undertaking various enforcement tasks than agencies pursuing strict or creative enforcement strategies.

The choices central cities make about enforcement have a direct effect on their ability to compete for housing construction within their metropolitan areas. In general, the more vigorously cities pursued code enforcement, either in terms of the use of strict or creative enforcement strategies, or in terms of the effort they devoted to enforcement, the less successful they were in capturing new housing construction. Enforcement strategies have this effect on the construction of single-family-detached housing units, while code enforcement effort suppresses multifamily housing. Contrary to our expectations, the greater flexibility and use of incentives that characterizes a creative enforcement strategy does not lessen the adverse effects of deterrent enforcement practices, which the creative and strict enforcement strategies have in common.

Our findings suggest that if central cities cut back on the use of deterrent enforcement practices, such as stop-work orders and fines, they will enhance their ability to capture a greater proportion of single-family-detached housing within their metropolitan areas. This is important, because our earlier research indicates that of all types of private-sector construction (i.e., single- and multifamily housing, retail, office, and industrial), central cities are doing worst in capturing single-family housing (Burby et al. 2000). The impacts of this poor performance are exacerbated by the fact that such housing accounts for about half of all private-sector construction activity within metropolitan areas. In contrast multifamily housing accounts for just over 10 percent of construction activity, and central cities have held their own with suburban areas in competition for multifamily projects.

Because of the importance of enforcement effort in attaining compliance, we think it would be unwise for central cities to cease being proactive about code enforcement in order to garner a higher proportion of multifamily housing within their metropolitan areas. If our supposition that effort reinforces the adverse effects of obsolete code standards that raise construction costs is correct, however, these findings do reinforce the need for central cities to take a hard look at the construction requirements embodied in their building codes. Our findings provide indirect support for the conclusion that multifamily housing construction could be stimulated if code standards were less onerous.

In conclusion the building code burden on central city housing construction is real. Code enforcement choices cities have made have reduced their ability to capture both single-family-detached and multifamily housing. Central cities can lessen this effect on the construction of single-family-detached housing if they de-emphasize the use of deterrence as a way to bring about compliance. This can be done without threatening the attainment of compliance with code standards, as long as cities continue to mount a vigorous enforcement effort. A continuing cost of vigorous enforcement, however, will be a somewhat reduced ability to capture multifamily housing. To counter this unwanted effect, cities should pay close attention to the cost implications of the code standards required in multifamily construction. We suspect that by eliminating costly building code requirements that contribute little to building safety, cities can enhance their ability to capture multifamily housing construction. In the meantime, however, we have shown that cities can begin to beat the building code burden for single-family housing by reorienting their enforcement practices to avoid the construction delays and nuisance effects that accompany the use of sanctions to bring about compliance with code standards. This would be no small accomplishment.

Appendix: Measurement of Variables

Variable	Source mean (s.d.)	Measurement
Construction activity		
Central city single-family housing success ratio—number of units	U.S. Census 1985–1995. 0.55 (0.38)	Number of central city single-family-detached houses constructed 1985–1995 per capita/number of metropolitan area single-family-detached houses constructed 1985–1995 per capita (sq. ft. transformation used in analysis). *Note:* In cases where data for a given year were missing, the mean of the eleven-year period was substituted for that value. In no cases was more than one year of data missing for a city in the sample.
Central city multifamily housing success ratio—number of units	U.S. Census 1985–1995. 1.06 (0.50)	Number of central city multifamily housing units constructed 1985–1995 per capita/number of metropolitan area multifamily housing units constructed 1985–1995 per capita (sq. ft. transformation used in analysis). (See *note* above.)
Enforcement		
Strict enforcement strategy	Derived by authors using approach explained in May and Burby 1998. 0.28 (0.45)	Derived from Cluster Analysis of indexes of enforcement practices (see May and Burby 1998). Coded as a dummy variable: 1—agency employs strict enforcement strategy; 0—agency employs another enforcement strategy.
Creative enforcement strategy	Derived by authors using approach explained in May and Burby 1998. 0.30 (0.46)	Derived from Cluster Analysis of indexes of enforcement practices (see May and Burby 1998). Coded as a dummy variable: 1—agency employs creative enforcement strategy; 0—agency employs another enforcement strategy.
Accommodative enforcement strategy	Derived by authors using approach explained in May and Burby 1998. 0.42 (0.49)	Derived from Cluster Analysis of indexes of enforcement practices (see May and Burby 1998). Coded as a dummy variable: 1—agency employs accommodative enforcement strategy; 0—agency employs another enforcement strategy.

Enforcement effort	Derived by authors from Burby, May, and Paterson 1998. 35.6 (6.2)	Index of overall effort a locality makes to enforce building standards. Mean of building official rating (scale 1 to 5) of degree of effort expended by the agency on seven tasks: public relations, surveillance, plan checking, inspection, legal prosecution, technical assistance, public awareness. Alpha = 0.69.
Deterrent enforcement practices	Derived by authors from Burby, May, and Paterson 1998. 53.2 (18.0)	Index based on use of thirteen different deterrent enforcement practices (see practices listed in Table 7.1). Alpha = 0.70.
Discretionary enforcement practices	Derived by authors from Burby, May, and Paterson 1998. (23.0)	Index based on use of five different discretionary enforcement practices (see practices listed in Table 7.1). Alpha = 0.57.
Incentive enforcement practices	Derived by authors from Burby, May, and Paterson 1998. 25.9 (21.2)	Index based on use of six different incentive enforcement practices (see practices listed in Table 7.1). Alpha = 0.45.
Technical assistance enforcement practices	Derived by authors from Burby, May, and Paterson 1998. (24.1)	Index based on use of six different technical assistance enforcement practices (see practices listed in Table 7.1). Alpha = 0.58.
Standardization and supervision enforcement practices	Derived by authors from Burby, May, and Paterson 1998. 65.6 (22.3)	Index based on use of nine different standardization and supervision enforcement practices (see practices listed in Table 7.1). Alpha = 0.60.
Demand for housing/buildings Population—proportion of metropolitan population living in central city, 1990	Derived by authors from U.S. Census (1993c) data. 0.64 (0.15)	Transformation: population of central city/population of metropolitan area (sq. ft.).

(continued)

156

Appendix (*continued*)

Variable	Source mean (s.d.)	Measurement
Income—ratio of central city to metropolitan area median per capita income, 1990	Derived by auathors from U.S. Census (1993c) data. 0.97 (0.10)	Transformation: population of central city/population of area median per capita income (sq. ft).
Spending power—ratio of city to metropolitan area median per capita income	Derived by authors from U.S. Census (1984) data. 1.29 (0.33)	Transformation: central city retail sales per capita income/ metropolitan area retail sales per capita income (sq. ft.).
Metropolitan population growth, 1980–1990	Derived by authors from U.S. Census (1993c, 1983) data. 823.47 (107.97)	1990 population—1980 population (sq. ft.)
Metropolitan income growth (per capita), 1980–1989	Derived by authors from U.S. Census (1993c, 1983) data. 84.46 (11.42)	1990 median per capita income—1980 per capita income/1980 median per capita income (sq. ft.).
Development opportunities Land area—percentage increase in city land area, 1980–1989	Derived by authors from ICMA, 1997. 3.89 (1.52)	Land area 1990—land area 1980/land area 1980 (sq. ft.).
Obsolescence—ratio of city to metropolitan area percentage of housing built prior to 1940	U.S. Census, 1993a. 1.00 (0.03)	Percentage of housing in 1990 built before 1980 (sq. ft.).
Metropolitan housing shortage, 1990	Derived by authors from U.S. Census, 1982, 1992b, 1993c). 6.98 (1.37)	Actual 1990 median house value—predicted 1990 median house value with 1990 predicted value = c + 1980 median house value + change in median family income 1980–199). Positive sign indicates housing shortage (sq. ft.).

Variable	Source (value)	Description
Development costs		
Cost of land—ratio of city to metropolitan area population density, 1990	Derived by authors from U.S. Census, 1993b. 1.83 (0.40)	Population density of central city/population density of metropolitan area (sq. ft.).
Metropolitan residential construction cost, 1993	Ferguson, 1996. 0.97 (0.063)	Metropolitan construction cost index based on relative cost of materials and labor (sq. ft.).
Metropolitan nonresidential construction cost, 1993	Ferguson, 1996. 0.97 (0.061)	Metropolitan construction cost index based on relative cost of materials and labor (sq. ft.).
Metropolitan property tax index, 1990	Boyer, 1989. 9.73 (2.99)	Places rated index of property tax rates (sq. ft.).
Quality of life		
Poverty—ratio of city to metropolitan area increase in percentage of persons in poverty, 1980–1989	U.S. Census, 1993c. 1 (0.03)	Central city percentage of census tracts with 20 percent + of households below poverty level income/metropolitan percentage of census tracts with 20 percent + of households below poverty level income (sq. ft.).
Crime—ratio of city to metropolitan area number of Part 1 crimes per capita, 1990	U.S. Department of Justice, 1992; U.S. Census, 1993c. 1.56 (0.42)	Total number of Part 1 crimes (murders, rapes, robberies, aggravated assaults, burglaries, larcenies, motor vehicle thefts, and arsons)/central city population.
Percent of metropolitan area students in public schools	Boyer, 1989. 9.45 (0.28)	Percent of students attending public schools (sq. rt)
Characteristics of metropolitan area		
Metropolitan population, 1990	U.S. Census, 1993c. 797.67 (496.13)	1990 metropolitan population (000) (sq. ft.).
Metropolitan unemployment rate, 1990	U.S. Census, 1993c. 6.15 (1.67)	1990 unemployment rate.
Development constraints: miles of metropolitan area shoreline	Calculated by authors from atlas maps. 0.066 (0.12)	Miles of shoreline (not including small inland lakes) bordering metropolitan area (sq. ft.).

* * *

We are grateful for the assistance of Joyce Levine and Sandra McMillan in assembling data on central city characteristics. Financial support for this research was provided by the National Center for Central City Revitalization at the University of New Orleans and by National Science Foundation Research Grant Number BCS-93311857 to the University of New Orleans. The findings reported in this chapter are not necessarily endorsed by the organizations that provided financial support.

Emil Maliza and Peter May were coinvestigators on this research project for the National Center. They have made substantial contributions in the writing of this chapter.

Note

1. See Aldendefer and Blashfield (1984) for an overview of cluster analysis. We employed the K-means statistical routine in the SPSS for Windows statistical package. The clustering is based on the Euclidean distance between the unstandardized measures of each of the five types of enforcement practices listed in Table 7.1 (each measured on the same scale of 0 to 100).

References

Advisory Commission on Regulatory Barriers to Affordable Housing. 1991. *"Not in My Backyard: Removing Barriers to Affordable Housing."* Washington, DC: U.S. Government Printing Office.

Aldenderfer, M.S., and R.K. Blashfield. 1984. "Cluster Analysis." *Quantitative Applications in the Social Sciences,* series number 07–44. Beverly Hills, CA: Sage.

Burby, R.J., and R.B. Paterson. 1993. "Improving Compliance with State Environmental Regulations." *Journal of Policy Analysis and Management* 12, no. 4: 753–72.

Burby, R.J., P.J. May, and R.B. Paterson. 1998. "Improving Compliance with Regulations: Choices and Outcomes for Local Government." *Journal of the American Planning Association* 64, no. 3: 324–34.

Burby, R.J., P.J. May, E. Malizia, and J. Levine. 2000. "Code Enforcement Burdens and Central City Decline." *Journal of the American Planning Association* 66, no. 2: 143–61.

Dowall, D. 1984. *The Suburban Squeeze: Land Conversion and Regulation in the San Francisco Bay Area.* Berkeley: University of California Press.

Dowall, D., and J.D. Landis. 1982. "Land Use Controls and Housing Costs: An Examination of San Francisco Bay Area Communities." *American Real Estate & Urban Economics Association Journal* 10 (Spring): 67–93.

Downs, A. 1991. "The Advisory Commission on Regulatory Barriers to Affordable Housing: Its Behavior and Accomplishments." *Housing Policy Debate* 2, no. 4: 1095–1137.

Field, C.G., and S. Rivkin. 1975. *The Building Code Burden.* Lexington, MA: Lexington Books. D.C. Heath.

Fischel, W.A., ed. 1990. "Special Issue: Land-use Controls." *Land Economics* 66, no. 2: 229–355.

Grabosky, P., and J. Braithwaite. 1986. *Of Manners Gentle, Enforcement Strategies of Australian Business Regulatory Agencies.* Melbourne: Oxford University Press.

Kagan, R.A. 1994. "Regulatory Enforcement," in *Handbook Of Regulation and Administrative Law,* ed. D.H. Rosenbloom and R.D. Schwartz, pp. 383–422. New York: Marcel Decker.

May, P.J. 1997. "State Regulatory Roles: Choices in the Regulation of Building Safety." *State and Local Government Review* 29, no. 2: 69–80.

May, P.J., and R.J. Burby. 1998. "Making Sense Out of Regulatory Enforcement." *Law and Policy* 20, no. 2: 157–82.

National Commission on Urban Problems. 1969. *Building the American City.* House Document no. 91–34. Washington, DC: U.S. Government Printing Office.

President's Commission on Housing. 1982. *Final Report.* Washington, DC: U.S. Government Printing Office.

Scholz, J.T. 1994. "Managing Regulatory Enforcement," in *Handbook of Regulation and Administrative Law,* ed. D.H. Roosenbloom and Richard D. Schwartz, pp. 423–63. New York: Marcel Decker.

Data Sources

Boyer, R. 1989. *Places Rated Almanac: Your Guide to Finding the Best Places to Live in America.* New York: Prentice Hall.

Burby, R.J., P.J. May, and R.B. Paterson. 1998. "Improving Compliance with Regulations: Choices and Outcomes for Local Government." *Journal of the American Planning Association* 64, no. 3: 324–34.

Ferguson, J.H., ed. 1996. *Mean Square Foot Costs, 1997: Residential, Commercial, Industrial, Institutional.* Kingston, MA: R.S. Means.

International City/County Management Association. 1997. The Municipal Yearbook. Washington, DC: ICMA.

U.S. Bureau of the Census. 1983. *1980 Census of Population: Characteristics of the Population/General Social and Economic Characteristics.* Washington, DC: The Bureau.

———. 1983. *1980 Census Of Population: General Social and Economic Characteristics.* Washington, DC: The Bureau.

———. 1984. *1982 Census of Retail Trade: Geographic Area Series.* Washington, DC: The Bureau.

———. 1993a. *1990 Census of Housing: Detailed Housing Characteristics.* Washington, DC: The Bureau.

———. 1993b. *1990 Census of Population: Social and Economic Characteristics.* Washington, DC: The Bureau.

———. 1993c. *1990 Census of Population and Housing: Summary of Population and Housing Characteristics.* Washington, DC: The Bureau.

U.S. Bureau of the Census, Manufacturing and Construction Division. 1985–1995. *Building Permits.* Annual series. Washington, DC: The Bureau.

U.S. Department of Justice, Federal Bureau of Investigation. 1992. *Uniform Crime Reports for 1990.* Series 55100. Washington, DC: The Department.

8

Sabina E. Deitrick and Stephen C. Farber

Citizen Reaction to Brownfields Redevelopment

Brownfields redevelopment is providing opportunities for urban revitalization in American regions, particularly in older industrial areas where the reorganization and abandonment of industrial production left behind open tracts of land for redevelopment. Because brownfields in older industrial regions are often located in close proximity to central cities and even within the dense fabric of urban neighborhoods, they may be viewed as "community assets," opportunities for communities to reshape the environment of their future.

Such a position stands in contrast from the deindustrialization focus on brownfields as constraints to regional revitalization. This view of brownfields focuses on the actual or perceived levels of contamination from former industrial uses, the liability constraints imposed on redevelopment from state and federal environmental regulations, and the loss of the region's economic base (Leigh 1994). Recent changes in state and federal laws have altered to some extent the cleanup and liability issues, changing cleanup standards to reflect different uses and extending liability protection for those in compliance with the law. Markets, likewise, have changed, with many successful brownfields projects completed, often spurred by public sector changes and additional incentives.

This research poses two questions:

1. What are the costs and benefits to brownfields redevelopment in urban communities?
2. How do community stakeholders perceive brownfields and actual or potential brownfields redevelopment within their community?

The research focuses on brownfields redevelopment in Pittsburgh, Pennsylvania; it first defines the community for brownfields redevelopment by establishing the stakeholders in five brownfields communities in Pittsburgh. Public cost-benefit analysis is applied in each case to determine what public investments have been made on the sites and what have been the returns. Next, the research seeks to discover what are the most important issues for communities faced with a brownfield in their midst. How do different stakeholders within the defined brownfields community evaluate these issues? What can policy and planning learn from understanding the complex issues involved in brownfields redevelopment and the differences among opinions expressed by various stakeholder groups? In this part of the research the main goals are to identify and interpret stakeholders' perceptions of brownfields redevelopment through a Q methodology. Because brownfields redevelopment encompasses a number of different concerns, the understanding and interpretation of them differ across constituencies. brownfields themselves are somewhat of a "chaotic conception," covered by subjective viewpoints of sites' redevelopment, public policies, and even definitions.[1] Q methodology provides a means to test this variance of opinion. For the purpose of this research, our working concept of brownfields is underutilized urban sites with environmental contamination problems.

The Pittsburgh region lost over 150,000 manufacturing jobs from the late 1970s forward, creating many brownfields. The city has seen a number of brownfields revitalization projects over the past decade, but still contains numerous small and large former industrial sites in varying stages of redevelopment. We presume that brownfields can be viewed as constraints to urban revitalization but also constitute opportunities for redeveloping old industrial sites and helping to revitalize communities. A second purpose of the study is to relate these findings to ongoing policymaking related to brownfields. We begin by reviewing the theoretical conceptions of brownfields and their redevelopment and then proceed to a description of the study sites and the communities within which they are located. Cost-benefit analysis is then conducted for the sites that have realized redevelopment. The next section discusses the Q methodology employed in the study. The results are then presented and analyzed. The chapter concludes with the importance of these findings to the brownfields literature and policymaking involved in revitalizing such sites in older industrial cities.

Context

Brownfields research, policy, and redevelopment practice have advanced rapidly over the past decade. From initial obstacles of legislation—most notably the Comprehensive Environmental Response, Compensation, and Liability Act of 1980 (CERCLA or Superfund)—government at all levels has enacted programs and policies to encourage the redevelopment of abandoned and contaminated lands in older industrial areas. More than forty states now have voluntary cleanup programs (VCPs) to provide incentives to remediate and redevelop brownfield sites. The U.S. Environmental Protection Agency (EPA) holds an annual brownfields conference. Lender liability concerns have been reduced with clarification of federal liability issues, and states offer liability protection for successful participants in its programs. Importantly, a wealth of case study information has been collected on successful projects and how they were accomplished (Leigh 1994, Bartsch and Collaton 1997, Pepper 1997, Davis and Margolis 1997, Simons 1998).

Nonetheless, the conceptualization of brownfields remains clouded by perspective. brownfields are unlike other urban redevelopment projects because of their actual or potential contamination. This involves a legal perspective on redevelopment, focusing on issues concerning liability to both property owners and lenders. The specter of contamination brings an important environmental component to the brownfields problem, unlike other urban redevelopment projects, involving remediation methods, standards for cleanup, and the costs of remediation. The costs of remediation introduce an overarching economic component to brownfields redevelopment, which extends from the cleanup costs to the costs of redevelopment to the market basis of projects, often located in underinvested parts of a metropolitan region. The legal component, likewise, is not costless, as new insurance programs have been introduced by private firms for brownfields redevelopment. Linked to this are other economic development concerns regarding the type of redevelopment and the goals, which can vary depending on perspective, such as increasing tax revenues for a municipality and increasing employment. The final concern involves community—who is the community, what are their concerns, what is their role? Unlike traditional redevelopment projects, brownfields may have different or larger implications for a community, particularly regarding health and environmental issues, along with economic and social concerns. This set of implications and concerns makes brownfields different from traditional property redevelopment. Their perceptions are shaped by both their own relation to the brownfield site and to the legal, environmental economic, and community issues associated with redeveloping sites.

Legal Issues

The earliest work on brownfields focused on their potential inclusion under Superfund legislation and the paramount issues of liability extending to owners and lenders of a site, regardless of the cause of contamination (Macfarlane et al. 1994). Liability under CERCLA and its followup, the Superfund

Amendment and Reauthorization Act of 1986 (SARA), extended liability as joint and several to all owners and lenders on a property, regardless of who was responsible for the contamination. Because of this, contamination or the possibility of contamination has constrained redevelopment of brownfields sites. Not only were developers reluctant to take on contaminated or potentially contaminated sites, but lenders were likewise adverse to engaging in brownfields projects, resulting in an unwillingness to foreclose on properties and requiring greater protection from liability (Toulme and Cloud 1991, Murphy 1997).

As more properties were becoming "brown" and redevelopment prospects were limited by liability uncertainties and cleanup costs for both developers and lenders, public officials recognized the constraints imposed by existing legislation. Most brownfields were not Superfund priorities, and the EPA cleared 27,000 sites from its National Priorities List (Kaiser 1998). In 1996 the Asset Conservation, Lender Liability, and Deposit Insurance Protection Act was passed to protect lenders, including public sector authorities, in compliance with current law and not actively participating in the management of a contaminated facility. Even so, lenders could still be liable under other federal or state environmental laws (Murphy 1997).

States likewise sought to stimulate investment in brownfield properties and passed legislation to promote redevelopment. In Pennsylvania, for example, Act 2 of its Land Recycling Program provides liability protection to those participating in the cleanup of a site, including current or future owners, the developer of the site, a successor, or a public utility (PADEP 1996). Act 3 of the program extends liability protection to financiers, including economic development agencies, lenders, and fiduciaries.

The changes in federal and state laws have created an environment providing greater security from liability issues for those participating in cleanups, but uncertainty still remains in the legal realm (Murphy 1997). Recently insurance companies have begun to offer environmental insurance for brownfields projects (McElroy and Davis 1997), though recent evidence suggests it is currently underused because of a lack of timely information both from underwriters and potential users (Meyer 1998). Differing perceptions about legal issues attached to brownfields remain, and these are explored in our model below.

Environmental Issues

How clean is clean? This is the question that prompted many studies of brownfields and the attendant cleanup involved on a site. The environmental issues of brownfields involve several components, none of which can be separated from the other concerns. First is the contamination on a site, which may pose health risks to the users of a site and to the nearby population; both groups will have concerns about brownfields contamination. Cleaning up the contamination involves economic costs, the degree subject to the amount and type of the contaminant. Complying with environmental laws also adds transactions costs to redevelopment, beyond the actual clean up (Gibson 1995). Finally, polluters or those causing the contamination are subject to the liability laws of the environmental agencies that regulate hazardous wastes.

Further impeding the redevelopment of brownfields sites is the issue of cleanup standards. Many laws required site remediation to "background" or pristine conditions, regardless of future use and the technical advances of risk-based assessments. Recognizing the limitations placed by a uniform standard, particularly by the growing number of brownfields sites, states changed laws. In Pennsylvania, for example, Act 2 of its Land Recycling Program sets a range of cleanup standards, none more stringent than the standards that were in place: The background standard returns sites to the level of cleanliness prior to contamination; the statewide health standard presents a list of cleanup levels for various contaminants; site-specific standards reflect the present or future use of the property based on site-specific risk assessment; and special industrial areas include standards for industrial properties where there is no financially viable responsible person to clean up contamination or land within state enterprise zones (PADEP, 1996).

Environmental issues also concern less technical features of the environment. Here the potential reuse of brownfields sites can be tied to the natural and built environments more generally. Reusing brownfields for new development can deflect demand for new sites on the urban fringe, commonly called greenfields. With accelerating sprawl development across the country, the focus on brownfields includes the need to protect open space and farmlands in regions by redeveloping former industrial sites. These considerations have entered into public brownfields policies. The Pennsylvania act, for instance, includes farmland and green space preservation as one of its three main goals, in addition to cleaning up and redeveloping sites (PADEP 1996). The redevelopment of brownfields in many regions also involves consideration of aesthetic uses, such as parklands and recreational uses. In Pittsburgh, where many brownfields lie along waterways, brownfields redevelopment involves new uses for the region's riverfronts, reflecting aesthetic, recreational, and economic values (Hirsch 1998).

Economic Issues

The economic issues further complicate the brownfields issue. Unlike other redevelopment projects, economic costs extend beyond the urban land market.

Economic issues overlap with the above environmental and legal concerns in ways already mentioned: the costs imposed on cleaning up a site, the transaction costs involved in working with the public environmental agency and perhaps a city planning department regarding rezoning issues, and costs from additional protection, such as environmental insurance.

Private sector economic issues also concern the current market for the property and its projected market and whether it is to be reused for industrial activity or transformed into new uses, such as housing, commercial development, mixed-use development, or recreational activities. From the public sector viewpoint there are opportunity costs to using limited public resources for subsidies and loans on brownfields redevelopment, particularly in regions and states with fiscal constraints.

In addition to costs, an economic perspective must determine the benefits that accrue to brownfields redevelopment. Developers will be concerned with cash flow on a project, both during the remediation and redevelopment phases, and expected returns from the completed project. Where public incentives are available, private developers can factor these into their development equation. Public benefits may include additional property tax revenues from upgrading properties, increased revenues from related sources, such as business, sales or personal income taxes, and other goals such as increasing employment.

Sprawl considerations can also be viewed in an economic framework. The costs of brownfields redevelopment, including their attendant cleanup and transaction costs, must be viewed against the total costs involved in developing greenfield sites, including the investments in basic infrastructure and congestion costs, along with actual project costs. In addition, ecological costs of greenfields development can be substantial. Debate ensues regarding these total costs and which development is more costly. Suffice it to say that individual projects may stack up differently, but nonetheless, the perception of the costs attached to redeveloping brownfields versus greenfields affects individual investment decisions.

Community Concerns

As with the issues discussed above, community concerns are varied and cover a number of areas. First, a brownfield may pose a public health risk that concerns the community, as could standing contamination on a former industrial site. Second, the community may have a historical attachment to the brownfield, especially if the industrial firm once located there was a major employer of community residents. Third, communities have a stake in the redevelopment of the brownfield property, no matter what outcome occurs.

Federal and state brownfields policies require community involvement. The EPA's brownfields programs require community participation for funding, and they establish models of community-brownfields participation and encourage redevelopment partnerships. The Pennsylvania program also requires a public involvement process for the redevelopment of properties under site-specific standards and for special industrial sites.

Communities surrounding brownfields can represent different, often competing, interests, since a community may have different perceptions of what should be developed and how, based on different preferences and priorities. Community members may rank economic development as one of the major concerns, particularly in economically distressed areas. Individuals active with environmental issues may view brownfields development from a different perspective. Furthermore, requiring community involvement does not necessarily ensure active participation: Some residents may be left out. In one of the sites examined below, an innovative public process revealed "an alternative public that had been without voice in the adversarial space of the official (public) hearings" (Collins and Savage 1998, p. 217).

Within these different community discourses is the understanding of how a community and its residents view their landscape. This mental landscape (Gould and White 1974) shapes how people in a community perceive and relate to their environment, which is further shaped by their current and historical environment. In the case of Pittsburgh, brownfields often resulted from a hundred years or more of industrial activities on a site. How does a community perceive not only the brownfield site itself, but its prospective or potential changed use?

These four concerns, legal, environmental, economic, and community, are not discrete components of a brownfields redevelopment, but are interrelated and form complex relationships. This adds to the complexity of brownfields redevelopment and to the complexity of understanding its context. The research analyzes these components and how they are perceived by different agents in the brownfields redevelopment process. The next section presents a brief description of the five study sites where the research was performed.

Study Areas and Sites

The five sites comprise different brownfields projects located within different neighborhoods in Pittsburgh. Three sites are associated with one neighborhood, and one site is encircled by three neighborhoods and another borough. We include in our study two separate, small projects in the fifth neighborhood, Lawrenceville, which differs from the others, since the industrial sites are small and varied across locations within the neighborhood.

Demographic and Economic Characteristics

The general population and employment characteristics of the neighborhoods in our brownfields sites typify what might be seen generally in older industrial areas. The sites, like the city of Pittsburgh, have been losing population for decades. Population loss was greater than the citywide average in four sites, and only the neighborhoods surrounding Nine Mile Run declined by less, at 4 percent. Most communities have predominately white populations, except one site. The elderly make up 20 to 25 percent of the neighborhoods' population, exceeding the city average of 18 percent. For all sites except one, poverty levels exceeded the county average. Per capita income is lower than the city's level in all sites but one.

These characteristics reflect the structural changes that occurred in the Pittsburgh regional economy during the 1980s. The steel and metals complex collapsed by the early 1980s, while manufacturing employment decreased by 45 percent, for a loss of nearly 121,000 jobs between 1980 and 1990. Over the same years the services sector added over 155,000 jobs, an increase of 55 percent. The impacts of these changes were hardest felt in older industrial neighborhoods, typical of our brownfields neighborhoods, where employment losses exceeded both city and county averages in all sites except Nine Mile Run. In general terms, our brownfields neighborhoods show a white population base, increasingly elderly, as employment and population decreased over the 1990s. Though neighborhood-based data are not available for the 1990s, we expect that the general trends have continued, with some exceptions, as noted below. The sites themselves are considered in more detail below, particularly regarding the community role in redevelopment.

Hays

The Hays neighborhood lies in the southeastern section of the city and is more properly culturally and geographically connected to the Monongahela Valley (the Mon Valley) the location of many former steel mill properties. Its brownfield was a single plant, a former U.S. Army munitions facility that was mothballed after the Vietnam War. An environmental assessment prepared for the army in 1991 found a variety of pollutants on the site, including total petroleum hydrocarbons, volatile organic carbons (VOCs), PCBs, and asbestos insulation in the soil. The 31st Ward Citizens' Council, the active community group in the neighborhood, approached the city about assuming control of the property for building a movie production facility. The Pennsylvania Department of Environmental Protection (PADEP) determined that only the petroleum hydrocarbons and PCBs would require remediation; the concentration of metals and VOCs were at acceptable levels. The army used federal funds to clean the site of asbestos, underground storage tanks, and other contaminants (TBC 1997).

In 1993 the army "sold" the site to the Urban Redevelopment Authority of the City of Pittsburgh (URA) for $1, though interest in the production facility waned owing to the types of contaminants present in the building. The city sought out a developer. The community opposed their first choice, an aluminum and scrap melting operation, because of contamination risks and low projected employment levels. The URA then attracted GalvTech, a galvanizing and coating metals firm, to the site, with a state grant of nearly $1,000,000 going to cleanup. The 31st Ward Citizen's Council became inactive after the project was completed.

Herr's Island

Herr's Island is a forty-two-acre island located in the Allegheny River, just three miles from the central business district. Its industrial history is a long one, extending back over a hundred years to a variety of industrial uses. By the early 1900s, however, it had become the region's stockyards and meatpacking center. Over the century, as the packing operations closed down, a number of other small-scale industrial uses cropped up. Beginning in the 1970s the city and state began acquiring properties, originally to develop a park. Reacting to continuing job losses among residents and public sector support of expanding industrial parks in suburban reaches of the region, activists and political leaders on the Northside pressured the city to finish acquisition and redevelop the island, led by the Northside Civic Development Corp., the neighborhood CDC. The redevelopment began with the CDC, a private developer, and the city proposing a mixed-use project, with commercial space, light manufacturing, recreational uses, and housing.

In 1988 an environmental assessment of several parcels of land on the island revealed toxic wastes, including excessive levels of aromatic hydrocarbons and PCBs. The soils bearing these toxic wastes were encapsulated on site in 1990. In addition, organic wastes from the rendering and stock facilities were discovered and had to be hauled off-site for disposal. Finally, several parcels were discovered to contain excessive levels of heavy metals and petroleum hydrocarbons. The contaminated soils were treated for pH and then covered with crushed stone to be used as a parking lot. (TBC 1997). With $3.4 million in public funds for remediation, development began in 1991, and the Urban Redevelopment

Authority of Pittsburgh (URA) assumed control for the public sector. Northside Civic's role diminished, however, as the project got under way and the CDC became less effectual in development efforts. The newly redeveloped island has been renamed Washington's Landing. The mixed-use development contains high-end residential units, recreational activities, and a mix of businesses that employ over 400 people. In terms of community, however, Washington's Landing constitutes a new community today, physically and economically isolated from its northern neighbors across the river, despite its initial roots in the community-building process of neighborhood organizations.

Lawrenceville

Lawrenceville itself is more properly an industrial district, in a nineteenth-century conception of the term, with residents and industry colocated or within close proximity. The neighborhood is a mix of manufacturing, warehousing, retail districts, and residential quarters lying on the south side of the Allegheny River. Part contains the city's traditional wholesale food district, which underwent transformation in the 1990s to comprise a new entertainment district, with retail operations, restaurants, and loft housing. In Lawrenceville we focused on two individual brownfields projects.

The first, the Lectromelt facility, was a former electroplating plant on a 6.2-acre site. It dates back to 1882, when an iron and steel, and a gasification plant were located there. Lectromelt went bankrupt in 1992, and a DEP inspection revealed drums of flammable, used oil and coolants, which were removed by a firm hired by the bankrupt trustee. The URA purchased the site in 1994 for $130,000 and $800,000 in accrued tax delinquencies. Under an EPA Regional Brownfields Pilot project grant, the building was cleaned up, demolished, and redeveloped as a new flexible-space building.

The second site is the Bathhouse and Stable buildings, a historically significant project with lead and asbestos contamination. The stable was built in 1888, and the bathhouse was built in 1891 and closed in 1961. The buildings were most recently used for automotive repair work and contained oil and grease and other contaminants. The Lawrenceville Development Corporation (LDC), the neighborhood CDC, targeted the buildings as part of its Doughboy Square rejuvenation and obtained an option on the buildings. Pittsburgh History and Landmarks Foundation, a local developer, assisted on the property. LDC plays an active role in revitalizing the neighborhood through new housing constructed at Doughboy Square, preservation efforts, environmental improvements, retail corridor development, and its industrial site inventory database for prospective manufacturers.

LTV—South Side

When LTV shut down its steel mill operation on the Southside in 1986, neighborhood and labor activists pursued plans to attract another steelmaker to the facility. Though their plans were never accomplished, the neighborhood remains one of most organized in the city, through the South Side Local Development Corp. (SSLDC), the South Side Planning Forum, and a number of business, neighborhood, and environmental groups revitalizing the former mill neighborhood. The main thoroughfare, Carson Street, has received awards for its success in the Main Street program. New housing has been constructed, as infill projects and redeveloped former commercial and industrial properties.

The former LTV site lies on the eastern edge of the city, bordered by the South Side neighborhood. The one hundred-thirty-acre mill site was acquired by the URA in 1993, with initial plans to develop part of the area for riverboat gambling (Deitrick et al. 1999). Neighborhood resistance and stalled passage of a state law thwarted gambling proponents, and the URA turned to a planned mixed-use project, South Side Works. Environmental assessments revealed that the site contained metals such as arsenic, chromium, nickel, lead, and zinc, as well as semi-volatile organics, PCBs, and petroleum hydrocarbons. The groundwater was contaminated in one location. Today, the project is under construction. The neighborhood remains actively involved, as all projects go through neighborhood review in accordance to the community plan (Fitzpatrick 1998).

Nine Mile Run

Nine Mile Run is a 238-acre slag dump, with 134 developable acres, located across the Mon River from the former Homestead Steel Works. The Run itself drains a 7.7 square mile watershed into the river. The Duquesne Slag Company dumped about eighteen stories of waste on the site over a fifty-year period (Collins and Savage 1998). It is bordered by the south Squirrel Hill neighborhood, among the more prosperous neighborhoods in the study, Swisshelm Park, Duck Hollow, Regent Square, and a large city park, Frick.

In 1994 the URA obtained a one-year purchase option on the site for $100,000. Environmental assessments found excess chromium, to be mitigated by ground cover. The URA purchased the property in 1995 for $3.8 million and assembled a planning team to prepare plans for a housing development of up to eight hundred units. Resistance in the community to the URA development surfaced among community groups, the Squirrel Hill Urban Coalition, the Swisshelm Park Community Organization, and the Regent Square

Community Organization, whose concerns centered on slag cleanup and removal and traffic congestion. A Carnegie Mellon University team, the STU-DIO for Creative Inquiry, was also involved in the project through a series of community meetings and a development plan to clean up the streambed and maintain sustainable open space in the redevelopment. Development plans have been altered, and the project, called Summerset, is now beginning.

The brownfields communities in this study face common problems—population loss, high proportion of elderly—as described above. They also differ in their organizing and advocacy related to brownfields. In two sites, Lawrenceville and the Southside, active and effective organizing through a CDC and other neighborhood groups promotes brownfields redevelopment through a community-based process. Neither community unconditionally blocks industrial reuses of brownfields, but community-based organizations are active partners in the brownfields redevelopment and their goals concern larger issues of community revitalization and environmental improvements rather than simply reuse. The Hays neighborhood organized around an employment-based reuse of a manufacturing facility, representing a specific activity rather than a range of community-based organizing. Nine Mile Run created two forms of community organizing. The first, leveled with charges of NIMBYism, saw neighborhood organizations protesting a new development but soon acquiring the force to alter the city's development plans. At the same time, another form of community organizing focused on the environmental aesthetics that could be attached to the proposed project. In Nine Mile Run there were no community development corporations, as the LDC or SSLDC, and organizing initially began as reactive. In the final case, Herr's Island, a CDC began the process for organizing around the redevelopment of the island; soon, however, it lost its position as the project grew larger and was subsumed by the public-private partnership. In the Herr's Island case the resulting project is largely disconnected from its northern neighbors. Below we examine the costs and benefits of the brownfields projects.

Cost-Benefit Analysis

At the time of this study, only the Hays GalvTech project was totally completed. Others were under way. We provide a fuller accounting for Hays and briefly mentioned costs and benefits for the other four projects.

Hays-GalvTech

Development costs have several possible perspectives. From a social perspective, costs are all resources that must be redirected toward the venture, which would include both privately and publicly funded resources. We refer to this as the Full Cost of Development (see Table 8.1). These full costs include both private and public investments in cleanup, plant and equipment, roads, training, and so forth, necessary to make the site economically viable. Public grants and loans financed real resource transfers to this site. The U.S. Army financed a minor share of cleanup. GalvTech financed the placement of equipment on the site. The full cost of creating an economically active site was $37.5 million.

However, one could argue that the cost of making it an economically viable site would exclude the equipment and training costs, which are specific to the particular activity. These site development costs would then include building and site cleanup, feasibility studies, site improvements, and road and rail access. This cost was $9,257,036.

A different cost perspective is the state and local public finance perspective. Presumably, public bodies seek to use publicly available resources to benefit their constituencies. A public finance perspective would then compare the financing costs to the public with the benefits to the public. In this case, costs would include those resources devoted to the venture through direct purchases, grants, and loans by public agencies. We refer to these resources as State and Local Public Development Costs (see Table 8.2). Grants are non-reimbursable costs. State and local grants totaled $4,457,036 through 1997.

State and local loans represent another financial instrument for site development. Loans totaled $4,950,000 through 1997. The cost of the loan is not its face value. Basically, one has to compare the lending terms with the foregone returns or capital costs of the public agency. These costs will vary across public agencies depending on their funding opportunities and sources of capital.

As in the case of costs, there are several perspectives on benefits of the Hays site development. First, there are narrow economic measures, including new employment and incomes, and economies of public services; and the broader, quality of life measures, related to well-being, aesthetics, social capital development, crime, and so forth. Second, there is a distinction between broad social benefits versus localized benefits; for example, new jobs in the Hays community at the expense of jobs elsewhere. Third, there are the public fiscal benefits if tax revenues exceed public finance and service costs.

In its first year of operation, 1996–97, GalvTech employed thirty-five full-time equivalent (FTE) persons, at an average annual wage of $36,020, for a total payroll of $1.261 million. In year two, 1997–98, employment increased to eighty persons, for an annual payroll of $2.882 million. In

Table 8.1

Full Cost of Development, 1991–1997 (current dollars)

Funded item	Private cost	Federal cost	State cost	Local cost	Total cost
Site cleanup		500,000			500,000
Feasibility study			58,000	5,286	63,286
Building cleanup			993,750		993,750
Improvements			1,600,000	4,850,000	6,450,000
Roads			750,000		750,000
Rail access			500,000		500,000
Equipment	27,957,000				27,957,000
Worker training			300,000		300,000
Total Cost	27,957,000	500,000	4,201,750	4,855,286	37,514,036

Sources: URA 1997; URA 1998. Urban Redevelopment Authority of Pittsburgh (1997a) *URA Factsheet, 1997.* Pittsburgh: Urban Redevelopment Authority of Pittsburgh. Urban Redevelopment Authority of Pittsburgh (1998) *URA Factsheet, 1998.* Pittsburgh: Urban Redevelopment Authority of Pittsburgh.

Table 8.2

State and Local Public Development Costs, 1991–1997 (current dollars)

Type of cost	Local grant	State grant	Local loan	State loan	Total cost
Feasibility study	5,286	58,000			63,286
Site improvements	2,350,000		2,850,000	1,600,000	6,800,000
Training of workers		300,000			300,000
Public roads		750,000			750,000
Private rail access				500,000	500,000
Building cleanup		993,750			993,750
Total Cost	2,355,286	2,101,750	2,850,000	2,100,000	9,407,036

Sources: URA 1997; URA 1998. Urban Redevelopment Authority of Pittsburgh (1997a) *URA Factsheet, 1997*. Pittsburgh: Urban Redevelopment Authority of Pittsburgh. Urban Redevelopment Authority of Pittsburgh (1998) *URA Factsheet, 1998*. Pittsburgh: Urban Redevelopment Authority of Pittsburgh.

addition, there were approximately one hundred fifty FTE jobs in construction for one year. It could be argued that the parent of GalvTech was seeking regional facilities to complement its other two existing plants in the region. Therefore, we cannot establish with certainty that these would be net new jobs in the region attributable to the brownfields development program. However, it is probably reasonable to argue that there was a net increase in local Hays community positions, although it is not possible to establish whether these positions were filled by local residents.

Public fiscal benefits accrue when the tax or other revenues to public agencies generated by the facility exceed the financial subsidies and public service costs associated with the site and its economic activities. Tax revenues would include property taxes, employment and income taxes, purchased materials taxes, and corporate profits and franchise taxes. The lease payments for the site were based on loan terms that equaled the local issuing agency's (URA) cost of capital, so there is no fiscal benefit there. Property taxes based on land and structure depend upon the tax status of the GalvTech land, structures, and equipment. The building and land are owned by PEIDC, a public agency. The fair market value of the land and building increased from zero in 1996 to $2.338 million in 1998. Assessed value is 25 percent of market value, or $0.585 million (Table 8.3). Property taxes collected from GalvTech by the city of Pittsburgh and Allegheny County increased from zero in 1996 to $75,483 in 1997 and $169,041 in 1998.

Business and employment related taxes do accrue. The city of Pittsburgh levies a business privilege tax, earned income tax, nonresident employment tax, and an occupation tax. These estimated city business and employment taxes are estimated below in Table 8.4. For purposes of estimation, we assume one-half of the workers are nonresidents. This shows the city collecting estimated non-property taxes from GalvTech of $27,596 and $63,082 in 1997 and 1998, respectively. The state collected an estimated $56,722 and $105,169 in these years.

The Hays site presents an interesting example of a combined public and private effort to redevelop urban property. The cost of bringing the site into full economic use was $37.5 million, including the costs of plant equipment and worker training. The cost of site redevelopment, including building and site cleanup, site improvements, and providing road and rail access, was only $9.3 million. State and local outright grants totaled $4.5 million, or roughly one-half the site development costs. Property tax collections to the city and county rose to an annual $169,000 after full development. The city also collected an annual $63,000 in other taxes (income, privilege, etc.) after full development, while the state collected an estimated annual $105,000.

176

Table 8.3

Assessed Value of Hays Site, Applicable Millage; Rates and Property Taxes Collected, 1997–1998

Assessed value		Millage rates on base						Property Tax	
1997	1998	Pittsburgh land	Pittsburgh building	Pittsburgh school	Allegheny County	W Homestead	Steel Valley	1997	1998
$ 27,908	$ 62,500	184.5							
$233,092	$522,000		32	59.7	25.2	56	100	$75,483	$169,041
$261,000	$584,500								

Source: Allegheny County, 1998, Office of Property Assessments.

Table 8.4

GalvTech City and State Non-Property Tax Revenues, 1996–1998
(in dollars)

	1996–1997	1997–1998
City		
Business privilege[a]	NA	NA
Wage and income[b]	24,776	56,632
Mercantile[c]	2,820	6,450
Total City	27,596	63,082
State		
Unemployment[d]	10,711	24,483
Personal income[e]	35,300	80,686
Corporate income[f]	NA	NA
Capital stock and franchise[g]	NA	NA
Total state	56,722	105,169
Total	73,607	168,251

Source: Authors' calculations.
Notes: NA—Not applicable since GalvTech is a partnership and not a corporation.
[a]Business privilege: 0.6 percent of gross revenues.
[b]Wage and Income: includes earned income tax (2.875 percent of total wages), nonresident tax (1 percent of total wages for nonresidents minus payments to other municipalities), and occupation tax ($10 per employee). The annual payrolls were estimated to be $1.26 million and $2.88 million in 1997 and 1998, respectively. This estimate was based on number of employees and average annual earnings.
[c]Mercantile: 1.5 mills on Gross Revenues minus Cost of Goods (excluding labor) with exemption on first $20K. This tax base was estimated to be $4.3 million in 1998 and $1.88 million, based on the ratio of 1997 to 1998 estimated annual payrolls.
[d]Unemployment: 3.83 percent of taxable wages, maximum of $8,000 per employee.
[e]Personal Income: 2.8 percent of taxable income.
[f]Corporate Income: 10 percent corporate net income
[f]Capital stock and franchise: complicated formula based on income and net worth.

This represents a total annual tax collection of $337,000 (105,000 (nonproperty) + 63,000 (property) = 168,000 (nonproperty) + 169,000 (property) = 337,000), which would pay off the state and local grants in roughly thirteen years. This implies an initial outright investment of $4.5 million in public funds, yielding increased taxes of $337,000 per year, implying a return of 7.5 percent, excluding increased income taxes. In addition, there were eighty full-time jobs created, plus one hundred fifty temporary construction jobs.

Herr's Island

Financial analysis of Herr's Island (HI) must distinguish between site development associated with cleanup and infrastructure, and building development. The URA arranged financing for the site development activities.

Table 8.5

Public Finance Sources for Site Development: Activities on Herr's Island

Funding source	Funds ($million)
Federal	
U.S. Economic Development Administration	2.28
Appalachian Regional Commission	1.85
Total federal and multistate	4.13
PA state	
Department of Community Affairs	2.3
Department of Commerce	2.4
Department of Environmental Resources	3.14
Strategy 21	3.0
Total state	10.84
City and regional	
City of Pittsburgh CDBG	4.4
Urban Redevelopment Authority	1.89
City of Pittsburgh Bond Funds	3.25
Port Authority Transit	0.8
Pittsburgh Water and Sewer Authority	1.2
Total city and regional	11.54
Grand Total	26.51

Source: Urban Redevelopment Authority, 1997b, Washington's Landing Fact Sheet.

Public financing came from a wide variety of sources (see Table 8.5), with a total of $26.5 million contributed from public funds for site development. The city and state contributed roughly equal shares of the costs. (However, city CDBG money is ultimately federal money, which, if allocated to federal sources, would make city and federal shares roughly equal.) The total site development cost of $26.5 million consisted of land assembly and demolition ($8.35 million), remediation ($3.4 million), grading ($2 million), bridges ($4 million), utilities ($2.35 million), roads ($3.4 million), and parks and trails ($3 million) (URA 1997). Total site preparation and development costs (excluding building structures) for the forty-two-acre HI site were $631,000 per acre.

In addition to the above cleanup and infrastructure costs, public agencies funded the relocation of Gamma Sports, a private company located on the island. The state of Pennsylvania, through grants and loans, financed $2.1 million in relocation costs for Gamma Sports in 1991. Of this total, $0.9 million was grants and $1.2 million in loans. These loans were made at 3.75 percent and 5 percent. Any subsidy on these loans would depend upon the state's cost of capital.

The benefits from the development come from several sources. Commercial building development on HI was undertaken mainly by private sources, totaling $20.3 million (see Table 8.6). Additionally, property values on Herr's Island have increased as a result of the redevelopment (see Table 8.7). Increased property tax collections between 1995 and 1998 were $231,224, based on total assessed value. New homeowners received tax abatements during their first three years of ownership; residential property climbed steadily as the residential phase was developed. New employment is also a benefit of the redevelopment. Occupants of the new buildings have brought permanent new jobs to HI, though it is difficult to determine the net addition. While there is likely to be job reshuffling around the region, there are also likely to be some new jobs created as a result of the HI development; how many is impossible to say.

The Herr's Island site represents an interesting case of public agencies fully financing the site preparation. A total of $26.5 million of public funds were used to redevelop the site, a cost of $631,000 per acre. Once the site was ready for use, the public agencies funded the relocation of one business there through a grant and loan combination. The public agencies have leased a large share of the developed land. Building construction totaled $20.3 million, of which public agencies funded roughly 10 percent. While public-owned lands and buildings are nontaxable, privately owned land and buildings constructed on the island have increased tax revenues. Increases in commercial-related property tax collections due to the redevelopment were estimated to be roughly $231,000 annually. Residential property tax collections on the island, attributable to the housing development, will increase over time, although the three-year tax abatement program would delay full collection. For residential property in place in 1997, full tax collections would be roughly $60,000 annually for the ten residences completed. Employment in site construction and preparation was estimated to be roughly three hundred workers. The ability to calculate the effects of regional permanent employment is limited since some of the businesses may have remained in the region even if the site had not been developed.

Other Sites

The full cost, private and public, of development for the Lectromelt site was $3,823,000 (Table 8.8). These costs include investments in cleanup, demolition of building, site preparation, improvements in infrastructure, structural cost, and so forth, necessary to make the site economically viable. State and local costs were all grants, totaling $1,014,000 through 1998. In addition to the state and local grants shown, a loan of $500,000 from the URA was made at 5 percent for one year to the company developing the site.

Table 8.6

Commercial Building Construction on Herr's Island, 1992–1997

Date of construction	Size (sq. ft.)	Private cost ($million)	Public cost ($million)	Owner	Status
1992	44,500	2.4	0	WLA	Lease to PADEP
1993	NA	1.5	0	TRRA	Owner-occupied
1993	28,000	2.9	0	WLA	Lease to PADEP
1993	37,000	3.3	0	Sports Technology, Inc.	Owner-occupied
	NA	3.0	0	WLM	URA leases land
	30,000	2.6	0	Rubinoff Co.	Lease to Silicone Graphic
1997	53,000	1.9	2.7	PEIDC	Lease to AHI
Total		17.6	2.7		

Sources: Urban Redevelopment Authority, 1997b, Washington's Landing Fact Sheet; PEIDC Annual Report, 1997.

Key: NA—Not available.
WLA—Washington's Landing Associates (private).
URA—Urban Redevelopment Authority (public).
PADEP—Pennsylvania Department of Environmental Protection (public).
AHI—Automated Healthcare (private).
PEIDC—Pittsburgh Economic and Industrial Development Corporation (public).
TRRA—Three Rivers Rowing Association (private).
WLM—Washington's Landing Marina (private).

Table 8.7

Assessed Values of Properties on Herr's Island, 1995 and 1998

Tax status	Land assessed value ($)	Building assessed value ($)	Total assessed value ($)	Fair market value ($million)
1995				
Non-taxable	432,785	215,210	647,995	2.6
Taxable	0	0	0	0
1998				
Non-taxable	276,240	162,500	438,740	1.8
Taxable	327,660	1,739,000	2,066,660	8.3

Source: Urban Redevelopment Authority, 1997b, Washington's Landing Fact Sheet.

Table 8.8

Full Cost of Development, 1991–1998 (current dollars)

Funded item	Private cost	Federal cost	State cost	Local cost	Total cost
Site cleanup	15,000	100,000	442,500	147,500	705,000
Demolition			394,000		394,000
Site preparation	84,000				84,000
Roads	30,000			30,000	60,000
Structural cost	2,580,000				2,580,000
Total Cost	2,709,000	100,000	836,500	177,500	3,823,000

Note: All public costs in this table were funded through grants.

Table 8.9

Project Costs for Proposed Development of Bathhouse and Stables
(in dollars)

Cost category	Bathhouse	Stable	Total
A. Site acquisition			
Property acquisition	120,000	100,000	220,000
Environmental (Phase I)	3300	1700	5000
Legal, survey, and taxes	8387	7097	15,484
Subtotal	131,687	108,797	240,484
B. Construction			
Non-environmental	203,950	356,367	560,317
Environmental remediation	30,000	25,000	55,000
Subtotal	233,950	381,367	615,317
C. Site development	9200	5500	14,700
D. Cost during construction	3782	2072	5854
E. Professional fees	41,689	50,100	91,789
F. Financing expense	9950	7250	17,200
Total project costs	430,258	555,086	985,344

Source: Lawrenceville Development Corporation, 1999.

For the Bathhouse and Stable, redevelopment of the properties shows total project costs of $985,344 (Table 8.9). Environmental Phase I costs are $5,000, and environmental remediation costs are estimated to be $55,000. By late 1998 LDC had entered into a lease-purchase arrangement with an architectural firm for the stable property.

We could not calculate full costs and benefits of all the projects; nonetheless, they are well enough under way to begin to estimate community perceptions to the redevelopments occurring. In the next section of the report we estimate community perceptions to brownfields redevelopment in our five brownfields neighborhoods. Empirical estimation of perceptions is conducted through a Q methodology.

Data and Q Methodology

The study undertook a Q-method analysis to understand community perceptions surrounding brownfields redevelopment in the sites. Q methodology allows for an ordered means to test subjectivity (Brown 1980). As shown in the sections above, redeveloping brownfields is subject to a number of perceptions regarding contamination, costs, the threat of liability, level of community involvement, and so on. The five sites described above represent communities in which brownfields redevelopment has occurred or is occurring.

In the Q method, perceptions about an issue are collected as a series of viewpoints on the subject. Each viewpoint is represented by a statement on the subject or activity. Subjects in the study—its variables—perform a rank-ordering of the statements along a continuum of their agreement or disagreement with the statements. These orderings are called Q sorts. Three sequential statistical procedures are then performed on the Q sorts. The raw data matrix of persons and their Q sorts are correlated to create a matrix of correlations between persons for all Q sorts. This shows correlation among persons on the basis of their ranking of the statements. Then factor analysis is applied to the matrix to reduce correlations to groups of persons with like Q sorts or clusters of opinions on the subject (McKeown and Thomas 1988). The factor analysis produces a series of factors for each person variable. Factor weights are then computed for persons who load significantly on a factor; thus individuals with higher factor loadings on a particular factor are more heavily weighted in the final, merged array. Factor weights for individual significant Q sorts are then merged to establish weighted scores for each statement. Persons whose Q sorts are similar will cluster together on the same factor. Thus, each factor cluster is made up of persons who represent a distinct perspective on the subject, which differs from other person clusters identified with other factors.

The Statement (Q) Sample

The Q sample is the collection of statements that relate to the area of investigation. We determined from our literature review and interviewing schedule that the four theoretical domains discussed above comprise the core perceptions held about brownfields redevelopment: economic, environmental, legal, and community issues. To develop the Q sample, we collected statements on brownfields redevelopment. The research employed a hybrid technique to develop the Q sample, using a set of statements drawn from a larger population (McKeown and Thomas 1988).[2] Statements were collected from interviews with brownfields stakeholders who would later perform the Q sorts, with additional statements from newspaper articles, editorials, letters to the editor, and other published material on brownfields redevelopment in Pittsburgh and the brownfields sites.

This process yielded an initial set of over one hundred and fifty statements, which were organized along the four theoretical domains. In seeking to analyze perceptions of brownfields redevelopment in Pittsburgh, the research sample covered the widest possible interpretation of opinion on the four theoretical concerns. The main effects of the research were to follow definitiveness across two levels, bias and wish/policy statements, and theoretical completeness across the four domains. This results in a factorial design of twenty-four combinations, (A)(B) x 3 replications (see Table 8.10).[3] A statement was selected to represent each combination.

Our set of statements revealed contradictory opinions on a number of important concerns about redeveloping brownfields, such as differing opinions about the costs of cleanups and hindrances caused by liability issues. Perceptions also encompassed desires for particular ends (wish) or for means for achieving an end (policy). These provide the second level of definitiveness of the study. Specifically, bias statements concern general preferences based on a particular interpretation of facts. An example of a bias statement would be (ae): "Clean up costs are usually the biggest obstacle to brownfields redevelopment." This statement reflects a bias, a "doubtful question," and represents an opinion of the holder, not a statement of fact (Brown 1980, 68). Perception about the statement will depend on one's experience with brownfields cleanups and how one views environmental costs.

Wish statements reflect a desire for a particular end. Since brownfields redevelopment involves interlocking, complex factors, wish statements could encompass desires to redevelop a site into a particular use or reflect a desire for participation in brownfields redevelopment, for example, (ac): "Residents of individual communities, no matter how small, should be able to stop any redevelopment scheme they did not like." We see here a strong

Table 8.10

Design of Community Perceptions to Brownfields Redevelopment in Pittsburgh

Main effects	Levels
A. Definitiveness	(a) bias
	(b) wish/policy
B. Theoretical completeness	(c) community
	(d) economic
	(e) environmental
	(f) legal

Replications $= m = 3$
$N = (A)(B)(m) = (2)(4)(3) = 24$ Q sample statements

desire that community residents should be able to block development that they view as intrusive or against values held in the community. The view reflects the desire that residents should have a voice in the redevelopment of their community, a statement suggesting a course of action for communities to achieve a desired outcome.

Policy statements center on beliefs as to the best way to reach a particular goal or end. Policy statements are important to understand in analyzing the perceptions of brownfields redevelopment, since redevelopment is intimately tied to public policy on a number of fronts, including all four of our theoretical domains. An example of a policy statement (be) reflecting the view that community involvement should be part of brownfields redevelopment is: "The real and perceived contamination issues surrounding most brownfields sites suggest that an informed public should be a prerequisite for brownfields development."

The Person (P) Sample

The study employed an extensive person sample in order to cover the range of stakeholders in the brownfields development. Organizations, firms, groups, and individuals were identified for the collection of stakeholders rather than random-sampling, as consistent with the method (Brown 1990, 260; McKeown and Thomas 1988, 37–38). The research team set up appointments to administer the Q sorts, and research was conducted in summer of 1998. The final P set realized n = 117 respondents who performed Q sorts.

Respondents were classified by their attachment to brownfields redevelopment (see Table 8.11).[4] We divided up participants in the study by private sector, public sector, and nonprofit sector employment that directly relates to brownfields redevelopment. A fourth category, community activist/resident, included volunteers, members of neighborhood and environmental groups,

Table 8.11

Stakeholders in Brownfields Revitalization

Respondents in Brownfields Q Study

Private sector	39	Public sector	22
Manufacturing	4	Federal	1
Property developers/mgt/owners	6	State—Pennsylvania DEP	7
Lenders	4	City	14
Environmental consulting	14	Urban Redevelopment Authority	5
Architecture/landscape arch.	6	Mayor's office	4
Legal	2	Planning	3
Journalism	3	Environmental education	1
		Council office	1
Nonprofit sector	31	Community activist/resident (nec.)	25
Community development corporation	5	Environmental affiliation	6
Community-based organization	5	CDC/CBO affiliation or resident	19
Environmental interest group	9		
Economic development organizations	7		
Education	5		

and residents. These distinctions were drawn from the participants' personal data sheets and respondents' self-categorization of their brownfields and community involvement. The goal in Q method is to represent a range of stakeholders, not randomly selected individuals.

Ranking the Statements: The Q Sorts

We initially pretested the experiment and refined the questions. The Q sorts were administered to the respondents in the study in the summer of 1998, using a scoring continuum from –4 (the statement the respondent least agrees with) to +4 (the statement the respondent most agrees with), with mean = 0. Respondents received directions on the procedure and performed the rankings of the statements. Computational values were substituted for the continuum score to transform all values to positive numbers ranging from 1 to 9 (with mean = 5, and s = 2.0851 the same as the Q-sort continuum). The research then followed statistical procedures to determine the final factor scores and interpret the results.

The responses were correlated in a 117x117 correlation matrix for all persons and their respective rankings of statements. The correlation matrix shows the relation among pairs of individuals in the study (rxy). Factor analysis is then used to determine how the respondents in the study are grouped together. The correlation matrix was factor analyzed by the principal components method with a varimax orthogonal rotation.[5] This yielded a rotated components matrix, which reveals each subject's correlation with a particular factor. Each significant factor represents a cluster of persons whose Q sorts, or rankings, are similar enough to be grouped together, though they will not perfectly agree for all statements. The factor analysis is then used to produce factor scores. Unlike R-based factor analysis, which then interprets the results of traits, or variables based on factor loadings, Q analysis uses the factor loadings to generate a factor array, or model Q sort, for each factor, ranging from –4 to +4. Only those individuals whose score is determined to be significant for the factor, are considered as part of the factor and only significant factors are included.

Our results yielded three significant factors; each represents a unique perspective on brownfields redevelopment, which is determined by analyzing the final ranking of the statements for each factor and the group of individuals who form each factor. Both personal characteristics and statement rankings are analyzed in order to understand what each factor implies.

The Results

Some general conclusions emerge at the outset. Men represented nearly three-quarters of our total P-sample (see Table 8.12). Though we attempted to achieve representativeness, women are underrepresented as brownfields stakeholders compared to the population at large. Our stakeholders are younger, on average, than the population of the brownfields neighborhoods. Furthermore, our P-sample is better educated than our brownfields communities, on average. This shows that not only are those whose work may involve some direct experience with brownfields redevelopment more highly educated on average than a brownfields neighborhood, as one might expect, but the community or environmental volunteers and activists are also more likely to be better educated. We find that though a higher than average proportion of elderly live in brownfields neighborhoods in Pittsburgh, they are less likely to be involved in their redevelopment, in either a professional or community volunteer capacity.

Factor 1: The Development Perspective

The Factor 1's perspective is dominated by what we label the Development Perspective. Respondents grouping in this factor represented more private sector interests and fewer activists than our P-sample. It included those in both public and nonprofit stakeholders centered in economic development work and involved persons across all five sites. Determining statements are shown in Table 8.13.

Table 8.12

Demographic Information on Respondents and Factors

	Number of persons				Percent of total			
	P-sample	F1	F2	F3	P-sample	F1	F2	F3
Male	87	37	13	7	74	77	52	78
Female	30	11	12	2	26	23	48	22
Age								
18–29	15	7	4	0	13	15	16	0
30–39	37	17	8	4	32	35	32	44
40–49	34	12	7	3	29	25	28	33
0–59	24	9	6	1	20	19	24	11
60+	7	3	0	1	6	6	0	11
Education								
High school or less	1	0	1	0	1	0	4	0
Some college	8	1	4	1	7	2	16	11
Bachelor's degree	43	15	6	5	37	31	24	56
Post bachelor's	65	32	18	3	56	67	56	33

Table 8.13

Q Sort—Factor Scores

Number	Statement	Factor 2 score	Factor 1 score	Factor 3 score
1	The public needs to know what contaminants there are and what the clean up is doing, but they don't have to be in on the business decision of redeveloping the site. 1CB	-3	0	0
2	The most important factor for a community when redeveloping brownfields is the intended use of the site, which includes what kinds of jobs will be there. 2CB	1	2	-3
3	Most brownfields redevelopment works best as a technical process carried out by specialists rather than a public participation process. 3CB	-2	-1	-1
4	Solving brownfield problems through economic development should not lead planners and developers to overlook the broader values of brownfield sites to a community. 4 CW	2	1	1
5	Residents of individual communities, no matter how small, should be able to stop any redevelopment scheme they did not like. 5CW	1	-3	-4
6	Before the bulldozers are unleashed on another former industrial site to build yet another imagined community, Pittsburgh's leaders and residents should find another way to invest in our future that doesn't involve further destruction of our community and past. 6CW	0	-2	-1
7	Clean up costs are usually the biggest obstacle to brownfield redevelopment. 7EnB	0	1	-2
8	The environmental issue really throws up a red flag—it scares a lot of developers away. 8EnB	-1	3	-1
9	The brownfields debate tends to center on speeding economic revitalization while environmental quality concerns, such as protecting public health, have become secondary considerations. 9EnB	0	-2	4
10	We simply should not go on destroying our farmland and green spaces while neglecting these abandoned or underutilized properties. 10EnW	4	4	3

Statement			
11	The real and perceived contamination issues surrounding most brownfields sites suggest that an informed public should be a prerequisite for brownfields development. 11 EnW	1	1	3
12	Put more brownfields in the Mon Valley back into trees, grass, and public spaces. 12EnW	0	-1	2
13	Older sites are more expensive to redevelop than greenfields. 13EcB	-1	2	-1
14	Major transportation improvements are needed for brownfields redevelopment to move faster. 14EcB	0	-1	-1
15	Even with government programs to help redevelop brownfields, developers still see it as a long process and are more willing to abandon the plan and find a clean site. 15EcB	1	2	0
16	We should not be investing in redeveloping brownfields in a time of tightening budgets, crumbling infrastructure, rising crime and declining education. 16EcW	-2	-4	-4
17	brownfields are simply developable sites—the contamination should be viewed as just the cost of doing business. 17EcW	3	0	-2
18	Redeveloping brownfields should not wipe out all trace of industry or manufacturing on former mill properties, only to set up tourist meccas. 18EcW	-2	0	1
19	The brownfields issue is a smoke screen for gutting clean up standards, environmental regulations, and liability standards. 19LB	2	-3	-1
20	Relaxing clean-up standards and releasing responsible parties from liability could create more contaminated sites in the future. 20LB	2	-1	3
21	With brownfields, local elected officials are being asked to solve problems that they are incapable of dealing with. 21LB	2	-2	-2
22	Even though brownfields projects are going ahead, people should be aware that there are unresolved issues regarding owner and lender liability. 22LW	1	0	1
23	They need to do something with the environmental laws so that you are only responsible for the contamination you cause and not contamination prior to your use of the site. 23LW	-3	1	-3
24	It should be easier to get more people to take advantage of the state's program and clean up brownfields as we get more successes with the new state brownfields program. 24LW	0	3	2

What distinguished Factor 1 individuals is their concern about development costs—both direct development costs plus costs associated with uncertainties around environmental issues. The Development Perspective views brownfields as more expensive to redevelop than greenfield sites, while both Factors 2 and 3 disagreed with this opinion (Statements 13 and 8).

The Development Perspective likewise supports a changed legal and policy framework for brownfields (Statements 9, 19, and 20). They view policies that encourage brownfields redevelopment positively and do not view the newer policies as increasing environmental threats. Furthermore, for the Development Perspective, brownfields policy represents development policy, not an attempt to weaken environmental laws. The strength of their views is reinforced in Statements 9 and 20, both by the difference between Factors 2 and 3, and by their differences on agreement and disagreement. In addition, though not a determining statement for Factor 1 respondents, their strong agreement with Statement 24 underscores their positive view of brownfields policy.

Echoing these sentiments is the Development Perspective's desire to reduce developers' uncertainty about brownfields even further. Though they did not strongly agree, the wide disparity between them and Factors 2 and 3 shows they believe brownfields policy could go further to reduce uncertainty (Statement 23).

One distinguishing factor of the Development Perspective is that most of the statements that determine the factor reflect bias, rather than wish or policy type statements. Except for Statement 23, which reflects a desire for changing environmental laws to reduce brownfields uncertainty further, the Development Perspective focuses on more tangible issues such as economic and environmental costs.

Factor 2: The Community-Environmental Activist Perspective

The second perspective reflects the Community-Environmental Activist Perspective (see Table 8.13 for determining statements). Nearly all the respondents that form this perspective either work in the nonprofit sector or are community or environmental activists in our formulation. Thus this perspective lies completely outside the public and private sector development realms. On the nonprofit side, many work in environmental interests groups, and as activists, they are more likely to be neighborhood-based. Additionally, unlike our P-sample, half are female and are more represented by the LTV-Southside neighborhood, though involvement in all is represented.

What distinguishes Factor 2 participants is their different views of what constitutes public involvement in brownfields redevelopment and what a community can do. Here they hold a strong stand on a community's right to be involved in brownfields redevelopment, revealed by both the statements they felt strongest about and the significant differences between them and Factors 1 and 3. A community should not be passive about redevelopment, in their view, but can take steps to be involved with choices of development. This is reflected in their strong disagreement on Statement 1. They believe that a community should be able to stop redevelopment it did not like (Statement 5), and differ significantly from Factors 1 and 3, who strongly disagreed with this. The strong association between this factor and the Southside LTV site is notable, also. The South Side Planning Forum reviews all proposed site developments, and, without their support, "developers could have a difficult time winning support from the City" (Fitzpatrick 1998, B-1).

Their activism extends to the role that knowledge plays in effective advocacy and organizing work. They strongly support a public participation process for brownfields issues. Though Factors 1 and 3 agreed that public participation is needed, Factor 2 takes an unambiguous stand (Statement 11). This reinforces the discussion above about what public participation means when required by law. Here we can see that the Community-Environmental Activist's perception is one of open processes with strong public input. The contamination is within their borders; they want to know about it.

Factor 2 individuals take the middle ground between Factors 1 and 3 on the brownfields-economic-environmental dichotomy. They do not view brownfields policy as a means to lessen environmental standards, as Factor 3, nor do they strongly disagree with these notions, as Factor 1. Their neutrality suggests that they do not perceive a tradeoff between environmental standards and economic development, or else they view it as a false dichotomy, unlike Factors 1 and 3 (Statements 9 and 10). For them other issues are more important.

Other statements reinforce Factor 2's conception of brownfields meaning more than economic development or gutting environmental policy. These individuals see alternative uses for brownfields that might involve uses not strictly defined as economic development. Reflecting the strength they place on the public's right to know about contamination is also their opinion about contamination itself—bad in its own right and not simply a cost to be borne.

Finally, the Community-Environmental Activist Perspective views the additional costs and time that brownfields redevelopment might entail in a different light from Factors 1 and 3. Statement 15, coupled with Factor 2's neutrality on certain cost concerns, suggests either a lack of concern by the Community Perspective on costs that developers face or a high degree of optimism about future redevelopment in their own neighborhood. Their disagreement on this issue is only slight, but it is significant when compared to Factors 1 and 3.

Factor 3: The Technical Environmental Perspective

Factor 3 is formed by their unified, strong support of environmental regulations (see Table 8.13 for determining statements). They do not share a perspective that includes community development issues as part of the brownfields problem. They likewise reject economic development as a goal of cleaning up brownfields. brownfields redevelopment is primarily an environmental issue. For these reasons, we have termed them the Technical Environmental Perspective.

The Technical Environmental Perspective supports strong environmental regulations (Statements 9 and 19). They feel that policies and laws designed to accelerate brownfields revitalization are reducing environmental quality and public health standards. Focusing on redevelopment prospects and economic costs for brownfields is pushing aside the concerns most important to them, the environmental regulations that determine cleanup standards.

Factor 3 maintains an environmental focus when other nonregulatory issues are factored in. Unlike Factor 1, Factor 3 firmly rejects a cost-based understanding of brownfields redevelopment and is less sympathetic to concerns of brownfields neighborhoods (Statements 2 and 7). The environmental cleanup is what is important, not the cost issues or community development concerns that arise (Statement 17). What gets redeveloped or what that redevelopment costs is not part of the Factor 3 perspective. Their perspective is almost a naive view of what developers face and a somewhat lack of concern of what urban neighborhoods confront with brownfields and neighborhood disinvestment. Consequently, they have little sympathy for more romantic notions of preservation or retaining links to an industrial past (Statement 18).

Because of their support for strong environmental regulations, Factor 3 individuals are skeptical of current policy changes. They believe that local elected officials, now brought into the brownfields arena with current policy changes, are not capable of understanding the technical environmental issues that brownfields entail (Statement 21). Furthermore, though neutral on prospects for new brownfields redevelopment under the state program, their difference from the strong agreement expressed by Factors 1 and 2 underscores their skepticism (Statement 24). Also, even though they disagree with Statement 16, their disagreement is less strong than Factors 1 and 2 and significant. They feel less strongly about the need for public sector support for redeveloping brownfields.

Common Perspectives Across Factors

The research results above point to three different views on brownfields redevelopment, what we have termed the Development Perspective, the

Community-Environmental Activist Perspective, and the Technical Environmental Perspective. With the interesting differences analyzed above, these perspectives conform, in part, to common views on brownfields redevelopment. The Community-Environmental Activist Perspective, however, is often missing from many brownfields studies. The research points to the need for this well-forged voice to be involved with planning and policymaking when brownfields are concerned. The Technical Environmental Perspective, likewise, suggests a lack of emphasis on the goal of getting brownfields redeveloped.

Across these different perspectives, however, we find common understanding about brownfields revitalization. Since brownfields redevelopment complicates an already complicated process, particularly in older industrial urban communities lacking new investment, shared viewpoints can help to shape a dialogue across these different perspectives.

1. All three perspectives agreed strongly with the need to redevelop brownfields as an alternative to expanding development into farmlands and exurban open space areas (Statement 10). Their shared desire to stem regional sprawl represents a significant unity of expression across disparate groups. This has important implications for policy in Pennsylvania, which is currently grappling with developing common land-use practices to manage urban and farmland growth. Despite opposition from organized development interests, containing urban growth through revit lizing urban brownfields has the support of our Development Perspective, along with the other two factors. Different constituencies might have different interpretations of this statement, but their strong common agreement presents a strong basis for forming alliances.

2. The Pittsburgh region is also engaged in a debate about new highway construction. The revitalization of brownfields, especially in the former steel areas of the Mon Valley, is often tied directly to building new roads. All three perspectives were largely neutral on this issue (Statement 14). None agreed strongly that transportation improvements were a necessary factor for brownfields revitalization, and all three perspectives felt that other concerns were more important in addressing the brownfields problem.

3. The three perspectives remained neutral about remaining liability uncertainties (Statement 22). This may be interpreted that all feel that new policies covering liability clarifications adequately address the issue. The perspectives may also vary on whether they feel that people are already aware of unexplored liability issues or that they don't view liability as important as other issues. We can't determine from these results, but their neutrality suggests that for the three perspectives here, lingering liability issues are not a main concern when compared to other brownfields concerns.

4. None of the three perspectives believed that no public participation is required in the brownfields redevelopment process (Statement 3). From our other statements we know that how each perspective views public participation strongly differs. We also know that what constitutes public participation in redevelopment does not conform to all desires. Nonetheless, the statement confirms that brownfields redevelopment requires more than technical understanding and public involvement is part of the process.

5. Each of the three perspectives viewed some type of public expenditure for brownfields redevelopment as generally positive, despite needs in other areas (Statement 16). Though the significant difference between the Technical Environmental Perspective and the other two was discussed above, all three supported public investments in brownfields. This suggests general public support for governmental policies that assist and encourage the cleanup and reuse of older industrial lands.

6. There was no support among the groups for historic preservation compared to the other brownfields issues (Statement 6).[6] This view may reflect an opinion that preservation does not have strong political support in Pittsburgh, despite outstanding efforts of revitalizing Pittsburgh neighborhoods through historic preservation (Moe and Wilkie 1997, Gratz 1998), including the Southside neighborhood. Of the sites in our study, one project—the Lawrenceville Bathhouse and Stable—involved historic preservation. Preserving the natural landscape that developed on the slag heap in Nine Mile Run became an important issue in determining the final project for the site. Though not historic preservation, brownfields revitalization through the reuse of an existing industrial facility occurred in Hays. Despite these examples, the three brownfields perspectives do not rank preservation issues highly. Either they feel them to be unimportant when confronted with older industrial sites or they cannot envision what preservation entails on older industrial sites.

7. Nonetheless, the perspectives shared slightly the view that brownfield sites might be attached to different values of a community, other than economic development issues (Statement 4). Often these sites were employment centers of a community, which developed and changed over a hundred-year period. Mild support for this statement could be interpreted as tempering the mild disagreement over preservation and brownfields redevelopment.

Conclusions

This research examined two implications of revitalizing brownfields: public benefits and costs of redevelopment and brownfields stakeholders' perceptions of redevelopment in five brownfields neighborhoods in Pittsburgh.

In all five cases, including those that are currently undergoing redevelopment, public-private partnerships were instrumental in getting projects off the ground. This includes issues around site acquisition and contamination and remediation, as well as other types of loans and grants available to users and developers. In a city such as Pittsburgh, where many brownfields do not get redeveloped by purely private market means, public investments and partnerships with nonprofit and private sector actors can stimulate brownfields redevelopment. Also in Pittsburgh, the Urban Redevelopment Authority is the major actor in the public sector for all the brownfields cases we examined. This suggests that public agencies can be effective in revitalizing brownfields in neighborhoods.

At the time of this study, public benefits and costs could only be fully estimated in the Hays case, which redeveloped the site into an industrial use. Given the data collected, the return seems reasonable over the long term. Other intangible benefits were not estimated, but should also be seen as including cleaning up a contaminated facility and reusing a former vacant plant that dominates the Hays neighborhood visually and economically.

The Q methodology was used to test concerns about brownfields redevelopment by brownfields stakeholders. The research reviewed four theoretical concerns that relate to brownfields redevelopment—legal, environmental, economic, and community. The research then tested stakeholders' opinions of these concerns through a Q methodology. The results yielded three different perspectives on brownfields redevelopment, each with its own orientations to how it views brownfields redevelopment and the underlying theoretical issues.

The Development Perspective encompassed both private and public sector economic development. Here cost issues were paramount. Changes in regulation and policy that encourage brownfields cleanups were viewed positively by this perspective. The perspective showed an understanding that some sort of public participation will occur with brownfields redevelopments, but drew the line on the extent of that participation. The perspective stands out starkly when compared to the Technical Environmental Perspective. They each represent the extremes of how brownfields legislation is viewed—as promoting increased revitalization of sites versus becoming a means to lessen environmental standards and weaken environmental regulation.

The Factor 2 perspective—the Community-Environmental Activist Perspective—puts community activism at the top of its priorities for brownfields redevelopment. The factor is not antidevelopment. Indeed it represents a middle position between Factors 1 and 3 on changing environmental laws to encourage brownfields reuse. It remains concerned about contamination in the community, but its preferences are different from those of the Technical Environmental Perspective.

The Technical Environmental Perspective takes a hard-line stand in favor of environmental regulations. brownfields policies are eroding the strength of current environmental standards, according to this perspective. In some statements this perspective seems to focus so intently on environmental regulations and standards that it is not clear that it understands or cares about the concerns of communities dealing with brownfields issues and community disinvestment.

The advantages of the Q method in testing subjectivity surrounding brownfields is highlighted in the statements regarding community involvement and community participation issues. All factors disagreed that brownfields redevelopment works best as a technical process rather than a public participation process (Statement 3: -1 -2 -1). We would expect the community perspective to disagree with this statement, but now that most new developments and environmental processes require public participation processes, both the development and technical environmental perspectives also disagreed with this. That might be the sort of result obtained from structured survey analysis. However, in our understanding of community we find that participation is not an unambiguous process; it means different things to different groups. The Q reveals this when stronger statements on community involvement are included. By forcing a ranking, we see that both the Developers Perspective and the Technical Environmental Perspective remain neutral to the idea that though the public needs to know about contamination on a site (probably they agreed with this), the pubic is not required for making business decisions (they probably disagreed with this). When stronger statements are included, the notion of what is participation diverges even further. Both Factors 1 and 3 strongly reject the notion that residents should be able to block unwanted redevelopment; while the Community-Environmental Perspective viewed this as part of participation.

Planning and policy can benefit from understanding these perspectives. Where public participation is required, it is understood that the public is diverse and approaches the brownfields issues differently with different concerns and understandings. Economic development officials in the public sector may already hold the Development Perspective and may not understand neighborhood and community concerns. Likewise the Community-Environmental Activist Perspective suggests that communities need to learn more about technical components of environmental and contamination issues to be able to work with Technical Environmental or Development Perspectives.

The research reveals areas of shared interests, which shows the possibility of consensus-building around brownfields redevelopment. The three perspectives agree on the need to use urban brownfields revitalization as a means to stem new land development. This unity among the perspectives points to a growing consensus against sprawl-type development and the need for governments to take action, however strongly resistance is felt. The research points to the possibility of building broad participation across these consensus areas. Coalitions promoting the containment of sprawl can build alliances among seemingly conflicting views to promote brownfields redevelopment.

Notes

1. Sayer (1984). At the governmental level we can see differences by viewing two U.S. federal agencies' definitions of brownfields. The Environmental Protection Agency (EPA) defines brownfields as "abandoned, idled or underused industrial and commercial sites where expansion or redevelopment is complicated by real or perceived environmental contamination that can add cost, time or uncertainty to a redevelopment project." The U.S. Office of Technology Assessment (OTA) takes a slightly different slant on brownfields to include "sites whose redevelopment may be hindered not only by potential contamination, but also by poor location, old or obsolete infrastructure, or other less tangible factors often linked to neighborhood decline." The EPA definition explicitly does not include Superfund National Priorities List (NPL) sites, whose cleanup comes under direct federal oversight (Kaiser 1998). Within the redevelopment community, whether explicitly acknowledged or not, the OTA definition provides a direct link to older, possibly distressed, communities faced with lack of investment opportunities, regardless of contamination.

2. Hybrid Q samples combine naturalistic samples, drawn from interviews of those performing the Q-sort experiment, and quasi-naturalistic Q samples, which are drawn from opinion statements external to the individuals in the study (Brown 1980, 173–74; McKeown and Thomas 1988, 26).

3. The number of multiples of the design of the experiment determines the size of the Q sample (Brown 1980, 189). Here the four theoretical concerns are replicated six times, for twenty-four statements. We determined that this number would serve both heterogeneity and replication, though it is smaller than many Q studies in the literature. During our pretest we confirmed the representativeness of the Q sample. We also rejected adding replications, as did the pretest group (The brownfields Center at Carnegie Mellon University and the University of Pittsburgh, June 1998). Following Dunn (1994), we determined the sample size to be "contextually appropriate," since the Q sorts would be performed by the P sample in a range of places—such as workplaces, community meetings, and committee meetings—where a time constraint would be evident.

Q methodology finds such n values needless. Typically a P set of forty to sixty subjects will yield enough people to define a factor, with four to five persons sufficient. The result here owes to the extensive approach to cover the stakeholders in the five communities. Subsequent tests of the model confirmed the factors as defined.

4. Many respondents wore two or more hats, such as an environmental lawyer active in the Sierra Club, an academic on a community planning board,

or an environmental consultant who volunteers expertise to a neighborhood association. Respondents were categorized by their primary employment status as it involves brownfields redevelopment. Community/environmental activists whose primary work does not involve one of the major brownfields employment categories, are classified under activist, such as a health-care worker who is a member of an environmental group, a construction worker who volunteers on a neighborhood organization's housing committee, or a designer with neighborhood volunteer experience.

5. Research has shown that choice of specific factor procedures makes little difference in the outcome, once the correlations matrix has been determined (Brown 1980, 208; McKeown and Thomas 1988, 49). Here, the principal components method was chosen.

6. The Emscher Park International Building Exhibition in the Ruhr region of Germany represents a creative model of addressing preservation issues while improving environmental and community quality (Kilper and Wood 1995).

References

Allegheny County. 1998. Office of Property Assessments. (This was a trip the author took to the actual office.)

Bartsch, Charles, and Elizabeth Collaton. 1997. *brownfields: Cleaning and Reusing Contaminated Properties*. Westport, CT, and London: Praeger.

Brown, Steven R. 1980. *Political Subjectivity: Applications of Q Methodology in Political Science*. New Haven, CT: Yale University Press.

The Brownfields Center (TBC). 1997. http://www.ce.cmu.edu/brownfields/NSF/ sites, Pittsburgh: Carnegie Mellon University and University of Pittsburgh.

Collins, Tim, and Kirk Savage. 1998. "Brownfields as Places: A Case Study in Learning to See Assets as Well as Liabilities, Opportunities as Well as Constraints." *Public Works Management and Policy* 2, no. 3 (January): 210–19.

Davis, Todd S., and Kevin D. Margolis, eds. 1997. *brownfields: A Comprehensive Guide to Redeveloping Contaminated Properties*. Chicago: Section on Natural Resources, Energy and Environmental Law, American Bar Association.

Deitrick, Sabina, Robert Beauregard, and Cheryl Zarlenga Kerchis. 1999. "Riverboat Gambling, Tourism, and Economic Development," in *Places to Play: The Remaking of Cities for Tourists*, ed. Dennis Judd and Susan Fainstein, pp. 233–44. New Haven, CT: Yale University Press.

Dunn, William N. 1994. *Public Policy Analysis: An Introduction*. Englewood Cliffs, NJ: Prentice Hall.

Durning, Dan, and Will Osuna. 1994. "Policy Analysts' Roles and Value Orientations: An Empirical Investigation Using Q Methodology." *Journal of Policy Analysis and Management* 13, no. 4: 629–57.

Fitzpatrick, Dan. 1998. "UPMC Moving on Sports Complex Seeks Backing for S. Side Medicine Hub." *Pittsburgh Post-Gazette* (November 10): B1.

Gibson, Jeremy A. 1995. "Remedial Reinforcements to the Rescue: The Brownfields Brigades Are on the March." *Journal of Environmental Regulation* 5, no. 1 (Summer): 29–42.

Gould, Peter, and Rodney White. 1974. *Mental Maps*. Middlesex, UK: Penguin.

Gratz, Roberta. 1994. *The Living City*. Washington, DC: Preservation Press.

Gratz, Roberta Brandes. 1998. *Cities Back from the Edge.* New York: John Wiley & Sons.

Hirsch, Eloise. 1998. City of Pittsburgh Department of City Planning, radio interview, WDUQ, Pittsburgh.

Kaiser, Sven-Erik. 1998. "brownfields National Partnership: The Federal Role in brownfields Redevelopment." *Public Works Management and Policy* 2, no. 3 (January): 196–201.

Kilper, Heiderose, and Gerald Wood. 1995. "Restructuring Policies: The Emscher Park International Building Exhibition," in *The Rise of the Rust Belt*, ed. Philip Cooke, 208–30. London: UCL Press.

Leigh, Nancey Green. 1994. "Focus: Environmental Constraints to Brownfield Redevelopment." *Economic Development Quarterly* 8, no. 4 (November): 325–28.

Macfarlane, Ross A., Jennifer L. Belk, and J. Alan Clark. 1994. "Confronting the Impacts of Environmental Strict Liability on Brownfield Redevelopment." *Environmental Claims Journal* 6, no. 4 (Summer): 459–80.

McElroy, William, and Todd S. Davis. 1997. "Environmental Insurance in the brownfields Transaction," in *brownfields: A Comprehensive Guide to Redeveloping Contaminated Property*, ed. Todd S. Davis and Kevin D. Margolis, chap. 11, pp. 144–53.

McKeown, Bruce, and Dan Thomas. 1988. *Q Methodology.* University Paper series on Quantitative Applications in the Social Sciences, series 07–066. Newbury Park, CA and London: Sage.

Meyer, Peter B. 1998. "Background Note on Insurance and Brownfield Reinvestment Decisions." *Public Works Management and Policy* 2, no. 3 (January): 243–50.

Meyer, Peter B., and Sabina Deitrick. 1998. "Brownfields and Public Works: An Introduction to the Focus Section." *JWMP* (Journal of Public Works Management & Policy). 2, no. 3 (January 1998): 202–9.

Moe, Richard, and Carter Wilkie. 1997. *Changing Places: Rebuilding Community in the Age of Sprawl.* New York: Henry Holt.

Murphy, Margaret. 1997. "brownfields Sites: Removing Lender Concerns as a Barrier to Redevelopment," in *brownfields: A Comprehensive Guide to Redeveloping Contaminated Properties*, ed. T.S. Davis and K.D. Margolis, pp. 100–20. Chicago: Section on Natural Resources, Energy and Environmental Law, American Bar Association.

Pennsylvania Department of Environmental Protection (PADEP). 1996. *Pennsylvania's Land Recycling Program: First Year Progress Report.* Harrisburg: Pennsylvania Department of Environmental Protection (July).

Pepper, Edith M. 1997. *Lessons from the Field: Unlocking Economic Potential with an Environmental Key.* Washington, DC: Northeast Midwest Institute.

Sayer, Andrew. 1984. *Method in Social Science: A Realist Approach.* London: Hutchinson.

Simons, Robert A. 1998. *Turning brownfields into Greenbacks: Redeveloping and Refinancing Contaminated Urban Real Estate.* Washington, DC: Urban Land Institute.

Swaffield, Simon R. and John R. Fairweather. 1996. "Investigation of Attitudes Toward the Effects of Land Use Change Using Image Editing and Q Sort Method." *Landscape and Urban Planning* 35: 213–30.

Toulme, N.V., and D.E. Cloud. 1991. "The Fleet Factors Case: A Wrong Turn for Lender Liability Under Superfund." *Wake Forest Law Review* 26, no. 1: 17–21.

Urban Redevelopment Authority of Pittsburgh. 1997a. *URA Factsheet, 1997.* Pittsburgh: Urban Redevelopment Authority of Pittsburgh.

———. 1997b. *Washington's Landing, Herr's Island Final Development Plan.* Pittsburgh, PA: Urban Redevelopment Authority of Pittsburgh. May 20.

———. 1998. *URA Factsheet, 1998.* Pittsburgh: Urban Redevelopment Authority of Pittsburgh.

U.S. Department of Commerce (USDOC). 1997. *Statistical Abstract of the United States, 1997.* Washington, DC: Government Printing Office.

9

PAMELA LELAND

Payments-in-Lieu-of-Taxes: A Revenue-Generating Strategy for Central Cities

As cities search for new or expanding sources of revenue, anecdotal evidence appears to indicate that they are increasingly turning to their own nonprofit community as a source of municipal income. Such efforts to solicit payments-in-lieu-of-taxes (PILOTs), municipal service fees, and/or voluntary contributions from nonprofit organizations are often highly publicized, with city administrators suggesting that these exempt organizations should pay for the municipal services they utilize, while nonprofit executives claim that precious organizational resources are being diverted from critical community needs. Research in 1996 into Philadelphia's PILOTs program indicates that millions of dollars could be added annually to municipal coffers through such efforts.

This chapter reports on research to determine the extent to which, across the United States, PILOTs, service fees, and voluntary contributions from local nonprofit organizations are a source of municipal revenue and whether such activities are a new trend or simply happening in a few high-profile places and states. The project utilized mail surveys and telephone interviews with public officials and key informants in seventy-three of the nation's largest cities to document the nature, extent, and impact of such activity as a revenue-generating strategy. Data collection for this national assessment was completed during the spring and summer of 1998.

The chapter is divided into five sections. After defining the research question and providing a general overview of the issue, the methodology, results, conclusions, policy implications, and future areas of research are discussed.

The Solicitation of PILOTs from Nonprofit Organizations: Defining the Research Question

Many urban governments are in fiscal crisis, and the options for generating new revenue are limited. Facing the results of suburbanization, de-industrialization, advances in technology, capital flight, and a growing urban underclass, urban governments must walk a tight balance between generating sufficient revenue through fees and taxes and creating structures that might act as a disincentive to economic growth and expansion. Policy choices are difficult and often conflicting (see Hanson 1983, Kantor 1988, Mollenkopf 1983).

Such crises in cities are occurring as the nonprofit sector is expanding— expansion that often results in the removal of additional property from local tax rolls. Public scrutiny of the sector is also increasing as the small business community suggests there is an "unfair competition" and as the public reacts to issues of excessive executive compensation and high-profile scandals within the nonprofit community. As society at large is struggling to define the meaning of charity in the 1990s, cities are simply trying to meet the need for services in a time of declining revenue.

This research project grew out of (seemingly) increasing anecdotal evidence and activities that suggested that local units of government were beginning to ignore long-established patterns of property tax exemption for nonprofit charitable organizations and were soliciting PILOTs. While the activity in some cities, for example, Boston and Philadelphia, were well known, prior to the research being presented here, there had been no effort to document this growth. This research has attempted to fill this knowledge gap by assessing the extent to which municipal governments are seeking PILOTs from nonprofit organizations, the nature of these activities, and whether this is a new trend or simply occurring in a few high-profile cities and states.

Parameters of the Research

Nonprofit charitable organizations are usually exempt by statute and/or state constitution from a host of state and local taxes. Depending on the type of nonprofit organization and the particular state, they may not be required to pay locally based property taxes, sales taxes, school taxes, road taxes, business privilege taxes, and so forth, or state income or sales taxes.

In this project, money paid by nonprofit organizations to local units of government for things from which they are legally exempt is termed PILOTs. These would include municipal service fees for such things as police and fire services because these are programs often paid for out of property tax revenue and are fees from which many nonprofits would be legally exempt. In this project, PILOTs would *not* include certain types of user or access fees charged to both for-profits and nonprofits (e.g., water, sewer, and/or cable) unless there was a legal basis for nonprofit exemption from such fees. It would *not* include payments by one unit of government to another, for example, payments by federal housing authorities to local governments. It would also *not* include fees and charges that nonprofits may pay in one state but not in another (if the reason for the payments is a tight or narrow granting of exemption privileges in that state, as in Colorado). Throughout the discussion it must be remembered that state definitions of "charity" vary as do state designations of exemption privileges and benefits; exemptions must be understood in the specific context of the local or state jurisdiction.

In some cases, local units of government, for example, Philadelphia, have allowed nonprofit organizations to provide services rather than money. These are referred to as SILOTs ("services-in-lieu-of-taxes").

Language is a complicating factor in discussing these issues. In Philadelphia after strong reaction from the nonprofit community, the city agreed to change the name of its PILOT/SILOT program. Members of the nonprofit community were adamant that they were *voluntarily* making these payments and that the phrase "in-lieu-of-taxes" suggested that they "owed" the city something. The program is now called the Voluntary Contribution Program. (For those familiar with the city of Philadelphia's program, the irony is evident. The city entered into legal agreements with more than forty large health and educational institutions, resulting in several million dollars annually in money and services. It is widely known that the "carrots"—or "the sticks"—in these agreements were a series of unfavorable or unclear court rulings that put many of these organizations at risk of losing their "charitable" status in the commonwealth if challenged in a court of law.)

Complicating matters even further is the fact that some states use the word PILOTs to refer to reimbursements *from the state* to those local units of government (typically counties) who hold a high percentage of exempt property. This is most common in terms of state game lands, where states have taken the property off local tax rolls. In both Connecticut and Rhode Island, however, the state reimburses cities for what is considered an extraordinary amount of exempt property held by the public sector and/or nonprofit organizations. As stated earlier, these kinds of payments from one unit of government to another are not included in this project.

Review of the Problem

Investigating what may be an emerging trend in the solicitation of PILOTs from nonprofit organizations requires that we consider a number of related topics. First is the role of the property tax in the generation of municipal revenue. This will be followed by consideration of the treatment of exempt organizations in property tax structures. Finally the apparent increase in these efforts to solicit PILOTs from nonprofit organizations will be reviewed, with particular attention paid to recent activities in the Commonwealth of Pennsylvania.

Property Tax as a Portion of Municipal Revenue

The property tax—both real and personal—has been the foundation of local revenue in this country for hundreds of years. Over time there has been a shift away from taxation of personal property (i.e., goods) toward real property (i.e., land). There has also been a decline as a portion of *overall* government revenue. For example, as a portion of *municipal* revenue it declined from 46 percent in 1957 to 26 percent in 1977 (Gold 1979, 30). However, at about one-quarter of all municipal revenue currently, property taxes remain a significant source of income for local units of government (Fisher 1990, Gold 1979, Bahl, Sjoquist, and Williams 1990). In 1996, $197 billion was produced via property taxes at the local level, representing 77 percent of locally generated revenue (ULI 1997, 13). And despite the decline in recent years—which was steepest between 1977 and 1982—property taxes as a proportion of revenue remained constant during the 1980s and will likely be maintained as a "significant feature of local finance" for the future (Bahl, Sjoquist, and Williams 1990, 371–72).

In general, though property tax hovers around one-quarter of municipal revenue overall, there is sometimes significant variation between cities and regions of the country. States in the northeast rely more heavily on property taxes than states in the southeast, and school districts and townships rely on it more than counties and municipalities (Fisher 1990). In New York City property tax revenue constitutes about one-quarter of municipal revenue; in Loudon County, Virginia, however, it was about 70 percent in 1994. In Dallas, Texas, property taxes have fallen from 50 percent to 35 percent of the municipal budget since 1990 (ULI 1997, 20–23).

Property Tax Exemptions

One of the ironies in the dependence on property tax revenue is the extent to which there is relief from these taxes. Students new to the issue of property tax exemption are often surprised to find that property tax relief or exemptions cover much more than religious or charitable nonprofits. There is a long history of relief practices that includes exemptions for businesses, homeowners, *and* public, charitable or religious purposes.

Steven David Gold in *Property Tax Relief* identifies eight different types of property tax relief including credits, exemptions, differential assessment ratios, and direct aid from higher levels of government (1979, 10–15). The strategy selected depends on the rationale and motivation for the particular policy, but the resulting picture is clear: Relief strategies have been and continue to be used extensively, though often inconsistently and conflictually.

While property tax exemption for charitable organizations has a long history, so do other models of relief. The first evidence of business exemptions occurred in 1649 in Connecticut, and a 1979 state survey indicated that twenty-six states had relief programs as a tool to attract or retain business development and/or expansion (Gold 1979, 131–32). Homestead exemption programs became common during the Great Depression, and today every single state (and the District of Columbia) has either a homestead exemption or circuit breaker program that benefits homeowners and/or renters. While these programs vary in size and type, they can result in significant lost revenue for their respective governments. Florida's program means $1.6 billion less money for local governments. (Fisher 1996, 193–94)

The practice of exempting property used for charitable, religious, and educational purposes precedes many of the uniform tax codes and systems set in place during the nineteenth century (Fisher 1996, Gold 1979). As found in other tax treatments of nonprofit and charitable organizations, legislation regarding property taxation for charities seemed to simply adopt longtime practice without specific articulation of motivation or rationale. Such practices (and reasons) were so commonly understood that specific articulation was (apparently) deemed unnecessary (Scrivner 1990). Thus many properties held by charitable organizations were never initially placed on tax rolls or have never been accurately assessed. This makes a precise determination of the value of property held by the nonprofit sector fraught with problems (Gold 1979, Bureau of Government Research 1996).

As a result of this long-standing practice of property tax exemption for multiple constituencies, many communities have a high percentage of exempt property; it is commonly asserted that one-third of potentially taxable real estate is exempt. Of this, Gold reported that 85 percent of fully exempt property was owned by government, with only 15 percent held by charitable institutions (1979, 240). The distribution of this exempt property is, however, highly uneven. Older cities and central cities have a much higher portion of nontaxable real estate.

In further understanding the impact of exempt property on a particular place, a brief discussion of one city might prove helpful. Consider the city of New Orleans. According to a 1996 study by the Bureau of Governmental Research, 65 percent of the total value of property in Orleans Parish is exempt.

This percentage represents almost $1.7 billion dollars. Of this amount, however, only $949 million is privately owned.

Of the privately owned portion, slightly less than half—$448 million—is covered by the homestead exemption. In fact, of the 79,527 households covered by that exemption, 68 percent are fully covered and 32 percent are partially covered. It was estimated that in 1996 if there were no homestead exemptions, an additional $55.4 million in taxes would have been generated.

This means that approximately $500 million in property is exempted for "other" purposes. Over 88 percent of this other property covers three types— religious, educational, or health-care property. About 6 percent is for various manufacturing exemptions, and the rest includes various miscellaneous organizations such as fraternal, cultural, philanthropic, and civic purposes.

The value of an examination of exempt property in a city such as New Orleans is the resulting awareness that a strategy of soliciting PILOTs from nonprofit organizations alone would not address the problem of a disproportionate level of exempt property in the generation of property taxes. In New Orleans only $440 million of a total assessed property base of $2.5 billion is held by the traditional nonprofit sector. And this portion includes the religious sector—typically sacrosanct in any PILOTs initiatives. In New Orleans (and likely in other cities) it is clear that the problem of lost revenue from exempt property is more largely driven by publicly owned property and homestead exemptions for private owners than by property held by charitable organizations.

Recent Attempts to Solicit PILOTs

Complicating a discussion on the growing solicitation of PILOTs is that in some cases, they have been a resulting compromise and alternative to long and expensive litigation over the issue of exempt status in whole or in part. It should be understood, therefore, that a discussion of PILOTs initiatives cannot be separated from a discussion of the debate about definitions of a charity and/or exemption privileges and benefits in general.

Also to be reiterated at the outset is that organizations are incorporated as nonprofit within a state context—definitions, privileges, and benefits vary by state. Only thirteen states have definitions of a charity that parallel the federal IRS tax code (Gallagher 1992). Most states, therefore, have their own definitions regarding what type of organization is considered worthy of various exemptions. Furthermore, most states vary the extent of exemptions by type of organization, so that different types of nonprofit charities may be exempt from property taxes, sales taxes, income taxes, and so forth, but not necessarily all of them. To put it simply, state tax treatment of nonprofit organizations is a very mixed bag.

In recent history the public scrutiny and challenge to property tax exempt status began in Utah in the 1970s. First there was a general narrowing of the interpretation of a charity, which limited property tax exemptions for certain organizations. This was followed by years of continued examination, administrative rulings, and challenge to the exempt status of hospitals and other health-care organizations. The Utah Supreme Court finally ruled in 1985 that nonprofit status does not necessarily qualify an organization (in this case a hospital) for property tax exemption. In reviewing what happened next, McDermott writes:

> The hospital industry quickly marshaled its forces and persuaded the [Utah Constitutional Revision Commission] and the legislature to propose a constitutional amendment specifically granting property tax exemption to nonprofit hospitals and nursing homes on the 1986 ballot. Despite an extensive campaign by nonprofit hospitals, and an early two-to-one lead in the polls, this amendment was defeated by a narrow margin.

> With the failure of this amendment, county assessors challenged the property tax exemption of virtually every nonprofit hospital in the state. In all but two counties the challenges were resolved at the local level for the hospital. (1989, 497)

These activities in Utah opened up a larger debate across the country about the continued eligibility of nonprofit hospitals for property tax exemption. This debate regarding hospitals, however, was less about an overall definition of a charity than it was a concern that nonprofit hospitals were not continuing to provide a sufficient level of "charity care" (White 1993). A Maine court ruled that the level of charity care was the primary determination of whether a hospital was, in fact, a charity. White wrote that local officials in twelve states were attempting to eliminate tax exempt status for hospitals (p. 73).

The PILOTs debate has now spread throughout the country. Gallagher (1997) reports that a number of cities—Syracuse, Buffalo, Hartford, New Haven, Wilmington (DE), Des Moines, Baltimore—and states—Kansas, Nebraska, New Hampshire—continue to discuss and attempt the collection of PILOTs from nonprofit organizations.

PILOTs Initiatives in the Commonwealth of Pennsylvania

Though Utah was the location of some early activity and there is an established program in Boston, it is the Commonwealth of Pennsylvania that has had the most (and the most significant) activity with PILOTs in recent years. Pennsylvania also is an excellent example of how legal issues play an important, if not essential, role in the success of PILOTs programs.

A 1985 Pennsylvania commonwealth court decision cleared the way for successful solicitations of PILOTs—or "voluntary contributions" as people like to say—throughout the state. In a case related to sales tax exemption for a health-related services (nonprofit) corporation, Commonwealth Court articulated five aspects to a "purely public charity." All five of these must be met in order to be considered a purely public charity in Pennsylvania and thus be eligible for various subsequent exemptions. The five are:

1. Advances a charitable purpose.
2. Donates or renders gratuitously a substantial portion of its services.
3. Benefits a substantial and indefinite class of persons who are legitimate subjects of charity.
4. Relieves government of some of its burdens.
5. Operates entirely free from a private profit motive.

The problems arising from this definition of a charity (now commonly known as the Hospital Utilization Project or HUP test) were not related to the criteria themselves. In fact, many organizations and groups came out publicly in support of this conceptualization of a nonprofit charity.

The problems related to the application and interpretation of the criteria by various boards of assessments and courts throughout the commonwealth during the early 1990s. As a result of ambiguity in these decisions, local units of government were very successful in soliciting PILOTs from nonprofit organizations. While nonprofit leaders were (and remain) unwilling to publicly discuss these efforts in terms of municipal "blackmail," research indicated that for some, a choice to settle was preferred, rather than risk a court battle which might result in the loss of charitable status. By 1994 more than 1,000 nonprofit organizations—from hospitals and colleges to social service agencies, youth-service organizations, and veterans groups—had been solicited for such payments. Given efforts by the city of Philadelphia and other known activities subsequent to 1994, these numbers have, no doubt, increased dramatically (Leland 1995).

State legislation adopted in 1997, which was supported by both the nonprofit community and municipal leaders, seems to have reduced the ambiguity of the five-point HUP test. The legislation as well as some recent favorable court decisions have led nonprofit leaders to believe that local units of government are in a much weaker position in forcing nonprofit organizations to pay PILOTs. Municipal leaders, however, assert that they are still able to raise such monies from nonprofit organizations. Only time will tell . . . at least one major city in the commonwealth continues to attempt to garner PILOTs from local health-care organizations.

Methodology: A Survey of Major U.S. Cities

The goal of this research project was to gather a national picture of efforts by local units of government to solicit PILOTs or other taxlike payments from local nonprofit organizations. A key question was whether these activities—which appeared to be growing in scope—represented a new trend in municipal revenue-generation or were simply high-profile activities in a relatively small number of locations. For those cities engaged in such activities, specific research questions included: the reason for the emergence of these activities, the level of revenue being generated, the measure of the success, and the impact on the nonprofit organizations themselves.

Given the extraordinary number and types of local governments—from school districts to counties to special districts to cities, towns, and townships, and so forth—a sample composed of the fifty largest cities in the United States plus the largest city in any state not represented by the fifty largest cities was created.[1] It was assumed that either these kinds of activities would more likely occur in the larger, more complex units of government or that respondents from the largest cities would know of such activities in other units of government within their respective states. A total of seventy-three cities comprised this sample.

Information regarding these activities in the sample locations were sought from two primary sources: municipal finance directors and community leaders/key informants. The primary source of information was the local municipal finance or budget director in the seventy-three cities in our sample. These names were purchased from the National League of Cities. Two information-gathering strategies were utilized. The first consisted of a mail survey that first asked a general question as to whether (a) these activities were currently taking place, (b) had occurred in the past, or (c) were anticipated for the future. If the answer to any of the above questions was affirmative, a series of more detailed questions about these activities were presented. The mail survey was fielded to municipal finance directors in March 1998; a second mailing to nonresponding finance directors took place in May 1998.

For these respondent groups the second strategy entailed a detailed phone interview with the finance director (or his designee). Conducted during summer 1998, the phone interviews not only attempted to confirm information provided on the mail survey but also solicited more specific information about current and future efforts to solicit payments, fees, or user charges from local nonprofit organizations. The interview also (1) verified the treatment of various organizations often thought to be nonprofit but which may not be in actuality (e.g., housing authorities, economic development authorities), (2) determined local mechanisms for funding water and sewer expenses, (3) determined the extent of these activities in other local units of government in that area or state, and (4) explored the use of abatements as an economic development strategy.[2]

The second source of information was local community leaders in the seventy-three sample cities. These key informants received a mail survey similar to, but more limited than, the mail survey sent to municipal finance directors. They were viewed as a source not only for verifying which cities might be engaged in soliciting PILOTs but also for general information about such activities.

In gathering the sample of community leaders, the goal was to contact approximately half a dozen key people for information about each city in the sample. Five different national mailing lists were gathered representing various constituencies. These lists included state and local United Way representatives, housing and development officials, community economic development professionals, statewide higher education association executives, and statewide nonprofit association executives. Five hundred and eighty-three surveys were mailed in March 1998. While some cities had significantly more potential respondents (given the size of local membership), most cities had four to six possible respondents; there were only a few cities with fewer than four potential respondents.[3]

Research Findings

Municipal Finance Directors Surveys

Seventy-three questionnaires were mailed the middle of March 1998. After the initial mailing and a second mailing to non-respondents, a total of forty-nine mail surveys were returned, for a response rate of 67 percent. While phone interviews were attempted with all seventy-three finance directors, contact was successful with only twenty-three individuals. Two of these were persons who had not responded to the mail survey.

Finance Director Nonresponse

Among the seventy-three sample cities, information was received from fifty-one municipal finance directors via either mail and/or phone. There was no response from twenty-two cities. These are listed in Appendix B. Among the twenty-two nonresponding cities, key informants indicate that only Portland, Maine, and Little Rock, Arkansas, may have PILOTs activities.

In 1996, $197 billion was produced via property taxes at the local level, representing 77 percent of locally generated revenue (ULI 1997, 13).

The Solicitation of PILOTs Payments

Only seven of the fifty-one responding cities indicated a solicitation of PILOTs, municipal service fees, or voluntary contributions specifically from (one or more) nonprofit organizations (see Tables 9.1 and 9.2). None of the responding cities reported past attempts to collect such fees, and only two cities—Billings and Boise—reported a likelihood that such fees would be collected in the future.

In both Billings and Boise water and sewer costs are already collected as user fees and applied to all persons and organizations. Billings's proposed program will impose an additional "franchise fee" on both for-profit and nonprofit entities. If this program is approved, this fee could produce approximately $4.5 million per year (on top of a $100 million budget). In Boise's case, there is no specific program in the works, but PILOTs are a regular topic of conversation and the city is currently in litigation over the exempt status of one hospital.

As for current activities, in addition to the seven identified cities, two other finance directors reported "possibly" receiving contributions from a single institution (a hospital in one city and a university in another). In both cases, however, the finance director indicated that (1) the city did not *solicit* these monies and (2) he/she did not know enough to be sure that a contribution was indeed paid. Given the tenuousness of the response, these two cities have been excluded from analysis.

Overview of Cities' PILOTs Activities

The number of organizations participating and the amount of money raised are reported in Table 9.3.

Efforts to solicit PILOTs vary widely, with more explanations for each situation needed. For example, in several of these cities, programs have been in existence for more than twenty-five years (Detroit and Baltimore); others are only one to two years old. Some of the programs cover a variety of organizations (Boston and Philadelphia), while others target specific types (Detroit solicits from housing and residential programs, while Minneapolis solicits only from nursing homes). A description of each of these seven cities (listed in alphabetical order) follows:

Table 9.1

Cities That Currently Solicit PILOTs from Nonprofit Organizations According to Municipal Finance Directors (n = 51)

Baltimore	Indianapolis	Philadelphia
Boston	Minneapolis	Pittsburgh
Detroit		

Source: Author's survey

Note: A number of other cities in the sample reported receiving payments from local (federal) housing authorities. These were not considered meeting the definition of PILOTs per this research project.

Table 9.2

Cities that Currently Do Not Solicit PILOTs from Nonprofit Organizations According to Municipal Finance Directors (n = 51)

Albuquerque	Fort Worth	Ogden
Anchorage	Houston	Phoenix
Billings	Jackson, MS	Portland, OR
Birmingham	Jacksonville, FL	Sacramento
Boise	Kansas City	San Antonio
Buffalo	Kansas City, MO	San Diego
Charleston, WV	Las Vegas	San Francisco
Cheyenne	Los Angeles	San Jose
Chicago	Manchester	Seattle
Columbia, SC	Memphis	Sioux Falls
Columbus, OH	Miami	St. Louis
Dallas	Milwaukee	Tucson
Denver	Nashville	Virginia Beach
Des Moines	New Orleans	Washington DC
El Paso	Oakland	

Source: Author's survey

Baltimore. The city's PILOTs program was initiated in 1974 and is specifically directed at housing facilities, nursing homes, and community development corporations. In 1998 there were forty-eight participating organizations, generating $3.4 million. Payments are based upon the organization's annual operating income, thus not changing from year to year unless there is a significant change in operating income.

Boston. Boston's PILOTs program, in its current form, was initiated in 1983, though the city has collected PILOTs since the 1930s. It is a broad-based program to which all property-owning nonprofit organizations are subject. In 1998 thirty-eight organizations made payments, generating $19.4 million. These payments are separately negotiated between the city and each

213

Table 9.3

A Summary of Programs to Solicit PILOTs from Nonprofit Organizations (n = 7)

City	Number of NPOs	Amount generated ($)	City budget ($)	Amount as percentage of annual budget
Baltimore	48	3.4 million	2.2 billion	0.15
Boston	38	19.4 million	1.42 billion	1.4
Detroit	95–100	4.16 million*	2.46 billion	1.17
Indianapolis	1	4.4 million	4.21 billion	1.05
Minneapolis	6	260,000	936 million	0.03
Philadelphia	43	6.5 million**	1.2 billion	0.54
Pittsburgh	10	2.5 million	323 million	0.77

Notes: *1997 figure; all other figures are for 1998.
**This is the amount of "cash only." Philadelphia collected a total of $8.75 million in 1998.

organization, with SILOTs included in some cases without a specific limit on contributed services. The city initiates discussion at 25 percent of the would-be tax amount, which is the percentage of the city budget spent on police, fire, and snow removal. Agreements have a built-in "inflation clause" and can be for a period of anywhere between ten and thirty years.

Detroit. Detroit's PILOTs activities began in 1966 and are directed to housing/residential facilities for the disabled and low-income. Approximately ninety-five to one hundred nonprofit organizations currently make payments, generating $4.16 million in 1997. All nonprofit organizations are subject to the same formula (4 percent of the net shelter rent generated).

Indianapolis. This program, initiated via city ordinance in 1994, is directed toward a single nonprofit organization, a wastewater treatment facility. The facility pays $4.4 million a year. A third-party consultant determined the assessed property value of the facility and applied the appropriate tax rate to determine the property's would-be tax amount. The $4.4 million fee is less than half of the would-be amount and was agreed upon after discussions between the facility and the city. This effort, supported by state legislation, allows the city to treat this nonprofit (for PILOTs purposes) similarly to a public utility.

Minneapolis. Approved in 1991, this program was implemented in 1992 and is directed only toward nursing homes. Currently six homes participate, paying the same percentage (estimated to be about 40 percent) of the would-be tax amount of the respective properties. These fees are fully reimbursed by the state.

Philadelphia. The city enacted its Voluntary Contribution Program by executive order in 1994. Currently less than fifty organizations (mostly educational and health-care organizations) make payments, though all nonprofit organizations in the city are subject to the program. Nonprofit organizations participating in the program were deemed by an independent panel of city employees to *not* meet the commonwealth's standards of a public charity. Nonprofit organizations pay 40 percent of the would-be tax based on the assessed value of the property; dollars may be offset by SILOTs up to one-third of the 40 percent. In 1998, $6.5 million was contributed in cash, with total dollars and services valued at $8.75 million.

Pittsburgh. Pittsburgh's PILOTs program is both temporary and informal, resulting from unique agreements between specific nonprofit organizations and the city. These agreements are usually for a period of eight to ten years, though the nonprofit organization can break the agreement by giving six months' notice. While Duquesne University has made payments for approximately twenty years, all other organizations began making payments in the late 1980s. In 1998 ten nonprofit organizations—from colleges and universities to hospitals to youth/recreation organizations—contributed approximately $2.5 million.

Key Informant Survey

Out of 583 questionnaires mailed in early March 1998, 159 were returned and usable, for a response rate of 27 percent. An additional 26 surveys were returned marked "undeliverable" or were filled out incorrectly.[4]

Tables 9.4 and 9.5 report feedback as to the sample cities' current efforts to solicit PILOTs. Key informants reported that 11 of the 73 cities currently received such fees from nonprofit organizations, while 56 cities did not. No key informant surveys were received from 10 of the 73 sample cities.

To be highlighted is the extent to which information from key informants was incorrect. For example, they failed to identify Baltimore and Detroit as cities that solicit PILOTs and incorrectly identified Boise, Los Angeles, Miami, and Milwaukee as doing so. The activities of Portland, Maine, and Little Rock, Arkansas, were unable to be verified.

Information from key informants was also conflicting for six cities, which are identified in Tables 9.4 and 9.5. For example, some respondents in Boston (accurately) reported that the city collects PILOTs; other respondents (inaccurately) said "no" the city does not *currently* collect payments now but will do so in the future. Indianapolis and Philadelphia are similar examples.

Comparison of Information from Key Informants and Municipal Finance Directors

Of the forty-five cities in which information has been received from both respondent groups, there is a general consistency of information regarding current efforts to solicit PILOTs. In only eight cities did information from finance directors conflict with information from one (or more) key informants. In four cities key informants indicated that the city did not collect PILOTs when, in fact, the city did so (Baltimore, Detroit, Minneapolis, and Philadelphia). In the other four cities key informants indicated the presence of PILOTs activities when, in fact, no such activities are in place (Boise, Los Angeles, Miami, and Milwaukee). As noted earlier, multiple key informants sometimes conflicted with one another.

Table 9.4

Cities That Currently Solicit PILOTs from Nonprofit Organizations According to Key Informants (n = 159)

Boise*	Los Angeles	Philadelphia*
Boston	Miami	Pittsburgh
Indianapolis	Milwaukee*	Portland, ME
Little Rock*	Minneapolis*	

Notes: Information from key informants was determined to be incorrect in some of these cities.

    *Conflicting information from key informants was provided.

Table 9.5

Cities That Do Not Currently Solicit PILOTs from Nonprofit Organizations According to Key Informants (n = 159)

Albuquerque	Des Moines	Newark
Anchorage	Detroit	Oakland
Atlanta	El Paso	Oklahoma City
Austin	Fargo	Omaha
Baltimore	Ft. Worth	Philadelphia*
Billings	Honolulu	Phoenix
Birmingham, AL	Houston	Portland, OR
Boise*	Jackson, MS	Providence, RI
Bridgeport, CT	Kansas City, KS	Sacramento
Buffalo	Las Vegas	San Antonio
Charleston, WV	Lexington, KY	San Diego
Charlotte	Little Rock	San Jose
Chicago	Manchester, NH	Seattle
Cincinnati	Memphis	Sioux Falls
Cleveland	Milwaukee	Toledo
Columbia, SC	Minneapolis	Tucson
Columbus, OH	Nashville	Virginia Beach
Dallas	New Orleans	Washington, DC
Denver	New York City	Wilmington, DE

Notes: Information from key informants was determined to be incorrect in some of these cities.

    *Conflicting information from key informants was provided.

There are four cities in the sample from which no surveys were received from either key informants or municipal finance directors—Burlington, Fresno, Long Beach, and Tulsa.

Discussion

The small number of cities—only seven among fifty-one major U.S. cities—that currently solicit PILOTs from nonprofit organizations was surprising.

Even more surprising is that only one city—Boston—solicits a wide range of nonprofit organizations. Philadelphia, Pittsburgh, and Baltimore largely target health-care and educational institutions. Detroit and Minneapolis target only one type of nonprofit, and Indianapolis solicits only one organization! Given that only two other cities in our sample saw this as a "likely" activity in the future, it would seem that the doomsayers have been wrong: There is no massive trend, among major cities at least, to "go after" the nonprofit sector.

With that said, however, there are a couple of caveats. The first is that while these activities may not be widespread, if they happen in your city or to your organization, it can be significant. In Minneapolis six organizations contribute an average of $43,000; in Pittsburgh ten organizations contribute an average of $250,000; in Boston thirty-eight organizations contribute an average of $510,000. In Indianapolis one organization contributes $4.4 million!

Another significant aspect in this potential for significance is consideration of those factors that drive such activities and the degree to which other cities are at risk of these forces. Six of the seven finance director respondents cited either or both the city's need for revenue and concern over nonprofits' "free" use of public services as contributing reasons for the implementation of PILOTs activities. Two respondents cited concern over the nonprofit sector's competition with the for-profit sector as a factor, and one respondent identified concerns over executive compensation and/or excessive nonprofit organizational revenue as contributing factors. All seven respondents, however, cited the need for revenue or the free use of public services as the single most important factor in these activities. The lesson here is that these activities could easily and quickly become more prevalent if either municipal revenue need or public sentiment changes.

The Issue of User Fees

Another qualification to this conclusion is the potential for user fees as a means to fund municipal services to emerge as an addition or alternative to property taxes. While some argue that user fees have become an attractive means to shift some of the costs of government to nonprofit organizations (see, e.g., Gallagher 1997), the shift to user fees for water and sewer has been a growing trend in the delivery of public services for decades and, for some cities, has been the model of funding from inception. It is difficult, therefore, to isolate the shift to user fees as a response and reaction to the exempt status of nonprofit organizations from the larger shift toward more efficient (and equitable) distribution of costs.

In this research the goal was to determine if any city has switched to a user fee structure specifically for the purpose of gaining participation from the nonprofit community. Only in Buffalo was this reported to have occurred distinctly as a response to the tax exempt status of nonprofit organizations. We did find that more than half the cities in our sample already charge for water, sewer, and/or waste disposal via user fees (see Table 9.6).

Indeed, five of the seven cities that solicit PILOTs *also* have the user fee structure for water and sewer.[5] Clearly, charging user fees does not preclude the solicitation of PILOTs.

A final caveat concerns the problems of language and definitions raised earlier in the chapter. Despite efforts to specify definitions and circumstances, there is evidence in some of the mail surveys that respondents may have included certain kinds of activities under the category of PILOTs that did not meet our research parameters (e.g., the monies that federal housing authorities pay to local municipalities). This inconsistency in the mail surveys was one reason that phone contact was attempted with all seventy-three finance directors. While we are confident in the results as to the extent of PILOTs activities in fifty-one major U.S. cities, any future research efforts should continue to focus on the clarity and consistency of language.

Conclusions, Policy Implications, and Future Research

As noted earlier, given anecdotal evidence, findings regarding the extent to which large cities in the United States solicit PILOTs from nonprofit organizations were surprising. However, the facts that some cities do successfully garner monies from local nonprofit organizations and that these activities are driven primarily by a local need for revenue and/or concern over nonprofit use of public services, keep this as an issue that warrants continuing scrutiny. Not only does this raise a number of related and important policy questions, our knowledge of PILOTs activities is far from complete. Related policy issues and further areas of research will be discussed below.

Policy Implications in PILOTs Activities

The fundamental policy issue raised in a study of PILOTs activities is the insufficiency in sources and level of municipal revenue. This research clearly indicated that each city's need for revenue was a primary determinant in the implementation of these programs. For some cities the monies generated are significant. Even though it may be a small percentage of the budget, as one respondent said, a million dollars is a million dollars! And yet the monies raised by PILOTs activities are not sizable enough to address the long-term revenue needs of local governments. Clearly other sources of funds need to be identified and developed.

Table 9.6

Cities That Collect User Fees for Water, Sewer, and/or Water Disposal per Phone Interviews with Municipal Finance Directors (n = 23)

Albuquerque	Columbia, SC	New Orleans
Anchorage	Dallas	Ogden
Baltimore	Ft. Worth	Phoenix
Billings	Indianapolis	Pittsburgh
Birmingham, AL	Miami	Portland, OR
Boise	Milwaukee	San Antonio
Boston	Minneapolis	St. Louis
Charleston, WV	Nashville	Virginia Beach

It is the willingness and perceived appropriateness of gathering these monies from exempt organizations that is the critical policy issue for advocates of the nonprofit sector. This concern is also embodied in the second most important reason cited for these activities, that is, concern over nonprofit organizations' "free use" of public services. Proponents of the nonprofit sector cite the long-standing partnership (which is represented in tax-exempt status) between the public and nonprofit sectors in meeting community needs. They specifically cite the "community benefit" rationale, which was first articulated in 1938, stating, "The exemption from taxation of money or property devoted to charitable or other purposes is based upon the theory that the government is compensated for the loss of revenue by its relief from the financial burden which would otherwise have to be met by appropriations from public funds and by the benefits resulting from the promotion of the general welfare" (Scrivner 1990, 128). For nonprofit sector proponents, citing "free use" implies that the public sector no longer understands and accepts the exchange in the relationship and the value of the services being provided by nonprofit organizations.

This leads to a third major policy issue—the conflict between historical definitions and structures of charities and the modern nonprofit corporation, and the subsequent debate over what privileges and exemptions should be granted to exempt organizations. As the reach of local nonprofit organizations expands beyond the local political jurisdiction, citizens ask (rightfully so) what benefit they receive for the subsidy of exempt activity beyond their borders. This disjuncture between *who pays* and *who benefits* is a critical one in the debate over nonprofit tax exemption.

But the privileges granted to exempt organizations extend beyond the property tax issue. As the character of many commercial nonprofit organizations becomes more competitive and business-like, there are fundamental questions related to privileges and exemptions from various kinds of taxes at *all* levels of government. For example, should all 501(c)(3) organizations be treated in the same manner from a tax perspective? Should membership nonprofits (i.e., non–501(c)(3) organizations) receive the same income tax exemption as charitable nonprofits? When both for-profit and nonprofit organizations can effectively compete in the same marketplace, what is the rationale (and benefit) of exempt status and why should *any* organization (in that industry) receive exempt status? Within the nonprofit community, these are unpopular, if not heretical, questions. Nonetheless, they warrant public examination.

A final policy issue highlighted in this research is the inconsistent treatment of exempt organizations across political jurisdictions, even though these jurisdictions may exist within the same state. Is it significant that a youth facility may be making payments in one part of a state but not the other? Is it appropriate that a hospital may make payments to a school district but not to the municipality? But this matter is more than equity within the nonprofit sector—though this is significant—it is also a matter of public accountability. For example, earlier research in Pennsylvania (Leland 1995) documented the presence of PILOTs agreements in which both parties are prohibited from discussing the terms of the agreement! Should not such activities be done "in the sunshine" given that they exist within a context of taxation and tax exemption? This activity of the solicitation of PILOTs raises equity issues for nonprofit organizations, coterminus taxing authorities, and local citizens and warranted greater public examination.

Areas for Future Research

As noted, given anecdotal evidence, the low number of large cities that seek PILOTs from nonprofit organizations was an unexpected result. This result alone raises an important question for future research, specifically, whether *size* is a significant and independent variable in the presence of these activities. This study focused on large cities as its unit of analysis on the assumption that they are more complex and often more sophisticated in their governance structures and therefore would be more likely to engage in these activities. It may be, however, that smaller cities, with fewer revenue choices and a more limited economic base, are *more* likely to engage in PILOTs activities. To what extent size matters is an important follow-up question.

There are a number of other related (direct and indirect) questions that emerge from this research. These include:

1. Why and how are some cities successful in their attempts to solicit PILOTs when other cities are not? For example, Philadelphia and

Boston have successfully implemented PILOTs programs that generate millions for city coffers. Washington, D.C., Wilmington, Delaware, and Iowa City, Iowa, were unsuccessful in their recent attempts. What are the local conditions that result in a successful implementation?

2. What, if any, is the impact of paying PILOTs on nonprofit organizations themselves? How do different types of nonprofits generate the monies to pay PILOTs (e.g., are these monies reimbursable by the state, as in Minnesota, or are the costs passed along to consumers)? Do different types of nonprofit organizations experience different results and impact?

3. What, if any, has been the impact of legislation recently adopted in the Commonwealth of Pennsylvania on local government efforts to solicit PILOTs? Has the legislation stalled municipal PILOTs activities, or are these efforts continuing on a widespread basis despite legislation favorable to the nonprofit sector? It is known that, in the city of Scranton, efforts continued (at least into 1998) to gather voluntary contributions from local health care organizations. Is this a common pattern?

4. In local tax and service fee treatment, how are different nonprofit organizations treated across different political jurisdictions? Are there patterns of treatment by type of nonprofit organization (e.g., hospitals versus educational organizations versus social service organizations)?

5. What is the PILOTs activity among nonmunicipal local units of government such as special tax districts or school districts? For example, does the anecdotal evidence of PILOTs activity in a number of Pennsylvania's 501 school districts represent a pattern among these independent taxing authorities (both inside and outside Pennsylvania)?

Summation

Research and discussion of the solicitation of PILOTs are fraught with myriad complications. What may seem like a fairly straightforward question—*do cities solicit taxlike revenue from exempt organizations?*—quickly becomes a single issue that raises (1) the complicated structure of our federal system, (2) the long-established interdependency and interconnectedness of public and nonprofit sectors, (3) the unsolvable conflict between economic development and redistribution politics, (4) changing social values and definitions of charity, and (5) the financial problems of central cities.

Ultimately, as with most issues, one's perspective on this subject is driven by where one sits. Cities with critical financial needs and growing revenue short-falls assert that local organizations that use public services should pay for those services. Unable and/or unwilling to further burden local taxpayers, municipal leaders view nonprofit organizations as a legitimate source of revenue.

Nonprofit organizations contend that they cannot afford to pay property taxes, PILOTs, service fees, or voluntary contributions. They charge that redirecting resources to local units of government will negatively impact clients and limit their ability to serve the public good.

Many other stakeholders including local citizens groups, however, point to the deep reserves and endowments held by some large nonprofit organizations and no longer accept this "we can't afford to pay" at face value. They further cite high executive compensation and national nonprofit scandals and assert that modern nonprofit organizations are not the charitable organizations of the past but simply another form of big business. As seen in Pennsylvania, the debate as to a modern definition of a charity can be fierce and furious. It also appears that the numbers of those who advocate or endorse a PILOTs program are growing. But advocating such policies does not translate to implementation: The data from this research indicate that not only are PILOTs activities not widespread in major U.S. cities, they are not likely for the near future.

Appendix A. Cities in Sample (n = 73)

Albuquerque, NM	Fargo, ND	Oakland, CA
Atlanta, GA	Fort Worth, TX	Ogden, UT
Anchorage, AK	Fresno, CA	Omaha, NE
Austin, TX	Honolulu, HI	Philadelphia, PA
Baltimore, MD	Houston, TX	Phoenix, AZ
Billings, MT	Indianapolis, IN	Pittsburgh, PA
Birmingham, AL	Jackson, MS	Portland, ME
Boise, ID	Jacksonville, FL	Portland, OR
Boston, MA	Kansas City, MO	Providence, OR
Bridgeport, CT	Kansas City, KA	Sacramento, CA
Buffalo, NY	Las Vegas, NV	San Jose, CA
Burlington, VT	Lexington, KY	San Francisco, CA
Charleston, WV	Little Rock, AR	San Antonio, TX
Charlotte, NC	Oklahoma City, OK	San Diego, CA
Cheyenne, WY	Long Beach, CA	Seattle, WA
Chicago, IL	Los Angeles, CA	Sioux Falls, SD
Cincinnati, OH	Manchester, NH	St. Louis, MO
Cleveland, OH	Memphis, TN	Toledo, OH
Columbia, SC	Miami, FL	Tucson, AZ
Columbus, OH	Milwaukee, WI	Tulsa, OK
Dallas, TX	Minneapolis, MN	Virginia Beach, VA
Denver, CO	Nashville-Davidson, TN	Washington, DC
Des Moines, IO	New Orleans, LA	Wilmington, DE
Detroit, MI	New York, NY	
El Paso, TX	Newark, NJ	

Appendix B. Sample Cities with No Response from Finance Directors

Atlanta	Little Rock*
Austin	Long Beach
Bridge Port	New York
Burlington	Oklahoma City
Charlotte	Omaha
Cincinnati	Portland, ME*
Cleveland	Providence, RI
Fargo	Toledo
Fresno	Tulsa
Honolulu	Wilmington, DE
Lexington	

*Only these two cities were cited by key informants as having PILOTs programs.

Notes

1. The original research proposal called for a survey of the fifty largest cities. Given the overrepresentation of some states in this sample, it was decided to broaden the sample to also include the largest city in any state not represented by the fifty largest cities.

2. Originally the research methodology called for detailed phone interviews with only those cities that indicated PILOTs activities. Due to the surprisingly large number of cities that indicated no such activities, a phone interview was attempted with each of the seventy-three finance directors. While response to the phone interview was less than the response to the mail survey (twenty-three phone interviews versus forty-nine mail surveys, respectively), the phone interviews did not reveal incorrect or misleading information in the mail surveys. The phone interviews only allowed us to better understand and expand upon the mail survey data. In some cases, it was decided after the phone interview that some activities did not fall under our definition of PILOTs activities (e.g., the receipt of monies from federal housing projects).

3. The original proposed research strategy called for phone interviews with local key informants in each of the sample cities. Given the expansion of the number of cities in the sample (from fifty to seventy-three), the desire to significantly broaden the pool of key informants, and the benefit of seeking similar information in similar format from both respondent groups, it was decided to send a mail survey similar in content to the survey sent to municipal finance directors.

4. Despite instructions to the contrary, some respondents who communicated no knowledge about the designated sample city provided us with information about some city about which they did know. This information—though minimal—will be evaluated at a later date.

5. User fee structures for water and sewer were unable to be verified in Philadelphia and Detroit.

References

Adams, Charles. 1988. "Tax-Base Composition and Long-Run Growth in City Taxes." *Urban Affairs Quarterly* 24, no. 2: 315–26.

Advisory Commission on Intergovernmental Relations. 1981. *IN BRIEF: Payments in Lieu of Taxes on Federal Real Property.* Washington, D.C.

Asquith, Christina. 1998. "Longwood ruling a Big Relief to Nonprofits," *Philadelphia Inquirer* (July 22): Sec. R, p. 3, col. 2.

Bahl, Roy, David Sjoquist, and Loren Williams. 1990. "The Property Tax in the 1980s and Prospects for the 1990s." *Public Budgeting and Financial Management* 2, no. 2: 351–76.

Bureau of Governmental Research. 1996. *Property Taxes in New Orleans: Who Pays? Who Doesn't? And Why?* New Orleans, LA.

The Chronicle of Higher Education. 1998. "N.H. Medical Center Loses Tax Exemption," April 10: A46.

Citizens League. 1988. *Cut Tax Exemptions, Boost Equity and Accountability.* Minneapolis, MN.

Fisher, Glenn W. 1990. "The Evolution of the American Property Tax." *Public Budgeting and Financial Management* 2, no. 2: 279–309.

———. 1996. *The Worst Tax? A History of the Property Tax in America.* Lawrence: University Press of Kansas.

Gallagher, Janne. 1992. *Sales Tax Exemptions for Charitable, Educational and Religious Nonprofit Organizations.* A Special Report from the Human Services Forum of the National Assembly and Independent Sector.

———. 1997. "When Local Governments Come Calling: The Movement to Tax Charities." *The Exempt Organization Tax Review* 18, no. 1: 25–33.

Gold, Steven David. 1979. *Property Tax Relief.* Lexington, MA: Lexington Books.

Hanson, Royce. 1983. *Rethinking Urban Policy: Urban Development in an Advanced Economy.* Washington, DC: National Academy Press.

Hospitalization Utilization Project (HUP). 1985. 507 Pa. 1, 487 A.2d 1306 (Pa. Commonw. Ct. 1985).

Jordan, George E., and Dan Weissman. 1998. "James: Let Our Cities Tax Hospitals and Colleges." *Star-Ledger,* Newark, NJ (June 24): 23.

Kantor, Paul, with Stephen David. 1988. *The Dependent City: The Changing Political Economy of Urban America.* Glenview, IL: Scott, Foresman.

Leland, Pamela. 1995. "The Extent of the Challenge to Property Tax Exemption in Pennsylvania: A Survey of 67 Counties." Unpublished Paper.

McDermott, Richard E. 1989. "Property Tax Exemption for Nonprofit Hospitals." *Hospital and Health Services Administration* 34, no. 4: 493–505.

Mollenkopf, John. 1983. *The Contested City.* Princeton: Princeton University Press.

Mullen, John K. 1990. "Property Tax Exemptions and Local Fiscal Stress." *National Tax Journal* 43, no. 4: 467–78.

Reese, Laura A. 1991. "Municipal Fiscal Health and Tax Abatement Policy." *Economic Development Quarterly* 5, no. 1: 23–32.

Scrivner, Gary N. 1990. "100 Years of Tax Policy Changes Affecting Charitable Organizations," in *The Nonprofit Organization: Essential Readings,* ed. David L. Gies, J. Steven Ott, and Jay Shafritz, pp. 126–37. Pacific Grove, CA: Brooks/Cole.

Shedlock, Lynne Slack. 1998. "Council Wants Hospitals to Pay for Fire Dispatches." *Scranton Tribune* (June 23): A5.

Urban Land Institute (URI). 1997. *America's Real Estate: Natural Resource, National Legacy.* Washington, DC.

Weisbrod, Burton A. 1997. "The Future of the Nonprofit Sector: Its Entwining with Private Enterprise and Government." *Journal of Policy Analysis and Management* 16, no. 4: 541–55.

White, Harvey L. 1993. "Fees and Services in Lieu of Taxes: Challenging the Tax Exempt Status of Nonprofit Hospitals." *Municipal Finance Journal* 14 (Fall): 66–80.

Part 4

Central City–Suburb Connection

10

VICTORIA M. BASOLO AND CHIHYEN HUANG

Central City and Suburban Policy Choices

Local policy decisions are critical to the sustainability of our living environments. In an era of intergovernmental devolution and funding cutbacks, decision makers in many central and suburban cities work to improve the local economy and the quality of life for their residents, often through housing and economic development programs. The policymakers in central cities, however, are confronted with significantly different housing and economic issues compared to their suburban counterparts.

The planning and policy literatures are rife with analyses of central city–suburban trends. Three areas of comparison are population growth, employment growth, and housing quality and affordability. Figures based on decades of population migration clearly show an increase in suburban city populations and a general decline in central city populations, even in metropolitan areas that experienced overall growth (Moss 1997, Kasarda et al. 1997, Gale 1987). These statistics also reveal a concentration of lower-income households, particularly African Americans and other minorities, in central cities (Downs 1997, Kasarda et al. 1997, Jencks and Peterson 1991).

Employment trends over the last few decades have disadvantaged central cities and favored suburban communities. Globalization of the economy and economic restructuring from a manufacturing to service economy resulted in a shift of employment opportunities from central cities to suburbia (Downs 1994, Imbroscio et al. 1995, Mollenkopf 1983). As a result, many central cities experienced higher than U.S. average unemployment rates during much of the 1990s.

Central cities also have more severe housing problems than suburban communities. Housing in central cities tends to be older, on average, than housing in suburbia, and older housing is likely to be in worse condition than newer dwellings. In fact, studies show that inner cities have a high number of structurally inadequate housing units compared to suburban communities

(Apgar et al. 1991). Furthermore, income disparities between central cities and suburbs result in a relatively higher housing cost burden for many lower-income renter households in central cities (Joint Center for Housing Studies 1994). Finally, central cities have more public housing (PH) units (approximately 68 percent of all PH units) than suburban communities (Reingold 1997). The location of public housing, therefore, concentrates the poor in central cities. This concentration of the poor is associated with a host of social problems including isolation, joblessness, and crime (Brophy and Smith 1997, Wilson 1987, Witte 1996).

Central city–suburban comparisons highlight the differences in needs and resources between the types of cities and their residents. The federal government has developed policies to address some of these problems. Examples of federal programs include a demonstration program (Move to Opportunity) to assist inner-city residents to relocate to areas of greater opportunity (Schwartz and Tajbakhsh 1997, Gabriel 1996) and the empowerment zone/enterprise community (EZ/EC) initiative to help depressed inner cities (and rural communities) establish and implement a revitalization strategy with the help of federal tax incentives and grants (U.S. Department of Housing and Urban Development 1997, Nenno 1997).

Many of the current federal programs support a philosophy of devolution and emphasize local leadership for urban policy solutions. Federal initiatives often require cities to plan, organize, and contribute local resources to revitalization programs. The rationale for local planning and program development relies on the argument that city officials know best the problems, needs, and resources of their communities. This knowledge should produce effective policies and programs to resolve local issues.

Significant contextual differences between central cities and suburban communities suggest that policy strategies would vary by type of city. For example, economic development and affordable housing policies, programs, and expenditures should be different in central cities compared to suburban cities. Public choice theory, however, suggests that intercity competition results in similar economic development and housing policy preferences across all cities (Peterson 1981, Schneider 1989). Many social scientists criticize the deterministic nature of public choice theory, and empirical studies offer mixed findings for this rational view of local policymaking (Logan and Swanstrom 1990, Swanstrom 1988, Basolo 1999, Schneider 1989). At the same time, most studies focus on one type of city and fail to distinguish between central cities and suburban communities.

This research examines economic development and affordable housing policy in a sample of central cities and suburbs in the United States. It investigates the effect of intercity competition on policy choices, the level of local commitment to economic development and affordable housing policy, and the fit of these policies to needs in central cities and suburban communities across the United States.

Trends, Theory, and Existing Studies

Many explanations are offered for population, income, and employment trends in central cities and suburbia. Scholars claim that population shifts from central cities to suburban communities reflect American values about private property and space, the influence of transportation and technological innovations, the influence of development interests, the impacts of federal transportation and housing policies, white flight, and racial discrimination (Bottles 1987, Monkkonen 1988, Kantor 1988, Kasarda et al. 1997, Citizens Commission on Civil Rights 1986).

Employment trends over the last few decades have disadvantaged central cities and favored suburban communities. Globalization of the economy and the market mechanism resulted in the loss of many traditional central city jobs, especially in the low-skilled manufacturing sector, to foreign countries with a large supply of cheap labor (Scott 1988, Bluestone and Harrison 1982). Furthermore, economic restructuring resulted in a shift of employment opportunities from central cities to suburbia (Downs 1994, Imbroscio et al. 1995, Mollenkopf 1983). The transmutation of local economies from a manufacturing base to service industries created a demand for more educated, higher-skilled labor. Central city labor pools, while critical to the traditional manufacturing industry, were ill suited to the new, service-based economies. The central city, therefore, lost jobs to higher-skilled labor pools in the suburbs (Kasarda 1995, 1990). John Kain (1968) argues that manufacturing decentralization from the central city to the suburbs and racial discrimination in suburban housing markets resulted in a spatial mismatch between suburban employment and central city workers. In other words, minorities, especially African Americans, lost job opportunities in the central city and were denied access through housing discrimination to opportunities in the suburbs.

The lack of employment opportunities and the concomitant rise in poverty in central cities are associated with housing affordability problems. Also, the housing stock tends to be older in central cities and therefore, more likely to be structurally inadequate. Furthermore, some central city renters experience both inadequate housing and a severe rent burden (Joint Center for Housing Studies, 1994).

The existing conditions in central cities and the suburbs reveal differences in needs between these types of cities. Presumably, local policies concerning economic development and affordable housing would be dissimilar in central cities and suburban communities as a result of disparate needs. However, public choice theorists argue that policymaking will not differ among cities, because of intercity competition. These scholars reason that cities provide services to residents and must maintain them at a certain level and at reasonable cost, or tax rate, to maintain their population base and fiscal health. If cities fail to deliver adequate services at an acceptable rate, residents will move to another city that better serves them. Moreover, cities will not be able to attract new residents and maintain economic health when more fiscally desirable alternatives exist for a mobile population.

The foundation for this argument was Charles Tiebout's theoretical article "A Pure Theory of Local Expenditures" (1956). Paul Peterson (1981) extended Tiebout's work to make conclusions about local decision making. Peterson presents three types of policies: developmental, allocative, and redistributive. Developmental and redistributive policies are the two extremes in this typology and are the key concerns of Peterson's argument. According to Peterson, intercity competition requires policymakers to act in the city's self-interest and as a result, severely limits local policymaking. Local decision makers favor developmental policies such as the attraction of industry and large employers, because these policies are aimed at improvement of the local economy. On the other hand, city officials will eschew redistributive policies such as affordable housing programs, because they shift resources from the middle- and upper-income groups to lower-income people and, as a result, are detrimental to the economic vitality of a city. As Peterson writes, "the pursuit of a city's economic interests . . . makes no allowance for the care of the needy and unfortunate . . . the competition among local communities all but precludes a concern for redistribution" (pp. 37–38).

Peterson investigated education policy, a redistributive function, in central cities versus suburbs. He concluded that central cities were more likely to implement redistributive activities, because historically, they were financially more prosperous than suburbs. However, Peterson argues that central cities no longer have the resources for the "luxury of redistribution" and "are slowly adapting to the more competitive circumstances of today" (p. 106).

Mark Schneider (1989) contributed to public choice scholarship with his study of public goods and services. Schneider focused on suburban communities only, and therefore, he offered no information about policy decisions in central cities. His work, however, provided an empirical test of Peterson's theory. Schneider performed pooled, cross-sectional analyses of the factors influencing developmental and redistributive expenditures in suburban communities. Among other factors in his model, he included demographic, intergovernmental, and competition influences. Schneider found some evidence that intercity competition limited redistributive expenditures; it was, however, not statistically significant in his model of developmental expenditures.

Anthony Downs (1994) agrees with the public choice theorists. He states "all communities compete" (p. 23) and emphasizes that cities must remain attractive and maintain a reasonable tax rate to attract residents and businesses. Redistributive policy is inconsistent with this goal regardless of the affluence level in the city. Although wealthier, fiscally healthy, cities can afford to shift resources from higher- to lower-income people, residents in these communities have social and political reasons for avoiding redistributive policies (Downs 1994).

Lower-income communities, such as many central cities, have a weak tax base, but typically a higher per capita cost for many public services. In these localities an increase in the tax rate to fund services yields a small return. Although these communities may elect officials sympathetic to their needs, these city decision makers still pursue economically beneficial policies, such as subsidies to for-profit developers, and discourage the attraction of additional lower-income people (Downs 1994).

Several studies have investigated the policy preferences of U.S. city mayors to determine the validity of the public choice hypothesis. Most of this research considers policy making across all types of cities and, therefore, fails to distinguish between central and suburban cities. For example, Basolo (1997) conducted a mail survey of mayors from a representative sample of U.S. cities with a population of 25,000 or more. Basolo's study focused specifically on economic development—a developmental policy—and on affordable housing—a redistributive policy. The study questionnaire asked respondents to identify their level of agreement with the following statement: "If it came down to choosing between supporting economic development programs or housing programs for the poor, I would support economic development efforts." Twenty-seven percent of the mayors strongly agreed with the statement and approximately 85 percent agreed with it to some extent. Only 2.5 percent of the respondents strongly disagreed with the statement (n = 322). Longoria (1994) and Saiz (1999) use factor analysis on a range of local services to match services to the categories of Peterson's policy typology and compare spending patterns for each category. Both researchers find that U.S. mayors' spending preferences favor developmental over redistributive policies.

Research rarely considers the validity of the public choice hypothesis by type of city. A study by Green and Fleischmann (1991), however, did compare central cities, suburbs, and nonmetropolitan cities on economic development policy. Using regression analysis, the authors investigated the factors that influence the level of local economic development activities, which they measure as an additive index of the number of programs used by cities to promote development. They ran three separate regressions, one for each type of city, which include a range of contextual factors as independent variables. The coefficient for the regional competition variable is positive and statistically significant ($p = .05$ or better) for all three types of cities. Therefore, these results suggest that competition in the region results in a higher level of economic development activities in cities.

Much of the research on city policy preferences indicates that competition plays a major role in the determination of local policy decisions. However, many researchers argue that political factors are important in explaining local policy decisions. Regime analysis, for example, identifies public/private coalitions in interdependent relationships in cities and views local governments as coordinators of resources. These coalition members share desired outcomes and establish long-term relationships and combine resources to effectuate these outcomes (Stoker 1995, Stone 1993, 1986). The nature of the relationships over time and the shared goals of regime members are thought to affect local policy choices. Regime studies often provide rich descriptive analyses of city activities. However, at this time, this research approach suffers from several weaknesses. First, the study of the nature of public/private relationships is a reformulation of community power theory; therefore, there is some question about the added value of regime analysis (Basolo 1998). Second, the identification of shared goals may be difficult, as all participants may not reveal their true preferences. In other words, a desired outcome may appear shared among parties, but, in fact, some participants may be working toward a different goal. Third, regime analyses typically focus on one or just a few cities, and generalization across cities is limited. Further development of the regime perspective is necessary before a regime theory can be presented as an adequate explanation of policy choices across cities.

Empirical studies have identified other factors as influencing local decision making. The fiscal condition of a city, for example, is thought to affect local government expenditures (Clark and Ferguson 1983). Also, some researchers have identified population, growth, minority and interest group representation, poverty level, and unemployment as important influences on city policymaking (Green and Fleischmann 1991, Waste 1989, Clark and Ferguson 1983, Greenstone and Peterson 1976).

Sample Methodology and Data

Public choice theory identifies a severe limitation on local policymaking. This literature suggests that cities experience a competitive constraint on local decision making. Therefore, the economic development and affordable housing policy choices made in central cities should be similar to the choices made in suburban communities. On the other hand, contextual factors such as demographic and employment trends, as well as housing conditions, can vary considerably between the two types of cities. These contextual differences between central cities and suburban communities suggest that needs and resources will result in different policy choices and levels of commitment in the two types of cities.

This research considers public choice theory in a comparative analysis of central cities and suburban communities. We explore the level of local financial commitment to economic development and affordable housing policy and the fit of these policies to needs in central cities and suburban communities. In so doing, the analysis considers contextual factors and the level of intercity competition for a sample of U.S. cities with populations of 25,000 or more.

The data come from several sources including a 1996 mail survey of city housing staff and economic development professionals in a probability sample of U.S. cities with a population of 25,000 or more. A disproportionate, stratified, random sample of cities (n = 709) was selected from the population of all cities with a 1990 population of 25,000 or greater in the United States (n = 1,070).[1]

Survey response rates varied by respondent group. These response rates were 61.6 percent (n = 437) for housing staff and 58.3 percent (n = 413) for economic development professionals. The elimination of nonmetropolitan or rural cities from the sample as well as the existence of missing values on key variables reduces the final data sets for this analysis to 366 and 308 cases respectively.[2] An analysis of the data sets reveals some bias in both of the samples after the reduction of cases.[3] However, the bias problem appears much more severe in the economic development sample. Furthermore, the economic development data set contains no northeastern cities with populations of 250,000 or more. Therefore, we recommend caution in generalizing the results to the population.

The survey data were combined with data from the U.S. Bureau of the Census: the 1990 U.S. Census of Population and Housing and the 1994 County and City Data Book. Policy variables such as expenditures and program type were collected in the sample survey. The city type and contextual factors were downloaded from the U.S. Bureau of Census sources.

Analysis of Economic Development Policy and Support

Central and suburban cities participating in the economic development survey vary on the contextual factors in this study. They differ, on average, in unemployment rates, population growth rates, poverty rates, and median household income. Table 10.1 displays the means and standard errors for each of these variables for central and suburban cities. As expected, central cities, on average, have lower median household incomes, experience higher levels of unemployment and poverty, and have slower population growth than suburban cities. However, suburban communities have higher levels of competition compared to central cities.[4]

Public choice theory asserts that higher levels of intercity competition result in public investment in developmental policies such as economic development programs. On the other hand, central cities clearly indicate a greater need for economic development programs based on lower median household incomes and lower growth rates, on average, and higher unemployment and poverty rates.

The effect of competition and the needs factors on cities may be revealed in spending decisions by city officials. Cities spend funds received from local sources such as property taxes, business taxes, and development fees as well as monies from other sources such as state and federal governments. Most intergovernmental funds place certain constraints on the local recipients. For example, the Community Development Block Grant (CDBG), a federal program used for both economic development and housing, requires the local government to spend program funding for at least one of the following objectives: benefiting low- and moderate-income persons, aiding in the prevention or elimination of slums or blight, and meeting other urgent community development needs (U.S. Department of Housing and Urban Development 1999). Another example, the Urban Development Action Grant (UDAG), was a federal program designed to leverage public funds with private dollars for the development of commercial, industrial, or housing projects. A minimum of 2.5 private dollars to every UDAG dollar was required, and the project had to be completed in no more than four years (Gist 1980). Therefore, cities have less discretion in their spending of intergovernmental funds. At the same time, cities may view federal and state grants as "free money," and therefore, expenditure of these funds may have less significance to decision makers than the localities' own source monies. Furthermore, cities may simply substitute intergovernmental dollars for local funds. For these reasons, we investigate the expenditure of funds for economic development from all sources as well as local sources only.

A majority of central cities and suburban communities spent funds for economic development in Fiscal Year (FY) 1994–1995. In fact, over 80 percent of the cities in both categories reported some expenditure on economic development. The expenditures of public funds for economic development, however, indicate that central cities spent more. Table 10.2 shows

Table 10.1

Economic Development Survey: Descriptive Statistics for Contextual Factors by City Type (n = 308)

	Central		Suburban	
Contextual factors	Mean	Standard error	Mean	Standard error
Unemployment rate, 1990	0.07	0.00	0.05	0.00
Growth rate, 1980–1990	0.14	0.02	0.34	0.05
Percentage below poverty, 1989	0.17	0.01	0.08	0.01
Median household income, 1989	27,090	507	40,288	888
Intercity competition, 1990	30.54	2.76	71.96	4.37

Source: U.S. Department of Commerce, Bureau of the Census. 1992. *1990 Census of Population and Housing Summary Tape File 1C.* Washington, DC (CD-Rom format).

Note: The intercity competition variable was calculated from the 1990 Census Bureau records of incorporated cities with populations at 25,000 or above within metropolitan areas.

the means for total economic development expenditures (all sources) and local economic development expenditures (own source monies) for both types of cities.

We would expect central cities to have higher levels of expenditures, because they tend to have larger populations than suburban communities. Once we normalize expenditures by population size, the mean values in Table 10.2 suggest, for both the total expenditures and own source expenditures, that central cities spend more dollars on economic development. However, the standard errors of the means are critical information to determine if the differences in means are statistically significant. We performed four t-tests to ascertain this information. The results of these difference of means tests are found in Table 10.3.

The t-tests reveal that there is no statistically significant difference in the means of per capita economic development expenditures between the two types of cities. In other words, we cannot say with confidence that the means of expenditures on economic development differ in central and suburban cities after we adjust for population size differences.

One common strategy used by cities to promote economic development is not represented in expenditure data. Many cities offer tax incentives or abatements to attract businesses to their jurisdiction. This type of approach results in a loss of future tax revenue and is not recorded "on the books." Following the reasoning of public choice theorists, the use of tax incentives for economic development should be more evident in suburban cities due to higher levels of competition. However, the problems of unemployment and disinvestment in central cities should provide some motivation to central cities to

Table 10.2

Expenditures on Economic Development by City Type (n = 308)

	Central		Suburban	
Variables	Mean	Standard error	Mean	Standard error
Total expenditures	3,386,599	653,406	986,034	271,083
Own source expenditures	2,457,170	635,725	809,927	244,011
Total expenditures per capita	36.72	16.22	18.40	4.59
Own source expenditures per capita	28.61	16.05	15.34	4.27

Table 10.3

Results of t-Tests on Economic Development Mean Expenditures (n = 308)

Variables	t	p-value
Total expenditures	3.41	0.00
Own source expenditures	2.42	0.02
Total expenditures per capita	1.09	0.28
Own source expenditures per capita	0.80	0.43

forego future tax revenue to attract employers and stimulate today's economy.

The data reveal that suburban cities use tax incentives far more frequently than the central cities. The chi-square (X^2) computed for the data supports that there is an association between use of tax incentives and type of city. Unfortunately, most survey respondents could not estimate the value of the tax incentives. Therefore, we cannot offer conclusions on the level of support associated with tax incentives. We can state, however, that the suburban cities in our sample used this policy more during the period 1992–1995 than did central cities (see Table 10.4).

Cities in both categories seem to support economic development policies. This finding is consistent with public choice theory, but recognizes that, in central cities, population needs also may influence developmental policy decisions. Regardless of the motivation for these decisions, we can conclude that economic development is a popular policy among cities and is widely supported by decision makers.

Analysis of Affordable Housing Policy and Support

Affordable housing needs in cities may be reflected in population factors as well as local housing market indicators such as quality of the building stock and housing values. The population factors and competition levels for the

Table 10.4

Use of Tax Incentives Between 1992 and 1995 by City Type (n = 302)

Variable	Central		Suburban	
	#	%	#	%
Tax incentives	63	40.6	93	63.3
No tax incentives	92	59.4	54	36.7
Total	155	100	147	100

Note: $X^2 = 15.81$ with 1 degree of freedom; p-value = 0.00.

Table 10.5

Affordable Housing Survey: Descriptive Statistics for Housing Market Indicators by City Type (n = 366)

Contextual factors	Central		Suburban	
	Mean	Standard error	Mean	Standard error
Median value of housing, 1990	36,698	1,533	30,616	1,497
Median monthly rent, 1990	363	7.18	550	9.69
Vacancy rate, 1990	0.08	.00	0.06	0.00
Housing conditions, 1990	0.93	0.18	−1.32	0.18
Homeownership rate, 1990	0.54	0.01	0.63	0.01

Source: U.S. Department of Commerce, Bureau of the Census. 1993. *1990 Census of Population and Housing Summary Tape File 3C.* Washington, DC (CD-ROM format).

Note: The housing condition indicator is an additive index of the Z scores for four structural conditions. In the full sample, the values range from −4.085 (better) to 12.175 (worse).

cities responding to the affordable housing survey are similar to the results from the cities in the economic development sample. The descriptive statistics for the housing market indicators are shown in Table 10.5. Central cities, on average, have higher median housing values, but lower median monthly rents compared to suburban cities. Vacancy rates are higher in central cities, housing conditions are worse, and home ownership rates are lower than in suburban communities.

The higher levels of intercity competition in suburbs should result in less support to affordable housing programs according to the reasoning of public choice theorists. At the same time, rents are higher in suburban cities and suggest some need for affordable housing. Central cities also appear to have housing needs with higher median housing values, lower home ownership rates, and worse housing conditions than suburban communities. We would expect central cities with the evident housing needs and lower competition levels to support affordable housing policy. Suburban cities, however, seem to have competing forces, high levels of competition, but some affordable housing needs.

The initial examination of city expenditures for affordable housing in FY 1994–1995 reveals a disparity in spending policy between the two types of cities. Almost all of the central cities (98 percent) spent funds on affordable housing, but fewer suburban communities (77 percent) reported expenditures in this policy area (see Table 10.6). In other words, approximately one-quarter of the suburban cities spent no funds on affordable housing. Still, the data reveal that the majority of both types of cities did spend dollars on affordable housing.

Total expenditures from all sources and expenditures from city sources only are shown in Table 10.7. In terms of total expenditures for affordable housing, central cities, on average, spent more than five times the funds spent by suburban communities. Also, central cities spent approximately 2.5 times more own source monies on affordable housing than the suburban cities. Again, per capita expenditures account for population size differences between the two types of cities. The per capita expenditures shown in Table 10.7 reveal that central cities, on average, spent more than suburban cities, both in total expenditures and own source funds.

The differences in the means of the housing expenditures variables seem rather dramatic. However, the variation in the distributions of the expenditures data is important to determine if the differences are statistically significant. We performed a t-test for each of the expenditures variables (see Table 10.8). The t-tests on the per capita affordable housing expenditures, both for total and own source expenditures, reveal that there is a statistically significant difference between the means of the two types of cities. Therefore, we find that central and suburban cities are different in their spending choices for affordable housing expenditures. In fact, central cities spend more per capita from their own source revenue and from all sources than the suburban cities.

Cities have devised a few affordable housing strategies that avoid direct expenditures of public funds. Some jurisdictions, for example, have passed rent control laws that limit the ability of private landlords to raise rents. While rent control has been discussed often in the housing literature (for example, see Salins 1992, Keating et al. 1998), this approach is not widely used by cities. In fact, less than 8 percent of the cities in our sample reported the use of rent control. Far more common among cities was the availability of a density bonus for low- and moderate-income units. A density bonus allows a developer who agrees to include low- and moderate-income units in the development to build more units than the zoning typically would permit. The size of the bonus as well as the number or percentage of low- and moderate-income units required for the bonus varies by jurisdictions.

Table 10.6

Propensity for Expenditures on Affordable Housing by City Type (n = 366)

	Central		Suburban	
Variable	Number	%	Number	%
Spent dollars	193	98.0	131	77.5
Spent no dollars	4	2.0	38	22.5
Total	197	100	169	100

Note: X² may not be reliable if any cell contains less than five cases; therefore, results for *X²* are not reported for this cross tabulation.

Table 10.7

Expenditures on Affordable Housing by City Type (n = 366)

	Central		Suburban	
Variables	Mean	Standard error	Mean	Standard error
Total expenditures	6,572,036	1,449,028	1,131,401	206,532
Own source expenditures	1,495,709	530,841	576,734	155,141
Total expenditures per capita	1,832.17	828.48	49.74	10.75
Own source expenditures per capita	126.13	50.99	23.55	6.22

Table 10.8

Results of t-Tests on Affordable Housing Mean Expenditures (n = 366)

Variables	t	p-value
Total expenditures	3.72	0.00
Own source expenditures	1.66	0.10
Total expenditures per capita	2.15	0.03
Own source expenditures per capita	2.00	0.05

Suburban cities use a density bonus approach more than central cities. Almost 40 percent of the suburban cities reported offering a density bonus, while only 20.5 percent of the central cities provided this incentive. The number of developers using the density bonus and the number of low- and moderate-income units built as a result of the bonus are unknown. As a result, for our sample of cities we cannot determine the effectiveness of this approach for the provision of affordable housing.

The majority of both types of cities support affordable housing to some degree. Central cities, however, spend more per capita on housing than suburban cities. According to public choice theory, we would expect this finding due to the relatively high level of regional competition for the suburban

Table 10.9

Use of Density Bonus in 1996 by City Type (n = 363)

Variable	Central		Suburban	
	Number	%	Number	%
Density bonus	40	20.5	62	36.9
No density bonus	155	79.5	106	63.1
Total	195	100	168	100

Note: $X^2 = 11.93$ with 1 degree of freedom; p-value = 0.00.

cities in our sample. Furthermore, central cities with lower incomes, worse housing conditions, and higher housing values, on average, appear to have more need for housing programs.

The similarities and differences among city types in their policy decisions cannot be explained definitively. However, the data from this sample provide several valuable observations. First, the economic and housing conditions in central cities are far worse, on average, than in suburban cities and support an argument for local housing and economic development programs. Second, per capita expenditures on economic development in central cities exceeded suburban cities as needs suggest; however, a t-test indicated that there is not a statistically significant difference by city type between the mean values for per capita expenditures on economic development. The latter finding may be a result of the difference in intercity competition between the two types of cities. Public choice theorists argue that cities will spend more dollars on policies to improve city economic interests as the level of competition increases in the region. In this study's sample, suburban cities experience far more competition than central cities on average, and therefore, their expenditures seem consistent with public choice theory. In addition, suburban cities compared to central cities are more likely to use tax incentives to attract businesses to their communities, which may also reflect the competition factor. Therefore, our results suggest that central cities' spending on economic development represents population needs, while suburban economic development expenditures may be a response to the structural process of intercity competition.

Finally, central cities spend more per capita on affordable housing than suburban cities do. Central cities exhibit a wide range of housing needs, and central cities' investment in housing programs appears to serve these needs. The results for suburban cities are less clear. Public choice theorists assert that cities in competitive regions will avoid redistributive expenditures such as affordable housing, because they benefit lower-income people rather than the middle-income residents sought by local governments. While our findings are consistent with this theory, our analysis does not answer the question of response to affordable housing needs in suburban cities. Suburban cities had higher rents, on average, than central cities, so affordable rental housing is likely to be a problem in many suburban communities. We do not know, however, if suburban housing expenditures are targeted to this particular problem or another program such as home ownership subsidies. Likewise, we cannot discern if density bonuses, a more common policy approach in suburban cities, are applied to multifamily (rental) or single-family (ownership) developments.

In sum, this research does not provide housing expenditure information by specific needs for each type of city. However, a wide range of housing needs exists in central cities. Therefore, the bulk of housing programs most likely serve at least one major need in these cities. In suburban communities, however, the primary need appears to be for affordable rental housing. If suburban expenditures and density bonus programs do not target the rental market, their programs may fail to serve the population in greatest need. Further research clearly is necessary to determine the match of housing needs to policies in the two types of cities.

Conclusion

Central cities generally have worse housing and economic conditions than suburban communities. Based on our sample of cities, central cities have lower median household incomes, higher levels of unemployment and poverty, and slower population growth than suburban cities, on average. In addition, central cities, on average, have higher housing vacancy rates, worse housing conditions, higher median housing values, and lower home ownership rates compared to suburban cities. Suburban cities in our sample, on the other hand, have higher median monthly rents and experience higher levels of regional competition compared to central cities.

The differences between central cities and suburban communities should result in a variation of policy strategies between the two types of city. If determined on a needs base only, economic development and affordable housing policies, programs, and expenditures should be different in central cities compared to suburban cities. Public choice theorists, however, claim that intercity competition influences local policymaking. Specifically, intercity competition will result in adoption of policies that improve the economic interest of the city, such as economic development, and avoidance of redistributive policies, such as affordable housing programs.

This research examined spending policies on economic development and affordable housing in central cities and suburban communities. Our results show that there is not a statistically significant difference between the mean values for per capita expenditures on economic development for the two areas. This finding suggests that needs as well as intercity competition affect city expenditure decisions for economic development. Similarly, expenditures on affordable housing appear to be influenced by both needs and competition levels. Central cities spend more per capita on affordable housing than suburban cities, and the difference in the means is statistically significant.

Many suburban cities use policy strategies that require no direct outlay of funds. For example, tax abatements for economic development and density bonuses for affordable housing were far more common in suburban cities than central cities. These approaches may serve the needs in suburban communities, but we cannot be certain without further investigation. Future research should link the economic and housing needs of cities to spending policies and programs, particularly, program outputs, to assess the fit to community needs as well as the effectiveness of local economic development and affordable housing policies.

* * *

This research received funding from the National Center for the Revitalization of Central Cities, the National Science Foundation under Grant No. SBER-9630638, and the U.S. Department of Housing and Urban Development. The substance and findings of that work are dedicated to the public. The author and publisher are solely responsible for the accuracy of the statements and interpretations contained in this chapter. Any opinions, findings, interpretations, and conclusions or recommendations expressed in this material are those of the author and do not necessarily reflect the views of the National Center for the Revitalization of Central Cities, the National Science Foundation, or the U.S. Government.

Notes

1. The initial sample was stratified with population size and geographic region as stratification variables. Stratification versus unstratified simple random sampling improves sample efficiency (Kish 1967). The largest category of cities (populations of 250,000 or more) was oversampled, because fewer cities in this category exist in the population. Oversampling increases the likelihood that larger cities are represented in the final results.

2. The cases were weighted to account for sample design and response rate.

Each case receives a weight equal to the inverse of the sampling proportion times the response rate in its stratification cell; cases with missing values on key variables were considered as nonrespondents. The sample design and weighting are used by STATA, a statistical program, to produce the correct statistical estimates.

3. The bias tests consisted of running logistic regressions on the included cases compared to the excluded cases in each of the data sets. The independent variables in the model for the economic development survey were as followed: total population (logged), growth rate (logged), unemployment rate (logged), percent below poverty (logged), and median household income (logged). The model for the affordable housing survey included total population (logged), growth rate (logged), percent below poverty (logged), median household income (logged), median housing value (logged), and housing conditions (logged) as independent variables.

4. Intercity competition was measured as the sum of all incorporated cities plus counties in a city's MSA (or PMSA if the city is in a CMSA).

5. Suburban cities compared to central cities typically have more land available for new residential subdivision development. The availability of land, therefore, may account for the higher use of density bonuses in suburbs.

References

Apgar, William C. Jr., George S. Masnick, and Nancy McArdle. 1991. *Housing in America: 1970–2000.* Joint Center for Housing Studies, Harvard University.

Basolo, Victoria. 1997. *U.S. Mayors' Views on Affordable Housing and Economic Development Policies: A Summary of Survey Results.* Working Paper Number 97–09, Center for Urban and Regional Studies Working Paper Series: University of North Carolina at Chapel Hill.

———. 1998. *Housing Policy in the Local Political Economy: Understanding the Support for Affordable Housing Programs in Cities.* Dissertation: University of North Carolina at Chapel Hill.

———. 1999. "The Impacts of Inter-city Competition and Intergovernmental Factors on Local Affordable Housing Programs." *Housing Policy Debate* 10, no. 3: 659–88.

Bluestone, Barry, and Bennett Harrison. 1982. *The Deindustrialization of America.* New York: Basic Books.

Bottles, Scott L. 1987. *Los Angeles and the Automobile.* Berkeley: University of California Press.

Brophy, Paul C., and Rhonda N. Smith. 1997. "Mixed-Income Housing: Factors for Success." *Cityscape* 3, no. 2: 3–31.

Citizens Commission on Civil Rights. 1986. "The Federal Government and Equal Housing Opportunity: A Continuing Failure," in *Critical Perspectives on Housing,* ed. Rachel G. Bratt, Chester Hartman, and Ann Meyerson, pp. 296–324. Philadelphia: Temple University Press.

Clark, Terry Nichols, and Lorna Crowley Ferguson. 1983. *City Money.* New York: Columbia University Press.

Downs, Anthony. 1994. *New Visions for Metropolitan America.* Washington, DC: The Brookings Institution.

———. 1997. "The Challenge of Our Declining Big Cities." *Housing Policy Debate* 8, no. 2: 359–408.

Gabriel, Stuart A. 1996. "Urban Housing Policy in the 1990s." *Housing Policy Debate* 7, no. 4: 673–93.

Gale, Dennis E. 1987. *Washington, D.C. Inner-City Revitalization and Minority Suburbanization.* Philadelphia: Temple University Press.

Gist, John R. 1980. "Urban Development Action Grants: Design and Implementation," in *Urban Revitalization*, ed. Donald B. Rosenthal, Beverly Hills, CA: Sage.

Green, Gary P., and Arnold Fleischmann. 1991. "Promoting Economic Development: A Comparison of Central Cities, Suburbs, and Nonmetropolitan Communities." *Urban Affairs Quarterly* 27, no. 1: 145–54.

Greenstone, J.D., and Paul E. Peterson. 1976. *Race and Authority in Urban Politics.* Chicago: University of Chicago Press.

Imbroscio, David, Marion Orr, Timothy Ross, and Clarence Stone. 1995. "Baltimore and the Human Investment Challenge." *Urban Revitalization*, ed. Fritz W. Wagner, Timothy E. Joder, and Anthony J. Mumphrey, Jr., pp. 38–68. Thousand Oaks, CA: Sage.

Jencks, Christopher, and Paul E. Peterson. 1991. *The Urban Underclass.* Washington, DC: The Brookings Institution.

Joint Center for Housing Studies. 1994. *The State of the Nation's Housing.* Joint Center for Housing Studies, Harvard University.

Kain, John F. 1968. "Housing Segregation, Negro Employment, and Metropolitan Decentralization." *Quarterly Journal of Economics* 82: 175–97.

Kantor, Paul with Stephen David. 1988. *The Dependent City: The Changing Political Economy of Urban America.* Glenview, IL: Scott, Foresman.

Kasarda, John D. 1990. "Structural Factors Affecting the Location and Timing of Urban Underclass Growth." *Urban Geography* 11: 234–64.

———. 1995. "Industrial Restructuring and Changing Job Locations." *State of the Union: America in the 1990s* (Volume 1), ed. Reynolds Farley, pp. 215–67. New York: Russell Sage.

Kasarda, John D., Stephen J. Appold, Stuart H. Sweeney, and Elaine Sieff. 1997. "Central-City and Suburban Migration Patterns: Is a Turnaround on the Horizon?" *Housing Policy Debate* 8, no. 2: 307–58.

Keating, W. Dennis, Michael B. Teitz, and Andrejs Skaburskis. 1998. *Rent Control: Regulation and the Rental Housing Market.* New Brunswick, NJ: Center for Urban Policy Research.

Kish, Leslie. 1967. *Survey Sampling.* New York: Wiley.

Logan, John R., and Todd Swanstrom, eds. 1990. Preface to *Beyond the City Limits.* Philadelphia: Temple University Press.

Longoria, Thomas Jr. 1994. "Empirical Analysis of the *City Limits* Typology." *Urban Affairs Quarterly* 30, no. 1: 102–13.

Mollenkopf, John H. 1983. *The Contested City.* Princeton, NJ: Princeton University Press.

Monkkonen, Eric H. 1988. *America Becomes Urban.* Berkeley: University of California Press.

Moss, Mitchell L. 1997. "Reinventing the Central City as a Place to Live and Work." *Housing Policy Debate* 8, no. 2: 471–90.

Nenno, Mary K. 1997. "Changes and Challenges in Affordable Housing and Urban Development." *Affordable Housing and Urban Redevelopment in the United States*, ed. W. Van Vliet, pp. 1–22. Thousand Oaks, CA: Sage.

Peterson, Paul E. 1981. *City Limits*. Chicago: University of Chicago Press.

Reingold, David A. 1997. "Does Inner City Public Housing Exacerbate the Employment Problems of Its Tenants?" *Journal of Urban Affairs* 19, no. 4: 469–86.

Saiz, Martin. 1999. "Mayoral Perceptions of Development and Redistributive Policies." *Urban Affairs Review* 34, no. 6: 820–42.

Salins, Peter. 1992. *Scarcity by Design: The Legacy of New York City's Housing Policies*. Cambridge: Harvard University Press.

Schneider, Mark. 1989. *The Competitive City*. Pittsburgh: University of Pittsburgh Press.

Schwartz, Alex, and Kian Tajbakhsh. 1997. "Mixed-Income Housing: Unanswered Questions." *Cityscape* 3, no. 2: 71–92.

Scott, Allen J. 1988. *Metropolis*. Berkeley: University of California Press.

Stoker, Gerry. 1995. "Regime Theory and Urban Politics," in *Theories of Urban Politics*, ed. David Judge, Gerry Stoker, and Harold Wolman, pp. 54–71. London: Sage.

Stone, Clarence N. 1986. "Power and Social Complexity." *Community Power: Directions for Future Research*, ed. Robert Waste. Newbury Park, CA: Sage.

———. 1993. "Urban Regimes and the Capacity to Govern: A Political Economy Approach." *Journal of Urban Affairs* 15, no. 1: 1–28.

Swanstrom, Todd. 1988. "Semisovereign Cities: The Politics of Urban Development." *Polity* 21: 83–110.

Tiebout, Charles. 1956. "A Pure Theory of Local Expenditures." *Journal of Political Economy* 64: 416–24.

U.S. Department of Housing and Urban and Development. 1997. "Community Planning and Development: Empowerment Zones." HUD Web page: http://www.hud.gov/budget99/ justif99/cpd/bcpdzone.html.

———. 1999. "Guides to HUD's Community Planning and Development programs." HUD Web page: http://www.hud.gov:80/local/atl/ atl_pgud.html#CPD1.

Waste, Robert J. 1989. *The Ecology of City Policy Making*. New York: Oxford University Press.

Wilson, William Julius. 1987. *The Truly Disadvantaged*. Chicago: University of Chicago Press.

Witte, Ann Dryden. 1996. "Urban Crime: Issues and Policies." *Housing Policy Debate* 7, no. 4: 731–48.

11

ALEX SCHWARTZ AND KIAN TAJBAKHSH

Mixed-Income Housing

Economic integration has become a top priority for housing policy in the United States. Responding in part to the failures of public housing and the social costs of concentrated poverty, housing programs increasingly try to blend extremely low-income households with more affluent neighbors. Governments pursue this strategy of economic integration in two basic ways. One approach, dispersal, is to help public housing residents and other extremely low-income households move into suburban middle-income neighborhoods. The other method, mixed-income housing (MIH) includes households with varying levels of income within the same building or development.

Of these two approaches for achieving economic integration, dispersal strategies are more dominant, although mixed-income housing is gaining momentum. Dispersal strategies are exemplified by Chicago's well-known Gautreaux program and the more recent federal Moving to Opportunities demonstration program, which was in large part inspired by Gautreaux (Rosenbaum 1995, HUD 1998). Both programs help public housing residents relocate to suburban communities, providing Section 8 vouchers, landlord outreach, counseling, and other forms of assistance. Similarly, HUD's Vacancy Consolidation and Regional Opportunity Counseling Initiatives, operating in more than twenty-five metropolitan areas, also seek to broaden the residential choices for residents of federal housing projects—including ones slated for demolition—by combining housing vouchers with counseling and other services (Turner 1998).

Federal interest in mixed-income housing is best represented in its policy shifts toward public housing. The federal HOPE VI program for the revitalization of severely distressed public housing increasingly favors plans that include mixed-income occupancy in addition to downsizing, reconfiguration, and integration of community services (Schwartz and Tajbakhsh 1997, HUD 2000). The Quality Housing and Work Responsibility Act of 1998, the most far-reaching federal housing legislation in years, also promotes greater income diversity within public housing. The law mandates that households with incomes below 30 percent of the area median cannot account for more than 40 percent of all new admissions into public housing. The law also specifies that at least 75 percent of all new tenant-based subsidies (Section 8) must go to households with incomes below 75 percent of median. When they exceed this percentage, housing authorities can reduce the number of extremely low-income households admitted to public housing on a one-to-one basis provided that the percentage of extremely low-income households does not fall below 30 percent of public housing admissions (HUD no date). HUD more recently proposed a regulation that would require all public housing authorities to change their admissions policies and practices to establish a mix of incomes within each building. They would classify buildings and prospective residents by income level and then use this information in deciding which tenant applications to accept for which buildings. The goal is to bring higher-income families into lower-income buildings and lower-income households into higher-income buildings ("Proposed Rule on Public Housing Income Deconcentration Published" 2000).

Mixed income housing dates back several decades and is extremely diverse. Developments vary in terms of the representation of different income groups, how these income groups are defined, the tenure of the housing (rental vs. ownership), and the financing of the housing. For example, what may be classified as high income in one mixed-income development could fall under the low-income category in another (Schwartz and Tajbakhsh 1997). Examples of mixed-income housing include the above-mentioned HOPE VI developments—the first of which have just recently been completed—so-called 80–20 programs built with low-interest financing, housing built to satisfy state and local inclusionary zoning requirements, and a small number of developments financed with federal Low Income Housing Tax Credits (see Schwartz and Tajbakhsh 1997, and Brophy and Smith 1997 for specific examples).

Despite its fairly long history and current salience, very little is known about the operational performance or social aspects of mixed-income housing. Most of the literature to date on the topic consists of case studies of individual developments (see Schwartz and Tajbakhsh 1997 for a review; also Brophy and Smith 1997). Very little research is available on the factors that make mixed-income housing financially viable or the social benefits of residing in mixed-income housing. The only study to date on the social side of mixed-income housing is an article on Chicago's Lake Parc Place, a mixed-income development created on the site of a former public housing project (Rosenbaum et al. 1998).

In a previous paper we raised a series of questions about the financial viability and social benefits of mixed-income housing (Schwartz and Tajbakhsh 1997). From an operations perspective, we discussed how the location, cost design, and condition of a mixed-income development, perhaps combined with its resident demographics, influence the degree to which upper-income tenants "cross-subsidize" their lower-income counterparts. In other words, location and other contextual factors, combined with the state of the regional housing market, shape the development's ability to attract and retain higher-income residents. When market rate units are subject to frequent and/or prolonged vacancies, they incur additional maintenance expenses and revenue losses that could potentially offset the higher rents collected from these units. Turnover expenses and vacancy losses are probably highest in weak housing markets. The greater the availability of affordable housing for middle-income families, the greater the range of housing options for these households, making it more difficult for a mixed-income development to attract and retain these households.

Unless the regional housing market is extremely tight and there is a severe shortage of affordable units, moderate- and middle-income households can easily opt not to reside in mixed-income housing. And they will decline to do so unless the development is appealing in some way—perhaps more appealing than conventional middle-income housing. Therefore the size, design, condition, location, and cost of the housing (and perhaps the demographic characteristics of its occupants) are extremely important in attracting higher-income households. These factors are important individually and in combination, but there has been little research on the way their interaction creates viable mixed-income housing (Schwartz and Tajbakhsh 1997, 76).

We also raised several questions about the social effects of mixed-income housing. To date, little or no research has been done on ways by which mixed-income housing may improve the lives of the low-income residents. For example, do low-income households need to interact with higher-income neighbors in order to achieve social or economic benefits? Or is the mere presence of stable working families sufficient, whether or not these households interact with lower-income households? If social interaction across income groups is desirable or necessary, it is also important to understand the likelihood of social interaction when different income groups are also characterized by racial and household differences. The Brophy and Smith study of seven mixed-income developments found that the upper-income tenants in most tended to be white and childless and had minimal interaction with their lower-income neighbors, who tended to be African American or Latino families with children. Given the diversity of income groups included in mixed-income developments, it is also important to examine the minimum necessary income of the highest-income group in order to achieve the desired social effects. "Need they be middle income, moderate income, or simply employed, regardless of their income?" (Schwartz and Tajbakhsh 1997, 74).

This chapter begins to address some of these questions. It examines the operational performance and social dynamics of different types of mixed-income housing in New York City (the Bronx), Massachusetts, and the Bay Area of California. It is based largely on interviews with the sponsors and managers of the developments, and, in the case of the Bronx, social service providers and residents. The sample of fourteen developments covers a wide variety of mixed-income housing, ranging from predominantly low-income housing located in the South Bronx to developments located in affluent suburbs where three-quarters of the residents pay market rents. After first presenting a brief overview of the mixed-income housing and the programs and organizations responsible for their development and management, the sections examine the operational performance and social dynamics of the housing in each of the three sites. The concluding section offers some preliminary conclusions and suggestions for additional research.

Overview of Selected Developments and Projects

In this section we present an overview of the MIH programs in three different sites and highlight their differences and similarities: the city-run Vacant Cluster Program in New York City, the statewide program run by the Massachusetts Housing Finance Agency through the SHARP (State Housing Assistance Production) program, and one run by the Bridge Housing Corporation, a nonprofit housing developer focused on the San Francisco Bay Area in California. Each of these produces or has produced MIH, but they differ in their design, financing, management, and scope. We chose these sites and these projects so as to cover as broad a range as possible of the settings within which mixed-income housing is being developed.

Vacant Cluster Program (Bronx, New York)

In 1986 New York City decided to invest more than $4 billion of its own resources for the development and rehabilitation of housing. In part a response to reduced federal housing assistance and mounting homelessness, the "capital budget" housing program helped produce more than 150,000 units of new and rehabilitated housing over the following ten years (Schwartz 1999). The city's housing programs primarily served moderate- and low-income households, including a large proportion of the formerly homeless.

Middle-income families received less than 10 percent of the housing (however, they did account for nearly 75 percent of all city-funded new construction). Several programs were specifically designed as mixed-income developments. The first and largest of these was the Vacant Cluster Program.

Created in 1987, the Vacant Cluster Program (originally called Construction Management Program) was one of the very first programs devised under the Capital Budget Program (see New York City Housing Partnership 1994, 133–38 for background on the program and project information). The city's Department of Housing Preservation and Development (HPD) designed the program to rehabilitate large clusters of vacant city-owned buildings, a reflection of abandonment (if not arson) and real estate tax delinquency, in the South Bronx and Harlem. These areas epitomized the urban devastation that the South Bronx had symbolized in the 1970s and 1980s. Swaths of vacant land surrounded vacant buildings. Needless to say, the population had declined precipitously and many local businesses and services had closed. In sum the Vacant Cluster program created new housing on a large scale in some of the city's most devastated zones of abandonment. In the words of an HPD planner who helped implement the program, the goal was to rebuild entire neighborhoods; the size, scale, and scope of the program was unparalleled in the city's history.

Three elements were critical to the success of the Vacant Cluster Program: scale, services, and income-mixing. In order to build new communities in these severely distressed surroundings, HPD felt it had to redevelop blocks of buildings; it would make no sense to rehabilitate one or two buildings that were surrounded by many other vacant buildings. Second, housing alone would not be sufficient to achieve the goal of neighborhood restoration. As buildings were restored and repopulated, they required schools, stores, medical offices, and other services. HPD worked with city agencies and nonprofit groups to establish new service facilities in the developments and surrounding blocks. In addition, the Vacant Cluster Program provided a modest level of funding for on-site social services. Finally, in order to stabilize the community, the city considered it crucial to include a mix of incomes among the residents. Otherwise, if every apartment in every building was allocated to low-income families, the city would have created new concentrations of poverty.

The Vacant Cluster Program funded six large developments—five in the South Bronx, one in Harlem—with more than 3,700 apartments. Except for the Harlem project, which is managed by the New York City Housing Authority, the Vacant Cluster developments are managed by nonprofit organizations. Each development has essentially the same income mix: 30 percent of the units are allocated to formerly homeless families (most of whom receive public assistance and Section 8 vouchers), 45 percent are assigned to low-income families (defined as having income up to 60 percent of the New York area's median), and the remaining 25 percent are rented to moderate-income families (earning up to 80 percent of the median). Each unit is designated to a particular income group; if a household leaves the development, it must be replaced by another household from the same income group. The income groups are spread randomly throughout the buildings. There are no differences between the income groups in the quality, size, or location of their units. The six developments were completed and rented out by the early 1990s. All units are covered by New York City's rent stabilization law, which determines the maximum allowable increase in rent per year and after each vacancy. Thus, depending on the amount of turnover, rents for units within the same income category can vary.

Four of the five Vacant Cluster developments in the South Bronx were included in the study (the sponsor of one development declined to participate). Appendix A profiles the participating developments. We interviewed staff from the nonprofit agencies that own the developments, the property managers, and social service providers. We also interviewed staff at HPD responsible for the development of the projects and for oversight of asset management, and we conducted resident focus groups at two of the projects—the oldest and newest.

Massachusetts Housing Finance Agency (MHFA)

The Massachusetts Housing Finance Agency (now called Mass Housing), has a long tradition of financing and otherwise supporting mixed-income housing. The state legislation authorizing the agency's rental development bond programs mandated that low-income persons or families occupy at least 20 percent, or in some cases 25 percent, of all units in bond-funded developments (Massachusetts Housing Finance Agency 2003, 16). In total, Mass Housing has financed the development of more than 56,000 units of housing, most in mixed-income projects. While some MHFA mixed-income rental buildings involve no subsidies beyond a below-market rate interest rate, many other projects carry additional subsidies for low-income units.

One of the largest such programs was the SHARP program. Created in the mid-1980s as a way to replace lost federal rental housing programs, SHARP financed over eighty mixed-income projects totaling about 10,000 units of housing. The program's design called for projects with a minimum of 20 percent low income, although there exists a wide range of mixes. In the mid-1990s the SHARP program experienced some financial problems (MHFA 2003). However, these difficulties stemmed not from the mixed-income character of the developments but from the overly optimistic assumption in the program's underwriting that "steadily escalating market rents in the late 1980s would continue indefinitely" (MHFA 2000, Smith 2002, 32–33). Indeed, mixed-income rental housing remains one of MFHA's "three primary business areas" (Mass Housing 2003).

Seven MHFA-financed developments were selected for the study. They were chosen to represent a mix of geographic locations, sizes, and income distributions. Projects ranged in size from forty-two to over two hundred units. Income distributions ranged from 70 percent/thirty percent low-income/market-rate to the more usual mix of 25 percent low-income/75 percent market rate. Rent levels in the projects reflected both the type of subsidy that was used for the subsidized units (e.g., Section 8, 236), and the tight housing market especially for those projects in and around cities such as Boston and Cambridge. The developments were located in varying urban and suburban settings in the Boston metropolitan area. They were supported through a wide variety of federal, city, and private financing. In only one development were units arranged according to their subsidized or market-rate status; otherwise, they were randomly assigned. The only exception was in the case of Newton's fifty-nine-unit Warren House, where penthouse units were reserved for market rate tenants.

Through structured phone interviews with site managers, we asked several questions regarding the differences between the subsidized and non-subsidized units within the development with regard to physical arrangement, provision of amenities, and access to services (see Appendix B for list of interviewees). In none of the cases studied were the units arranged in an explicit manner according on their status as subsidized or not. They were randomly assigned. In a few instances some of the units had been picked by the state housing agency (Massachusetts Housing Finance Agency) and thus were "fixed," that is, did not move around within the building depending on the tenant. However, even in these cases, there was no set pattern to the arrangements. Only in one case, of a fifty-nine-unit building, were the penthouse units specifically reserved for market rate tenants.

The absence of explicit differentiation between units, according to degree of subsidy, was reflected in all other dimensions also. While there was a range of services offered on-site, in none of the cases was there a difference in amenities provided in the apartments or a difference to access to services or amenities within the building with respect to the income of tenants. Most managers pointed out that it was necessary to provide a high quality of amenities to attract the market rate or higher-income tenants. This suggests that in these cases, the poorer households received higher amenities and quality of services than they might have otherwise received in a non–mixed-income development.

In only two of the six projects were social services provided. These also had a high proportion of ethnic and racial minorities. Overall, however, there appear to be no significant difference in general project characteristics between subsidized and non-subsidized units.

Bridge Housing Corporation (California)

In California we studied four projects sponsored by the Bridge Housing Corporation and one owned and managed by a private real estate firm. Bridge Housing Corporation is a well established and large nonprofit housing developer based in the San Francisco Bay area. It was founded in 1981 by the Bay Area Council, a consortium of three hundred of the region's largest corporations, as a way to direct a large pool of charitable donations toward the goal of building affordable housing for households with annual incomes of between $18,000 and $35,000. Since 1983 Bridge has built over ten thousand homes valued at over $1.4 million. These range from single-family owned housing to elderly and mixed-income rental properties. In addition, Bridge Property Management Company manages sixty-four properties totaling over 6,800 units. (Bridge did not supply the names of the developments.)

In California our sample covered five projects with a range of sizes and differing income mix configurations, and located in different types of neighborhoods. In terms of the demographic characteristics, blacks and whites made up a smaller proportion of residents in all income categories compared to Massachusetts and New York City. There was a higher proportion of Hispanic and Asian tenants.

The projects in the three different sites clearly differ in significant ways. The most important variables are the size of the projects, the income mix, the financing, and the locations. The Vacant Cluster projects in the Bronx section of New York City were located in a low-income inner-city neighborhood with a predominantly minority (African American and Hispanic) population. While there was a range of incomes represented in the projects, all could be considered low-income and thus were, compared to Massachusetts and California, quite similar. In the Bronx perhaps the major distinction was between working and nonworking households. In California the projects we studied were located in suburban areas and in neighborhoods of generally higher incomes than in New York. In Massachusetts, by contrast, the mixed-income housing projects were located in a broader range of neighborhood types, in terms of both urban and suburban settings, and working-class versus more affluent suburbs. Clearly, MIH projects can be designed with a broad set of characteristics.

The question we will explore in the following sections is the degree to which these differing characteristics impact the operational feasibility and hoped for positive social effects of residential income mixing.

Financial Feasibility/Management Performance

An important aspect of the financial and management feasibility of mixed-income housing concerns the effects on certain key performance indicators of units with different levels of subsidy. Thus we were interested in seeing if there are significant differences between subsidized and non-subsidized units with respect to vacancy rates, average duration of occupancy, turnovers, arrears and vacancy losses, and per unit maintenance costs. These can potentially contribute considerably to the cost of managing these developments and thus can ultimately impact the feasibility of maintaining mixed-income housing over the long term.

In New York City, four Vacant Cluster developments all seem to function well from a financial and managerial perspective. Vacancy rates are low and rental arrears are not severe. The developments consistently produce positive net operating income; none have deficits. Rent collection, for example, at the Mount Hope development averages between 90 and 95 percent of gross potential rent. According to the organization's executive director, the Vacant Cluster buildings consistently outperform its rental properties developed through other city programs. According an asset manager at New York City's Department of Housing Preservation and Development, who had recently assessed the operational performance of Vacant Cluster developments, the buildings have done well in terms of rent collection, vacancy losses, stability of reserve funds, and physical upkeep.

To what extent do the Vacant Cluster developments' strong financial performance stem from their mixed-income occupancy? Unfortunately, the developments' management information systems are not set up to provide data by income category on rent collection, vacancies, maintenance expenses, or other property management indicators. For insight into the operating costs and revenues connected to different income groups, we must rely on the judgment of the developments' owners and property managers.

There appear to be few significant differences across the income groups in any indicator of financial performance. If anything, the moderate-income groups may put more stress on the developments' finances than the lower-income groups. Two managers felt that moderate-income residents account for a disproportionate share of units in rent arrears. Perhaps because they have more disposable income and thus more choices in how they spend their money, moderate-income households are at greater risk of coming up short for the rent. "The more choices one has with money, the greater the chance one will make the wrong choices," says a manager of one Vacant Cluster development.

Managers at all four developments concur that moderate-income units turn over somewhat more frequently than other units and stay vacant longer. It takes slightly longer to find qualified families that can afford the higher rents of the moderate-income units; management must process more applications per vacant unit to find an acceptable tenant. The developments' location in the very low-income neighborhoods of the South Bronx most likely makes it harder to attract moderate-income households, who have more residential choices, even in New York's tight housing market. It is important, however, not to exaggerate the revenue losses associated with turnover expenses and vacancy losses for moderate-income units. All four developments have waiting lists for each income category. Had the Vacant Cluster Program earmarked a higher portion of the units to moderate-income households, this income category would most likely pose a much more serious challenge. "I'm just glad the moderate-income units are only 25 percent of the total," says one manager.

Ironically, if there is any cross-subsidy within the Vacant Cluster developments, it comes not from the higher rent moderate-income units but from units reserved for formerly homeless families—30 percent in total. These families all received Section 8 certificates or vouchers, which generate considerably more income than the moderate-income units. For example, the Fair Market Rent in fiscal 2000 was $920 for a two-bedroom apartment, compared to an average of about $700 for low-income units of equivalent size in the Vacant Cluster developments. Section 8, according to one manager, accounts for $1 million of the project's $4 million budget. Without it, the developments would not be financially viable.

At times, however, the Section 8 revenue stream has been diminished by delays in issuing Section 8 to formerly homeless families, especially in the mid- to late 1990s when the federal government did not fund any incremental Section 8 subsidies. As a result, when units designated for homeless families were vacated, the developments' managers faced the frustrating choice of either keeping the units vacant for months on end until the city came up with Section 8 assistance for prospective homeless tenants, or to allow these families to move in, hoping that the families would eventually receive Section 8 and that retroactive rent payments could be collected eventually.

If the managers perceived few differences across the income groups in terms of revenue, they saw even less with respect to operating costs. They saw no relationship at all between household income and the need for maintenance and repairs. Some property managers did believe that some formerly homeless families are harder on their apartments than other households, but other managers saw no such pattern at all. Damaged appliances and fixtures, clogged drains, and excessive wear and tear, in other words, are no less prevalent within moderate-income units than in units reserved for lower-income families.

When asked to explain their developments' solid finances, the managers and owners of the Vacant Cluster projects emphasize such factors as underwriting, scale, and social services. None of them referred to the mixed-income aspect of the Vacant Cluster Program.

The city funded extensive gut rehabilitation of the Vacant Cluster buildings, reducing the need for major new repairs and maintenance. Most of the projects were financed with a 2 percent mortgage from the city, payment of which was deferred for a minimum of five years to allow for the accumulation of maintenance and capital reserve funds. The absence of market rate financing obviously reduced the developments' total operating costs. (Significantly, the absence of Low Income Housing Tax Credits enhances the long-term stability of the Vacant Cluster developments since there is no need to refinance after fifteen years, when tax credit projects reach the end of their occupancy restrictions.)

The size and scale of the developments allowed for economies of scale in purchasing supplies and services. It also gave the sponsors and property managers more control over the immediate neighborhood and thus a greater sense of safety. The development's security guards—all of the developments' budgets provide for security guards—help keep watch around the clock. The physical concentration of Vacant Cluster buildings allows for a critical mass in achieving neighborhood stability. With several buildings on a block, and some blocks consisting almost entirely of Vacant Cluster buildings, the developments may be less vulnerable to vandalism, drug dealing, and other forms of crime. It is much more difficult, in other words, to maintain a subsidized building on a block surrounded by problem buildings. An HPD asset manager emphasized the importance of scale in comparing the Vacant Cluster Program with another city-funded mixed-income program, the Special Initiatives Program (SIP), which also combined formerly homeless families with low- and moderate-income households (albeit in different proportions). Unlike Vacant Cluster, SIP buildings tend to be scattered across many neighborhoods, typically being the only city-funded buildings on their block. As a result, the HPD asset manager believes it is much more difficult for building staff, despite their best efforts, to keep the buildings secure and vandalism at bay.

Finally, site managers believed that the availability of social services contributed to the developments' financial stability. Property managers work closely with social service staff, especially in dealing with tenants that fall into arrears. They seek to understand the tenant's situation and to help develop a feasible strategy for paying the back rent and keeping up with future rent payments.

In Massachusetts, in general, we found only minor variations in the operational characteristics across the units. However, vacancy rates and periods, and turnovers were consistently higher among the market rate than the subsidized units. On reflection, this makes sense: low-income households, and especially racial minority households, have fewer housing choices and would thus tend to move less often. Given the large demand for affordable housing by low-income households (reflected, for example, in long public housing waiting lists), the average duration of turnover (i.e., the time units stay vacant between move out and move in) in low-income units tends to be minimal. These differences imply that in this respect, the market rate units present comparatively higher per unit maintenance costs than the subsidized units. On the other hand, we found that low-income units in Massachusetts typically have higher arrears.

In only a minority of cases did site managers report that maintenance costs were appreciably higher in the low-income units. At the same time, they did not suggest that this was connected directly to the behavior or income level of the tenants. Rather they pointed to the larger size of families and to the fact that these households spent more time in the units (due to a higher proportion of persons, including children, not working). Overall, the more general result was that there were no apparent differences in per unit maintenance costs across different income groups.

Only in the case of a project in the South End of Boston did the site manager feel that the major challenge was attracting and maintaining market rate tenants. She emphasized that in this case the subsidized units did not offset or cross-subsidize the higher costs associated with the greater vacancy and turnover in the market rate units. She claimed that some market rate tenants did prefer to live in an all market development for the high rents they were paying. As a result, this development was unable to maintain their goal of 75 percent minority tenants in the market rate units.

In terms of marketing of units, most projects in Massachusetts reported that they did not market the subsidized units because they used referrals from the local PHA waiting lists; the market rate units were marketed using the conventional channels. Unless different marketing strategies lead to different perceptions on the part of residents, which in turn makes it harder to maintain a stable group of tenants, this aspect of the mixed-income housing projects seems unlikely to impact its feasibility.

In California there appear to be broad similarities with the cases in New

York and Massachusetts in terms of the management aspects. All four projects are well managed, financially viable, and almost fully occupied. Vacancy and turnover rates were higher for the market rate units. In none of the projects was there a difference in maintenance costs across different units. According to a Bridge project manager, "Apartments at various rates are completely integrated . . . there are no differences between the units. They all have the same amenities and are integrated." In California most tenants were aware of the mixed-income nature of the development through word of mouth as well as via marketing materials. In only one case, sponsored by a private developer, the manager reported that tenants were generally unaware of the mixed-income nature of the developments.

Social Effects

If concentrated poverty is at the root of welfare dependency, teenage pregnancy, violent crime, failure to complete high school, and other social problems of inner-city neighborhoods, it is logical to expect income mixing to foster a more positive social environment. All levels of government along with many influential policy experts look to mixed-income housing as a key element in the nation's fight against poverty. Despite its conceptual appeal, there is little evidence to show that mixed-income housing actually helps alleviate the social ills of poverty. The most convincing case for the social benefits of mixed-income housing would require rigorous longitudinal analysis, ideally along the lines of the current Moving to Opportunity for Fair Housing Demonstration Program, through which the federal government is assessing the benefits of residential dispersal strategies for low-income families (HUD 1998).

Our examination of the social effects of mixed-income housing does not come close to an experimental design or a longitudinal analysis. Like Brophy and Smith's review of mixed-income housing developments, our knowledge of the social aspects of this form of housing derives from interviews with property managers, project sponsors, and service providers. In addition, we conducted focus groups with residents of two of the Bronx's Vacant Cluster developments as a way of exploring in greater depth the issue of social effects and interaction within the developments.

In New York property managers and service providers claim that resident interaction has much more to do with shared interests and personal affinities than household income. Households are as likely to have social ties with a neighbor from another income group as from their own group. Participation in on-site social services programs encompasses all three income groups. Personal relationships seem based on physical proximity, the friendships of children, shared interests, and mutual affinity. When asked about the direct benefits of income mixing in terms of employment or educational outcomes, building managers and social service providers point out examples of residents sharing job tips, forming car pools, and the like, but there is no way of extrapolating from these anecdotes. Site managers and social service providers also say substantial numbers of formerly homeless mothers are now employed or in school. However, there is no way of attributing these improvements to mixed-income housing. After all, welfare rolls have declined dramatically in the past few years throughout New York City (and the nation), reflecting welfare reform and economic growth. Moreover, it is impossible to view the effects of income mixing in the Vacant Cluster developments separately from the developments' social service programs. As noted above, three of the four developments provide a range of services on-site, including childcare, counseling, and advocacy.

In Massachusetts interviews with site managers familiar with the social interactions within the development revealed two key factors. First, there was in general minimal interaction in the apartment buildings among residents. This appears to be a general characteristic of apartment living and not specifically associated with mixed-income developments. Furthermore, according to the managers, social interaction did not vary in a noticeable way by income category. That is, when it did occur, it tended not to be markedly more or less restricted to one group. In one case, in which the majority of tenants were African American and Latino, interaction was high and general among the residents. Second, regarding the effects of interaction, or even of the copresence of a variety of a income groups on low-income households, the managers could not report definite findings. It was hard to glean the necessary type of information through phone interviews with managers to be able to say anything certain about this issue. Several managers did, however, point to the presence of activities on-site (usually organized by the management) as a catalyst and arena for interaction. Only in one case did this include an economic development component, a "college access program" (which provided information about school and college programs); participation in these activities (rather than interaction perhaps) may have led to job tips or other referrals that may have had a positive economic outcome. In some cases the managers said they did not track such detailed aspects of their developments. In California managers felt that it would be a violation of Fair Housing Laws to maintain records on this. Presumably, this arose from the differing ethnic or racial composition of the different income groups.

We also asked about the extent to which residents were aware of the mixed-income nature of their developments, that is, that the developments were explicitly designed to accommodate households of different incomes (rather than simply housing households of different incomes). In almost all cases in Massachusetts, the tenants were aware of the fact that their developments included both subsidized and non- or less-subsidized units. Only in a few cases were there reports of any resentment on the part of market rate tenants against the subsidized tenants. Those cases were handled straightforwardly by the site manager. They pointed out that the mixed-income nature of the development had been explained to prospective tenants and that there were therefore no grounds for complaints. In a few projects managers estimated that not all market rate tenants were aware of the presence of subsidized units.

In general, therefore, it appears that while awareness of the MIH aspect was clear to most tenants, it rarely led to tension or other forms of problems. Similarly, tenant satisfaction was reported to be generally high. This is no doubt a consequence of the fact that most of the projects screened prospective tenants. Of more central concern for our research, there was apparently little difference in either awareness or satisfaction across income groups.

These seem plausible claims on the part of site managers. First, in almost all cases, the mixed-income nature of the development was clearly explained to all prospective residents. Second, given the need to attract market rate or higher-income households, in conjunction with the fact that units were neither segregated by income group or provided different levels of amenity, tenant satisfaction was generally even across income groups.

Do the demographic characteristics of the residents affect these results? Our sample covered a range of demographic characteristics, such as race and ethnicity, age, and size of household. Based on our field research and focus groups with residents, some factors do seem to have an impact on variables such as social interaction. In some cases where the market rate units were generally occupied by students or young professionals, who tended to be single and relatively mobile, these populations contrasted strongly with the subsidized households. If interaction in apartment buildings is usually minimal at best, it becomes even weaker in these cases. In general it appears that the relative cultural homogeneity of residents, in addition to the availability of opportunities to interact (usually organized by management), seemed to increase the propensity to interact. This seems to echo the case of the housing projects in the Bronx.

Information about the extent of social interaction in the California developments was not as detailed as in the other sites. Bridge did not track this variable. In the case of El Cerrito there was little interaction. In the view of the site manager this was a function of the different lifestyles of the different income groups rather than their incomes per se. For example, market rate tenants include students who do not spend much time in the developments and thus as a result do not interact with the older, minority tenants in the subsidized units.

To gain further insight into the social aspects of Vacant Cluster developments, we convened two focus groups for residents at the two such developments in New York City. Consisting mostly of unemployed women, some formerly homeless, the focus groups discussed several aspects of mixed-income housing. Participants were sharply divided in both groups as to the benefits of raising children in a mixed-income environment. Some felt the presence of working families helped children become more aware of the world of work and the need for self-discipline. Others sharply disputed these assertions, arguing that parents and other family members matter vastly more than neighbors in providing appropriate role models. When asked whether neighbors help each other obtain jobs, some participants could identify specific examples, but the overwhelming consensus was that many more residents owed their jobs to the developments' social service staff than to their neighbors.

The participants were all aware of the mixed-income nature of their housing. Few if any, however, considered income mixing to be a defining characteristic of their housing. Much more prominent were the availability of social services, the presence of security guards, the quality of building management, and maintenance, affordability, and location. Most participants said they socialized in some way with other residents, as did most of their neighbors. No one felt that social interactions were confined within particular income groups. How well residents got along, or didn't, had everything to do with their personalities and nothing to do with their income.

The apparent sociability of Vacant Cluster residents contrasts sharply with the observations of site managers of almost all the mixed-income developments studied in Massachusetts and California, where there was much less social interaction. This may in part be explained by the higher degree of racial and ethnic homogeneity in the New York cases.

Conclusions

Several conclusions can be drawn from the analysis presented above. First we examined the two key issues of financial and management feasibility and of the social effects of mixed-income residency. In general we found that the range of incomes represented in the development, the nature of the neighborhood in which the development is located, the commitment of the sponsor to high-quality affordable housing, and the state of the local housing market all contribute to the ability of MIH development to attract and retain the market rate tenants that are often necessary for the maintenance of the development. This, of course, varies with the range of incomes represented. In cases such as New York City, for example, in which the highest rents are relatively low, and where the development is located in a relatively undesirable inner-city neighborhood, the reliance on the rental subsidies associated with the low-income units is greater. In Boston, by contrast, high housing costs and declining subsidies put pressure on developers and managers to raise rents of the subsidized units and to make extra efforts to attract and retain market rate units. In sum, it is fair to say that the feasibility of the MIH development appears to depend more on "external" factors (such as subsidy levels, location, and the local housing market) than "internal" factors (such as vacancy rates, per unit maintenance costs, development costs, and so on). (We use the internal/external distinction loosely. Clearly some variables, such as vacancy rates, can be considered as both internal and external.) Finally, it should not be taken for granted that the only management challenge in MIH concerns the subsidized units and the low-income tenants. Attraction and retention of market rate tenants can in some circumstances be a critical issue. However, this factor again appears to be related principally to external market factors and not to the difficulties associated with having households of different income groups in the same building.

The second key issue we explored was the extent to which social interaction took place within the developments across income groups and if it did, the evidence for the hypothesis that this interaction had led to positive economic and/or social outcomes for members of the lower-income households. This is perhaps the most difficult aspect of our research. This hypothesis was derived from the literature on the problems associated with concentrated poverty. The behavioral hypothesis associated with this literature is that greater interaction of lower-income households, and especially their children, with higher-income households within the residential environment will influence the goals, perceptions, and opportunities of the former toward greater labor market participation and "mainstream" social behavior (Schwartz and Tajbakhsh 1997).

Contrary to the expectation arising from the literature on the problems associated with concentrated poverty that the dynamics and effects of income mixing should be readily identifiable, our research reveals a much more ambiguous picture. Although there is some anecdotal evidence to support the hypothesis, overall our research in three sites around the country did not reveal any clear or direct results. A fair assumption is that if income mixing is indeed the remedy that proponents suggest, we should have found clearer evidence of the mechanisms and effects. Our research did not reveal such patterns.

A further point worth considering is the possibility that income mixing only indirectly contributes to improved outcomes. It is important to point out that in addition to the behavioral hypothesis summarized above, critiques of concentrated poverty and proposals for dispersal of the poor also rest on an institutional hypothesis regarding income mixing. This holds that the positive outcomes purported to be associated with the economic integration of households arises not from the altered perceptions and behavior of poor households, but rather from the greater stability of building or neighborhood supporting institutions (churches, schools, voluntary organizations, CDCs) that act as important mediating factors for poor households' connections with the labor market and other "social capital" creating institutions (Gittell and Vidal 1998, Ferguson 1999). For example, the fact that mixed-income housing developments often provided a high degree of amenities seems to be a positive spin-off for the poorer households. For poorer households, living in a residential environment that is safe and dependable may provide the stepping stone they require to enter and remain in the job market.

Our research should be viewed as preliminary; without conducting a longitudinal analysis with an experimental control group it is not possible to reach more robust conclusions. Furthermore, the hypothesized relationships we are attempting to explore are both complex and subtle, requiring ethnographic and detailed case studies and more comparative statistical methods. The addition of other sites would expand the types of mixed-income housing and the local market conditions in our sample, and would allow us to draw more generalizable conclusions concerning the linkages and effects underlying the mixed-income housing model.

However, given the absence of strong evidence demonstrating these linkages and effects, we suggest that, by itself, mixed-income housing is not the "silver bullet" for improved social outcomes in dealing with poverty. Indeed, our research, as well as the tentative results of studies such as of the Lake Parc Place development (Rosenbaum et al. 1998), suggests a case for diminished expectations for mixed-income housing as a social policy tool. This is not to say that it plays no role. But it is important to emphasize that other factors such as the availability and extent of low-income rental subsidies, the state of the local housing market, the racial and ethnic mix of the tenants, and the availability of on-site social services play an equally if not more significant role in allowing mixed-income housing developments to succeed as both an affordable housing strategy and as an approach to social and economic development of poor inner-city households.

Appendix A. Profiles of Projects Studied

New York City

Crotona Park West

Sponsor:	Phipps Houses (citywide nonprofit)
Size:	563 units in twenty five-story walk-up buildings.
Development also includes open space, a day care center, a health clinic, and other community space.	
Racial composition of residents:	Latino and Black, including growing African immigrant population.
Completion date:	1993
Services provided:	Youth and teen programs, tenant counseling and advocacy, health clinic.

Highbridge Heights Unity Apartments

Sponsor:	Housing Development Institute (New York Archdiocese/Catholic Charities)
Size:	722 units in twenty-three five- and six-story buildings, some with elevators. Development also ncludes six playgrounds, almost 10,000 sq. ft. of community space, and 5,700 sq. ft. of commercial space. Sponsor has since acquired and/or developed six additional buildings, with almost three hundred units.
Racial composition of residents:	Roughly 60–65 percent Latino; 35–40 percent Black.
Completion date:	1992
Services provided:	The development has an extensive array of services, including an Even Start early childhood program, drug treatment and domestic violence programs, a children's choir, a 4,000-sq.-ft. health clinic, and credit unit, GED and immigration services. After-school and summer-school programs, including an award-winning children's choir, Highbridge Voices (Stewart 1999). There is a tenant association in almost every building as well as a council of association presidents.

Mt. Hope/BUILD Vacant Cluster

Sponsor:	Mt. Hope CDC and Build, Inc. (another CDC)
Size:	416 units in twelve buildings, six controlled by Mt. Hope and six by Build, Inc. All buildings include community space.
Completion date:	1992
Services provided:	The development does not provide any on-site social services. However, Mt. Hope runs several programs in the immediate neighborhood that are available to residents of the development. These include a job services center, and Individual Development Account program, homeownership counseling, tenant counseling, and advocacy.

New Settlement Apartments

Sponsor:	Settlement Housing Fund (citywide nonprofit)
Size:	893 units in fourteen six-story buildings on eight contiguous blocks. Commercial and community space account for about 15 percent of project floor area.
Completion date:	1991
Services provided:	A wide of educational and recreational programs for children and youth. Tenant counseling and advocacy. Sponsors and supports tenant organizations, including parents seeking to reform local schools.

Massachusetts

Cast Associates (Cambridge)

Sponsor:	MHFA
Type of subsidy:	236, CHA (Cambridge Housing Authority) rent subsidy, HUD rent subsidy.
Size:	42 units.
Income mix:	29 low income, 13 moderate, 0 market
Racial composition of residents:	95 percent, Black and Hispanic, 5 percent white.
Services provided:	The project provides minimal services such as a laundry. There are no social services.

Chapman Arms (Cambridge)

Sponsor:	MHFA
Type of subsidy:	SHARP
Size:	50 units.
Income mix:	50 percent low, 50 percent market
Racial composition of residents:	38 percent minority, including four Asian households.
Services provided:	One social service coordinator comes once a week to talk mainly with seniors. Laundry, no parking.

Kimball Court (Woburn)

Sponsor:	MFHA
Type of subsidy:	SHARP
Size:	187 units.
Income mix:	75 percent market, 25 percent low income
Racial composition of residents:	N/A
Services provided:	Nothing special.

Stone Brook Farm (Burlington)

Sponsor:	MHFA
Type of subsidy:	SHARP
Size:	203 units.
Income mix:	25 percent very low, 75 percent market
Racial composition of residents:	N/A
Services provided:	This project provides some recreational amenities such as a pool room and tennis courts. There are no social services.

Warren House (Newton)

Sponsor:	MHFA
Type of subsidy:	80/20 bond financing
Size:	59 units.
Income mix:	36 percent very low, 64 percent market
Racial composition of residents:	Mixed racial and ethnic composition: White, Russians, two Black, two Hispanic, Asians. Manager reported that there was an "even distribution of ethnic groups across the income categories."
Services provided:	TAP (Tenant Assistance Program-MHFA), community room; laundry, and so forth.

Langham Court (South End) mixed race and income neighborhood

Sponsor:	MHFA
Type of subsidy:	SHARP
Size:	84 units.
Income mix:	33 percent low, 33 percent moderate, 33 percent market
Racial composition of residents:	60 percent Latino (Dominican and Puerto Rico), 40 percent Black (including Caribbeans, Senegal, Ghana).
Services provided:	There are no social services provided on-site.

Roxbury Corner (Roxbury). Need to complete interview.

California

Dev A (Richmond, Contra Costa County; project on outskirts of town but not suburban)

Sponsor:	Bridge
Type of subsidy:	Sale of 501(c)3 tax-exempt bonds; private sources.
Size:	240 units.
Income mix:	60 percent market, 20 percent moderate, 20 percent very low.
Racial composition of residents:	N/A
Services Provided:	Community room. No social services on-site.

Dev B (Oakland, Alameda County, inner-city area)

Sponsor:	Bridge
Type of subsidy:	HUD FHA Up-front grant; Bridge investments.
Size:	295 units
Income mix:	50 percent market, 50 percent very low.
Racial composition of residents:	N/A. Still under construction, not fully rented.
Services provided:	This project provides extensive social services: a computer learning center, an on-site social worker, girls and boys club, extensive employment services.

Dev C (Emeryville, Alameda County, urban)

Sponsor:	Bridge
Type of subsidy:	Bank of America tax-exempt bond.
Size:	260 units.
Income mix:	60 percent market, 20 percent-low, 20 percent-very low.
Racial composition of residents:	N/A
Services provided:	Extensive recreational amenities. No social services.

Dev D (Milpitas, Santa Clara County, suburban)

Sponsor:	Bridge
Type of subsidy:	Local public funds; redevelopment loans.
Size:	416 units.
Income mix:	50 percent market, 25 percent low, 25 percent very low
Racial composition of residents:	50 percent Asian and Hispanic in all income categories; 15–20 percent white; the rest very mixed.
Services provided:	Community room, computer learning center. No social services. Extensive recreational facilities.

El Cerrito

Sponsor:	John Stewart Company
Type of subsidy:	Tax credit.
Size:	137 units.
Income mix:	755 market, 25 percent low
Racial composition of residents: Market units:	Asian, White, Black, 30 percent each, Hispanic 10 percent; 15–20 percent
Affordable units:	Black 60 percent, White 30 percent, Asian and Hispanic 5 percent.
Services provided:	Gym, older adult clinic for senior units, food court.

Appendix B: Interviews

Jack Doyle
Director
Settlement Houses
November 1999

Carol Lamberg and Susan Cole
Settlement Housing Fund
May 1999

Shaun Bell
Executive Director
Mount Hope Housing Company
August 1999

Norberto Otero
Director of Property Management,
Mount Hope Housing Company

Keith Slater
Chief Financial Officer
Mount Hope Housing Company

Andrea Herman
Director of Social Services
Mount Hope Housing Company

George Morris
Property Manager
Crotona Park West
July 1999

Harry Scanlon
Phipps Houses
July 1999

Ilene Popkin, Gary Sloman, and
    Yvette Shiffman
New York City Department of
  Housing Preservation and
  Development
    December 1999

Jorge Batista, Director,
    Highbridge HDFC
Fred Camerata, Wavecrest
    Management
Carmen Negron, Wavecrest
    Management
July 1999

Mary Manuel
Site Manager
Langham Court Properties
South End, Massachusetts
November 1999

Sara Gross
Site Manager
Cast Associates
Cambridge, Massachusetts
February 2000

Nancy Finnerty, Site Manager
Charles Maneickas, Regional
    Manager
Chapman Arms
Cambridge, Massachusetts
February 2000

Richard Murphy
Regional Manager
Kimball Court Apartments
Woburn, Massachusetts
March 2000

Debra Serneraro
Site Manager
Stone Brook Farm
Burlington, Massachusetts
April 2000

Alyson Walsh
Site Manager
Warren House
Newton, Massachusetts
November 1999

Loren Sanborn
The John Stewart Company
San Francisco, California
May 2000

Lydia Tan, Vice President and
  Director of Development Operations
Susan Johnson, Vice President
Bridge Housing Corporation
February 2000

* * *

References

Brophy, Paul C., and Rhonda N. Smith. 1997. "Mixed-Income Housing: Factors for Success." *Cityscape* 3, no. 2: 3–31.

Ferguson, Ronald F. 1999. "Conclusion: Social Science Research, Urban Problems, and Community Development Alliances," in *Urban Problems and Community Development*, ed. Ronald F. Ferguson and William T. Dickens, pp. 569–610. Washington, DC: The Brookings Institution.

Gittell, Ross, and Avis Vidal. 1998. *Community Organizing: Building Social Capital as a Development Strategy.* Thousand Oaks, CA: Sage.

Massachusetts Housing Finance Agency. 2003. Mass Housing Information Statement, June 27, www.mhfa.com/homepage/financial_pubs/info%20statement.pdf.

Mass Housing. 2003. www.mhfa.com/ (See "Background").

New York City Housing Partnership. 1994. *Building in Partnership: A Blueprint for Urban Housing Programs.* New York: Author.

"Proposed Rule on Public Housing Income Deconcentration Published." 2000. HDR Headlines (April 17), Internet List Server. New York: NYC Housing Partnership.

Rosenbaum, James. 1995. "Changing the Geography of Opportunity by Expanding Residential Choice: Lessons for the Gautreaux Program." *Housing Policy Debate* 6, no. 1: 231–69

Rosenbaum, James, Linda Stroh, and Cathy Flynn. 1998. "Lake Parc Place: A Study of Mixed-Income Housing." *Housing Policy Debate* 9, no. 4: 703–40.

Schwartz, Alex. 1999. "New York City and Subsidized Housing: Impacts and Lessons of the City's $5 Billion Capital Budget Housing Plan." *Housing Policy Debate* 10, no. 4: 839–77.

Schwartz, Alex, and Kian Tajbakhsh. 1997. "Mixed-Income Housing: Unanswered Questions." *Cityscape* 3, no. 2: 71–92.

Smith, Alastair. 2002. "Mixed-Income Housing Developments: Promise and Reality." Cambridge, MA: Harvard Joint Center on Housing Studies.

Stewart, Barbara. 1999. "A Choir Director in the Bronx Has Big Dreams." *New York Times* (July 4).

Turner, Margery Austin. 1998. "Moving Out of Poverty: Expanding Mobility and Choice Through Tenant-Based Housing Assistance." *Housing Policy Debate* 9, no. 2: 373–94.

U.S. Department of Housing and Urban Development (HUD). 1998. *Moving to Opportunity for Fair Housing Demonstration Program: Current Status and Initial Findings.* Washington, DC: U.S. Dept. of Housing and Urban Development.

———. 1998. "Public Housing Reform Act: The Quality Housing and Work Responsibility Act of 1998 (QHWRA)," http://www.hud.gov:80/pih/legis/titlev.html

———. 2000. *Hope VI: Building Communities, Transforming Lives.* Washington, DC: U.S. Dept. of Housing and Urban Development.

12

JILL SIMONE GROSS

CyberCities

What is the future for cities in an increasingly digital world? In 1995 alarmists told us that it was just a matter of time before fiber-optic infrastructure and digital capacity made central cities obsolete (Peters and Gilder 1995, Negroponte 1995, Naisbitt 1995). In the same way that technological innovations in transportation had facilitated the movement of people and then manufacturing to more distant suburban locations, digital technology would free business from its urban moorings (Cohen 2000). As business became more "footloose," central cities would cease to be "central." The inner city, as Anthony Downs (1994) points out, would be caught in a spatial and social gap between low-income people stuck within the city limits and jobs moving beyond the city limits. Technology, in this view, exacerbates problems of sprawl and punctuates the ongoing plight of inner-city residents left behind.

In this chapter I present data on New York City's efforts to counteract these trends through investment in fiber-optic infrastructure and digital capacity in the inner city. What follows is first a discussion of recent trends in the distribution of business and employment in the digital sectors of the New York metropolitan region's economy over the past decade. With this as our framework we then explore Digital NYC: Wired to the World, a cyber development partnership program designed to alter these economic trends and bring high-tech industry to underutilized parts of the central city.

New York City's cyber development policy is multifaceted. The program incorporates a variety of promotional economic development tools such as incentives, rebates, and grants. It is structured around a public-private partnership designed to induce private partners to invest in technical upgrading of buildings and the placement of digital infrastructure. Public sector partners market the areas and provide incentives, grants, rebates, and technical assistance. Nonprofit local development corporations manage the zones, mediate the relationships, and create linkages to local labor pools.

In this chapter I examine the impact of Digital NYC: Wired to the World on high-tech industry location in the New York metropolitan region. Our analysis of county business patterns, census data at the tract level and detailed accounts of activities within the Digital NYC zones of Brooklyn leads us to support the view that investments in digital infrastructure can bring new life to underutilized parts of the city (Moss and Townsend 2000). However, while these policies are breathing new life into previously digitally dead parts of the city, preliminary data also indicate that they are not directly affecting patterns of sprawl induced by the digital economy. Our data suggest that the businesses going to these inner-city and downtown technology zones are from niches of the digital economy that do not appear to be as footloose as other researchers have suggested (Peters and Gilder 1995, Negroponte 1995, Naisbitt 1995). Before turning to the analysis and findings, I present an overview of the research questions, data, and methods. I begin, however, with a brief discussion of the literature on the changing implications of sprawl and technology on cities over time.

Problem Definition

Sprawl: The Changing Impacts on the Central City

Central cities have long been sites for capital accumulation, innovation, and entrepreneurialism. The successful city of the twentieth century was one that could entice manufacturers to locate within the city limits. Location theory suggested that firms seeking to maximize their profits chose a setting in which the market for their product was strong, and the costs of land, labor, and capital were favorable (Friedrich 1929). Distance between the manufacturer, its production inputs (raw materials and labor), and product outputs (markets for goods) were considered to be the key factors underlying location decisions (Moses 1958). In turn, the successful industrial city was that which could offer affordable space, good transportation access, and a plentiful labor pool. Businesses opted for urban locations because they offered a competitive edge (McCann 2001). Not surprisingly, cities became magnets for people, investment, and growth.

With the advent of advances in transportation, technology, and government support of homeownership, there came a gradual dispersal first of people and then of jobs from the central city (Schneider 1980, Downs 1973). The overcrowding and high cost of land in urban cores exacerbated these trends. The result, by the middle of the twentieth century, was the emergence of the sprawl phenomenon—the unplanned deconcentration of business, industry and population beyond the city limits.

The sprawl phenomenon has occurred in several phases. In the first round of movement out of the central city during the early twentieth century, it was population that led the outward flow (Jackson 1985, Warner 1978). Middle- and upper-class urbanites sought more bucolic residential locations, away from the congestion that characterized industrial cities, assuming that the good life was most available in small communities. As Figure 12.1 illustrates, the movement of population outward to the suburbs in the New York metropolitan region has been ongoing since the turn of the century.

Though population began to settle in suburban locations, jobs and industry continued to opt for urban locations.

During the postwar period manufacturing began to move outward in search of larger and more affordable union-free production spaces. The process was helped along by technological advances that de-linked industries from dependence on rail, alongside governmental investments in vast road systems (Nivola 1999). Changes in manufacturing production processes made single-story horizontal production facilities more economical than vertical multistory plants (Judd and Swanstrom 1994). Suburban areas with an abundance of space and access to road transportation became powerful lures for manufacturers. In cities such as New York, "A pattern that has become familiar emerged: employment in goods handling activities (manufacturing, wholesale trade, freight transportation) declined as jobs moved out of the city to the surrounding metropolitan region, as well as to other parts of the country and the world, while office and service jobs increased, particularly in Manhattan" (Netzer 1990, 30).

As Jewel Bellush (1990, 317) points out, between 1958 and 1975 New York City saw a 40 percent decline in manufacturing jobs, representing some 400,000 actual jobs. Some 8,000 manufacturing jobs went to the surrounding suburban areas between 1980 and 1985. While in 1980 there were a total of 285,894 manufacturing jobs in New York City, in 2000 that figure had dropped to 145,562 (Bureau of Economic Analysis 1980, 2000).

The contemporary postindustrial city is one dominated by service-related industries at both the high-skill end (finance, insurance, real estate, management, and professional) and the low-skill end (wholesale and retail activities, administrative, and other supportive services such as restaurants and amenities).

According to the Bureau of Economic Analysis (2002), the largest industries in New York City in 2000 were finance, insurance, and real estate, 40.1 percent of earnings; services, 30.9 percent; and state and local government, 9.0 percent. In 1990 the largest industries were services, 33.8 percent of earnings; finance, insurance, and real estate, 25.7 percent; and state and local government, 13.6 percent. Of the industries that accounted for at least 5 percent of earnings in 2000, the slowest growing from 1990 to 2000 was

Figure 12.1   **Population of New York City Compared to New York Suburbs, 1900–1990**

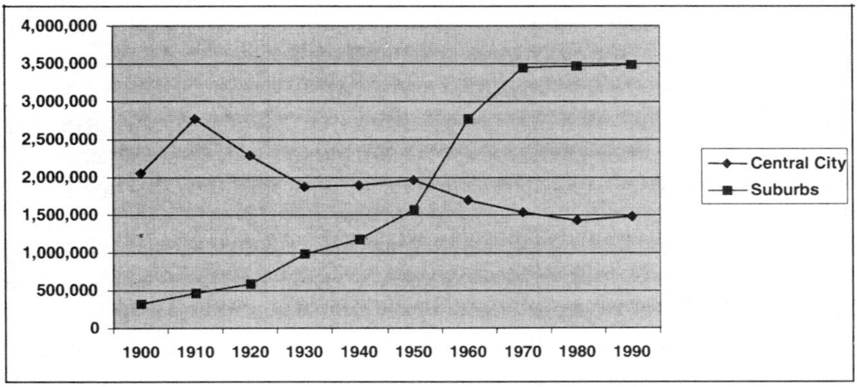

Source: New York Population of Counties by Decennial Census: 1900 to 1990, compiled by Richard L. Forstall, Population Division, U.S. Bureau of the Census, Washington, DC 20233.

Note: Central City = New York County; Suburbs = Nassau, Suffolk, and Westchester counties.

state and local government, which increased at an average annual rate of 2.3 percent; the fastest was finance, insurance, and real estate which increased at an average annual rate of 11.4 percent.

Technology and Sprawl

Today researchers suggest we may be approaching a new phase in urban restructuring. Technological advances in communications and information handling have made distant locations feasible as places for the white-collar service sector business as well as manufacturing (Fishman 1987). Some analysts argue that cities will no longer be able to anchor high-tech, office, and high-end service jobs. The central city will increasingly compete with suburban and exurban locations for their share of business and industry (Cohen 2000). Like manufacturing in the 1950s, businesses, jobs, and population will increasingly locate in suburban and perhaps even more distant satellite locations, facilitated by advances in digital infrastructure. Digital technology in this view promotes sprawl. Alongside this, by some accounts, inner-city residents are left with a shrinking job base and an inability to follow the jobs to more distant locations (Downs 1994). This makes cities, in the words of George Gilder and Tom Peters (1995), "leftover baggage from the industrial era."

Gilder, as mentioned above, was arguing that in time, technological innovation would enable service- and information-based industries to situate outside the urban agglomeration. These arguments were premised on a view that virtual interaction would eventually replace face-to-face interaction. Fiber-optic technological infrastructure would facilitate this process by allowing for the rapid exchange of information across distances. Businesses would no longer need to be located in the urban core. Business could be conducted in cyberspace—a "virtual" location, which brings workers and businesses together via networks of fiber-optic cable and allows for the rapid exchange of information among users, buyers, and sellers of information and services in the absence of face-to-face contact (Wheeler, Aoyama, and Warf 2000).

Others, however, reminded us that though businesses may technically have the capacity to locate outside the city limits, there are still significant centripetal pulls to be found in the central city. Indeed, as Gaspar and Glaeser (1998, 137–38) found in their analysis of communication technology on life in the city: "Cities are linked to face-to-face interactions since a common urban location drives down the cost of personal meetings. If new electronic media are complementary to face-to-face interactions, they will be complementary to cities as well . . . we find that improvements in telecommunications technology may increase the number of face-to-face interactions and the relevance of cities."

The conduct of business, therefore, still requires face-to-face interaction and a range of infrastructure and amenities that most suburban and rural areas simply cannot support. This view was in keeping with theorists such as Saskia Sassen, who argues that globalization is producing a new geography of centers and margins.

We find here a new logic for agglomeration and key conditions for the renewed centrality of cities in advanced economies. Information technology often thought of as neutralizing geography, actually contributes to spatial concentration (Sassen 2000).

This research sought to explore one city's effort to capitalize on advances in digital infrastructure and to consider the degree to which these efforts could contribute to spatial concentration and diversification of local opportunity structures by bringing high-tech industry to underutilized parts of the city.

Urban Growth and Development: Regulation versus Promotion in New York

Local governments in the United States have most commonly sought to control urban growth via regulatory measures such as land-use controls.

Though the goals of the efforts may vary—environmental protection, quality of life, and economic vitality—the tools utilized are somewhat uniform. The most direct approaches include zoning regulations to limit and/or separate uses of land, greenbelt policies to prevent uses, and preservation legislation to preserve uses. Cities have also utilized promotional strategies such as tax incentives, rebates, and grants to influence the location decisions of business as an indirect vehicle through which to guide urban spatial development.

In New York, for example, regulatory measures such as zoning have had a profound affect on the urban form. Traditionally, zoning has been utilized to segregate activities such as manufacturing and commerce from residential uses. These earlier zoning restrictions allowed the city to develop many of its underutilized areas for other more productive economic activities. However, over time it was precisely these same zoning laws that led to their decline. Many areas zoned for manufacturing alone were prevented from being able to adapt to the changing economic demands. Indeed, restrictive zoning became one of the key contributing factors in explaining long-term decline of the older industrial areas of Brooklyn that lie at the center of this research. It was these areas that suffered most directly when manufacturing left the city; their decline was exacerbated because they could not diversify their job bases due to the restrictive zoning. In turn many areas, particularly along the Brooklyn waterfront, suffered from abandon and neglect.

This research focused on digital upgrading efforts in four underutilized industrial waterfront areas in Brooklyn, rezoned in the late 1990s to allow for mixed uses (manufacturing, commercial, and residential)—DUMBO (Down Under the Manhattan Bridge Overpass), Red Hook, Sunset Park, and the Brooklyn Navy Yard. Each had suffered over the long term by virtue of the fact that once manufacturing moved from the city, these spaces ceased to be viable sites for alternative uses. In interviews with long-term property owners in these areas, we were told that efforts had been made to alter the zoning designation since the late 1970s to allow for mixed uses. It was not until 1997, however, that these areas were rezoned.[1] While the alteration of zoning laws was an important first step in the process of revitalizing these areas, by many accounts it was too little too late. After twenty years of decline and neglect these locations were in need of significant investment. For property owners and developers the risks of investment outweighed the potential benefits. In turn the city began to shift its focus away from restrictive use and regulation and toward the creation of a series of promotional policies designed to offset some of the perceived risks of investing in these areas—via incentives, rebates, and grants.

Deregulation of the area by easing zoning restrictions created the conditions for change. Incentives were needed to encourage owners and developers to upgrade their buildings for mixed uses, and to lure businesses back. New York already had some success with this policy combination in the central city, though it was as yet untested in the inner ring surrounding the central city.

In 1997 New York sought to lure digital industry to a lower Manhattan neighborhood known as Tribeca. The area was characterized by many underutilized industrial spaces. A program was implemented known as "plug 'n' go." Matching grants were offered to developers and property owners to encourage the upgrading of these buildings for digital use. Buildings had to be made "smart"—addressing the wiring, ventilation, and access needs of digital industry. The city also created a series of incentives whereby large amounts of office space were leased at below-market rents for start-up and expanding high-tech companies. The city made loans available for upgrading and provided supportive services, amenities, and marketing. The timing for the introduction of this program was key. It came just as the wave of dot-com growth was cresting.

One surface indicator of the success of plug 'n' go in Tribeca is that the area came to be known as Silicon Alley. A more important sign was the growth in the number of high-tech-related companies that located there. From 1997–1999 the overall number of high-tech businesses in Manhattan grew from 2,600 to 4,000. The high-tech community employed more than 138,000, and revenue from new media jumped from 2.8 billion in 1997 to 9.2 billion in 1999 (Hevesi 1999).

It was the success of this program that led policymakers to promote a similar strategy in the boroughs surrounding Manhattan. In the spring of 2000 New York City's Economic Development Corporation (EDC) introduced Digital NYC: Wired to the World. This is a public-private partnership program in which private partners finance the upgrading of industrial spaces and provide fiber-optic infrastructure and broadband access to tenants. Public partners offer matching grants of up to 250,000 dollars to market the areas and spaces, locally and nationally. The public partners also assist in branding the areas and marketing to international investors. Local nonprofit development corporations (LDCs) manage the day-to-day needs of the technology zones and link up new businesses with local labor pools and technical assistance. With the assistance of EDC and the Small Business Administration of New York (SBA), LDCs also provide information to new businesses on related tax rebates and incentives that local businesses are eligible for by virtue of locating in the zones.

The goals of this digital development partnership program were threefold.

First, to facilitate the placement of digital infrastructure in digitally "dead" areas of the New York metropolitan region. Second, to entice businesses with digital needs to locate therein and to hire locally. Last, to forge digital development partnerships that link together public and private partners in the effort to minimize the risks of digital investment in these areas. A total of seven zones were created—one in Queens, one in Staten Island, one in Harlem, and four in Brooklyn. Our study focused on the Brooklyn cases.

Before moving on to a discussion of our methods and findings, a few points must be raised regarding several environmental factors that had significant implications for our analysis. The program being studied was implemented in the year 2000. Though it was conceptualized at the height of the dot-com wave, it was implemented in the wake of the bursting of the dot-com bubble. Then, less than one year into the program, New York City's economy was rocked by the events of 9/11.

In 2000 the New York City economy was significantly outperforming the nation primarily because of a robust financial services sector. By mid-2000, however, the nation's and the city's economies began to slow. The slowing in the New York City economy was primarily attributed to declining capital markets activity that was, in part, a response to failures in the dot-com and telecommunication industries as well as the general slowdown in the nation's economy. After declining to near-zero growth in second quarter 2001, the New York City metropolitan area economy contracted sharply following 9/11. In the third quarter of 2001 the gross metro product of the city decreased at an annual rate of approximately 15 percent, compared with a 1.3 percent annual rate of decline in the nation's gross domestic product (Crain's New York 2002).

As a result of these factors, we felt it important to measure success not only in the aggregate for the city as a whole, but in a disaggregated way as well (see the section on methods below). By looking at the changes regionally as well as locally, we were better equipped to explore the implications of these geographically and digitally targeted programs for the four zone areas in Brooklyn. That said, we would suggest that the program has been moderately successful in facilitating the development of high-technology industry in underutilized sections of the city, although some areas have fared better than others.

Key Research Questions

We hypothesized that these cyber-development policies could be used to generate conditions that might enhance the city as a place to do business (particularly for the so-called footloose IT-intensive industries), preventing sprawl via promotion rather than regulation. We began with two basic research questions:

1. Can local governments utilize geographically targeted cyber-development policies as a means of counteracting the sprawl tendency in "footloose" industry?
2. Can these same policies promote a more equitable distribution of economic activity in the metropolitan region by bringing high-tech industries to underutilized parts of the city such as the older downtowns and the inner city?

Research Methods and Data

Regional Trends in High-Tech Industry and Sprawl

In order to explore our first research question, we gathered County Business Patterns data and analyzed trends in high-tech/digital industry in the New York metropolitan region over time. Our original research delineation of high-tech/digital industry was derived from the Department of Commerce, which defines the digital economy as the convergence of three sectors—information, computing, and communications. In an effort to better understand where digital industry was situating in the New York metro area, we looked at the numbers employed, and numbers and sizes of establishments in high-tech industry in the five boroughs of New York and the geographically contiguous suburban areas from 1994 to 2000.[2]

We were also interested in exploring "footloose" trends. To be footloose suggests that a business is not geographically bound to a specific area. Thus we felt that movement in the distribution of industry over time or lack of movement as indicated by growth or decline in employment in these sectors would provide us with a regional overview of the sector. We then analyzed county business patterns data in the following sectors: High-tech Manufacturing, Communications Services, Software and Computer Related Services (see Appendix A for a detailed listing of SIC and NAICS codes).[3]

Our research on the businesses locating in Brooklyn's Digital NYC zones led us to expand our definition of the digital sector beyond that provided by the Department of Commerce. We found that other related digital technology users were being drawn to these areas. As one zone manager commented, "How do you define 'high-technology'? Really, this sort of infrastructure is integral to any twenty-first-century business. Bringing the infrastructure and stating that it is specifically for high-tech use is silly because almost every business has a Web site, and every business needs high-speed Internet connections to facilitate their business. Who's to say?" (Personal communications, Brooklyn Chamber of Commerce, March 2002)

In turn we felt it important to attach a broader lens to our analysis of NYC's efforts to promote the inner city as an area for digital investment, and so we also explored a range of related sectors involved with the dissemination and transfer of information through digital infrastructure. These were industry sectors that utilize digital infrastructure but are not themselves captured by much of the literature exploring the "digital economy" (i.e., related professional uses such as advertising, graphic design, and architects; healthcare and social support services; finance, insurance, and real estate).

To be "footloose" also suggests that a business is not tied to local sources of raw materials or to local markets (Lyons and Hamlin 2001). To explore the question of raw materials, we also gathered census data on what Richard Florida (2000) refers to as the "economic geography of talent." We explored the relationships between the kinds of businesses locating in the area to local labor pools (focusing specifically on local education levels and skill bases). We explored this input side of production as opposed to market outputs for several reasons. Primarily, we looked at this because this was the data most accessible to us. We found digital markets to be far more difficult to track given that the markets do not tend to be geographically tied to the production sights, and data on digital commerce was not available at either the tract or the zip code level for the time period we were assessing. This will be the focus of future research.

Brooklyn's Digital NYC Zones

Our second research question focused on the degree to which New York City government could promote a more equitable distribution of economic development activities in the New York metropolitan area by producing development in underutilized parts of the central city—such as deteriorated downtowns and the inner city. Data on the local economies at the zip code and tract levels was drawn from the U.S. economic census, county business patterns, New York State Department of Labor, the Federal Communications Commission, and the Empire State Development Corporation. Our more localized research analyzed tract and zip code level data on employment and skill bases, and local industry patterns within the Digital NYC zones in Brooklyn. We explored all of these areas using both descriptive statistics, and we conducted location quotient analysis to better understand the degree to which there was or was not clustering of talent, employment, or business in high-tech and the related high-tech areas mentioned above.

More detailed data on the types of businesses locating in the zones, the amount of space being leased, and numbers of employees per business was derived from leasing statistics provided by the Economic Development Corporation of the city of New York and from each of the Brooklyn local development corporations managing the zones.

In an effort to better understand the reasons why businesses were locating in the zones and the factors explaining differences between the zones, we analyzed the original program goals articulated in the accepted zone proposals. We made multiple site visits to each of the zones, and we conducted twenty-five semi-structured interviews with policymakers, zone managers, realtors, property developers, and businesses. We also attempted to survey (electronically and via telephone) all of the businesses leasing spaces within the zones, with a 15 percent response rate to date.[4] With this data we then began the process of triangulation. Convergent analysis or triangulation is a method through which qualitative and quantitative data can be linked.

Knowing a single landmark only locates one somewhere along a line in direction from the landmark, whereas with two landmarks, one can take bearings on both and locate oneself at their intersection (Fielding and Fielding 1986, 23).

The method is driven by the underlying assumption that measurement of a complex phenomenon such as local economic development requires more than one method. In this research we utilized semi-structured survey interviews with stakeholders inside and outside designated zones; we also conducted a structured survey of businesses located in the zones. We explored macro and micro data on the number and types of businesses and employment within the aforementioned sectors of the digital economy.

Findings

Regional Trends[5]

As mentioned above, scholars suggest that digital technology may enable high-tech industries to move outside the urban area. Given that these kinds of industries and the related industry users are central to the New York economy, and that Digital NYC is specifically targeted toward anchoring these very same businesses to the inner city, we felt it important to begin by exploring the broad trends in these industries over time. This information provides a historic context to help us better understand the degree to which high-tech and related users are moving out of the urban core and then to explore the degree to which Digital NYC was or was not countering these trends.

Figures 12.2, 12.3, and 12.4 offer an interesting picture of the distribution of employment in high-tech industry between 1994 and 1997 (see

Appendix A for a detailed listing of specific industry classifications used). First, these tables illustrate that there is, in fact, a significant degree of differentiation in location patterns over time within niches of the high-tech industry itself. Manufacturing, high-tech, and software services show the least change in the overall distribution of employment within the New York metropolitan region over time, while communications services shows significant change over the period analyzed.

Trends in High-Technology Manufacturing

In the case of high-tech manufacturing, as with manufacturing in general, the suburban regions clearly dominate, as Figure 12.2 illustrates. In the year 2000, for example, despite its declining share in the state as a whole, the suburbs of New York captured over 25 percent of high-tech manufacturing in the state as compared with less than 5 percent in both the inner ring and the central city of New York. As for the consistent decline since 1994, this is in keeping with broader trends statewide. This data suggest that suburban locations are better able to anchor this sector of the digital economy. To fully understand the factors that account for these trends, direct analysis of the location decisions of suburban high-tech manufacturers would need to be conducted; this was beyond the scope of this analysis.

This data on broad trends in the manufacturing sector of high tech offer us an indicator of locational preferences within this particular sector. These tendencies in the sector are in keeping with the findings of other research on the manufacturing side of high-tech outside New York. Schneider and Kim (1996), for example, found that high-tech manufacturing did not rely on the urban core for labor and goods. This enables these businesses to locate outside the central city. Hackler (2000) argues that this form of manufacturing is, in fact, distinct, in that it occurs over time and across several phases. In turn Hackler points out that high-tech manufacturing lends itself to a more dispersed location pattern, in that it has the ability to conduct different phases of its production process at different locations, differentiating it from other forms of manufacturing. In turn he points out that high-tech manufacturing can be more footloose. We would also suggest that the suburban locations continue to offer comparative advantages to manufacturing more broadly, due to availability of space, good road transportation for tangible goods, and other factors that shaped the earlier outward flow of manufacturing that began in the 1950s.

The central city continued to hold a very small proportion of this sector, with no change over the time period studied. Interestingly there was a spike in employment in this sector in the inner city in 1997. We speculate that

Figure 12.2   **Percent Employed in High-Tech Manufacturing in New York State by New York Metropolitan Area, 1994–2000.**

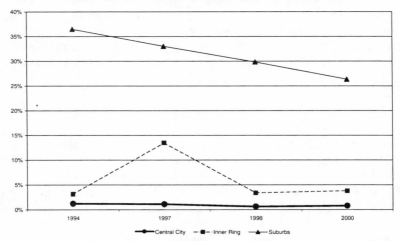

Source: County business patterns data, U.S. Census Bureau.
Note: Central City=New York County; Inner Ring=Bronx, Kings, Queens, and Staten Island Counties. See Appendix A for listing of industrial classification codes.

there are several reasons for this trend. According to the Federal Reserve, there was a glut in commercial and industrial space in the central city in 1997, due to residential conversions, facilitated in part by a myriad of alterations in zoning allowing for mixed use (Federal Reserve 1996). In the central city, developers at the time tended to turn spaces from commercial and manufacturing uses to residential, which offered the largest profit margin. This may partially account for the brief growth in high-tech manufacturing in the inner ring at the time, as it was one of the few areas with available and more affordable spaces for manufacturing. Also in 1997, as a result of an international campaign launched by the Brooklyn Chamber of Commerce, several design-related manufacturers moved into some of the industrial waterfront spaces (McCall 1999). The spike was short-lived though, and by 1998 many of the industries had actually moved out of the state altogether (Federal Reserve 1997).

Trends in Communications Services

As Figure 12.3 illustrates, the trends in communications services are quite different. The regular changes in the distribution of employment over time would suggest that this sector is less anchored to a specific metropolitan region than was the case for manufacturing. The graph also suggests that there is an interaction effect shaping employment distribution in this sector.

Figure 12.3   **Percent Employed in Communications Services in New York State by New York Metropolitan Area, 1994–2000**

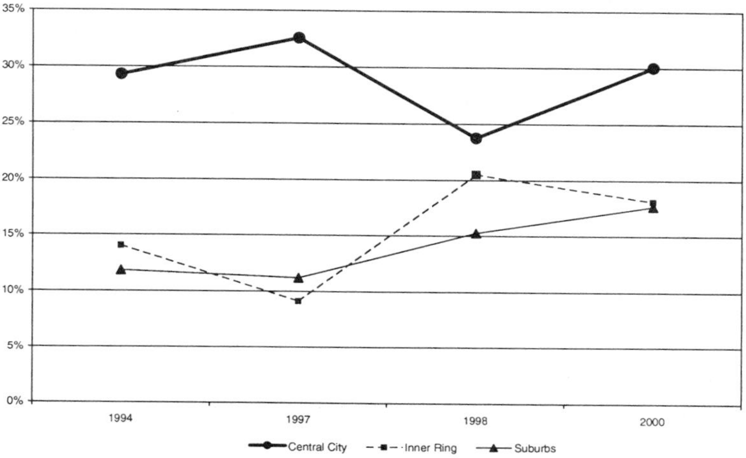

Source: County business patterns data, U.S. Census Bureau.
Note: Central City=New York County; Inner Ring=Bronx, Kings, Queens and Staten Island Counties. See Appendix A for listing of industrial classification codes.

Increases in the proportion of communication services employment in the central city tend to occur at the precise moments when there are decreases in the proportion employed in these inner-ring areas.

The reverse is also true. In 1998, when the inner ring saw a growth in this sector, the central city saw a decline; the reverse was true in 1997. This would suggest that movement in one area is at the expense of other areas; thus we see redistribution as opposed to an increase for the city as a whole. We also see that the suburban areas have showed a steady increase in communications services since 1994 and began to surpass the inner ring in the year 2000.

The growth in the central city's share of this sector between 1998 and 2000 can be explained in part by the introduction of plug 'n' go, as mentioned above. The spike in employment levels in 1997 and drop by 1998 we propose, is tied to legislative changes at the federal level (McDowell 2000). The Telecommunications Act of 1996, among other things, promoted competition within this sector and led to a flurry of new companies entering the market in the central city to test the waters. Many of these companies were short-lived, thus the decline by 1998.

Trends in Software and Technical Services

Figure 12.4 portrays the trends in employment distribution in the software and technical services sector (the soft side of the digital economy). Here it is only the central city that experienced an increase in employment share in recent years. The suburbs have seen little change, and the inner ring has shown a small decline. Indeed, location quotient analysis suggests that, in fact, New York City has the highest concentration of employment in this sector of high tech for the state as a whole, with a location quotient of 1.77.

As with communications services, we would suggest that recent central city increases in employment (1998–2000) were tied in part to the plug 'n go program and the dot-com bubble of the late 1990s.

Trends for Related High-Technology Users

The trends for related users can be summarized as follows. First, in the areas of advertising, architecture, graphic design, public relations, and Finance, Insurance, and Real Estate (FIRE) we found significant concentrations in the central city. In the aggregate, since 1994, 68–80 percent of the employment in these areas for the state of New York is accounted for by the central city. In terms of the trends across these sectors for the inner and suburban rings—the suburbs have experienced regular increases since 1994, moving from an 8 percent share in 1994 to a 12 percent share by 2000. The inner ring saw little movement over this time period in these areas with only 2–3 percent shares of employment in this sector. The limited movement between regions in these areas and the ongoing concentration in the central city suggest that these sectors are not as footloose as Gilder believed; rather they are concentrating in the central city as Sassen and others argued. By many accounts, human contacts remain a key need in this niche of the digital sector. As Gary Abramson (1998) comments, "In spite of all the IT innovations that have created global networks, encouraged wave after wave of international mergers and globalized consumer culture, what matters now—and will matter even more in the future—are genuine, tangible relationships."

The only sector in which the inner ring outperformed both the suburban and central city areas was in health care and social support services. Maintaining on average a 27 percent share since 1994, the suburbs captured 20 percent with a very small decrease over time, and the central city saw a small increase over time moving from a 16 percent share in 1994 to a 19 percent share in 2000.

With these historic trends in mind we now turn our attention to a look inside the Digital NYC zones and explore the location trends within the zones themselves. We sought to assess the degree to which the zones were able to lure each of the aforementioned high-tech sectors and the related sector users, and consider why. We then explore the relative implications of these new businesses on diversifying the economic activity in the local areas.[6]

Figure 12.4 **Percent Employed in Software and Technical Services in New York State by New York Metropolitan Area, 1994–2000**

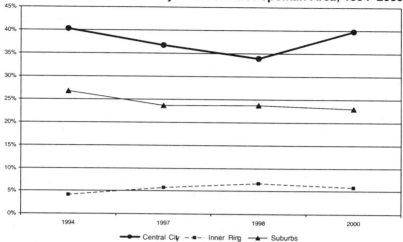

Source: County business patterns data, U.S. Census Bureau.
Note: Central City=New York County; Inner Ring=Bronx, Kings, Queens and Staten Island Counties. See Appendix A for listing of industrial classification codes.

Table12.1

Location Quotients (Soft Side of the Digital Economy) for Select New York Counties Relative to New York State, 2000

	Number of employees
Brooklyn	0.70
Nassau	0.85
Suffolk	0.72
Manhattan	1.77

Source: County business patterns data, U.S. Census Bureau.

Digital NYC and High-Tech Business Location

Aggregate Outcomes

Overall, as of June 2002, eighty-seven leases were signed in the Brooklyn zones, representing some 2,900 jobs,[7] a total of 295,505 square feet of space was converted and leased. Interviews and surveys suggest that just under half of the businesses going to the Brooklyn zones areas are new businesses.[8]

Of those who moved from other locations, the majority came from Manhattan. The businesses that left Manhattan did so due, in large part, to the high cost of space and dislocation caused by the World Trade Center disaster. Preliminary findings suggests that Digital NYC is shifting employment between the core and the inner ring, rather than acting as a regional growth control or sprawl neutralizer. Interviews suggest that these Brooklyn-based businesses would have opted for locations elsewhere in Brooklyn over suburban locations. However, again given the unique circumstance of the post-9/11 business environment, we feel further analysis over time is warranted.

The features identified as the most important reasons why the businesses chose the Brooklyn zones were rental costs (see Table 12.7 below), digital infrastructure, good transportation, proximity to Manhattan, and a desire "to be in this neighborhood." Interestingly, cluster factors, such as the desire to be near supportive businesses or industry partners, were of less importance to locational choice. Analysis of the geography of talent suggests that skill bases are also important to firm location. In accordance with research on site selection, as will be illustrated below, we found that skill base needs varied by the niche of the high-tech sector—software and technical services versus related users (Rex and Walls 2000).

Figure 12.5 is an aggregate view of the industry sectors currently represented in Brooklyn's Digital NYC zones. This data indicates that Digital NYC has not altered the trends in communications services or manufacturing in any way for the inner ring, as represented by the Brooklyn cases. Indeed, in the case of communications services, the downswing in the New York economy mentioned above seems to have had a particularly harsh effect. As one of the zone managers commented,

> The property owners started developing one of their buildings for use as a telecom hotel. A large telecom provider came in and took 80,000/square feet. They signed the lease but then they went bankrupt and never took possession of the space. This happened during conversion. So, that is pretty much a bust, as far as preparing the building for telecom uses. Now our landlords are trying to figure out what they want to do with it. They're considering putting it back to manufacturing (Personal communication, Brooklyn Information and Technology Center, April 2002).

Aggregate Impacts on Footloose Trends and Sprawl

The primary goal of Digital NYC was to create high-technology districts that could attract communications services, software and computer-related services, and high-technology manufacturing. To date, two of these sectors

Figure 12.5   **Aggregate Distribution of Businesses by Type in Brooklyn
Digital NYC Zones**

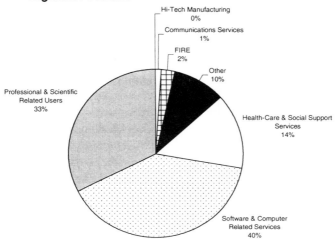

are for the most part absent from the zones—high-tech manufacturing and communications services. At the same time there has been some success in bringing software and computer-related services. Out of a total of eighty-seven leaseholders, thirty-three come from this sector. Thus, our aggregate data on the Brooklyn zones suggest that these areas are not attractive location sites for high-technology manufacturing or communications services. They have been more effective in luring software and computer services and other high-tech related users. We would argue that these small successes are important for the inner ring, which saw a small decline in this sector between 1998 and 2000.

Digital NYC Businesses and Local Revitalization Process

Program Outcomes by Zones

We were also interested in exploring the degree to which Digital NYC was able to promote a more diversified economic base for the areas. We looked at zip code level data on the number of establishments in each of the high-tech and related high-tech sectors, and census data on local demographics. We then disaggregated our zone data in order to compare the zones against each other and explore the impacts of the program by zone since 2000, and considered what, if any, lessons could be learned regarding geographically

Table 12.2

Number of Signed Leases, 2000–2002

	Initial target	Outcomes	Achieved (in %)
Brooklyn Navy Yard	25	13	52
Silicon Harbor	80	4	5
Downtown Brooklyn Connected	30	59	197
Brooklyn Information Technology	None specified	11	NA

Source: Zone project proposals and current leasing statistics (Personal communications, Economic Development Corporation of the City of New York, February 2002, Department of Small Business Services, June 2002).

Table 12.3

Square Feet Available/Square Feet Leased, 2000–2002

	Initially available	Actually leased	Achieved (%)
Brooklyn Navy Yard	58,500	37,699	64
Silicon Harbor	57,500	6,500	11
Downtown Brooklyn Connected	183,000	179,714	98
Brooklyn Information Technology	100,000	71,592	72

Source: Zone project proposals and current leasing statistics (Personal communications Economic Development Corporation of the City of New York, February 2002, Department of Small Business Services, June 2002).

targeted cyber development programs on diversifying and bringing new kinds of jobs and industry to the areas.

Tables 12.2 and 12.3 illustrate some program outcomes by zone. As can be seen, Downtown Brooklyn Connected (DBC) has been the most successful both in terms of the overall number of leases and square footage leased. We would suggest that there are two key reasons that underlie this. This zone has a single private property owner who had begun upgrading in 1997, prior to the introduction of the program. The other zones tend to have more than one property owner as partners, or, in the case of the Navy Yard, the land is city-owned. In DBC, property was digitally upgraded and ready to lease in 2000, while the other zones began upgrading in 2000. As one private sector partner comments: "One reason I think we're successful as opposed to everyone else, we put more money into it. We spent millions of dollars to upgrade these buildings. Others haven't done that. The nature of this company is to be very aggressive and invest" (Personal communication, Two Trees Management, March 2002).

DBC therefore had a head start, which is key in light of the fact that the dot-com bubble had begun to burst in 2000. Smaller businesses in these sectors began searching to cut costs, and DBC may have indirectly benefited from the fallout. In addition, the fact that this zone is controlled by a single property holder also means that negotiation and decision-making processes are often faster than in the other zones where decisions frequently require negotiations among a larger pool of public and private partners. Streamlining the decision-making processes made DBC a more viable location choice for many.

Interviews with zone businesses suggested that transportation, digital infrastructure, and proximity to Manhattan were important aspects of their location decisions. Comparatively, DBC is geographically the closest zone to Manhattan, has the best access to public transportation, and had digitally upgraded before most of the other areas. In contrast, Silicon Harbor in Red Hook, the area with the fewest leases, has poor public transportation access and has had the most difficult time in bringing in digital services because providers are more responsive to areas that have a denser network of business users.

Taking a Niche-Centered View of the Zones

While these overall programmatic indicators are interesting, they tell us little about local revitalization processes. In the aggregate, for example, the overall numbers of businesses going into these areas are not significant by regional standards. According to the Cyberstates 2002 report, there were some 2,500 new high-tech establishments overall in New York in 2001 (American Electronics Association 2002). Thus eighty-seven businesses in Brooklyn would appear to be a drop in the bucket. However, given that one of the goals of the program was to bring high-tech industry to underutilized areas, we felt it important to consider the relative impacts of business location in each zone on its local area. We began by looking at the distribution of businesses by zone to determine if there was any differentiation in the kinds of businesses going to each of the zones, and if so why. Figures 12.6, 12.7, 12.8, and 12.9 illustrate the distribution of businesses within each zone.

As can be seen, each zone has attracted a unique combination of businesses. Silicon Harbor (SH) and Downtown Brooklyn Connected (DBC) have tended to attract professional users and software and computer-related services to their areas. The related users are predominately graphic designers and other high-skill, creatively oriented professionals (such as architects and news media). Interestingly, these two zones have in large part lured those

Figure 12.6   **Types of Businesses Located in Silicon Harbor**

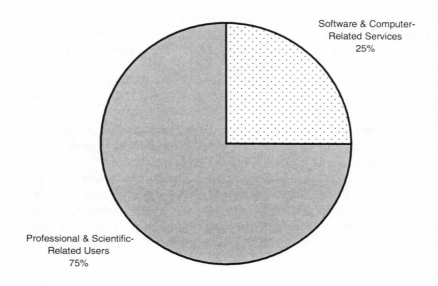

Figure 12.7   **Types of Businesses Located in Downtown Brooklyn
Connected**

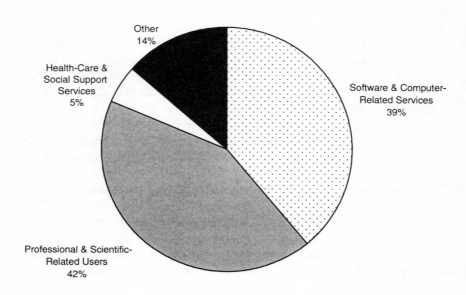

Figure 12.8 **Types of Businesses Located in the Brooklyn Navy Yard Tech Zone**

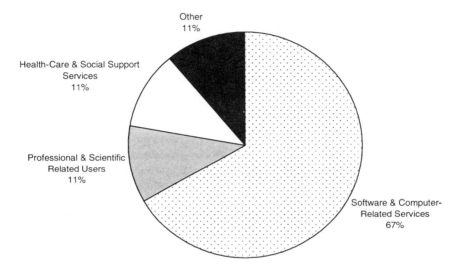

Figure 12.9 **Types of Businesses Located in Brooklyn Information Technology**

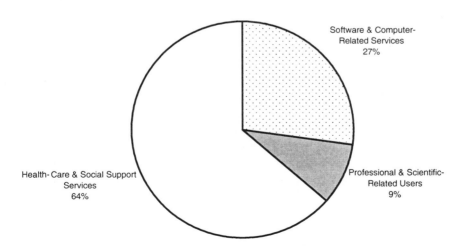

businesses that the program was predominately designed to attract. For the Brooklyn Navy Yard, though a large proportion of its Digital NYC businesses are software and computer-related services, the internal makeup of this group is largely drawn from the lower-skilled end of the sector (i.e., administrative support services). Brooklyn Information Technology, after losing its largest communications provider during the start-up phase (it went bankrupt) of the project, has been dominated by health-care and social support services—an industry that also draws its labor force from the low-skill end.

Geographies of Talent

What is particularly interesting about these trends is that they are highly reflective of the local geographies of talent. That is, the areas that have attracted high-skill businesses tend also to be areas with concentrations of highly skilled residents. Conversely, the areas attracting businesses that employ lower-skilled workers are also those areas with lower-skilled population bases. Tables 12.4 and 12.5 below are designed to illustrate the talent clusters within each of the Digital NYC zones. A location quotient figure greater than one indicates the existence of a concentration of individuals with the referenced educational levels relative to the borough of Brooklyn as a whole. Interestingly, those areas that have exhibited the greatest success as magnets for new digital business are also those that displayed concentrations of more highly educated and skilled residents. Conversely, Brooklyn Information Technology (BITC), the area that to date has been the least successful as a lure for digital industry, but highly successful in attracting health-care support businesses, is also an area with a higher concentration of low-skilled and less-educated residents.

This data is an important reference point to policymakers seeking to attract high-tech industry, for it points to the existence of differences in the needs within the high technology economy and its related users. The spectrum of needs among businesses with digital needs varies according to the niche of the sector they occupy. This is important in that it suggests the need to recognize that, in fact, the digital economy is far more diverse and attracting these businesses may require a more niche-specific approach. Blanket appeals, such as Digital NYC's to all digital users, may be less effective than more targeted approaches that seek to connect up businesses with local labor pools and local amenities. The nonprofit partners reiterated the importance of attracting businesses that would connect up with local labor pools. As the one zone manager pointed out,

Table 12.4

Education Location Quotient by Zone (for population over twenty-five years of age relative to the borough of Brooklyn as a whole)

	Less than 9th grade	HS graduate or higher	BA or higher
Downtown Brooklyn Connected	0.122	1.312	2.839
Silicon Harbor	0.000	1.210	1.816
Brooklyn Navy Yard	0.851	2.056	0.926
Brooklyn Information Technology	2.366	0.687	0.155

Source: U.S. Census 2000, Summary File 3 (SF 3), Sample Data—Borough and Tract Level.

Table 12.5

Skills Base Location Quotient by Zone (relative to the borough of Brooklyn as a whole)

	DBC	SH	BNY	BITC
Managerial/Professional	2.264	1.421	1.341	0.335
Service Occupations	0.331	0.698	2.188	0.509
Sales and Office	0.516	0.971	1.384	1.722
Construction/Maintenance	0.458	0.000	1.680	1.736
Production/Transportation	0.178	1.040	0.955	1.512
Manufacturing	0.472	1.391	0.405	0.972

Source: U.S. Census 2000, Summary File 3 (SF 3), Sample Data—Borough and Tract Level.

We're about opportunity, creating opportunity in the area for people who live here. Our goal is to link people in the adjoining residential neighborhood with jobs in the area. It's about increasing the competitiveness of local companies so that they can take advantage of the opportunities so that they can add more jobs. We have people who can use Word and can type 50 wpm and a lot of the jobs are inputting, data processing. They can do the data processing and we are placing people in these jobs and there are a lot more jobs per square foot for uses like that (Personal communication, Brooklyn Information and Technology, April 2002, project interviews).

Interviews with businesses illustrate these niche-specific needs. In Downtown Brooklyn Connected, dominated by software and related high-skill professional users—adequate space, high-speed Internet access, rental costs, proximity to related businesses, and proximity to Manhattan were highlighted. Silicon Harbor, with a similar niche of the sector but very few leaseholders, was highlighted as the place that had the best access to road transport but the worst access to public transportation, which might also explain the difficulty the area has had in increasing the number of businesses coming to the zone. SH lacks the amenities that this niche demands. Interestingly, both of these zones are located in areas currently considered hot creative spots. Both had preexisting artist clusters, which have also been established to be important lures for the high-skill ends of the digital sectors (Florida 2000, 2001). In both of these areas businesses indicated that being in "this neighborhood" was important to them.

In Brooklyn Navy Yard, with a concentration of lower-skill software users and health-care and social service providers, emphasis on cost of space and security tended to be rated a high priority for location. Limited access to business at BITC prevented us from fully exploring location from the perspective of the business owners there; we are, however, continuing our efforts at data-gathering in that zone.

Targeted Cyber Development and Local Revitalization

This research was also concerned with the degree to which programs such as Digital NYC could serve as tools of urban revitalization. As indicated above, I felt it important to look at the relative impacts of the zones on the locality itself. The most recent local data on employment and establishments available to us was from the year 2000. Given that Digital NYC was implemented in 2000, we decided to look at what, if anything, the businesses added overall to the local areas. Leasing data indicates that the majority of zones' businesses came from other local areas, and thus we know it was not captured by the 2000 county business patterns data for the zone areas. In Table 12.6 we can begin to see the relative impacts by high-tech niche of zone businesses on the locality.

This data suggests that the zones are indeed bringing new businesses into their areas, and diversifying existing job and employment bases. For example, though the relative number of businesses in software and technical services in the Brooklyn Navy Yard's immediate area is small, the new businesses that went to the Navy Yard represent a significant change vis-à-vis this high-tech niche for the local area. The same is true for health-care support services in the Sunset Park area of Brooklyn, where BITC is located. We would argue that diversity is important for local areas, especially in difficult economic times. In a recent article in Crain's New York, Digital NYC participants commented, "Digital NYC has helped diversify Sunset Park's economy and helped create affordable modern space outside Manhattan" (Shockney 2002).

Table 12.6

Impacts of Digital NYC Business by Sector on Local Economy

	County bus.# establishments in zip code area 2000	Master lease list	
		Lease list (# leases) in zones 2000–2002	Increase to zip code by zones (%) 2000–2002
Professional/scientific-related users			
SH	58	3	5.2
DBC	304	24	7.9
Navy Yard	22	1	4.5
BITC	19	0	0.0
Software and technical services: high-skill end			
SH	16	1	6.3
DBC	50	17	34.0
Navy Yard	5	5	100.0
BITC	10	0	0.0
Software and technical services: low-skill end			
SH	30	0	0.0
DBC	15	6	40.0
Navy Yard	59	1	1.7
BITC	28	3	10.7
Health-care and social support services			
SH	47	0	0.0
DBC	45	3	6.7
Navy Yard	45	1	2.2
BITC	18	7	38.9

Source: County business patterns data is from U.S. Census Bureau, and zone-based leasing statistics is from personal communications.

And another:

> Defining the programs success in terms of only high-tech tenants recruited misses the picture. The fact is that well over 100,000 square feet of space was wired and nearly three-quarters of that space is now leased in just under two years. And those leases brought new jobs, new investment and have breathed new life into a neighborhood, and indeed, New York's economy (Claro 2002).

Redistribution or Revitalization

We would be remiss at this point if we did not point to one of the potential downsides of programs such as these for local revitalization. As indicated

Table 12.7

Changes in Median Rental Rates per Square Foot, 2000–2002

	Initial listing ($)	Current listing ($)	Change (in %)
Brooklyn Navy Yard	15.00	21.50	+43
Silicon Harbor	10.00	10.00	0
Downtown Brooklyn Connected	15.00	20.00	+33
Brooklyn Information Technology	16.00	19.00	+19

Source: Personal communications, Economic Development Corporation of the City of New York, February 2002, Department of Small Business Services, June 2002

previously, the trend in the New York region vis-à-vis communications services was one of redistribution. This suggests that the benefits for one neighborhood may well be at the expense of others. We know for example that many of the businesses that relocated moved from areas they considered to be either too expensive, as in the case of those coming from Manhattan, or considered to be unsafe or poorly serviced as in the cases of those coming from other parts of the inner city.

In addition, in some of the zones there are fears that the program will be used to simply displace what little manufacturing there is in the city. The upgraded spaces enable the owners to charge higher rents than those charged for manufacturing or warehousing.

As Table 12.7 illustrates, even since the introduction of the program there have been significant increases in rental rates in several of the zones. These rates are well below Manhattan prices of $45 per square foot in 2002 and suburban rates, which were on average $28 per square foot (Crain's 2002). However, relative to the local areas and existing businesses, the current zone listings are far higher than prior to the program's introduction. As one zone manager pointed out, "An industrial user in this building has paid $6/square foot. Now the tenants are paying $19/square foot (Project interview).

And another, "at least until recently, real estate costs were usually within the price range of small manufacturers and other industrial businesses— rental prices are typically $5 to $10 per square foot for warehouse and about $2.50 per square foot for land" (Personal communication, Silicon Harbor at Red Hook, May 2002).

Conclusions and Recommendations

Our analysis of digital industry in the New York metropolitan region broadly and of the businesses that have located in the Digital NYC zones of Brooklyn lead us to argue that geographically focused cyber development can be an effective way of bringing digital infrastructure to digitally dead parts of the city and diversifying local job bases. At the same time, in its current form the program does not function as a growth control.

The hard side of digital economy (i.e., high-tech manufacturing) continues to opt for suburban locations. The soft side of the digital economy (communication, software, and technical services) has a more differentiated pattern—concentrating in central city and suburban locations. Related users such as back office and support services (i.e., administrative, social, and health care) are divided between inner-city urban and suburban locations. In all cases, we found that the inner city tends to attract smaller businesses and start-ups. In data processing, by way of illustration, our location quotient analysis of establishment concentration by number employed found a location quotient of 1.21 in Brooklyn for small business, while the Long Island suburb of Nassau had a location quotient of 1.03 for large business in this sector—those employing a hundred or more. This leads us to wonder whether these inner-city zone areas will become transitional places for emerging high-technology business, which in the long run, with growth, will move to suburban areas. Regional data from the past illustrated the continuing growth in the suburban proportion of high-tech employment relative to the inner city. At the same time, interviews and surveys of the Digital NYC businesses does indicate that the Brooklyn zone businesses want to be in Brooklyn for the long term. We will have to revisit them in five years time to see if these perspectives change.

We would suggest that effective digitally oriented economic development policies should be niche focused—to recognize that there are a wide range of businesses that utilize digital infrastructure and that the needs of those businesses vary. Across the sector, digital infrastructure, adaptable space, low rent, and good communications all mattered. Interestingly, business incentives were rarely considered to be key.

Different locations will be more or less suitable based upon matching the competitive advantages of the location to the needs of the high-tech sector niche. For the high-skill end of the high-technology sector—relevant talent, creative environments, infrastructure, and quality of life were important priorities. For the low-skill end—relevant talent, affordable space, security, and good public transportation access were key. It was the poorer area that tended to draw the low-skill end of the sector.

In terms of the impacts on local area economies, we would again suggest benefits and weaknesses. There are clear indicators that these programs are bringing jobs and business to areas that sorely need it. And in many cases they are also helping to expand and diversify local opportunity structures. Evidence also suggests that the investments are bringing digital infrastructure to areas that were digitally dead. According to FCC zip code data, these areas experienced significant increases in the number of customers provided high-speed Internet access; between 1999 and 2002, in the area where BITC is located, there was a 400 percent increase, in DBC a 120 percent increase, SH 100 percent, and the Navy Yard 71 percent (FCC 2003). At the same time there is concern that eventually these kinds of investment may actually lead to displacement of what remains of the urban manufacturing sector. As one zone manager commented: "This is one of the key issues, or one of the downsides of the digital program, is that it isn't an abandoned area. It's an area that has manufacturing, warehouse distribution and other industrial related jobs and there is a competition for the real estate" (Personal communication, Brooklyn Information and Technology, April 2002).

The partnership strategy has also had both strengths and weaknesses that revolve around differences in the degree of commitment to the program itself. The benefits have been in terms of sharing some of the risks of upgrading.

> As far as using public money to leverage private investment, it's been a huge success here. For a paltry fee, really just my salary for the past two years and a couple thousand marketing dollars, we've leveraged millions of dollars in private investments. Not just the landlord's money in improving the buildings but the improvements paid for by the tenants" (Personal communication, Brooklyn Information and Technology, April 2002).

The role of public partners in marketing the areas has also been highlighted as one of the significant benefits.

> The program has been an invaluable assistant, in terms of guiding us through the marketing process or actually handing us tenants" (Personal communications, Brooklyn Information and Technology, April 2002).

Difficulties have revolved around differences in the levels of commitment among private sector partners. As one policymaker pointed out,

> There's the layer of the infrastructure providers where in the early stages of development everyone's like, Digital's great, we want to be able to access these new clients and so we're definitely going to go out there. But as time wore on in dealing with, the providers—who make it possible for people to even go out there, it became a little bit difficult to get them to provide service out there, due to a low concentration of businesses. That's been a struggle." (Personal communication, Economic Development Corporation of the City of New York, February 2002)

Thus we would suggest that programs such as these are important from the perspective of revitalization, though less relevant in their current form as growth controls. We would argue that, given the diversity within the sector, a more niche-centered approach might be better able to tap into the needs of those businesses moving out of the central city and affect patterns of sprawl. The findings shed light on the cyber geography of the metropolitan region, and the effects that targeted cyber policy can have on the location of high-technology users.

Appendix A. Digital Sector

Standard Industrial Classification (SIC) Codes Analyzed for 1994–1997 Period

High Tech Manufacturing

3570 Computers and Office Equipment
3670 Consumer Electronics
3660 Communications Equipment
3670 Electronics Components and Accessories
3674 Semi Conductors
3820 Measuring and Controlling Devices

Communications Services

4812 Radio Telephone Communications
4813 Telephone Communications
4840 Cable and Other Pay Television Services
4890 Other Communications Services

Software and Computer-Related Services

7371 Computer Programming Services
7372 Prepackaged Software
7373 Computer-Integrated System Design
7374 Computer Processing and Data

Preparation

7375 Information Retrieval Services
7376 Computer Facilities Management

Services

7377 Computer Rental and Leasing
7378 Computer Maintenance and Repair
7379 Other Computer-Related Services

North American Industrial Classification System (NAICS) Codes Analyzed for 1998–2000 Period

High-Tech Manufacturing

3341 Computers and Peripheral Equipment
3343 Consumer Electronics and Components
3342 Communications Equipment
3344 Semi Conductors
3345 Measuring and Control Instruments

Communications Services

513110 Wired Telecommunications Carriers
513211 Paging Services
513212 Cellular and Other Wireless

Telecommunications

513310 Telecommunications Resellers
513410 Satellite Telecommunications
513510 Cable and Other Program

Distribution

513910 Other Telecommunications

Software and Computer-Related Services

51120 Software Publishers
514511 Custom Computer Programming
514512 Computer Systems Design
514513 Computer Facilities Management
514519 Other Computer-Related Services
51419 Online Information Services
514210 Data Processing, Hosting, and Related Services
514330 Engineering Services
514710 R&D
514380 Testing Laboratories
611420 Computer Training

High-Tech Users

Analysis of the Digital NYC Zones demonstrated that a much wider range of industries were utilizing digital infrastructure and in turn contributing to the digital economy. This led us to also explore the following additional sectors. These sectors are heavily represented in the Digital NYC zones:

Advertising
Graphic Design
Heath-Care and Social Support Services
Engineering and Architecture
Management and Public Relations
Finance, Insurance, Real Estate

* * *

Thanks to the National Center for the Revitalization of Central Cities for financial support of this research and to Edward T. Rogowsky, whose spirit remained an inspiration throughout. The Economic Development Corporation (EDC) of the city of New York and the Department of Small Business Services (SBS) provided invaluable data. In particular, Commissioner Robert Walsh (SBS), Florence Adu (EDC), Stephanie Vecciarelli (SBA), and Jennifer Watler (SBA) provided us with data, candid advice, and insight. We thank Professor Lynne McCormick at Hunter College for her incredible assistance in reviewing drafts of this research. A number of students from the Hunter College Department of Urban Affairs and Planning have provided valuable assistance at different stages of the research. Katherine Bowman, Gemma Futterman, and Amanda Christon provided assistance with interviews, site visits, and literature reviews. We are grateful to Christopher Cardinal and Mark Leavitt for their technological expertise and assistance in the development and dissemination of an electronic survey to zone businesses.

Notes

1. The battle to rezone these areas is complex and beyond the scope of this chapter. By way of overview, conflicts revolved around the very real fears that rezoning would escalate the outward flow of manufacturing to suburban locations, causing additional displacement. Communities feared the added traffic and environmental consequences that mixed-use areas might bring. Interviews also suggested that the process of re-zoning in New York was slow and often caught in the shifts in leadership at both the local, city, and state levels.

2. As we sought to understand the movement of business between different areas of the metropolitan region, we grouped out county data together as follows. Central City = New York County; Inner Ring = Bronx, Kings, Queens, and Richmond counties; Suburbs = Nassau, Suffolk, and Westchester counties. We

selected this time frame based in large part on the availability of detailed economic data on the digital sector.

3. We analyzed data between 1994 and 2000. Given that a wide range of industries make up the digital sectors, and that County Business Patterns data changed their industrial classifications in 1997, we adapted the categorizations utilized in the Cyber States Reports produced by the American Electronics Association. See Appendix A for a full listing of the sectors analyzed.

4. In an effort to gather additional data on the location decisions of businesses locating in the zones we created a survey that was electronically distributed. We thought that, as these areas were digital, a digital survey would be the most expeditious way of gathering data. We found, however, that though it is easy and inexpensive to conduct surveys in this format, it is equally easy for respondents to delete surveys and block further transmissions. After four rounds and assistance from the Brooklyn zone managers, we decided to attempt to conduct the survey over the telephone. To date we have achieved only a 15 percent response rate electronically but are now supplementing this with telephone outreach. These findings will be reported in a broader study under way of all the zones in the five boroughs of New York.

5. Regional data are all derived from County Business Patterns—SIC data for 1994 and 1997, NAICS data for 1998 and 2000.

6. Success can be measured in the aggregate—overall numbers of jobs and establishments that Digital NYC brought to the Brooklyn areas. For the purposes of this research, however, we felt that in addition to the aggregate data, we needed a more detailed analytic approach. As we sought to better understand the implications of these zones for local revitalization efforts, we felt success also needed to be looked at in a relative way. We disaggregated our data by sector and zone. This method allowed us to look at relative success vis-à-vis the locality in which the zone was situated.

7. Of the eighty-seven leaseholders, four did not provide information on their industry sector and seventeen did not provide data on the number of employees. The seventy businesses on which we have this data reported employing a total of 2,865 individuals. The median number of employees was 4 per business. We used the median as our measure of central tendency because we had several outliers employing over 100. Thus if the seventeen nonreporting businesses reflect the median, they would account for an addition 68 employees; in turn we approximate that overall 2,900 individuals are employed in these zones.

8. Data on the age of businesses came from leasing statistics, while data on actual factors underlying firm location are derived from survey interviews with thirteen Brooklyn zones' businesses. Thus, we emphasize that these underlying factors are indicators and that further research is required. We are currently conducting a survey of all the businesses in all the Digital NYC zones in an effort to generate more statistically rigorous findings on location choices. Contact the author for this data.

References

Abramson, Gary. 1998. "Cluster Power." *CIO Enterprise Magazine.* Framingham, MA: CXO Media Inc. Online: www.cio.com.

American Electronics Association. 2002. *Cyberstates 2002.* Washington, D.C. American Electronics Association.

Atkinson, Robert D., and Paul D. Gottlieb. April 200. *The Metropolitan New Economy Index: Benchmarking Economic Transformation in the Nation's Metropolitan Areas.*, Washington, D.C. Progressive Policy Institute, Technology & New Economy Project and Case Western Reserve University, The Center for Regional Economic Issues.

Bellush, Jewel. 1990. "Clusters of Power: Interests Groups," in *Urban Politics. New York Style*, ed. Jewel Bellush and Dick Netzer, pp. 296–338. Armonk, NY: M.E. Sharpe.

Bureau of Economic Analysis. 2002. *BEAR Facts New York, New York.* Washington, DC: U.S. Department of Commerce.

———. 1990–2000. Regional Economic Information System, Bureau of Economic Analysis. Washington, DC: U.S. Department of Commerce.

———. 1980. *CA25–Private employment: Manufacturing (number of jobs).* Washington, DC: U.S. Department of Commerce.

———. 1990. *CA25–Private employment: Manufacturing (number of jobs).* Washington, DC: U.S. Department of Commerce.

———. (2000. *CA25–Private employment: Manufacturing (number of jobs).* Washington, DC: U.S. Department of Commerce.

Claro, Cesar J. 2002. "Letters to the Editor: Digital NYC reboots local jobs." New York: Crain Communications, February 25.

Cohen, Natalie. 2000. *Business Location Decision-Making and the Cities: Bringing Companies Back.* A working paper for the Center on Urban and Metropolitan Policy. Washington, DC: The Brookings Institution, April.

Crain's New York Business. 2002. *Market Facts 2002.* New York: Crain Communications, July 1.

DiChaira, Robert, and Norman Gertner. 2002. *The New York City Economy: Post 9/11.* FDIC, Bank Trends Analysis of Emerging Risks in Banking. New York: FDIC Division of Insurance, May.

Downs, A. 1973. *Opening Up the Suburbs: An Urban Strategy for America.* New Haven: Yale University Press.

———. 1994. *New Visions for Metropolitan America.* Washington, DC: The Brookings Institution.

Empire State Development. 2001. "New York State's Technology Driven Industries: Electronics Manufacturing." Albany, NY: Division of Policy and Research.

Federal Communications Commission. 2003. Reported *Number of Customers Provided High-Speed Internet Services by Select Zip Codes.* Reported in Form 477. Washington, DC: Federal Communications Commission.

Federal Reserve Bank of Minneapolis. 1996. *The Beige Book: Second District– New York*, www.federalreserve.gov/FOMC/BeigeBook/1996/19961030/2.htm.

Fielding, N., and J. Fielding. 1986. *Linking Data, Qualitative Research Methods*, vol. 4. Newbury Park, CA: Sage.

Fishman, Robert. 1987. *Bourgeois Utopias: The Rise and Fall of Suburbia.* New York: Basic Books.

Florida, Richard. 2000. *The Economic Geography of Talent.* Pittsburgh: Heinz School of Public Policy and Management, Carnegie Mellon University, florida@cmu.edu.

————. 2001. *The Geography of Bohemia.* Pittsburgh: Heinz School of Public Policy and Management, Carnegie Mellon University, florida@cmu.edu.

Friedrich, C.J. 1929. *Alfred Weber's Theory of the Location of Industries.* Chicago: University of Chicago Press.

Gaspar, Jess, and Edward L. Glaeser. 1998. "Information Technology and the Future of Cities." *Journal of Urban Economics* 43: 135–256.

Hackler, Darrene. 2000. "Industrial Location in the Information Age: An Analysis of Information-Technology-Intensive Industry," in *Cities in the Telecommunications Age,* ed. James O. Wheeler and Yuko Aoyama, and Barney Warf, pp. 200–218. New York: Routledge.

Hall, Peter. 1997. *Megacities, World Cities and Global Cities.* The Hague: The First Megacities Lectures, http://www.megacities.nl/lecture_hall.htm.

Heilbrun, James. 1981. *Urban Economics and Public Policy,* 2d ed. New York: St. Martin's.

Hevesi, Alan G. 1999. *The New York City Software/IT Industry: How NYC Can Compete More Effectively in Information Technology.* New York: Office of the Comptroller.

Jackson, Kenneth T. 1985. *Crabgrass Frontier: The Suburbanization of the United States.* New York: Oxford University Press

Judd, Dennis R., and Todd Swanstrom. 1994. *City Politics: Private Power and Public Policy.* New York: HarperCollins College Publishers.

Lyons, T.S., and R.E. Hamlin. 2001. *Creating an Economic Development Action Plan.* Westport, CT: Praeger.

McCall, H. Carl Spring. 2002. "Recent Trends in the New York City Economy," *Report 2–2002.* New York: Office of the State Comptroller.

————. 1999. "Brooklyn: An Economic Review," *Report 1–2000.* New York: Office of the State Comptroller.

McCann, Philip. 2001. *Urban and Regional Economics.* Oxford: Oxford University Press.

McDowell, Stephen D. 2000. "Globalization, Local Governance, and the United States Telecommunications Act of 1996," in *Cities in the Telecommunications Age,* ed. James O. Wheeler, Yuko Aoyama, and Barney Warf, pp. 112–29. New York: Routledge.

Moses, L.N. 1958. "Location and the Theory of Production." *Quarterly Journal of Economics,* 78: 259–72.

Moss, Mitchell L., and Anthony M. Townsend. 2000. "How Telecommunications Systems are Transforming Urban Spaces," in *Cities in the Telecommunications Age,* eds. James O. Wheeler, Yuko Aoyama, and Barney Warf, pp. 31–41. New York: Routledge.

Naisbitt, R. 1995. *The Global Paradox.* New York: Avon Books.

Negroponte, N. 1995. *Being Digital.* New York: Vintage Books.

Netzer, Dick. 1990. "The Economy and the Governing of the City," in *Urban Politics New York Style,* eds. Jewel Bellush and Dick Netzer, pp. 27–59. Armonk, NY: M.E. Sharpe.

New York City Department of Small Business Services. 2002. "Master Lease List for Digital NYC Program," June.

New York New Media Association and PricewaterhouseCoopers. 2001. "New York New Media Industry Survey Climate Study." New York: Price WaterhouseCoopers LLP.

Nivola, Pietro S. 1999. *Laws of the Landscape.* Washington, DC: The Brookings Institution.

Personal Communications. May 2001–October 2002. Author's study conducted for National Center for the Revitalization of Central Cities: "High Technology and Local Economic Development in Brooklyn."

——. 2002a. Brooklyn Chamber of Commerce, March.

——. 2002b. Brooklyn Information and Technology Center, April.

——. 2002c. Brooklyn Navy Yard, February.

——. 2002d. Downtown Brooklyn Connected, April.

——. 2002e. Economic Development Corporation of the City of New York, February.

——. 2002f. Economic Development Corporation of the City of New York, April.

——. 2002g. Economic Development Corporation of the City of New York, June.

——. 2002h. Economic Development Corporation of the City of New York, October.

——. 2002i. Silicon Harbor at Red Hook, May.

——. 2002j. Two Trees Management, March.

——. 2003. New York City Department of Small Business Services, January.

Peters, Tom, and George Gilder. 1995. "City vs. Country: Tom Peters and George Gilder." *Forbes*, February 27.

Rex, Tom, and Katrina S. Walls. 2000. "Site Selection Factors Vary Widely by Economic Cluster." *AZB: Arizona Business, Nov. 2000* 47, no. 11: 6–8. Arizona: Center for Business Research.

Sassen, Saskia. 2000. *Cities in a World Economy*, 2d ed. Thousand Oaks, CA: Pine Forge Press.

Schneider, Mark. 1980. *Suburban Growth: Policy and Process.* Brunswick: Kings Court Communications.

Schneider, Mark, and Duckjoon Kim. 1996. "The Effects of Local Conditions on Economic Growth, 1977–1990: The Changing Location of High-Technology Activities." *Urban Affairs Review* 32, no. 2: 131–56.

Shockney, Bill. 2002. "Letters to the Editor: Digital NYC Reboots Local Jobs." New York: Crain Communications Inc., February 25.

Warner, Sam Bass. 1978. *Streetcar Suburbs: The Process of Growth in Boston, 1870–1890*, 2d ed. Cambridge: Harvard University Press.

Wheeler, James O., Yuko Aoyama, and Barney Warf. 2000. "Introduction: City Space, Industrial Space, and Cyberspace," in *Cities in the Telecommunications Age*, eds. James O. Wheeler, Yuko Aoyama, and Barney Warf, pp. 3–17. New York: Routledge.

Part 5

Conclusion

13

ALAN F.J. ARTIBISE

Conclusion: Opportunities and Challenges for Containing Sprawl and Revitalizing the Core

This collection of detailed studies of one of North America's major challenges—suburban sprawl in combination with central city decline—is designed to set forth strategies and policies that effectively address several issues. Can sprawl be contained? What combination of incentives and disincentives, policies and regulations can achieve this goal? And if sprawl can be contained, will the result also be the revival of central cities? How can policies designed to contain sprawl also result in central city revitalization? There are no easy answers.

Previous volumes produced by the National Center for the Revitalization of Central Cities have attempted to address these complex issues from a variety of perspectives. The first, published in 1995, analyzed the successes and failures of urban revitalization programs during the 1970s, 1980s, and early 1990s by focusing on detailed case studies in seven American cities. *Urban Revitalization: Policies and Programs* (Wagner et al. 1995) concluded by providing a discussion of policy implications and recommendations that touched on six areas: leadership capacity building, promotion of regional cooperation and problem solving, federal financial commitment to central city revitalization, human investment strategies, lessons for federal interagency cooperation, and federal support for local planning efforts. The second volume—*Managing Capital Resources for Central City Revitalization* (Wagner et al. 2000)—reviewed several strategies for managing the central city's capital resources in light of reduced federal and state spending. In this context of a "postfederal" environment, the volume concluded that five factors are advisable for successful central city revitalization: public-private partnerships, physical revitalization, taking a regional perspective, involving all actors (public, private, and community) in the process, and crafting strategies that recognize the unique features of each central city.

This volume was followed by an analysis of *Human Capital Investment for Central City Revitalization* (Wagner et al. 2003). The failure to develop human capital was explored and determined to be an essential element in any comprehensive program for central city revitalization. Strategies examined included upgrading education and school-linked services, enhancing tenant-based housing management programs, and fostering community reinvestment agreements. Together these recommendations were put forth as the core of an integrated program to improve the quality of education, skills, and general daily life of central city residents.

In this volume the opportunities and challenges are again addressed but with the benefit of a decade of research and with a focus on policies and approaches that citizens and elected officials can study and implement. In addition, a new dimension is added to the challenge of central city revitalization by coupling this issue with the equally challenging matter of containing sprawl.

Setting the Context

Part 1 of the volume investigates the nature of urban growth, providing a useful and concise review of the issues addressed in subsequent chapters. Krishna Akundi's discussion of the patterns of suburban expansion and metropolitan development begins by noting that "few, if any, metropolitan regions in the United States are dense or compact." Instead, the "urban landscape is marked by wide stretches of vacant land." This phenomenon, usually referred to as suburban sprawl, has many consequences, but perhaps none more important that the concomitant decline of the core or central city of the metropolitan region.

Akundi's concise overview provides a valuable history of sprawl, the consequent changes in metropolitan patterns of growth and decline, as well as an analysis of the social, economic, and spatial impacts. This analysis is critical to this volume since it sets a context for subsequent discussions. Notably, Dr. Akundi acknowledges that suburbanization—at least at first glance—has considerable appeal to consumers. Indeed, it has been argued that sprawl, like development, provides multiple benefits: freedom of automobile use, living and shopping opportunities removed from the problems of central cities, rising home values, better and safer schools, lower property taxes, and so on.

Nonetheless, this positive view of the benefits of suburban sprawl as a market phenomenon with strong consumer support is seriously and effectively challenged by those citizens who are left behind and by those public officials who must manage the entire metropolitan region, not just the suburbs. In 1998, for example, the Council of State Governments addressed the plethora of problems attributable to suburban sprawl. A partial list includes the following: loss of open space, fiscal disparities, income and racial segregation, leap-frog development, growing traffic congestion, and increased demand for expensive highway investment, environmental degradation, and unsightly strip development.

In short, left unattended, suburban sprawl can lead to critical problems for metropolitan regions—problems that sooner or later must be addressed by all residents of a region. The challenge is how to contain sprawl and at the same time revive core cities. The fact is that healthy regions can have both vibrant central cities and well-planned suburban communities. But why is this combination so rare? If achieved, a balanced pattern of urban central cities and compact suburban communities can result in economic growth and appropriate social and environmental patterns of development—in short, in sustainable development.

The Path to Sustainable Development in Metropolitan Regions: Federal and State Roles

Achieving balanced urban development patterns in North American urban regions is no easy task. There are no panaceas or silver bullets. The patterns that have been evolving for over five decades cannot be easily undone. Yet, research presented in this volume indicates that the invisible hand of the market will not fix problems. Instead, regions must explicitly adopt and implement policies designed to contain sprawl and revive the core. After all, metropolitan regions—like humans—must constantly evolve to survive. Those that do change will thrive; those that stubbornly stick to old patterns of development will decline.

Professor Bright's detailed and persuasive contribution reviews issues relating to vacancy, poverty, and abandonment in central cities, a ubiquitous problem in the vast majority of central cities. She carefully sets a context by noting that regional containment strategies—in and of themselves—are still rare in the United Sates (although more common in Canada). And given the antipathy of many Americans to effective metropolitan government, it is recommended that central cities focus on job creation based on the demonstrated fact that jobs result in revival. The author also notes that changing urban growth patterns provide opportunities for revitalization as immigration, an aging population, and the Internet all generate new and welcome pressures for infill as opposed to suburban sprawl.

Bright's partial prescription for central city revitalization—central city job creation—strongly suggests that local governments cannot alone achieve the desired results. Programs and policies effected by states and federal governments—policies that often encouraged sprawl in the first place—must now be redirected or at least balanced to encourage central city redevelopment.

This emphasis on the need for aligned policies at all levels of government is strongly supported by the case study of "smart growth" in the San Diego region. Just as adjustments in federal policy are necessary, state governments must step up to the plate. The authors of the San Diego study contrast the relatively effective state support for regional planning efforts and initiatives in Washington, Oregon, and New Jersey with the lack of such support in California. The analysis of San Diego's Association of Governments (SANDAG) over the past several decades demonstrates how critical state support and state mandates are for success. In recent years SANDAG has both adopted a leadership role and "sounded the alarm." While progress has been made, the conclusion reached is that in the San Diego region, without greater state involvement, progress will be both slow and piecemeal. The nature and intensity of the problems require a long-term, comprehensive, cooperative response by local and regional officials, but the challenges also require an engaged state government.

The Importance of Regional Governance

While the second and third chapters in this volume note the role of local and regional government in the context of state and federal policies, the next three explicitly address the challenges of regional governance. All three studies conclude—albeit with varying degrees of assertiveness—that regional governance does make a difference. In metropolitan St. Louis—one of the United States' most politically fragmented regions—suburban expansion has continued unabated even while efforts at the regional level to deal with both sprawl and central city revitalization have been present. There have been many efforts at regional cooperation, but while there have been successes, they are few in number. Nevertheless, this study suggests that regional issues can be addressed as long as the regional "table is set." In other words, in an obvious reference to an often neglected fact, Dr. Tranel notes that containment and revitalization at the regional level can take place only if local and county governments from throughout the region meet together on some regular basis. This evolution of regional governance—if not regional government— eventually leads to ongoing intergovernmental relations and, occasionally, effective regional cooperation. Many in the St. Louis region would argue that this evolutionary model works too slowly and therefore requires critical support in the form of a state mandate and state policies if the problems are to be addressed. Even though some progress is being made, an increased pace of regional solutions to regional problems will come only if the political will is present. A starting point is the need to understand that the sustainability challenge—thinking globally and acting locally—must be revised to allow—indeed encourage—regional actions. Only at this level can many of the social, economic, and environmental challenges be transformed into opportunities.

While the St. Louis story is a cautionary tale about the many bumps on the road to regional cooperation, the Vancouver, B.C., story—told in a dramatically different setting and context—indicates how regional governance can evolve into a reasonably effective mechanism. Like St. Louis, the Greater Vancouver Regional District (GVRD), works within a political tradition where local autonomy is very strong and provincial involvement in urban affairs is weak. Few in the region argue for radical changes in the mandate or powers of the regional government. Yet the results in Greater Vancouver have been to produce containment and revitalization policies—at a regional level—that work quite effectively. But even in this context challenges remain. The remarkable growth of the region and its reputation for livability are constantly under threat. The GVRD will continue to thrive only if—as has been the case since the earliest forms of regional cooperation in 1911—the structure of regional government continues to evolve. Notably, in Greater Vancouver what motivates the regionalists is continuing faith in three truisms that drives the quest for regional sustainability; truisms that would be wisely followed in other metropolitan regions. First, knowledge is power. The knowledge resource of the GVRD, sustained and nurtured over the decades, serves the regional body well in ongoing debates. Second, good ideas will triumph over bad. Once at the regional table, the decision-making officials can usually be convinced by the power of good and sensible ideas, provided they are advocated convincingly and consistently. Finally, a thorough and inclusive consensus will produce the regional interest. There are few examples where a thorough and open decision-making process—although agonizingly slow—has not produced a strongly supported concept of the regional interest. In short, communities can forge regional institutions if the effort is inclusive.

The final discussion of regional government moves beyond specific regional case studies to a preliminary assessment of issues relating to containment and revitalization in thirty-five of the United States' largest MSAs during the 1990s. Comparing jurisdictions with "business as usual" policies to those that adopted various forms of "smart growth" policies, the authors make several important, if preliminary, conclusions. Smart growth policies do make a difference, at least in terms of building activities. Coupled with evidence that Professors Nelson and Burby cite indicating how smart growth improves public health, income levels, land preservation, and so on, this conclusion supports the view that explicit policies can improve the urban environment in measurable ways. While more research is called for to fully understand the complex trends discussed in this chapter, the research does suggest that smart growth governmental policies and regulations at the regional level can result in sustained growth, while also maximizing benefits and minimizing costs.[1]

The Dilemma of the Central City

If effective regional governance can make a difference, what policies provide the best results? Chapters 7, 8, and 9 dissect three particular strategies that have been touted as important pieces of the central city revitalization puzzle. Dr. Burby first examines the effects of building code enforcement strategies. The choices made by local government—varying from lax to strict enforcement—can have a measurable impact on capturing housing construction starts. Generally, more rigorous enforcement of codes leads to reduced levels of success in terms of capturing new housing construction. In short the building code "burden" for central cities is real. The lesson, however, is not that central cities should rapidly shift from strict to lax enforcement; rather, the chapter strongly suggests that the careful and creative revision of codes is what is necessary. This might include eliminating costly building requirements that contribute little to building safety, and reorienting enforcement practices to avoid costly construction delays and nuisance effects that accompany the use of sanctions to bring about compliance.

This strong evidence is followed by discussion of a problem common to most central cities—the redevelopment of brownfield sites. Based on an examination of five such sites in Pittsburgh, the author notes that if sprawl on new land is to be contained, inner-city brownfield sites must be redeveloped. To achieve this laudable goal it is critical to build broad participation processes—utilizing such techniques as public-private partnerships—if brownfield redevelopment is to proceed in a timely fashion. It is also critical to understand the various perspectives and concerns that relate to brownfields redevelopment: legal, environmental, economic, and community. Once understood, planning and policy initiatives can move forward, since there are many shared interests among these interest areas. However complex these challenges are, authors Sabina Deitrick and Stephen Farber argue that coalitions that work to contain sprawl and revitalize the central city can build alliances that result in achieving the desired goal.

Another discreet strategy for central city revitalization addresses the ever-present need for financial resources. One trend, present in many metropolitan regions, has been to turn to the nonprofit community for payments in lieu of taxes (PILOTs) as a source of municipal income. While Professor Leland's study recognizes the need for additional research, she states that PILOTs efforts—driven by the need for more resources and the "free rider" concern—are not as prevalent as anecdotal evidence suggested prior to this research effort that involved seventy-three of the largest cities in the United States. In other words, although PILOTs are being pursued, the debate—sometimes fierce debate—has not yet reached any widespread consensus. While advocates of PILOTs appear to be growing, to date there have been few cases of implementation. It can be concluded that this important policy issue needs more time to evolve before a clear sense of direction can be determined.

Revitalizing the Region

Discussions of containment and revitalization are critical components of sustainable metropolitan development. But what can be done to have both sides of the equation in balance? The next section of the volume suggests several important policy initiatives.

To begin, the concern of this volume about the need for both containment and revitalization is in large part driven by the fact that central cities have demonstrably worse housing and economic conditions than their surrounding suburban communities: lower median household incomes, higher levels of unemployment and poverty, slower population growth, higher housing vacancy rates, and lower home ownership rates. The obvious conclusion is that significant contextual differences should lead to significantly different policy strategies. In short, policy initiatives—from federal to state to regional to local—must address the specific problem in the right context. One size does not fit all. Metropolitan regions must, therefore, develop sophisticated and targeted policies and programs if the entire metropolitan area is to benefit. This lesson, while hardly new or radical, needs constant emphasis given the propensity for senior governments in particular to design a program or legislate a policy and apply it evenly across a differential landscape. It simply does not work. As Professor Basolo concludes: "the differences between central cities and suburban communities should result in a variation of policy strategies between the two types of city."

Supporting this evidence calling for a sophisticated program and policy tool kit is research on mixed-income housing. Professor Schwartz's research, somewhat surprisingly, suggests that a mixed-income housing strategy is no silver bullet when it comes to addressing pockets of poverty in central city neighborhoods. While mixed-income housing strategies do play a role as a social policy tool, other factors must be considered at the same time if the goal of developing affordable housing and achieving sustainable development is to be reached.

In the final chapter Professor Gross examines the evolving landscape of the digital world. This research adds an additional positive note to this volume by concluding that cyber development can be quite effective in revitalizing central city neighborhoods, providing further evidence to Professor Blight's earlier comments in Chapter 2. In particular Gross argues that policies designed to support start-up and small business expansion can be effective, since, for many reasons, these activities opt for central city locations. This niche market may, in fact, be a manageable and strongly supportive inner-city revitalization strategy, both containing urban sprawl and revitalizing the central city.

The Shape of Future Policy Initiatives

Revitalizing the City: Strategies to Contain Sprawl and Revive the Core is focused on identifying and assessing potential policy initiatives in the ongoing challenge of shaping metropolitan development patterns. Taken together, the research in this volume prescribes a policy context that must involve the following elements. Efforts must be intergovernmental in nature. The programs and policies of federal and state/provincial governments are critical to success, and local activists attempting to contain sprawl and revive the core must work continuously to obtain resources and mandates from senior governments. No matter how committed or competent local and regional governments are, they face difficult paths to success if direction and support are not forthcoming from federal and state capitals. At the same time, the policies and mandates sought must be tailored to the needs of both particular regions and particular communities; all regions and all central cities are not the same. This need for more finely calibrated policy development is acute, but if it can be achieved—as it has been in a few instances—it has quickly demonstrated the value of such an approach.

This is not to say that similar attention must not be directed to local and regional initiatives. It must. Indeed, even without federal and state/provincial support, progress toward the goal can be made. The key point is that the synergy that can come from policies at several levels operating in concert is the ideal. In this regard it is essential to keep in mind the adage that good ideas will succeed—given enough time and effort.

In this context aggressive local policies—such as building code revisions, brownfields redevelopment, mixed-income housing policies, PILOTs, and cyber development—can lead the way.

In short, while smart growth policies can be effective redevelopment tools, it is even more important to practice smart politics by developing a regional consensus, pursuing deliberate and effective policies at all jurisdictional levels, and working toward realistic common goals. The fact is that livable communities do not just happen. They are created by the people who live in them.

Note

1. These views are supported by other, recent research (see, for example, E.J. Jepson, Jr. (2004).

References

Jepson, E.J., Jr. 2004. "The Adoption of Sustainable Development Policies and Techniques in U.S. Cities." *Journal of Planning Education and Research* 23, no. 3 (Spring): 229–41.
Muro, Mark, and Robert Puentes. 2004. *The Smart Money Is on Smart Growth.* Washington, DC: Center on Urban and Metropolitan Policy, The Brookings Institution.
Wagner, Fritz W., Timothy E. Joder, and Anthony J. Mumphrey, Jr., eds. 1995. *Urban Revitalization: Policies and Programs.* Thousand Oaks, CA: Sage.
———. 2000. *Managing Capital Resources for Central City Revitalization.* New York: Garland.
———. 2003. *Human Capital Investment for Central City Revitalization.* New York: Routledge.

About the Editors and Contributors

Krishna M. Akundi, senior planner with the Research and Technology Center, Maryland National Park and Planning Commission. He previously served as an economic research specialist with the Office of the Governor, Texas Economic Development and Tourism Division. Akundi was also research fellow to the National Center for the Revitalization of Central Cities. He holds a Ph.D. in urban studies with a concentration in regional analysis from the University of New Orleans and a master's in urban and regional planning from the University of Pittsburgh.

Alan F. J. Artibise, dean of the College of Urban and Public Affairs, University of New Orleans. He has published and taught in the areas of urban history, regional planning, public policy administration, and urban studies. His research interests include comparative urban development; urban and regional planning; transportation planning and public policy; governance issues; community visioning, planning and implementation; community development and revitalization; and tourism and resort planning and development. Before joining CUPA in 2002, he served in academic and administrative positions at the University of Missouri–St. Louis and at the universities of Victoria, Winnipeg, and British Columbia. Artibise has a doctorate in urban history from the University of British Columbia.

Victoria M. Basolo, assistant professor, Department of Urban and Regional Planning, University of California–Irvine. Her research interests include housing and economic development policy, intergovernmental relations, urban politics, public choice theory, institutional theory, and environmental policy. Her work has been funded by the National Science Foundation, and the U.S. Department of Housing and Urban Development as well as local governments and nonprofit organizations. Basolo teaches undergraduate and graduate courses in housing policy and local economic development policy. She holds a Ph.D. in city and regional planning from the University of North Carolina–Chapel Hill.

Elise Bright, associate professor at the School of Urban and Public Affairs, University of Texas–Arlington. She is recipient of the 2000 Paul Davidoff Award for her book *Reviving America's Forgotten Neighborhoods* (Taylor and Francis, 2000). Her areas of teaching and research are in economic development and urban redevelopment, land-use planning, and environmental planning. She received her doctorate from Texas A&M University.

Raymond J. Burby, professor of City and Regional Planning, University of North Carolina–Chapel Hill. He also serves as Director of Undergraduate Studies and Coordinator of the minor in Urban Studies and Planning curriculum. His research interests are in land use and environmental planning. Burby is an internationally recognized expert in the field of disaster planning. He has written several articles on this subject and has authored or edited fourteen books. Burby holds a Ph.D. from the University of North Carolina–Chapel Hill.

Nico Calavita, professor in the Graduate Program in City Planning at San Diego State University and adjunct professor in the Urban Studies and Planning Program at the University of California–San Diego. Professor Calavita's areas of interest include affordable housing and community development, growth management, the politics of growth, and comparative planning.

Roger W. Caves, professor of City Planning and director of the Graduate Program in City Planning at San Diego State University. He has published a number of articles on planning and public policy topics. He is the author of *Land Use Planning: The Ballot Box Revolution* (Sage 1992), editor of *Exploring Urban America: An Introductory Reader* (Sage, 1995), coauthor with Barry Cullingworth of *Planning in the USA*, 2d ed. (Routledge, 2003), and editor of the forthcoming *Encyclopedia of the City* (Routledge, 2004).

Chihyen Huang, Ph.D. assistant professor in the Department of Land Management and the Graduate Institute of Landscape and Recreation at Feng Chia University in Taiwan. His research interests include local economic development, public management, and urban political economy.

Sabina E. Deitrick, associate professor in the University of Pittsburgh's Graduate School of Public and International Affairs. Deitrick also serves as codirector of the Community Outreach Partnership Center and Urban and Regional Analysis Program—both housed in the University Center for Social and Urban Research. Her teaching areas include economic and community development, industrial geography, and urban and regional planning methods. Her current research interests include brownfields revitalization. She holds a Ph.D. in city and regional planning from the University of California–Berkeley.

Stephen C. Farber, professor of Public and Urban Affairs and International Development at the University of Pittsburgh. Dr. Farber's interests include microeconomics and environmental economics. His Ph.D. in economics is from Vanderbilt University. His master's in economics is from Grinnell.

Kathleen Ferrier, project manager at Carter Reese & Associates, one of San Diego's most progressive small developers, known for its innovative, mixed-use urban infill projects. She has BA degrees in Spanish and music from Millsaps College in Jackson, Mississippi; a master's in city planning from San Diego State University, and has pursued international studies at American University in Washington, D.C. She worked for the San Diego Association of Governments and Rick Engineering before joining Carter Reese in 2002.

Jill Simone Gross, professor, Urban Affairs and Planning Program, Hunter College. Her broad research areas are comparative international urban development and social capital formation. She teaches courses on citizen participation, comparative international urban economic and community development, urban governance and leadership. Current special policy focuses include culture, tourism, and "cyber-development" in American and European inner cities. Dr. Gross holds a Ph.D. in political science from the Graduate School and University Center, City University of New York, and a master's from the London Schools of Economics and Political Science.

Timothy E. Joder, associate dean of Business Affairs and executive director of Sponsored Research at the College of Urban and Public Affairs, University of New Orleans, serves as deputy director of the National Center for the Revitalization of Central Cities. Before joining the University of New Orleans in 1981, he served as chief planner, State Planning Office, Office of the Governor of Louisiana; community development planner with the City of Baton Rouge and East Baton Rouge Parish; and coordinator of the Boca Raton, Florida, Community Development Block Grant program. He holds a BA in urban affairs/geography from the University of Pittsburgh and a master's in public administration from the University of New Orleans.

Pamela Leland, assistant professor and associate policy scientist, Center for Community Research and Service. Her research interests include Management and governance of nonprofit organizations, tax-exempt status of charitable nonprofits, outcomes based evaluation, and nonprofit leadership. Leland received her Ph.D. in urban affairs and public policy from the University of Delaware.

John Meligrana, assistant professor of urban and regional planning at Queen's University. He has published extensively on issues of municipal government and urban development in Canada. He recently published *Redrawing Local Government Boundaries: An International Study of Politics, Procedures, and Decisions* (Vancouver: UBC Press, 2004). Dr. Meligrana received his Ph.D. from Simon Fraser University and a master's degree in urban and regional planning from Queen's University at Kingston.

Anthony J. Mumphrey, Jr., president of the Mumphrey Group Inc., a professional consulting firm that specializes in engineering, architecture, and planning services. He holds B.S. and M.S. degrees in civil engineering from Tulane University, and the M.A. and Ph.D. in regional science from the University of Pennsylvania. Mumphrey served as an executive assistant for planning and development to the mayor of New Orleans (1978 to 1984). He was a professor of urban and regional planning at the University of New Orleans and research director of the National Center for the Revitalization of Central Cities. His research interests include creative public-finance techniques, solid-waste management, the impacts of annexation and defensive incorporation, city-suburban development relationships, and the decision-making process in the public sector.

Arthur C. Nelson, professor and director of Urban Affairs and Planning, and Senior Fellow with the Metropolitan Institute at Virginia Tech's Northern Virginia Center in Alexandria. His research interests include land-use policy, economic development, growth management, public finance and administration, and real estate. He has served as a consultant to federal, state, and local government agencies, businesses, and nonprofit organizations on management, development policy, and regional economic analysis issues. Nelson received his doctorate in urban studies with concentrations in regional science and regional planning from Portland State University.

Alex Schwartz, associate professor, New School University. He also serves as senior research associate with the Community Development Research Center and as Chair of the Urban Policy and Analysis Program. Dr. Schwartz teaches courses in housing policy and policy analysis. His primary research interests are in the fields of housing and economic development. His work is published in *Housing Policy Debate, Journal of Urban Affairs, Journal of the American Planning Association,* and other publications. Before joining the New School, Schwartz was an assistant professor at Rutgers University, where he conducted research at the Center for Urban Policy Research. He received his doctorate from Rutgers University.

Kian Tajbakhsh (Ph.D 1993, Columbia University) is a social scientist and urban planner currently based in Tehran, Iran. He is involved in applied-policy-related research and consulting as well as academic research. He has worked as a consultant and researcher on local government and social policy in Iran with several organizations including the Ministry of Interior, the Social Security Organization, and international organizations such as the World Bank.

Since returning to Iran in 2000 he has been conducting research on two main areas: local democracy and governance in Iran and social theory and citizenship. Currently, Dr. Tajibakhsh is a member of the steering committee of the Urban Studies Research Group at the Cultural Research Bureau in Tehran, a private research organization. He has taught as a visiting professor at Tehran University (2001–2002). From 1994 until 2001, Dr. Tajbakhsh was assistant professor of Urban Policy and Politics at the Milano Graduate School, New School University, New York City, where he is now a senior research fellow (adjunct).

Mark Tranel, executive director, Public Policy Research Center, University of Missouri–St. Louis. He has served as principal investigator or research project manager on over forty applied research projects in the metropolitan St. Louis area. Dr. Tranel received his doctorate in public policy and administration from St. Louis University.

Fritz W. Wagner, dean emeritus of the College of Urban and Public Affairs at the University of New Orleans and research professor in the College of Architecture and Urban Planning, University of Washington. Dr. Wagner is founding director of the National Center for the Revitalization of Central Cities. He holds a bachelor of science degree from Michigan State University, and a master's and Ph.D. in urban planning from the University of Washington. His areas of interest include small-town and neighborhood planning, environmental planning, land use and zoning, policy analysis, and planning issues in developing countries.

Index

P

Palumbo, G., 6
Park, Julie, 50
Park, Keeok, 73–74, 77
Parks and recreation, 82, 89–90, 114, 119, 164
Paterson, R.B., 143, 144, 155
Payments-in-lieu-of-taxes (PILOTs), 201, 202–203, 206–219, 220–221, 319
Peace, Steve, 50
Pennsylvania
  brownfields redevelopment, 163, 164, 166–197
  payments-in-lieu-of-taxes (PILOTs), 207–208, 220, 221
  See also Philadelphia; Pittsburgh
Pepper, Edith M., 162
Peterman, D., 136
Peters, Tom, 274, 275, 277
Peterson, Paul E., 229, 230, 232, 234
Philadelphia, 11, 130
  payments-in-lieu-of-taxes (PILOTs), 211, 212, 213, 214, 216, 217
  services-in-lieu-of-taxes (SILOTs), 203
Phoenix, 29, 129, 130, 212, 216, 219
Pierce, Neil, 71, 105
Piesen, Ann, 45
PILOTS (payments-in-lieu-of-taxes), 201, 202–203, 206–219, 220–221, 319
Pittsburgh
  brownfields redevelopment, 160–161, 166–197
  growth rate, 130
  one-person households, 80
  payments-in-lieu-of-taxes (PILOTs), 212–217
  user fees, 219
Policy decisions
  affordable housing, 238–243
  developmental *vs* redistributive expenditures, 232–235, 242–243
  economic development, 235–238
  intercity competition and, 230, 232, 233, 236, 243

Policy decisions *(continued)*
  public choice theory, 230, 232–235, 242–243
Population growth, 76–77, 129–131, 229
  See also Sprawl; Suburbs, growth
Portland, Maine, 211, 216
Portland, Oregon, 27–28, 129, 130, 132, 212, 216, 219
Poverty rate, 29, 33–35
Preserving the American Dream (Wells Fargo), 17
President's Commission on Housing, 141
Price, E., 6
Property tax
  abatement, for brownfield redevelopment, 179
  assessment, 111
  base, 6, 233
  brownfield redevelopment sites, revenue from, 175–177, 179
  exemptions, 202, 204–206
  payments-in-lieu-of-taxes (PILOTs), 201, 202–203, 206–219, 220–221, 319
  percentage of municipal revenue, 204
  rate, 54, 56
  services-in-lieu-of-taxes (SILOT), 203
  vs user fees, 217–218, 219
Property Tax Relief (Gold), 205
Property values, 80–81, 179, 181
Proposition 13, 54, 56
Public choice theory, 230, 232–235, 242–243
Public facilities, in smart growth plan, 58–59, 63
Public housing, 248–249
Public policy. *See* Policy decisions
Public relations employment, 288
Pyatok, Mike, 64

Q

Q method analysis, 182, 195, 196
Quality Housing and Work Responsibility Act of 1998, 248–249